Cost–Benefit Analysis and Health Care Evaluations

Cost–Benefit Analysis and Health Care Evaluations

Edited by

Robert J. Brent

Professor of Economics, Fordham University, USA

Edward Elgar
Cheltenham, UK • Northampton, MA, USA

Published by
Edward Elgar Publishing Limited
Glensanda House
Montpellier Parade
Cheltenham
Glos GL50 1UA
UK

Edward Elgar Publishing, Inc.
136 West Street
Suite 202
Northampton
Massachusetts 01060
USA

A catalogue record for this book
is available from the British Library

Library of Congress Cataloguing in Publication Data
Brent, Robert J., 1946–
    Cost-benefit analysis and health care evaluations / Robert J. Brent.
      p. cm.
    Includes index.
    1. Medical care – Cost effectiveness – Research – Methodology.
  2. Cost effectiveness.   I. Title

    RA410.5 .B74 2003
    362.1'068'5 – dc21   2002029830

ISBN 1 84064 844 9 (cased)

Printed and bound in Great Britain by MPG Books Ltd, Bodmin, Cornwall

To my nieces and nephews: Eleanor, Olivia, Richard, Judith, Helen, Vienna and Eliot

Contents

Figures

Tables

Abbreviations

AC : Average cost per unit
AFDC : Aid to Families With Dependent Children
CA : Conjoint analysis
CBA : Cost–benefit analysis
CEA : Cost-effectiveness analysis
CM : Cost minimization
CUA : Cost–utility analysis
CV : Contingent valuation
DALY : Disability adjusted life year
DRG : Diagnostic related group
E : Effect from an intervention
ε_p : Price elasticity of demand
g : Growth rate of per capita income
η : Society's aversion to income inequality
λ : Growth rate of life expectancy
LEDR : Life expectancy discount rate
LOS : Length of stay
MB : Marginal benefits
MC : Marginal costs
MCF : Marginal cost of public funds
MU : Marginal utility
NHS : National Health Service (UK)
P : Price of a good or an effect
PACT : Program for Assertive Community Treatment
PTO : Person trade-off
Q : Quantity of a good or service
QALY: Quality adjusted life year
Q–F : Quantity–frequency index
QoL : Quality of life
QWB : Quality of Well-Being Scale
r : Interest rate used for discounting
RBRV : Resource based relative value
RC : Regular care
RCC : Cost-to-charge ratio
RS : Rating scale

RVU : Relative value unit
SG : Standard gamble
STPR : Social time preference rate
t : Time or year
TTO : Time trade-off
WS : Worksite program
WTP : Willingness to pay
Y : Income

Preface

Why write a third text on cost–benefit analysis (in addition to *Applied Cost–Benefit Analysis* (1996) and *Cost–Benefit Analysis of Developing Countries* (1998)), and why devote this text to just one area of application? First, as I regard CBA (cost–benefit analysis) as covering half of economics (the half that deals with how the economy should be changed, as opposed to the other half that explains how the economy operates in theory and practice), it would be silly to claim that everything that needs to be said is included in two volumes. Even though the previous texts are, like this one, geared to the basic principles of social evaluation (and how many basic principles can there be?), this does not mean that, because the basic principles do not change much, therefore the field does not change much. CBA is inherently an applied one; as applications grow in number and diversity, one's understanding and appreciation for the basic principles develops. In this context, a new set of applications is sufficient to help the discipline progress. Reassembling the same basic principles in new ways can also provide useful insights.

Second, the health care field is all encompassing. Matters of life and death are central to the field and it is hard to imagine any important policy issue not appearing here in some guise. Perhaps because of the recognition of its importance, the health care field is not content to leave matters in the hands of economists. Probably most of the applications in this area are done by non-economists (for example, psychologists, sociologists, statisticians and political scientists). This has (as one may now have expected) benefits and costs. The advantage is that insights from many different disciplines have been incorporated that look at ingredients anew and in creative ways (especially quality of life issues). The disadvantages are that there has been some 'reinventing of the wheel' whereby basic principles are rediscovered (for example, measuring costs and allowing for discounting) and, worse still, some basic principles have been ignored. For example, income distribution weights and the welfare cost of financing public expenditures are rarely included.

The aim of this text is therefore to build a bridge between the evaluations that occur in the health care field and those that take place in other areas of application. We attempt to achieve this by reinterpreting the work done by the non-economists and putting this into a common evaluation framework.

Then we add to that framework the missing necessary ingredients that economists have utilized in other areas. The level of economics introduced is at the introductory level (and not the intermediate level as with the other two texts). The material is intended to be self-contained with all the key concepts explained as and when required. These key concepts (such as demand, supply and elasticity) are used frequently and become mutually reinforcing. Given the applied nature of the book, some fundamental statistical concepts (such as confidence intervals) are included in as non-technical a fashion as is feasible. The content should be accessible to non-economists as well as economists. Researchers and practitioners in health institutes and hospitals may especially benefit from the approach taken and base courses or workshops on this material. For health economists looking for a second, policy-based, course to complement the standard health economics course, the book should be especially attractive.

The book is structured in the same way as the pioneering text by Drummond et al. (1986, 1997) that opened up the evaluation field to non-economists. Hence there are parts that cover cost-minimization (CM), cost-effectiveness analysis (CEA) and cost–utility analysis (CUA) as well as CBA. In this way the reader is placed in a familiar setting. The big difference in our approach, however, is that from the outset, and at all stages, CBA is imposed as the foundation stone for economic evaluation. In reality, there is only CBA. The other three methods CM, CEA and CUA are, at best, short-cut CBAs or, at worst, incomplete CBAs. The nature of the short-cuts and what is necessary to complete the evaluation are made clear. At the same time, the legitimate concerns of non-economists with traditional CBA are discussed fully. Hopefully, the reader will reach the same conclusion as the author: that CBA may have many weaknesses, but it is still the best evaluation framework. Should readers wish to go deeper into the economic theory underlying CBA, I can refer them to my other two CBA texts.

I wish to thank the many students at Fordham University who participated in the health care evaluations courses I taught. It is from them that I learned the costs and benefits of the simplification of economic explanations. I started the project when I worked part-time at the Nathan Kline Institute of Psychiatric Research (NKI) and much of my work on mental health evaluations was initiated there. I would like to acknowledge the three years of support I was given at NKI. I also wish to thank Fordham University for giving me a semester off to write the book, and Georgetown University School of Nursing and Health Studies where I visited and completed the book.

Acknowledgements

The author wishes to thank the following who have kindly given permission for the use of copyright material.

American Economic Association for Table 5.1 first published in Ballard, C.L., Shoven, J.B. and Whalley, J. (1985), 'General Equilibrium Computations of the Marginal Welfare Costs of Taxes in the United States', *American Economic Review*, **75**, 128–138.

American Medical Association for Table 3.5 first published in Hsiao, W.C., Braun, P., Kelly, N.L. and Becker, E.R. (1988), 'Results, Potential Effects, and Implementation Issues of the Resource-Based Relative Value Scale', *Journal of the American Medical Association*, **260**, 2429–2438; for Table 8.2 first published in Eddy, D.M. (1991a), 'Oregon's Methods. Did Cost-Effectiveness Analysis Fail?', *Journal of the American Medical Association*, **266**, 2135–2141; for Table 8.7 first published in Chang, R.W., Pellissier, J.M. and Hazen, G.H. (1996), 'A Cost-Effective Analysis of Total Hip Arthroplasty for Osteoarthritis of the Hip', *Journal of the American Medical Association*, **275**, 858–865; for Table 11.3 first published in Weisbrod, B.A., Test, M.A. and Stein, L.I. (1980), 'Alternative to Mental Hospital Treatment', *Archives of General Psychiatry*, **37**, 400–405.

American Psychiatric Association for Table 2.10 first published in Meltzer, H.Y., Cola, P., Way, L., Thompson, P.A., Bastani, B., Davies, M.A. and Switz, B. (1993), 'Cost-Effectiveness of Clozapine in Neuroleptic-Resistant Schizophrenia', *American Journal of Psychiatry*, **150**, 1630–1638.

Aspen Publishers Inc. for Table 3.4 first published in Schimmel, V.E., Alley, C. and Heath, A.M. (1987), 'Measuring Costs, Product Line Accounting Versus Ratio of Cost to Charges', *Journal of Health Care Finance*, **13** 76–86.

BMJ Publishing Group for Table 2.6 first published in Harper, D.R. (1979), 'Disease Costing in a Surgical Ward', *British Medical Journal*, **1**, 647–649; for Table 10.9 first published in Hyder, A.A. and Morrow, R.H. (1999), 'Steady State Assumptions in DALYs: Effect on Estimates of HIV Impact', *Journal of Epidemiology and Community Health*, **53**, 43–45.

Brookings Institution Press. for Table 11.2 first published in Klarman, H.E. (1965), 'Syphilis Control Programs', in Dorfman, R. (ed.), *Measuring Benefits of Government Investments*.

Cambridge University Press for Table 8.1 first published in Torrance, G.W., and Feeny, D. (1989), 'Utilities and Quality-Adjusted Life Years', *International Journal of Technology Assessment in Health Care*, **5**, 559–575.

Canadian Medical Association for Tables 9.2 and 9.3 first published in Churchill, D.N., Torrance, G.W., Taylor, D.W., Barnes, C.C., Ludwin, D., Shimizu, A. and Smith, E.K.M. (1987), 'Measurement of Quality of Life in End-Stage Renal Disease: The Time Trade-Off Approach', *Clinical and Investigative Medicine*, **10**, 14–20.

Elsevier Science for Tables 3.2 and 3.3 first published in Grannemann, T.W., Brown, R.S. and Pauly, M.V. (1986), 'Estimating Hospital Costs, A Multiple-Output Approach', *Journal of Health Economics*, **5**, 107–127; for Table 4.1 first published in Phelps, C.E. (1988), 'Death and Taxes', *Journal of Health Economics*, **7**, 1–24; for Table 4.3 first published in Weimer, C. (1987), 'Optimal Disease Control Through Combined Use of Preventative and Curative Measures', *Journal of Development Economics*, **25**, 301–319; for Table 6.5 first published in Garber, A.M. and Phelps, C.E. (1997), 'Economic Foundations of Cost-Effectiveness Analysis', *Journal of Health Economics*, **16**, 1–31; for Table 7.6 first published in Siegel, C., Laska, E.M. and Meisner, M. (1996), 'Statistical Methods for Cost-Effectiveness Analysis', *Controlled Clinical Trials*, **17**, 387–406; for Table 8.5 first published in Drummond, M., Torrance, G. and Mason, J. (1993), 'Cost-Effectiveness League Tables: More Harm than Good', *Social Science and Medicine*, **37**, 33–40; for Table 9.1 first published in Sackette, D.L. and Torrance, G.W. (1978), 'The Utility of Different Health States as Perceived by the General Public', *Journal of Chronic Diseases*, **31**, 697–704; for Table 9.5 first published in Nord, E. (1992), 'Methods for Quality Adjustment of Life Years', *Social Science and Medicine*, **34**, 559–569; for Tables 9.6, 9.7, 9.8 and 9.9 first published in Bleichrodt, H. and Johannesson, M. (1997), 'Standard Gamble, Time Trade-Off and Rating Scale: Experimental Results on the Ranking Properties of QALYs', *Journal of Health Economics*, **16**, 155–175; for Table 10.1 first published in Murray, C.J.L. and Acharya, A.K. (1997), 'Understanding DALYs', *Journal of Health Economics*, **16**, 703–730; for Table 10.7 first published in Johannesson, M. and Johansson, U.-G. (1997), 'Is the Valuation of a QALY Gained Independent of Age? Some Empirical Evidence', *Journal of Health Economics*, **16**, 589–599; for Table 12.2 first published in Donaldson, C. (1990), 'Willingness to Pay for Publicly-Provided Goods: A Possible Measure of Benefit?', *Journal of Health Economics*, **9**, 103–118; for Table 13.1 first published in Gertler, P.J., Locay, L. and Sanderson, W. (1987), 'Are User Fees Regressive? The Welfare Implications of Health Care Financing Proposals in Peru', *Journal of Econometrics*, **36**, 67–88.

R.J. Hannum for Table 4.2 first published in Hannum, R.J. (1997), 'Using an Expected Utility Model to Analyze the Social Costs and Benefits of Childhood Immunizations', PhD Thesis, Department of Economics, Fordham University, New York.

John Wiley & Sons Limited for Table 1.1 first published in Cook, J., Richardson, J. and Street, A. (1994), 'A Cost Utility Analysis of Treatment Options for Gallstone Disease, Methodological Issues and Results', *Health Economics*, **3**, 157–168; for Table 10.8 first published in Politi, C., Carrin, G., Evans, D., Kuzoe, F.A.S. and Cattand, P.D. (1995), 'Cost-Effectiveness Analysis of Alternative Treatments of African Gambiense Trypanosomiasis in Uganda', *Health Economics*, **4**, 273–287.

Kluwer Academic Publishers for Table 9.12 first published in Bayoumi, A.M. and Redelmeier, D.A. (1999), 'Economic Methods for Measuring the Quality of Life Associated with HIV Infection', *Quality of Life Research*, **8**, 471–480.

Lippincott-Raven Publishers for Table 1.3 first published in Elixhauser, A., Luce, B.R., Taylor, W.R. and Reblando, J. (1993), 'Health Care CBA/CEA, An Update on the Growth and Composition of the Literature', *Medical Care*, **31**, JS1–JS11; for Table 2.8 first published in Stern, S.H., Singer, L.B. and Weissman, M.M. (1995), 'Analysis of Hospital Cost in Total Knee Arthroplasty', *Clinical Orthopaedics and Related Research*, **321**, 36–44.

Lippincott Williams & Wilkins for Tables 1.2 and 6.3 first published in Logan, A.G., Milne, B.J., Achber, R.N., Campbell, W.P. and Haynes, R.B. (1981), 'Cost-Effectiveness of a Worksite Hypertension Treatment Program', *Hypertension*, **3**, 211–218; for Table 2.9 – Hurley, S., Kaldor, J.M., Gardiner, S., Carlin, J.B., Assuncao, R.M. and Evans, D.B. (1996), 'Lifetime Cost of Human Immunodeficiency Virus-Related Health Care', *Journal of Acquired Immune Deficiency Syndromes and Human Retrovirology*, **12**, 371–378; for Table 3.7 – Weintraub, W.S., Mauldin, P.D., Becker, E., Kosinski, A.S. and King III, S.B. (1995), 'A Comparison of the Costs of and Quality of Life after Coronary Artery Disease', *Circulation*, **92**, 2831–2840.

Massachusetts Medical Society for Table 1.4 first published in Neuhauser, D. and Lewicki, M. (1975), 'What Do We Gain from the Sixth Stool Guaiac?', *New England Journal of Medicine*, **293**, 226–228; for Table 1.5 first published in Boyle, M.H., Torrance, G.W., Sinclair, J.C. and Horwood, J.C. (1983), 'Economic Evaluation of Neonatal Intensive Care of Very Low Birth-Weight Infants', *New England Journal of Medicine*, **308**, 1300–1307; for Table 6.8 first published in Doubilet, P., Weinstein, M.C. and McNeil, B.J. (1986), 'Use and Misuse of the Term "Cost-Effective" in Medicine', *New England Journal of Medicine*, **314**, 253–256; for Table 7.1

first published in Weinstein, M.C. and Stason, W.B. (1977), 'Foundations of Cost-Effectiveness Analysis for Health and Medical Practices', *New England Journal of Medicine*, **296**, 716–721.

Sage Publications Inc for. Table 13.4 first published in Nord, E. (1995), 'The Person-Trade-Off Approach to Valuing Health Care Programs', *Medical Decision Making*, **15**, 201–208.

Springer-Verlag for Table 5.3 first published in Wildasin, D.E. (1992), 'The Marginal Cost of Public Funds with an Aging Population', in Dressen, E. and van Winden, F. (eds), *Fiscal Implications of an Aging Population*.

Taylor & Francis AS for Table 2.7 first published in Ashton, T. (1991), 'Cost-Effectiveness of Alternative Medications in the Treatment of Duodenal Ulcer', *Scandinavian Journal of Gastroenterology*, **26**, 82–88, www.tandf.no/gastro.

The University of Chicago Press for Table 4.4 first published in Weisbrod, B.A. (1971), 'Costs and Benefits of Medical Research', *Journal of Political Economy*, **79**, 527–544.

Every effort has been made to trace all the copyright holders, but if any have been inadvertently overlooked, the publishers will be pleased to make the necessary arrangements at the first opportunity.

PART I

Introduction

1. Introduction to health care evaluation

1.1 INTRODUCTION

The aim of this book is to explain how the theory and practice of cost–benefit analysis apply in the context of making health care expenditure decisions. We start by explaining why evaluation is necessary, defining an evaluation and identifying the main ingredients. Then we show how the ingredients are put together to form four alternative types of economic evaluation. Cost–benefit analysis will be demonstrated to be the primary evaluation technique, so the basic concepts behind this approach will be outlined. We proceed to supply applications (case studies) which illustrate some of the main evaluation principles and provide an overview of the health evaluation field. We close with sections that include problems, a summary, and a look forward that provides a guide to the book.

1.1.1 Why One Needs to Evaluate Programs

To many non-economists working in the health care field, the idea of taking the trouble formally to evaluate treatment programs seems a total waste of time and effort. Surely, they would ask, health care is absolutely necessary, so we know in advance that one must spend on what is necessary?

However, an economist would counter that it is doubtful that every item of health care expenditure was really indispensable. Moreover, even if it were true that every health expenditure were necessary, it is a fact of life that there are not enough resources to meet every health care demand. It is probable that, in the present state of knowledge, all the world's resources would not eliminate cancer. Even if this cancer goal were feasible, what about resources for other deadly diseases, such as AIDS? Also, what about resources for non-health necessities, such as food? Very soon one reaches the conclusion that some necessities are more necessary than others and so we must choose amongst the necessary items to decide which ones to finance from our limited resources.

Economic evaluation as a subject has been developed to provide a framework for helping to make the choices with which we are faced in the health care field. Only by making an economic evaluation can one be sure that all the other ways of making people better off have been considered and resources allocated to the areas that give the highest satisfaction.

If anyone needs to be convinced that one ever needs to carry out an economic evaluation in the health care field, consider this case. The American Cancer Society endorsed the protocol of having six sequential stool tests for detecting cancer of the bowel. Five sequential tests were previously the standard practice. 'Hey', you can imagine doctors saying, 'one can never be too careful when it comes to matters of health'. However, it was found that for every extra case detected by the sixth test, the cost was $47 million! One may not know exactly what is the value of detecting the one case of colon cancer. But one can suspect that it is not as high as $47 million, given that for the same amount society can instead feed over 12 000 people for a year (at $10 a day). Only by subjecting health care expenditures to an economic evaluation can we uncover the basis for making worthwhile decisions.

1.1.2   Definition of an Economic Evaluation

An economic evaluation tries to assess the social desirability of a program relative to some other alternative. If no other alternative is being considered, then the program is being described, but not evaluated. A good example of an analysis in health care that does not include alternatives explicitly is that contained in estimating the 'cost of a disease'. Consider the $65 billion estimate of the cost of schizophrenia in the US in 1991 by Wyatt et al. (1995). This estimate seems to be implying that, if schizophrenia were eliminated, then $65 billion would be saved. But, although such a figure is interesting in an abstract sense, involved with making a 'thought experiment' whereby one would like to know what would happen if the world were different than it actually was, the figure has little relevance for public policy purposes. There is no set of programs that exist today that can actually eradicate completely this mental illness. So no current choices are clarified by knowing the total cost of a disease.

The existence of alternatives is at the heart of an economic evaluation because making choices is central to economics. In fact, economics can be called the 'science of choice'. When there are no alternatives to consider, there is no need to make a choice, and there is no need to make an evaluation. It is important to understand from the outset the need to make choices, as much confusion over the nature of economic evaluations can then be avoided.

In the first place, it explains why economists carry out evaluations. Economists try to value a life in monetary terms not because they want to 'play God', but because one needs to choose how much of the world's resources should be devoted to saving lives. To claim that a life is infinitely valuable is not helpful (no matter how true it is in a spiritual sense). Devoting all the world's resources to save one life does not leave any for the rest of the 6 billion on the planet who would also desire to survive. The existence of finite resources forces us to make choices and undertake evaluations based on finite valuations.

Secondly, the need to make choices explains why an approach to evaluation can be adopted as 'best' even though one may have major reservations with the approach. Some approach must be adopted or else choices cannot be made. A flawed approach may be better as a guide to choice than one that is incomplete because difficult measurement issues have been avoided. Refusing to make difficult estimation decisions does not make the problem of having to make difficult choices disappear.

Prior to an evaluation, one must always check the effectiveness of the programs. That is, one has to establish whether a treatment does actually have an effect on the complaint. As Drummond et al. (1987) point out, 'There is no point in carrying out an ineffective program efficiently'. Nonetheless, having a controlled clinical trial, where one tries to control for all major influences (such as age, sex and severity of illness) when comparing the effectiveness of alternative treatments, may not be a good basis for collecting data for economic evaluations. There are very few health care interventions that work identically for all individuals. Recognizing individual differences is a very important part of conducting an economic evaluation because individual preferences greatly determine outcomes. For example, a medication that is more effective than another may not be better if people choose not to take it (because they do not like the side-effects).

1.1.3 Components of an Economic Evaluation

Health care programs take inputs (labor, capital, etc.) and transform them into outputs. In order to aggregate the inputs, one usually values the labor and capital using market prices to produce a measure of all the resources taken up in the health care intervention. This aggregate input measure is called 'costs' and is in monetary units. The outputs of the evaluation can come in different forms and these are the consequences of the intervention. The most obvious output to consider is what the health care industry immediately works with, such as a diagnostic test outcome or an operation successfully completed. These outputs are called 'effects' and expressed in natural units (such as a percentage detection or completion ratio). A broader measure of effects relies on 'utilities' (i.e., estimates of the satisfaction of the effects) and the output unit is called a 'quality adjusted life year' (the satisfaction of the time that a person has left to live). Lastly, the output can be expressed in the same monetary units as the costs, in which case the consequences are now called 'benefits'.

In the health care field (see Drummond et al. (1987)) the costs and benefits are disaggregated into three categories: direct, indirect and intangible. 'Direct' means directly related to the health care industry (the doctors, the hospitals and the patients). So physician and nursing expenses, and any hospital cost savings, are called direct costs and direct benefits respectively. 'Indirect' refers to inputs and outputs that pass outside the health care industry. The main measure of these indirect effects is via earnings forgone or enhanced due to treatment, as the earnings reflect the value of production lost to, or gained by, the rest of society. 'Intangible' refers to the pain and suffering that are caused or alleviated by a health care intervention.

Corresponding to the costs and consequences just identified, there are four types of economic evaluation that incorporate some or all of the components. All four evaluation types make use of costs. The type that only uses costs is called a cost minimization study. The other three differ according to what kind of consequence they incorporate along with the costs. A cost-effectiveness analysis uses the effects, a cost–utility analysis uses the utilities, and a cost–benefit analysis uses the benefits. This book is devoted to explaining, analyzing and developing these four types of evaluation, a process that we begin in the next section.

1.2   TYPES OF ECONOMIC EVALUATION

As we have just seen, there are four main types of economic evaluation that exist in the health care literature as recognized and understood by economists. The four methods are: cost–benefit analysis (CBA), cost-effectiveness analysis (CEA), cost–utility analysis (CEA) and cost minimization (CM). However, most of those who carry out the health care evaluations are non-economists. They actually do use one of the four types of evaluation, but they label their work differently. We need to be aware that many studies are called CBAs when in fact they correspond to a different evaluation category.

The distinguishing characteristic of a CBA is that it places a monetary value on the consequences. Forming 'benefits' means that the consequences are in the same units as 'costs'. One can tell whether the benefits are greater than the costs and thus know whether the expenditure is worthwhile. The main organization principle of this book is that the three other types of economic evaluation can be best understood as special cases of CBA. We are now going to give a brief summary of the four evaluation types using this principle. We start with an outline of CBA and then introduce the other three methods in terms that make their relationship to CBA clear from the outset.

1.2.1 Cost–Benefit Analysis

Consider the simplest type of health care intervention (or treatment), that is, taking an aspirin, which we designate by the subscript 1. This medication leads to advantages and disadvantages. When the advantages and disadvantages are measured in monetary terms, we will call them benefits B_1 and costs C_1. The aspirin would be worth buying (make a person better off) if the amount of the benefits exceeded that of the costs:

$$B_1 > C_1 \tag{1.1}$$

Equation (1.1) presents the basic cost–benefit criterion. It is this relation that determines whether a health care expenditure should be approved or not.

The CBA approach can be thought of as dealing with the final result of a health care intervention (consumer or patient satisfaction). In the process of arriving at the end result, there is an intermediate stage, which involves transforming the treatment from an input into an output that can be represented as E_1. Here E is called the effect of the intervention. In the aspirin example the effect might be pain (headache) relief. Benefit estimation can then be thought to have occurred in two steps: first there was an effect of an intervention, and then a monetary value was assigned to it. Let the second step be interpreted to be 'pricing' the effect and denoted by P_1. The two steps combine to construct the benefit measure in the form of a product of the effect times the price, that is: $B_1 \equiv P_1 . E_1$. In which case, equation (1.1) can be rewritten as:

$$P_1 . E_1 > C_1 \tag{1.2}$$

This criterion can be expressed in an equivalent way by dividing both sides of equation (1.2) by C_1. We then obtain the requirement that the benefit–cost ratio must exceed unity:

$$\frac{P_1 . E_1}{C_1} > 1 \tag{1.3}$$

The CBA criterion has an alternative formulation when there is a financial budget constraint, which limits how much costs can be expended. The logic is that if there is a budget constraint, then using funds for one purpose precludes their use for another. Let the alternative health care intervention, which could be something unrelated to providing headache relief, such as a diagnostic test for cancer, involve benefits B_2 (equal to $P_2.E_2$) and costs C_2. Then it is not sufficient that the benefit–cost ratio for intervention 1 exceeds unity; it must also exceed the benefit–cost ratio of the alternative intervention:

$$\frac{P_1.E_1}{C_1} > \frac{P_2.E_2}{C_2} \tag{1.4}$$

Criterion (1.4) ensures that if one spends on intervention 1, then one receives more benefit per dollar spent on costs than with the alternative use of the funds.

1.2.2   Cost-Effectiveness Analysis

In the health care evaluation field there has been a general unease with the step in CBA which entails the pricing of the effects, that is, with setting P_1 and P_2. The most popular approach is CEA, which tries to continue without the prices and work on the consequences side only with effects E_1 and E_2. In the classical version of CEA, there is envisaged to be a budget constraint, which means that treatments cannot be considered in isolation. However, treatment effects must be the same kind across alternatives. For example, one can compare either different ways of providing headache relief, or different ways of diagnosing cancer, but one cannot consider both effects at the same time. This means that the only difference between E_1 and E_2 is that E_1 (the effect coming from intervention 1) is at a different level of the same effect as E_2 (the effect coming from intervention 2). The aim now is to choose the intervention that supplies a unit of effect at lowest cost. Under a CEA, treatment 1 would be more cost-effective than treatment 2 if:

$$\frac{C_1}{E_1} < \frac{C_2}{E_2} \tag{1.5}$$

Rather than requiring the lowest cost for a given effect, one can instead try to achieve the most effect per dollar of cost. By inverting equation (1.5), we can see that the CEA is equivalent to requiring that:

$$\frac{E_1}{C_1} > \frac{E_2}{C_2} \tag{1.6}$$

Now compare equation (1.6) with (1.4). The only difference involves the inclusion of prices in the CBA criterion. Thus, if the prices of the effects are considered the same, which is valid in a CEA since it is a common effect that one is comparing with the two treatments, we can set $P_1 = P_2 = P$ in equation (1.4). Dividing both sides of this equation by P, we obtain the CEA criterion (1.6).

Clearly, in principle, CEA can be regarded as a special case of a CBA. The requirements, however, are very stringent. The effect must be *exactly* the same for the treatments being compared. This means that not only must there be a single effect that is common to the treatments; the quality of the effect also must be identical across treatments in order for the value, or price, of the effect to be the same.

1.2.3 Cost–Utility Analysis

Note that, in a CEA, the only difference between E_1 and E_2 is that the quantity of the effect is different in the two treatments. It is not the effect itself that is different. If we want to compare entirely different effects (as with headache pain relief and the precision of a diagnostic test) and we do not want to use prices explicitly, then one needs to have a process that enables all effects to be converted to a common unit.

In a CUA, the common unit is a quality adjusted life year (a QALY). The idea is that any health care intervention either enables one to live longer (that is, have more life years) or to live healthier (that is, have a better-quality life). Thus, the aspirin by relieving pain adds to the quality of life, and the more accurate diagnostic test would (if it leads to preventative action that reduces the chances of dying) add to the quantity of life. The essence of a QALY then is entailed in finding out how much quantity of life someone is willing to give up in order to live a higher quality of life (as is the case when deciding whether to have life-threatening surgery that would remove an obstacle to living normally).

With the QALY as the common effect, the evaluation exercise returns to the CEA framework. A CUA is therefore the special case of a CEA where the effect E is measured by a QALY, and the following criterion is used to replace equation (1.6):

$$\frac{QALY_1}{C_1} > \frac{QALY_2}{C_2} \qquad (1.7)$$

Since a CEA is a special case of a CBA, and a CUA is a special kind of CEA, it means that a CUA is a restricted CBA, where the restrictions are that to result in (1.7) from equation (1.4) we have $E = QALY$ for each treatment, in addition to $P_1 = P_2 = P$ (where P now relates to the price of a QALY).

Just as with a CEA, a CUA differs from a CBA in practice, not in principle. A CBA relies on the fact that individuals are used to purchasing goods on a market at a price. Individuals are familiar with the process of trading off valuations in terms of how much money they are willing to give up to receive more of a good. On the other hand, individuals are not used to buying a QALY and are therefore unfamiliar with the process of trying to obtain a QALY at lowest cost. Deriving meaningful estimates of QALYs is therefore at the heart of the CUA evaluation exercise.

1.2.4   Cost Minimization

In a CM, consequences play no part in the evaluation. The 'trick' therefore is to make disappear both parts of the benefit term, P and E. This does *not* mean setting $P.E = 0$, for then criterion (1.4) would be totally undefined. Rather it means that 'somehow' $P.E = 1$. With this specification of benefits for all treatments, equation (1.4) becomes:

$$\frac{1}{C_1} > \frac{1}{C_2} \tag{1.8}$$

Equation (1.8) is equivalent to requiring:

$$C_1 < C_2 \tag{1.9}$$

There is no unique way to satisfy the condition $P.E = 1$. For example, one could assume $P = 1/E$ (though I know of no one who actually does employ this assumption). What would be logical is that one treat a CM as a special case of a CEA. The restriction then would be that all effects are the same, $E_1 = E_2 = E$, *and* that the common effect would be standardized as a single unit, i.e., $E = 1$. This restriction, together with the assumption of an equal valuation per unit of effect ($P_1 = P_2 = P$), would be sufficient to reduce equation (1.4) to (1.8) and ensure that a CM is also a special case of a CBA.

If it is difficult in practice to justify the requirements of a CEA, it is going to be even more difficult to justify a CM. The quantity of an effect must be exactly the same for all treatments; but also the quality of an effect must be the same. Unless consequences are identical across treatments, a CM would not constitute a valid evaluation of treatments.

1.3   THE BASICS OF COST–BENEFIT ANALYSIS

Since CBA is the primary evaluation method, that the other types of evaluation only approximate, it is necessary to outline some of the fundamentals of the approach before we see it in action throughout the book. As we shall see in the applications section, there is a widespread (and increasing) reluctance to use CBA for health care evaluations. Outlining the fundamentals of CBA is especially important in order to dispel false perceptions of the weaknesses of CBA.

1.3.1   Why Cost–Benefit Analysis?

There are two parts to the answer to the question 'why CBA?'. The first involves explaining why, in general, CBA should be used rather than some other method of allocating resources. The second part involves explaining why, in the health care context, one should use CBA rather than the other types of economic evaluation. We consider each part in turn.

CBA is the core of a public policy course. Roughly, half of economics is trying to explain how the economy operates, and the other half is concerned with trying to *alter* how the economy operates. It is this second half that constitutes the public policy domain. Very few people would be interested in economics as a subject if there were not perceived some need to intervene in the economy. Policies to eliminate inflation, unemployment and poverty are all driven by this perceived need.

It is in this context of government intervention that CBA is most useful, for it provides a consistent framework for deciding when interventions are desirable or not. Considering whether to introduce a tariff reduction, a labor subsidy, an agricultural price support scheme, an environmental regulation, an interest rate change, or supply new funds for AIDS research are all matters for a CBA. When areas of economics, both within and outside the field of health care, do not employ the principles of CBA they engage in 'bad' public policy, in that their findings are based on incomplete analyses of what is socially desirable.

What, then, are the alternatives to using CBA? One could allow the market mechanism to allocate resources without any government intervention. But markets do have their imperfections and fairness/equity is not a market objective, even though in the health care field fairness is probably considered as important as efficiency. On the other hand, one could leave it to the political system to allocate resources. This has the drawback of government imperfections, in that voter preferences may be made secondary to political agent preferences. Even without government imperfections, it is not feasible to have a national vote every time a government intervention is to take place.

A CBA is designed to be a better reflection of what is socially desirable than market forces or direct government determination. As we shall see, CBA incorporates the efficiency rationale behind markets and makes adjustments for situations where market failure exists. It is efficiency that non-economists often ignore when in the health care field evaluators violate fundamental CBA principles. In addition, CBA *can* incorporate distributional considerations, which markets ignore and the health care field considers an essential ingredient in an evaluation.

In the health care context, CBA should be used rather than the other types of economic evaluation because it is the only method that can tell whether an intervention is worthwhile. Even the most cost-effective intervention may not actually be socially desirable, especially when we compare it with alternative uses of funds. It is not sufficient that we concentrate only on the health care sector. Our evaluation framework must ensure that health care programs are evaluated on a consistent basis with those in education, nutrition, the environment and social security. The objective is that all of public funds be spent wisely, not just those allocated (perhaps arbitrarily) to the health care sector.

The logic of this need to keep our perspective as general as possible comes out clearly even if health is the only social priority. For there are many different ways of achieving good health from areas not considered a part of the traditional health care sector. For example, the high rate of female literacy in Kerala in India is a main reason why that state (with only average levels of income per head) has one of the lowest rates of infant mortality and one of the highest rates of life expectancy.

1.3.2   The Social Perspective in Cost–Benefit Analysis

The perspective in CBA is a very broad one as it embraces the effects on everyone in society. A social evaluation does not consider just the parties directly involved with an intervention, that is, the firms (the hospitals and the physicians) and the consumers (the patients as clients). It also covers those indirectly affected, including the family members of the patients and even the general taxpayer. Strictly, then, CBA should be called 'social' CBA to recognize the all-inclusive nature of the evaluation. However, this usage is not widespread either within or outside the health care field. So we shall just refer to the analysis as CBA, leaving the social connotation implicit.

It is interesting that in the health care field it is considered good practice to make the perspective explicit at the outset of a study. That is, it is thought necessary to specify whose perspective the study is from. Is it from the perspective of the hospital, the client, the government taxpayer or whatever? Although it is true that an economic evaluation has usefulness from each and every one of these perspectives, it is only the social perspective that is important for social decision-making. A study that ignores the costs for the families of patients with psychiatric problems is not very useful for making choices about the best place to house the seriously mentally ill. Consequently, one should always adopt the social perspective in an economic evaluation if one wishes to try to influence social decisions.

Even though the social perspective is primary, other perspectives are not irrelevant. In a mixed economy, where the government makes decisions recognizing its interaction with the private sector, it is important to know whether the social outcome is in accord with outcomes from a more narrow perspective. If it is socially worthwhile for people to be inoculated for TB, but it is not worthwhile from an individual's point of view (as the benefits to the non-inoculated population who have a lower chance of contracting TB are ignored), then there could be an 'incentive compatibility problem'. Which is to say that the socially desirable outcome will not in this case be chosen by the individual. Therefore some government incentive must be given to induce individuals to adopt the socially optimal outcome if they do not think it is in their best interests. (Chapter 4 explains this further.)

1.3.3 Efficiency Costs and Benefits

Whether an effect of a health care service is a 'benefit' or a 'cost' depends on what is the purpose of the expenditure. For example, a reduction in the number of persons born stemming from a population control program may be considered an advantage if one is trying to ensure that existing food supplies enable the most people to survive; but it would constitute a disadvantage if one were trying to build a large (human) army for defense purposes.

In welfare economics (the theoretical base for all policy economics) the objective is usually assumed to be to maximize (aggregate) consumer satisfaction (also called utility). It is this sense of maximizing satisfaction (something to be made more precise in later chapters) that is meant by saying that programs are efficient. People get satisfaction if they are willing to pay for something. With resources (income) limited, purchasing health care precludes the purchase of other goods and services, which also give satisfaction. There would be no point in people purchasing the health care if it did not make them better off. Because it is the individuals themselves who are to decide how to spend their income, and in the process make themselves better off, the basic value judgment behind the welfare economic approach to valuation entails the assumption of 'consumer sovereignty'. That is, the individual is assumed to be the best judge of his/her own welfare.

If one does accept the assumption of consumer sovereignty, there is no good reason not to accept willingness to pay (WTP) as a measure of benefits, and therefore no good reason not to use CBA to evaluate health care expenditures. This has to be borne in mind when one considers the criticism of CBA that it is based on the questionable use of earnings to measure health benefits. The use of earnings (what was labeled 'indirect benefits' in section 1.1.3) is a part of 'traditional' CBA. The economic philosophy behind this valuation method is embodied in the 'human capital' approach. A person's earnings are meant to reflect a person's productivity. A health intervention by restoring a person's productivity thereby provides a benefit to society.

The complaint has been that the inclusion of earnings biases programs in favor of those who work and earn, against those that affect children, housewives and the elderly. The traditional CBA approach thus is thought to be inequitable. However, the main criticism of the human capital approach by economists is that this approach ignores the preferences of the individual him/herself, and clearly does not fit in with the usual welfare economic base behind CBA, which is based on an individual's WTP. Thus, one can be an opponent of the human capital approach, yet still be an advocate of modern (efficiency based) CBA.

The equity issue is also something that is not outside CBA, even though it may not be a part of traditional CBA. When one uses WTP, one can weight effects according to their social significance. Thus, if one person is in poverty, their WTP can be given a premium so that their lack of 'ability to pay' can be allowed for. The real problems of CBA are therefore: (a) dealing with cases when consumer sovereignty does not apply (as with programs geared to the severely mentally ill); (b) trying to measure WTP when market valuations of WTP do not exist or are greatly distorted (which is often the case in the health care field); and (c) trying to obtain meaningful measures of the equity weights. The human capital approach is the 'fall-back position' that one should rely on only when other approaches cannot be applied. Traditional CBA is not necessarily 'best practice'.

1.4   APPLICATIONS

We begin our applications with two studies typical of those in the health care evaluation field. In the first we consider an evaluation of gallstones procedures using a CUA, and in the second we present a CEA of alternative sites for hypertension treatment. The emphasis in both of these studies will be on allowing for the side-effects of health care interventions. We also use both these studies to reinforce the point that only a CBA can tell whether a treatment or intervention can be accepted or not. Despite the apparent superiority of CBA, CBA is not the method of choice in the health care evaluation field. The third application reports on a recent survey that finds that non-CBA evaluations predominate and that their share is increasing over time. We use this survey to give an overview of health care evaluations in practice. We close the applications section with an account of exactly how the $47 million estimated cost for the sixth stool guaiac protocol was obtained.

1.4.1 Evaluating Gallstone Treatments

Whether to include indirect costs (forgone earnings due to the patient's time being taken up by treatment) is a controversial issue. As we remarked earlier, there are those who consider its inclusion as inequitable. Other opponents stress its conflict with WTP principles. Even if one does endorse the inclusion of indirect costs, there are a whole host of measurement issues involved with estimating the extent to which society's output will actually fall when a person cannot show up for work. In a CUA of gallstone treatments by Cook et al. (1994), they focus on establishing the quantitative importance of including indirect costs.

Indirect costs impact the choice of gallstone treatment in the following way. The standard treatment for gallstones was removing the gallbladder itself (called a cholecystectomy). This causes considerable post-operative sickness (pain, diarrhea and nausea) and a lengthy recovery period (hence a lengthy period away from work). As an alternative to this 'open' surgery, one could have the gallstone removed by a laparoscopic cholecystectomy (a laparotomy is a surgical incision into any part of the abdominal wall), which is a minimal access surgery where the post-operative morbidity (sickness) is greatly reduced and patients can resume normal duties within two to three days. Finally, there is now available a way of fragmenting the gallstones by external shock waves, called an extracorporeal shock wave lithotripsy or ESWL (lithotripter is Greek for 'stone crusher'). With an ESWL being non-invasive, post-treatment sickness is minor and the patient can leave the hospital on the same day as treatment. The work disruption is thus least with an ESWL.

A CUA was a more appropriate evaluation technique than a CEA because there did not exist a single outcome to use as 'the' effect. A QALY covers the post-treatment sickness as a quality of life (QoL) issue, and the chance of dying from the operation as a quantity of life dimension. In the gallstone case, the chance of dying from surgery was thought to be 1 in 1000. The QALY outcomes therefore depended mainly on the QoL component (with life expectancies from gallstone patients set at 25 years, 0.001

times 25 produces a QALY amount of 0.025, that is, the *quantity* of life years element was about nine days).

Living (having time) with severe pain was judged by the patients to be worth 89% of time without pain. So an 11% reduction in QoL was assigned to any life years spent in pain. Having severe diarrhea had a QoL loss of 19%. For the three symptoms combined that were associated with time after open cholecystectomy, the QoL loss was 56%.

Table 1.1 (based on Tables 3 and 4 of Cook et al.) presents the results for the three kinds of gallstone treatment. Cook et al. used two different perspectives for estimating the QALYs. To simplify matters, we record only the approach that had the higher QALY magnitudes.

Table 1.1:   Costs and effects for alternative gallstone treatments

Cost variables and QALYs	Open cholecystectomy	Laparoscopic cholecystectomy	ESWL
Hospital cost	$3366	$2581	$4007
Patient cost	$992	$395	$254
Cost of conversion	$4358	$3154	$4962
Indirect cost	$2564	$1268	$574
Total cost	$6922	$4422	$5536
Effect (QALY loss)	0.1650	0.1200	0.1205

Source: Cook et al. (1994)

Open cholecystectomy has higher costs and lower outcomes (a larger QALY loss) than laparoscopic cholecystectomy and so it cannot ever be more cost-effective than the non-open form of surgery, no matter how one values a QALY. The additional total cost ($1114) of ESWL over laparoscopic cholecystectomy (that is, $5536 − $4422) divided by the additional effect of 0.005 QALYs (or 0.1210 − 0.1205) produces an estimated incremental cost of $2228000 per QALY gained from ESWL. If one omits the indirect costs, the incremental cost per QALY from ESWL would be 62% higher at $3616 000. Cook et al. therefore found that omitting or including indirect costs makes a big difference to the gallstone treatment outcomes.

There are two aspects of the gallstone treatment study that we wish to highlight. On one hand, we see the strength of a CUA in that it quite naturally includes treatment side-effects in the determination of outcomes. As we shall see in the next case study, trying to measure side-effects in monetary terms for use in a CBA is very difficult. On the other hand, we see the inherent weakness of any CUA study. Cook et al. found that the cost per

QALY gained from ESWL was $2228000 when indirect costs were included (and as high as $3616 000 when indirect costs were omitted). The authors state, 'it is doubtful that any authority would consider buying QALYs at the costs reported here'. While this judgment is undoubtedly correct, with a CUA we need to know exactly what cut-off point would make a QALY worth buying. The authors suggest that a cost per QALY of $13 573 might be worthwhile (which would be obtained if we omit laparoscopic cholecystectomy from consideration and look at ESWL over open surgery). But how can one know this for sure? Only a CBA can tell whether a treatment is worth undertaking.

Whether to include indirect costs can be resolved as follows. In a traditional CBA, restoring one's earnings ability is included as a benefit (indirect) and forgoing earnings in order to undergo treatment is included as a cost (indirect). So, clearly, ignoring indirect costs would not be valid in a traditional CBA because negative earnings are as important to record as positive earnings. Would it be valid to omit such costs from a CUA where the consequence is not measured in earnings?

Relative to a traditional CBA, a CUA can be interpreted to be omitting indirect benefits from the denominator of the cost-effectiveness ratio, but including indirect costs in the numerator. Omitting indirect benefits would be valid in a CUA because the consequence side has an all-inclusive outcome measure in a QALY. Quality-adjusted time can be used for any purpose one likes, including earning income. Using time for work is not an additional consequence. There would then be no question of trying to add earnings measured in dollars to the QALYs. Indirect costs, on the other hand, are not subsumed in the input side by some non-monetary index and so should be included on the denominator of a CUA.

1.4.2   A Worksite Hypertension Program

One of the intangible effects of taking medication is that there are side-effects to the treatment. The medications for hypertension (high blood pressure) particularly had this drawback as people were refusing to take the required medication. Low compliance and high treatment dropout rates were mainly responsible for the fact that, in the 1980s, only 30% of the US population had their blood pressure under good control. If one were going to conduct a CBA of hypertension treatments, an important part of the analysis would then involve putting monetary valuations on the side-effects of the medications. But little work actually has been done in this direction.

As an alternative to trying to find precise estimates of these intangible costs of treatment, one could try to side-step the issue by focusing on compliance as a separate treatment program and trying to achieve greater compliance at least cost. This in effect has been the approach adopted by Logan et al. (1981) who examined whether the greater convenience of worksite treatment programs would increase compliance. The relevance of Logan et al.'s CEA study for CBA is that if one can find a way to make the side-effects issue 'go away', a standard CBA that ignored compliance effects would be more valid. In effect, by providing a worksite location for treatment that is more convenient, one is lowering the disutility of the side-effects (in the sense that the side-effects occur in a more comfortable setting and hence become more tolerable) and thereby increasing compliance with the medication regime.

Table 1.2: Cost and effect per patient for worksite care and regular care

Variable	Worksite care (WS)	Regular care (RC)	WS − RC
Health system costs	$197.36	$129.33	$68.03
Patient costs	$45.50	$82.00	($36.50)
Total costs	$242.86	$211.33	$31.53
Effect (mm Hg)	12.10	6.50	5.60

Source: Logan et al. (1981)

Table 1.2 (based on Tables 3 and 4 of Logan et al.) shows the costs and effects of worksite care (WS), where a person is treated by a nurse at a person's worksite, compared to regular care (RC), where a person has to make an office visit to a physician. The effect of the treatment is recorded as a mm Hg reduction in the diastolic blood pressure (BP) of the patient. The direct costs are called here the 'health system costs'. As we can see in the table, the direct costs are higher for the worksite program, but the patient costs are lower. When we add the two categories of cost we find that total costs are $31.53 higher for the WS program. For this additional cost, the WS program obtains a 5.6 mm Hg additional reduction in blood pressure (which means that a 1 mm Hg reduction in BP can be purchased for $5.63).

The hypertension study highlights a number of principles concerning how to carry out an incremental analysis for a CEA (and these principles will be presented in Part III). However, we are more concerned here with discussing the study's relevance to the CBA principles established in this chapter.

The most important point to note with a CEA is that it does not establish whether *any* procedure is worthwhile. As Logan et al. acknowledge with their conditional statement: 'If conventional treatment of hypertension (RC) is considered worthwhile, it is clearly more cost-effective to replace RC with WS treatment.' We know that a 1 mm Hg reduction in BP can be purchased for $5.63 in the WS program. But we do not know whether this is a price that individuals (or society) are willing to pay. Moreover, even though the RC program is less cost-effective than the WS program (the C/E ratio is lower), the RC program could still be worthwhile if it is thought that $32.51 ($211.33/6.5) is worth paying for a 1 mm Hg reduction in BP.

Worth mentioning are the different results from alternative perspectives shown in the study. Logan et al. were careful to distinguish the total costs that are incurred by society as a whole from those related to the persons being treated for hypertension. In this case, costs for society moved in the opposite direction from those for the patients. The total cost increase of $31.53 from having the WS program consisted of a $68.03 increase in health system costs and a $36.50 reduction in patient costs. Clearly, patients will be more enthusiastic supporters of WS programs than the rest of society.

The fact that patients had the $36.50 saving from the WS program is vital information in understanding how a CEA can supplement a CBA. Recall that the problem was how to incorporate into an evaluation the side-effects of the hypertension medication. The CEA comparison of WS with RC can be interpreted as a way of minimizing the costs for overcoming the side-effects. Patients in the WS program received greater convenience. Not having to make an office visit translated into a cash equivalent saving of $36.50. One could argue that patients' behavior revealed their preferences over side-effects and so produced an estimate of what the side-effects were worth. That is, $36.50 was sufficient to overcome the adverse side-effects of the medication, or else the patients would not have taken the medication, and there would not have been the BP reduction observed.

The result is that we are suggesting the use of a two-stage evaluation process. First we employ a CBA to evaluate treatment ignoring the side-effects. Then we add to the cost side a sum of money to minimize the side-effects, which entails finding the most cost-effective way to overcome those side-effects. For the hypertension case, the most cost-effective way was to use the WS program, and the total amount of money to add to the costs was the $68.03 increase in health system costs for the program. The most informative way to view the $68.03 figure is to consider the second stage to be taking the $31.53 amount, reflecting the total additional resources required by the rest of society to set up the nurses at the worksite, and add to this the $36.50 to compensate the patients for taking the medication and putting up with the side-effects.

1.4.3   A Survey of Health Care Evaluation Practice

In this case study we provide an overview of the health care evaluation field using the survey by Elixhauser et al. (1993). Specifically, we report which type of economic evaluation is most used in practice and what kinds of treatment or service are being evaluated. In this way the reader can get a feel for the scope of the health care evaluation field and obtain an idea of what applications to expect later in this book.

Elixhauser et al. compiled a list of 1897 reports of health evaluation studies and 1309 other articles (reviews, editorials, methods and comments) for the period 1979–90. We will concentrate on the results for the study reports. To be included in the list the study must cover both the inputs (the costs) and the outputs (the consequences). As a consequence they exclude all cost minimization studies. Because authors called their studies CEAs even when they used QALYs as the effect, CEAs and CUAs were combined and all called CEAs. What then took place was a comparison of CBAs and CEAs. Most (66%) of the studies were for the US. Studies originated in the US that used foreign data were classed as non-US. There was a large growth in the number of economic evaluations over time (the annual number of studies grew from five in 1966 to 251 in 1990).

Prior to this study period, from 1966 to 1978, Elixhauser et al. claimed that CBAs and CEAs were roughly in equal numbers in the literature. This parity then changed and CEAs became the evaluation technique of choice. During 1979–85, the share of CEAs rose to 58.9%, and increased even further to 64.5% for the most recent period, 1985–90. The authors of the survey suggested that the controversy involved with putting a monetary value on life and limb that takes place in a CBA contributed to the relative appeal of CEA.

Table 1.3 (based on Tables 1 and 3 of Elixhauser et al.) summarizes the health care evaluation field for the 1979–90 period as it relates to CBA and CEA and to the two combined (called 'all'). From the outset we need to be aware that components do not sum to the correct totals (because the classification scheme used does not have categories that are mutually exclusive and collectively exhaustive).

The 1897 studies are split into three categories according to their medical function: (1) preventative (334 studies); (2) diagnostic (612 studies); and (3) therapeutic (761 studies). The first entry in Table 1.3 (listed as the 'medical function') presents the aggregate figures for the three categories, and the other headings deal with the detailed breakdown for these categories. We now cover the details for each category in turn.

Table 1.3: Comparison of CBA and CEA study reports from 1979 to 1990

Dimension	All reports	CBA	CEA
Medical function			
Prevention	333.7 (20.0%)	134.5 (23.1%)	171.5 (16.5%)
Diagnosis	612.2 (35.9%)	160.5 (27.6%)	421.5 (40.4%)
Treatment	761.2 (44.6%)	287.5 (49.4%)	449.5 (43.1%)
Prevention function			
Medically oriented	272.5 (80.4%)	106.5 (76.3%)	140.5 (74.5%)
Education / behavior	66.5 (19.6%)	33.0 (23.7%)	48.0 (25.5%)
Diagnosis function			
Symptomatic	353.5 (55.6%)	81.0 (46.6%)	254.0 (58.0%)
Screening	282.5 (44.4%)	93.0 (53.4%)	184.0 (42.0%)
Treatment function			
Cure	319.0 (44.6%)	103.0 (39.3%)	205.0 (48.4%)
Rehabilitation	58.0 (8.1%)	24.0 (9.2%)	29.0 (6.8%)
Maintenance	339.0 (47.3%)	135.0 (51.5%)	190.0 (44.8%)
Treatment modality			
Medication	233.0 (38.3%)	100.0 (44.8%)	128.0 (35.3%)
Device / procedure	152.0 (25.0%)	43.0 (19.3%)	99.0 (27.3%)
Surgery	133.0 (21.9%)	47.0 (21.1%)	83.0 (22.9%)
Education / behavior	58.0 (9.5%)	22.0 (9.9%)	33.0 (9.1%)
Other	30.0 (5.3%)	11.0 (4.9%)	20.0 (5.5%)

Source: Elixhauser et al. (1993)

1. *Preventative*: There are two types of preventative intervention, namely, medically oriented (consisting of traditional clinical interventions, such as physical check-ups, vaccinations and providing antibiotics) and education/behavior interventions (such as smoking cessation classes and community heart disease programs). The medically oriented prevention programs greatly predominated, with a share of around 80% for both CBAs and CEAs.
2. *Diagnostic*: This category comprises symptomatic (diagnosing patients with the symptoms of a disease by such devices as laboratory tests) and screening (diagnosing illness in asymptomatic patients, which includes tests for such things as cervical cancer). Symptomatic testing outnumbers screening testing overall and for CEAs, but not for CBAs.
3. *Therapeutic*: This type of intervention (listed under the heading 'treatment' in Table 1.3) is subdivided using two different classification schemes. First, treatments are classified by their function, whether cure (as with treating infectious diseases), rehabilitation (for example,

providing physical therapy after a stroke), maintenance interventions which do not eliminate the underlying conditions (as with hypertension treatment in the case study we have just covered) and multiple functions (for example, interventions in an intensive care unit). There are more maintenance studies than those related to cure for CEAs, but the reverse holds for CBAs. There were very few studies of rehabilitation whether it be CBA or CEA. Secondly, treatments were classified by treatment modality. For both CBAs and CEAs, roughly 40% of the modalities concern medications (pharmaceutical interventions), 20% are for procedures (such as venous compression stockings), 20% for surgery (invasive procedures) and the remaining 20% are for education (exercise regimens) and 'other' (nutritional interventions).

A useful way of providing some perspective about the Elixhauser et al. survey is to use as a reference point Drummond's (1981) observations comparing and contrasting economic evaluations in the health care field with those in other sectors. Drummond made his points in the context of evaluations prior to 1980, but they seem to be just as valid today.

In some respects, evaluations in the health care field are most suitable for the standard type of economic appraisal. Economic evaluations rely on 'partial equilibrium analysis', assuming that income and all other prices are held constant. Strictly, then, only 'small' projects are appropriately evaluated by economic appraisals. In the health care field this has definitely been the case. Evaluations have been applied to limited and tightly defined problems, such as whether hernias should be treated by inpatient or outpatient surgery, or whether one should screen for a particular disease.

A major difference between health applications and those elsewhere is over the selection of alternatives chosen for evaluation. In other fields, evaluations have been of large capital projects (e.g., airports). In the health care field the applications are of procedures (treatments) and not capital expenditures, such as hospitals. This has advantages and disadvantages.

The advantages are that:

(a) Decisions over procedures are at the heart of resource allocation in the medical field and so it makes sense to focus on activities that are of most concern to those involved in the field.
(b) Consequently, the health care field has an edge over other areas that have neglected to evaluate procedures, for example in the transportation field, where there is a need to evaluate whether standby flights are worthwhile.

The disadvantages of concentrating evaluations on procedures are:

(a) Health evaluators have had to deal with the difficult issues of measuring outputs.
(b) Important issues have been missed, for example, decisions over where to site hospitals.
(c) There is no direct link between the evaluation and the making of expenditure decisions. For example, it has been shown that kidney transplants are more cost-effective than any form of dialysis. The issue is: who is the client for this information? The question of transplants and kidney treatment as a whole is dealt with by health planners (hospital administrators, insurance companies, health maintenance organizations, and public officials) who take a broad view, and would need a lot wider evaluation than just knowing about a particular set of procedures.
(d) The narrow focus has led to the neglect of other health producing measures, such as changes in lifestyles and government agricultural policy, which may affect health just as much as the medical procedures.

1.4.4 The Sixth Stool Guaiac Protocol

The sixth stool guaiac protocol is a classic in the health care field as a case study in showing what happens when apparently sensible health regulations or procedures are imposed without first undertaking a thorough economic evaluation of the costs and effects of those procedures. Neuhauser and Lewicki published their work in 1975. More recently, there has been a reevaluation of the case study (see Brown (1990), Neuhauser (1990) and Gatsonis (1990)). Our view is that a lot can be learned from this study even if everything was not as assumed by Neuhauser and Lewicki. We first explain exactly how such a large figure of $47 million per case detected was obtained. Then we explore some of the wider implications following from the case study.

In earlier work, D.H. Greegor had studied asymptomatic colonic cancer, which involved testing the stool for occult blood. Unfortunately, some of those with cancer were not detected by a single test. Greegor therefore recommended, and the American Cancer Society endorsed, a protocol of six sequential tests. If a positive outcome for a test were found, the existence of cancer would be confirmed by a subsequent barium-enema examination.

The cost of an individual test was very small. The first stool test was assumed to cost $4, and each subsequent test cost $1. The barium-enema procedure was considered to cost $100. Clearly, so it seemed in a CM-type framework, it would be cheaper to use the stool tests than to use the barium-enema procedure on everyone. The issue was, though, how many extra cases would be detected by the sixth test.

Neuhauser and Lewicki used Greegor's results, which were based on a screening of 278 people, and extrapolated them for a hypothetical study of 10000 people. Thus, because two cases were confirmed out of the 278 cases, there would be 72 cases in a population of 10000. They treated each one of Greegor's tests as an independent event with a 91.67% chance of detecting cancer. After one test, with 91.67% of the cases detected, there would be 8.33% of the cases undetected. Test two would have a 91.67% chance of detecting the remaining cases, which means there would be an additional 7.64% cases detected (i.e., 0.9167 times 8.33% equals 7.64%). And so on. What this means is that of 72 cases of colonic cancer, 66 cases would be detected after one test, and 71 cases after two tests. Clearly, there were very few cases left undetected (precisely one) after two tests. By undertaking test six, only 0.0003 extra cases were detected. The cases detected and the corresponding costs are indicated below in Table 1.4 (see their Table 2). (The 'incremental' cost is the cost of one more test, while 'marginal' cost is the cost per case detected from one more test.)

Table 1.4:   Detection rates for successive stool guaiac tests

Number of tests	Cancer detection			Screening costs ($)		
	Number of cases	Incremental gain	Total	Incremental	Marginal	Average
1	65.9469	65.9469	77511	77511	1175	1175
2	71.4424	5.4956	107690	30179	5492	1507
3	71.9004	0.4580	130199	22509	49150	1810
4	71.9385	0.0382	148116	17917	469534	2059
5	71.9417	0.0032	163141	15024	4724695	2268
6	71.9420	0.0003	176331	13190	47107214	2451

Source: Neuhauser and Lewicki (1975)

The final line is what interests us. It shows that for an extra 0.0003 of a case detected, the extra cost involved with the sixth test was $13190. In other words, an extra case detected by the sixth test was $47 million ($13190/0.0003). Note that if the occult blood testing were bypassed and the barium used as the screening procedure for 10000 persons, the total cost would be $1 million (10000 times $100). The (marginal and average) cost would have been $13900 per cancer case detected. Thus, the sixth stool guaiac protocol was not even cost minimizing.

One general issue concerning the guaiac protocol that is often found in health care evaluations is the importance of assuming that treatments are divisible and that a proportional relationship concerning outputs and costs applies. One needs to be aware that $47 million was not actually at stake and could have been devoted elsewhere. The extra cost of the sixth test was only $13190. The point was that for this $13190 very little was obtained (0.0003 of a case detected). *If* one purchases cases at this rate, and *if* there were this proportional relation between cost and cases, then one would end up paying $47 million if one stopped when one purchased exactly one case. But, actually, only $13190 would have been saved if the protocol had not been introduced. CEAs and CUAs are especially vulnerable to relying on this proportionality assumption because their outcome measures are always expressed in ratio form.

In terms of the specifics of the case study, the main message (emphasized by Gatsonis) is the need to obtain precise estimates of clinical and economic outcomes when making economic evaluations. The Neuhauser and Lewicki study was based on working with the assumption that only two cases of colonic cancer were found in the study population. However, these were just the *proven* cases. Some of the people who had negative test results could have had the disease (Gatsonis writes: 'the possibility that further cancers may have existed among them is not negligible'). If instead of two cases there were three cases, all the numbers would change dramatically and the sixth test would not have been nearly so costly. One of the real problems therefore was in the Greegor data (concerning the prevalence of the disease), which Neuhauser and Lewicki used to carry out their evaluation.

The evaluation of the sixth stool guaiac protocol had a widespread impact. Not only did the study greatly affect the whole field of clinical decision-making, but it also changed actual policy. As pointed out by Getzen (1997), the study (and its aftermath) caused the American Cancer Society to amend its recommendations: 'Now, routine stool guaiac screening is recommended only for individuals over age 50, or whose family history makes them at high risk for colorectal cancer'.

1.5   FINAL SECTION

All chapters will contain a problems section, a chapter summary, and a section indicating where some of the unresolved issues will be covered in later chapters.

1.5.1   Problems

The four main methods for making an economic evaluation in health care have been introduced in this chapter. The problems that follow require the reader to select and assemble from a set of categories of costs and outcomes the necessary ingredients to conduct each of the four kinds of evaluation.

Table 1.5:   Evaluation of neo-natal intensive care treatment

Cost or consequence	Before intensive care	With intensive care	Incremental effect
1. Cost per additional survivor (to hospital discharge)	$5400	$14200	$8800
2. Cost per additional survivor (to death)	$92500	$100100	$7600
3. Survival rate (to hospital discharge)	62.4%	77.2%	14.8%
4. Survival time (per live birth):			
a. Life-years	38.8	47.7	8.9
b. QALYs	27.4	36.0	8.6
5. Earnings	$122200	$154 000	$32000

Source: Boyle et al. (1983)

The evaluation being considered in Table 1.5 is Boyle et al.'s (1983) study of neo-natal intensive care in Canada. (All monetary figures cited are in Canadian dollars.) The provision of neo-natal intensive care involves increased current capital expenditures (to control the respiratory, nutritional and environmental circumstances of the baby) in order to increase a baby's future survival chances. The costs and consequences for babies with birth weight 1000–1499 g are listed in Table 1.5 (all figures are undiscounted).

1. Undertake a cost minimization comparison of neo-natal intensive care (before versus with intensive care) from: (a) the hospital's perspective and (b) society's perspective.
2. Undertake a CEA comparison of neo-natal intensive care from society's perspective. (Hint: more than one category of consequence could be used to form the CEA comparison.)
3. Undertake a CUA comparison of neo-natal intensive care from society's perspective. (Hint: only one category of consequence can be used to form the CUA comparison.)

4. Undertake a traditional CBA comparison (that is, use the human capital approach) to evaluate neo-natal intensive care from society's perspective. (Hint: only one category of consequence can be used to form the CBA comparison.)

1.5.2 Summary

This chapter started with a definition of a health care evaluation that stressed the need to consider alternatives. It was argued that one needed to carry out evaluations in order to ensure that funds were put to their best use. We then introduced the four main types of economic evaluation that comprise the health care evaluation field. In explaining the logic of each type of evaluation, we first set up CBA as the primary evaluation method, and then showed that the other types of evaluation could be considered to be special cases of a CBA. It was the fact that CBA measured both inputs and outputs in common, monetary terms that made CBA the only method that can actually tell whether a health care intervention should, or should not, be undertaken.

Although there is this unity from a theoretical point of view, the focus in all cases was on identifying the practical circumstances necessary to validate a particular method. This focus will be the defining characteristic of the book. That is, we are trying to develop an understanding of the strengths and weaknesses of trying to apply each of the evaluation types.

In the outline of the basics of CBA, we identified consumer sovereignty as the main value judgment. Whenever it is sensible to assume that the individual is the best judge of his/her welfare, modern CBA based on WTP is the appropriate evaluation framework. How practical WTP is as an approach to estimating benefits is a separate issue and one that will be explored in depth in this book. The modern approach has to be contrasted with the traditional approach to CBA based on the concept of human capital. Traditional CBA, which uses earnings to measure the benefits, has the merit that data on production are readily available. This largely accounts for its popularity in the health care field. But it is not based on firm welfare economic principles that depend on individual preferences for their validity. Also the human capital approach has its critics on equity grounds.

The applications section revealed the strong preference in the practice of health care evaluations for non-CBA types of evaluation. Thus the applications covered the three main alternatives to CBA, that is, CUA, CEA and CM. The CUA study of gallstone treatments highlighted the strength of CUA to be able to include routinely in its evaluations quality of life issues, such as pain and suffering; something which CBA often fails to incorporate.

In the CEA of hypertension treatment locations, we showed how a CEA could be used in a back-up role to a CBA to help it include treatment of side-effects. However, with both applications, we emphasized the inherent weakness of using any non-CBA type of evaluation. One could not say whether any of the treatment alternatives were worthwhile. The final application, which was conducted in a CM-type framework, returned to the theme introduced at the beginning of the chapter. That is, why it is necessary to explicitly carry out a health care evaluation. Without a formal evaluation, one could be wasting dollars that could be used elsewhere to save lives or otherwise make society much better off.

1.5.3   Looking Ahead

With only the introductory chapter (Part I) covered at this stage, looking ahead involves providing a guide to the rest of the book. Each of the four evaluation types will be analyzed in depth. Part II deals with CM; CEA forms Part III; CUA is in Part IV, and the final Part V is on CBA.

Since all four evaluation types depend on costs, and this is all there is in a CM, we start with Chapter 2 defining costs from an economic perspective and examining the rationale of CM as a type of economic evaluation. Chapter 3 explains some of the problems of measuring costs and examines whether hospital and physician charges can be used. The concept of costs is then broadened in Chapters 4 and 5 to include the costs on the rest of society, whether they are people not directly involved with treatment (generating so called 'external costs') or general taxpayers.

Chapters 6 and 7 are on CEA. They analyze its relationship to CBA and cover the controversial issues involved with discounting effects. Chapter 8 starts the part on CUA and examines its link to CBA. Chapter 9 describes the main instruments used to estimate the utilities, and Chapter 10 examines other alternatives to a QALY in an equity context. The two different kinds of CBA, traditional and modern, are discussed in Chapters 11 and 12. The final chapter explores how to include equity considerations in CBA.

PART II

CM and CBA

2. Cost minimization and the definition of 'cost'

2.1 INTRODUCTION

We begin our account of health care evaluations with the cost part of CBA. All four evaluation types rely on these costs, which makes an analysis of costs common to all. We will be focusing on CM because an estimation of costs is all that is required to use this evaluation type. We start by defining economic costs and explain how they depend on the time period being considered. The role of discounting is then introduced. From there we present a detailed account of how CM fits in with economic theories explaining cost curves in the short and long runs. The first section closes with an analysis of how discounted costs at different times are combined into a present value figure. CM and its relationship with CEA and CBA criteria are explored in the next section. CM applications follow and the chapter ends with the final comments section.

2.1.1 Definition of 'Cost'

To a non-economist, 'cost' is what you pay for a good or service. Backing up the idea of paying for something is the existence of a receipt. This is a tangible record of incurring cost. So accountants and tax authorities implicitly define cost as an expense for which you have a receipt. However, to an economist, cost refers to the sacrifice of benefits by using resources for a particular use rather than for some other (best) use. That is, by using a resource for a particular use one is forgoing the opportunity of using that resource elsewhere. For this reason, economists refer to the sacrifice of benefits as 'opportunity cost'.

The existence of forgone opportunities may have nothing to do with money payments. Payments may be incurred for which there is no use of resources and hence no economic cost (as with sales tax payments to the government); and no money payments may be involved yet resources may be utilized (as when industries cause pollution by dumping waste products into rivers that require filtering).

Opportunity cost also may have nothing to do with receipts. A clear example involves charitable tax deductions in the US. A person who bakes and donates cookies for a hospital sale of refreshments for an open day can get a tax deduction for the gift, if they can get a receipt from the hospital. But if a person gives up their time actually to sell the refreshments, then the value of that time given up does not have a receipt and is therefore not tax deductible. The opportunity cost of time is a major component in many health care interventions, but is often excluded from economic evaluations, whether it be the time of volunteers or the time given up for patient care by family members.

2.1.2 Costs in the Short and Long Runs

We have just seen that time is a resource like any other that has value in an alternative use. The alternative use value of any resource is itself something that depends on time. The way that this works is as follows. The main factor that determines the magnitude of costs is the volume of output (or the scale of the effects). This relation between costs and output (the 'cost curve') is different the longer the time period we consider. In economics, time is classified in a way that need have no bearing on calendar time. The short run is that period when at least one input is fixed and the long run is the period when there are no fixed factors. An input is fixed if it does not vary with output.

For most health care evaluations that relate to hospital activities, one assumes that the cost of building the hospital has taken place and does not have to be replicated in order to accommodate the new mode of treatment one wishes to evaluate. The hospital building costs are then fixed costs for the purpose of the treatment mode evaluation. This means that one is not contemplating using the hospital building as, for example, a factory for making shoes. Since for the time being it has no alternative use, the hospital building expense will have been incurred irrespective of any particular treatment. The building cost will not be greater or lower if treatment does not take place. On the other hand, the costs of nursing, physician services and medication will be greater the larger the treatment scale we wish to introduce, and these then are variable costs.

In the long run, all costs are variable. Thus, when we vary the scale of a treatment, all costs must be included. We must now recognize that the hospital could close down if the building could be renovated and used for another activity. An interest payment for the use of the capital invested in the building must be added to the staff and medication expenses to determine the cost of treatment. It is in the determination of the long run cost curve that the concept of CM is important. For each output level, we find that combination of inputs that results in the least cost. As we shall attempt to explain in the next section, working with a cost curve obtained by cost minimization is a necessary condition for ensuring that we obtain the most worthwhile use of our resources.

2.1.3 Discounting Costs over Time

Although the short and long runs vary by industry and, within health care, according to the particular treatment we are evaluating, calendar time *per se* does have an important impact on an economic evaluation. A dollar of costs today is worth more than a dollar of costs in the future and we need to incorporate this fact. The process of reducing the value of future costs is called discounting and this relies on a parameter called the discount rate.

Exactly why, and with what rate, we discount are covered in detail in Chapter 7 when effects as well as costs are brought into the picture. For now, all we need to acknowledge is that banks and other financial institutions provide an interest rate on funds they borrow from savers. So if one puts a dollar in the bank today, then next year it will accumulate to a sum that includes the bank's interest rate. This would be one reason why a dollar today would be more valuable than one in the future.

2.2 COST MINIMIZATION AND ECONOMIC THEORY

Let us assume in this section (something we will check in the next chapter) that the price paid for an input measures its opportunity cost. For ease of exposition, we will consider the case where there are just two inputs, say capital K and labor L. If we represent the price of capital as P_K and the price of labor as P_L, then we can write total costs C as:

$$C = P_K K + P_L L \qquad (2.1)$$

where $P_K K$ is the amount spent on capital and $P_L L$ is the expenditure on labor. All the main principles concerning the construction of cost curves can be made in terms of the average cost per unit AC that is defined as:

$$AC = C/Q = P_K (K/Q) + P_L (L/Q) \qquad (2.2)$$

To calculate costs on the basis of equations (2.1) or (2.2), we need to be given two pieces of information. First one needs to know the prices of the inputs P_K and P_L. Then one requires knowledge of how many units of the two inputs K and L will be purchased at these prices. Throughout we will assume that the input prices are market determined and therefore known. How many inputs to use is found from the relationship linking inputs and outputs that is called the production function as represented by:

$$Q = F(K,L) \qquad (2.3)$$

For each and every combination of K and L, the production function indicates the maximum output Q that can be obtained. Since the production function depends on the time period being considered, we need to analyze separately the short run and long run cost curves.

2.2.1   Short Run Cost Curves

It usually makes most sense to think of capital as being the fixed factor in the short run. This makes labor the variable factor. Consequently, we can decompose total costs in equation (2.1) into two components: $P_K K$ is the fixed costs and $P_L L$ is the variable costs.

The production function in the short run can be written as:

$$Q = F(\bar{K}, L) \qquad (2.4)$$

where the bar over the variable K indicates that it is being fixed at a particular level. Using this notation, we can write the short run average cost equation as:

$$AC = (P_K \bar{K})/Q + (P_L L)/Q \qquad (2.5)$$

From equation (2.4), it is plain that the only way to obtain more output Q in the short run is to use more of the input L. However, the relationship between Q and L in the short run is such that, although it is true that generally one can expect that Q will increase with increases in L, it is also true that the increases in Q will often be smaller the more units of L one utilizes. This property of short run production functions is called by economists *the law of diminishing returns* and roughly corresponds with the adage: 'too many cooks spoil the broth' (where the space in the kitchen is, presumably, the fixed factor and using extra cooks just means that they get in each other's way).

The diminishing returns property of short run production functions implies that the average product of labor Q/L will (eventually) fall. Equivalently, we can say that the reciprocal of Q/L, i.e., L/Q, will rise. Note that L/Q is a part of the second term defining average costs given by equation (2.5), a term that is called average variable costs. So the law of diminishing returns requires that the component of average costs related to average variable costs must rise as output increases.

On the other hand, the first part of average cost in equation (2.5), which is called average fixed costs, always declines with an increase in output. The fixed costs are $P_K \bar{K}$. Dividing these fixed costs by Q (a process called in business 'spreading one's overheads') will be a force lowering AC. At low levels of output, one can expect the force lowering fixed costs per unit to be greater than that raising the variable cost per unit; hence AC will fall. However, the law of diminishing returns will get progressively more powerful as Q gets larger, and the advantages of spreading overheads will get progressively weaker. So at high levels of output AC will rise. Overall, then, there will be this 'U-shaped' relation between AC and Q in the short run.

To clarify the ideas that have just been presented, let us consider an example based on the hospital cost study by Stern et al. (1995) of total knee arthroplasty, i.e., artificial joint replacement ('arthro' means joint and 'plastos' is Greek for molded). We have created numbers that reproduce the total cost figures in that study of an average stay in a 580-bed teaching hospital. The full study will be one of the case studies in the applications section. They consider eight inputs. We will collapse them into two. We can regard the operating room to do the knee surgery as the fixed capital input K and the number of nurses as the variable input L. Their output Q is the length of stay LOS in the hospital measured in days.

The capital input (the operating room) is measured in minutes per hospital stay. The starting point in the Stern et al. analysis was 1992, when the operating room minutes were 202. So we will use $K = 202$ as the level of the fixed factor. Total fixed costs in 1992 were \$8872. If this entire sum involves capital expenditures, then the capital cost per minute, P_K, was \$43.92 (i.e., \$8872/202).

As there was no information on units for variable inputs, we deduced a hypothetical number of nurses by first assuming an input price for labor. If it costs \$100 a day to hire a nurse, and the average LOS in 1992 was 8.7 days (i.e., $Q = 8.7$ days), then having a nurse for the full hospital stay would fix $P_L = \$870$. Total variable costs in 1992 were \$8543. Again assuming all of this expense is devoted to just labor results in approximately 9.82 nurses being hired (on average). For four other LOS, we make up plausible numbers for L. Then the short run production function given by equation (2.4) can be represented as a table consisting of five output levels that correspond with five variable input levels for L. This relation is shown in the first two rows of Table 2.1.

Line 3 of Table 2.1 depicts the implication of the law of diminishing returns. It shows that, as labor increases, output per unit of labor decreases, i.e., the average product of labor (Q/L) falls. The last line confirms that, as Q/L falls, its inverse L/Q will rise. When we multiply the rising L/Q by the fixed price of labor P_L, we obtain $(P_L L)/Q$, which is average variable costs, and this must also be rising as L increases.

Table 2.1:   Short run production function for lengths of stay (LOS)

1. Length of stay, Q	1.50	5.00	6.10	8.70	9.00
2. Labor, L	1.25	5.00	6.20	9.82	12.00
3. Average product of labor, Q/L	1.20	1.00	0.98	0.89	0.75
4. Labor per day, L/Q	0.83	1.00	1.02	1.13	1.33

Source: Created by the author related to Stern et al. (1995)

The values calculated for average variable costs when $P_L = \$870$ are listed in Table 2.2. With total fixed costs equal to \$8872, Table 2.2 also presents average fixed costs and average variable costs for the five output levels given in Table 2.1. We see that the short run AC curve has the postulated U shape, as (eventually) the rising average variable costs offset of the falling average fixed costs.

Table 2.2:   Short run cost curves for lengths of stay (LOS)

1. Length of stay, Q	1.50	5.00	6.10	8.70	9.00
2. Average fixed costs, $(P_K \bar{K})/Q$,	\$5914	\$1774	\$1454	\$1020	\$986
3. Average variable cost, $(P_L L)/Q$	\$725	\$870	\$887	\$983	\$1160
4. Average costs, C/Q $= (P_K \bar{K})/Q + (P_L L)/Q$	\$6640	\$2644	\$2341	\$2003	\$2146

Source: Created by the author related to Stern et al. (1995)

The same production function is also displayed as a continuous curve in Figure 2.1. There one easily can see that the curve becomes flatter as units of labor increases, which is the property due to the law of diminishing returns. As drawn, we can see that maximum *LOS* corresponds with a number of nurses around 11.

2.2.2   Long Run Cost Curves

In the short run, the only way to increase output is to hire more labor. But in the long run there is more than one way to achieve this. One can alter capital as well as labor. It is in deciding the optimal mix of inputs that the

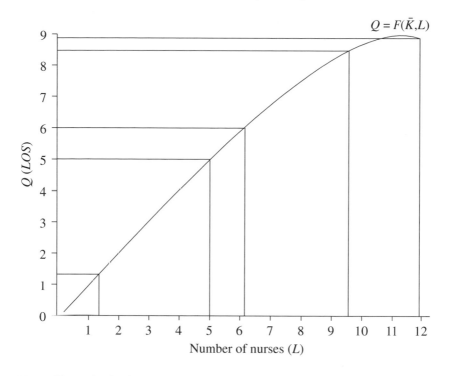

Note: The production function links units of output Q (*LOS*) with units of input L (number of nurses). In the short run (with capital fixed), the law of diminishing returns operates and this makes the production curve become flatter as the number of nurses increases. The flatter curve eventually will lead to a decline in the output per unit of labor (LOS/Q). This fall in the average product of labor will cause average variable costs to rise as labor increases and ultimately this will cause AC to rise with output.

Figure 2.1: The production function relating length of stay to the number of nurses

principle of cost-minimization becomes important. For, to be most efficient, one should choose the input combination that produces any given level of output at lowest cost. The law of diminishing returns does not apply in the long run and there is no necessity for AC eventually to rise with output.

We again illustrate the main ideas by using the Stern et al. study. They considered a 1994 output level as well as the 1992 one we have just analyzed. The length of stay over the two years fell from 8.7 to 6.1 days. Fixed costs (which we treat as capital costs) declined from $8872 to $6379. Assuming that the price of capital remained at its 1992 level of $43.92, we can deduce that K fell from 202 to 145 minutes (i.e., $6379/$43.92). Variable costs rose from \$8543 to \$8821. With labor as the only variable input, and with $P_L =$ \$870 assumed to remain at its 1992 level, the number of nurses would have increased from 9.82 to 10.14. The two actual values just mentioned for Q, K and L have been inserted into Table 2.3, together with other constructed possibilities. Table 2.3 represents the long run production function in tabular form (a three-dimensional diagram for Q, K and L is harder to draw and more difficult to visualize).

Table 2.3:   Long run production function for lengths of stay (LOS)

Labor, L (Number of nurses)	Capital, K (Number of operating minutes)		
	145	202	230
8.00	0.70	6.10	8.70
9.82	5.80	8.70	9.40
10.14	6.10	9.00	9.50

Source: Created by the author related to Stern et al. (1995)

Table 2.3 can be interpreted as follows. The outer row gives three capital alternatives and the outer column gives three labor options. The numbers in the inner three-by-three matrix in the center of the table indicate output levels. These output levels correspond to different pairs of values of the inputs K and L that are given by the column and row entries. Thus, the output level 0.70 in the first row and first column in the inner matrix of the table results from having 145 of K and 8.00 of L.

Because Table 2.3 represents a long run production function, we can see that there is more than one way to produce a given output. Consider the output $Q = 8.70$. Table 2.3 indicates that one can either use the combination of inputs: $K = 202$, $L = 9.82$, as we did in the short run with K regarded as fixed; or we can use the input combination: $K = 230$, $L = 8.00$, which has a higher K to L ratio and is therefore called the *capital intensive* input combination.

Whether one chooses the higher K/L ratio or not to produce $Q = 8.70$ depends on the objective. As we pointed out earlier, in a long run situation we are assuming that the aim is to achieve any given output at lowest cost (i.e., cost minimization). This was not an option in the short run because, with only one way to achieve a given output level (by altering the variable input), there was only one cost figure to consider. In our case, to apply the cost minimization principle, we need to calculate the cost of each input combination. If we substitute the input prices $P_K = \$43.92$ and $P_L = \$870$, along with the inputs $K = 202$, $L = 9.82$, into the cost equation (2.1), then the cost of the labor-intensive combination would be $17 415 (as was found by Stern et al.). However, for the hypothetical capital-intensive combination (using $K=230$ and $L=8.00$ with the same input prices), the cost would have been $17 062. Thus, in the long run, in order to choose the cost-minimizing combination to produce $Q=8.70$, one would use the more capital-intensive combination. The AC for using this lowest cost combination would be $1961 ($17 062/8.70).

Using exactly the same method, we can calculate the lowest cost way of producing the 1994 output level, $Q=6.10$. Table 2.3 reveals that either the input combination: $K=202$, $L=8.00$, or: $K=145$, $L=10.14$ are technically feasible ways of producing this level of output. With the input prices as before, the total cost of producing $Q=6.10$ would be lower using the second input combination (i.e., $15 190 as opposed to $15 832). Using the second input combination, the AC for producing $Q=6.10$ would be $2490.

The long run AC curve is defined as the lowest cost per unit for each output level. Because the law of diminishing returns does not apply in the long run, it cannot be stated *a priori* whether the long run curve will be falling (called 'economies of scale' by economists), rising ('diseconomies of scale') or horizontal ('constant returns to scale'). (The word 'scale' comes from the notion that one is varying inputs in the same proportion, like one does in making a model airplane to scale.) In the *LOS* costing example, we have just seen that the most efficient AC for producing $Q=6.10$ was $2490, and previously we found that it was $1961 for producing $Q=8.70$. In this case, AC was lower with the higher level of output. Thus, hospital stays for total knee arthroplasty is characterized as having economies of scale.

2.2.3 The Present Value Approach

Here we explain how one can determine exactly how much a dollar in the future is worth today, an amount called the *present value*. Say one has to pay 1 dollar's worth of costs next year. Why is this not worth a dollar? The reason is that, if one has a dollar today and puts it in the bank to earn interest at a rate r, then one would accumulate $1+r$ dollars next year. One could pay the dollar of costs and have a positive remainder (i.e., the interest r). So in order to pay $1 next year, one needs to put aside less than $1 today. How much less? As $1 accumulates to $1+r$, and one only requires $1, then $1/(1+r)$ would be the answer (seeing that $(1+r)/(1+r)=1$). The magnitude $1/(1+r)$ is called the *discount factor* to signify the extent to which future dollars are given lower values (i.e., discounted). Should future costs be $2 and not $1, then 2 times the discount factor produces the present value.

The logic of moving from next year's cost to this year's cost holds as between any two years. Thus, if one has to pay a cost of $1 in two years' time, one needs to put aside $1/(1+r)$ next year, but only $1/(1+r)$ times $1/(1+r)$ today. In other words, $1 in two years' time has a present value of $1/[1/(1+r)^2]$. For any year t in the future, the present value of a sum of money $S would be $S[1/(1+r)^t]$, where the expression in square brackets is the discount factor. That is:

$$Discount\ factor = \frac{1}{(1+r)^t} \tag{2.6}$$

Equation (2.6) makes clear that the discount factor that helps determine the present value is a function of two variables, r the rate of discount, and t the number of years into the future one is considering the cost. Table 2.4 below gives the calculated values of the discount factor for a range of discount rates and time horizons. Clearly, the higher the rate of interest, and the longer the future horizon, the lower the discount factor.

Table 2.4:   Discount factors for alternative time horizons and interest rates

Discount rates (r)	Number of years (t)					
	1	2	5	10	20	50
2% (i.e., 0.02)	0.980	0.961	0.906	0.820	0.673	0.372
5% (i.e., 0.05)	0.952	0.907	0.784	0.614	0.377	0.087
10% (i.e., 0.10)	0.909	0.826	0.621	0.386	0.149	0.009
15% (i.e., 0.15)	0.870	0.756	0.497	0.247	0.061	0.001
20% (i.e., 0.20)	0.833	0.694	0.402	0.162	0.026	0.000

Source: Created by the author from equation (2.6)

Typically, when one pays a cost in one year (like renting a nursing home for an aged parent) one has to pay that cost in a number of future years. In this case there is a stream of future costs to discount. The present value here is the sum of the present values in each year. With S_t denoting the cost S in year t, the present value PV of a stream of costs would be given as:

$$PV = \frac{S_1}{(1+r)^1} + \frac{S_2}{(1+r)^2} + \dots + \frac{S_t}{(1+r)^t} + \dots + \frac{S_n}{(1+r)^n} \tag{2.7}$$

The study by Lightwood and Glantz (1997) of the direct (medical) cost savings from the prevention of acute myocardial infarction (AMI) and stroke from the cessation of smoking illustrates the PV calculations. They looked at the 'benefits' of a quitter over a seven-year period. Year 1 was regarded as the current year and the costs at this time were not discounted. The cumulative year-by-year undiscounted cost savings are shown in the top line of Table 2.5 (based on their Table 4). The discounted cost savings, using a discount rate of 2.5%, are shown in line 3. To help explain how one moves from line 1 to line 3, we have inserted line 2 which shows the discount factors for each year using the 2.5% rate. This line was obtained by substituting $t = 1, ... , 6$ and $r = 0.025$ into equation (2.6). Thus, for year 2 considered to be one year into the future, the discount factor is $1/(1 + 0.025) = 0.0976$. Multiplying \$155 by 0.0976 produces the year 2 cumulative cost savings of \$151. When one multiplies line 1 by line 2, one obtains line 3. The cumulative cost savings after seven years were reduced by 14% even with such a low rate of discount as 2.5%.

Table 2.5: *Cumulative expected savings per quitter at time of cessation ($)*

Discount rates (r)	Years						
	1	2	3	4	5	6	7
1. Undiscounted	47	155	299	462	634	811	990
2. Discount factor	1.000	0.976	0.952	0.929	0.906	0.884	0.862
3. Discounted at 2.5%	47	151	284	429	575	717	853

Source: Based on Lightwood and Glantz (1997)

2.3 COST–BENEFIT ANALYSIS AND COST MINIMIZATION

We explain how a CBA operates and what must hold for CM (and CEA) to be a valid CBA.

2.3.1 Cost–Benefit Analysis

When we enquire whether $B > C$, we are asking whether the *total* benefits from all units of output that we are contemplating are worth more than the total costs. This question seeks to establish whether levels we are currently evaluating are worthwhile. The much larger issue is to know how many units give the most satisfaction, i.e., the greatest difference between benefits and costs. To obtain this desired output level, we need to look at how benefits and costs vary at the margin. Marginal benefits (MB) and marginal costs (MC) are the additional benefits and costs from producing one more unit of output.

The difference between using marginal and total evaluations of output in CBA can be explained by reference to Figure 2.2. Q_1 is the output level from a particular treatment. The *MB* curve is drawn downward sloping from left to right, and the *MC* curve is drawn upward sloping. As we have just seen, a rising *MC* is just one possibility. But, as will be explained in Chapter 3, the *MB* curve must be downward sloping.

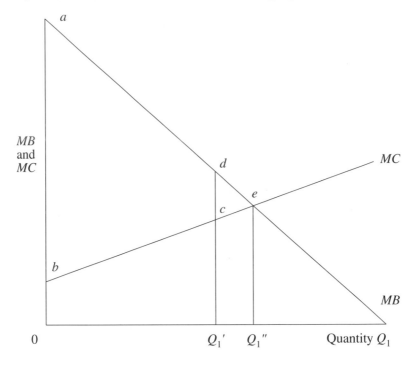

Note: To determine whether quantity Q_1' is worthwhile, one compares the area under the *MB* curve with that under the *MC* curve. A positive difference between the two (shown as area *bcda*) indicates that net-benefits are positive. But, to determine the best possible level of output, *MB* must equal *MC*, as it does at output level Q_1.

Figure 2.2:   A CBA of a particular intervention

To ascertain whether quantity Q_1' is worthwhile, we must compare the benefits and costs for all units up to Q_1'. The satisfaction from all units up to Q_1' is called the total benefits of Q_1'. As the *MB* curve indicates the satisfaction from a unit more (or a unit less) of output, total benefits B (being the sum of all units) are represented graphically by the area under the *MB* curve. Thus, the total benefits for Q_1' are given by the area $0 Q_1'da$ in Figure 2.2. Similarly, total costs C are the sum of marginal costs and represented graphically as the area under the *MC* curve. In Figure 2.2, the total costs of Q_1' are equal to the area $0\ Q_1'cb$. The difference between *B* and *C* is *net-benefits* and, for Q_1', they are given by the area *bcda*. Since the net benefits are positive, we can conclude that quantity level Q_1' is worth providing.

By approving the quantity Q_1', it does not necessarily mean that we have identified the best output level. When output is raised from Q_1' to Q_1'', benefits would increase by the area $Q_1'\ Q_1''ed$, and costs by the area $Q_1'\ Q_1''ec$, leading to a further net gain given by the area *ced*. Once one has achieved the output level Q_1'', any additional output would produce an incremental net loss $MB < MC$. The fact that $MB = MC$ at Q_1' guarantees that Q_1'' is the optimal level of output (as it *maximizes* net benefits).

2.3.2 Cost Minimization as a Cost–Benefit Analysis

In Chapter 1, equation (1.1), we expressed the basic cost–benefit criterion as equivalent to checking whether the net benefits were positive:

$$B_1 - C_1 > 0 \tag{2.8}$$

The aim was to see whether it was desirable to use aspirin to alleviate a headache rather than do nothing (i.e., let the headache disappear eventually of its own accord). When there is a choice of interventions, we wish to ascertain whether there are greater net benefits with aspirin than, say, ibuprofen (denoted by subscript 2). We need to check whether:

$$B_1 - C_1 > B_2 - C_2 \tag{2.9}$$

If the medications were equally effective, then they would remedy the headache to the same degree, at the same speed, and with the same side-effects. This means that the benefits would be identical, $B_1 = B_2$, and, on multiplying the inequality by minus 1, equation (2.2) simplifies to the cost-minimizing criterion given by equation (1.9):

$$C_1 < C_2 \tag{2.10}$$

The prototype situation for a CM, which ensures that net benefit differences are exactly equal to the cost differences, would be if the quantity of output is held constant at a particular level Q'. Two alternative treatments 1 and 2 would be able to produce this output level, so $Q_1 = Q_2 = Q'$. Figure 2.3 summarizes the logic.

When output is Q', total benefits are the area $0Q'ca$ irrespective of the type of medication taken. Costs using method 1 are the area $0Q'ed$. So

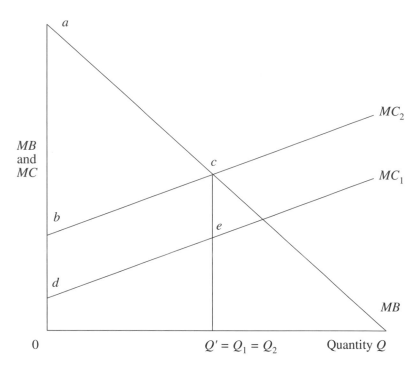

Note: A CM involves seeing whether the total cost of producing a specified output level
Q' is least when using method 1 (with a cost $0Q_1ed$) rather than method 2 with a cost 0
Q_1cb. Notice that if method 2 has larger costs, then the difference in areas *cbde* is positive.
This area is completely under the demand curve and so the change in benefits is also
positive.

Figure 2.3:   A CM as a CBA

net-benefits from medication 1 are represented by the area *adec*. On the
other hand, the costs from using method 2 are the area $0Q'cb$ with net-
benefits *abc*. The relative gain or loss is the difference between the two net
benefits, or area *cbde*. This is exactly the same amount as that given by the
difference between the two cost areas $0Q'cb$ and $0Q'ed$. Thus, there is this
one-for-one correspondence between cost differences and changes in net
benefits.

Although benefits seem to be side-stepped in a CM, it is perhaps just as
valid to use Figure 2.3 to think of a CM comparison expressed in terms of
cost changes as working through benefit changes. The difference in costs is
the area *cbde*. This area is a part of the total benefits $0Q'ca$. The CM exercise can be thought to be taking this part of benefits and converting them

into net benefits. In this way one could argue that costs are being side-stepped. However, there is no real contradiction as in the CM framework; as can be seen by equation (2.7), costs are really just negative benefits.

2.3.3 Cost Minimization and Cost-Effectiveness Analysis

To facilitate discussion of CEA using the notation of CEA, we will switch from calling the outcome variable 'output' Q and start calling it an 'effect' E. Again we focus on a particular effect E_1 (like administering an inoculation for tuberculosis).

A CEA allows for variations in outcome. Thus, unlike a CM, one does not assume that the scale of an effect is fixed. Say treatment 1 has a marginal cost curve MC_1 with an effect E_1' and treatment 2 has a marginal cost curve MC_2 with a higher effect E_1''. In terms of Figure 2.4, one is comparing a point such as a on MC_1 with a point such as e on MC_2.

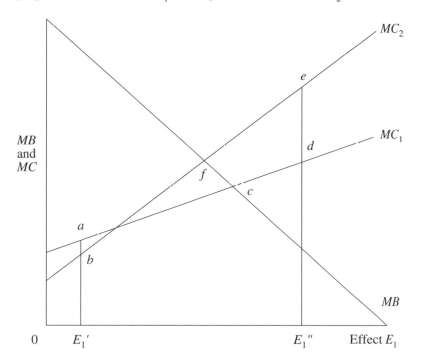

Note: A CEA involves comparing point a with point e, while a CM compares points such as a and b. Point e could be more cost-effective, yet still not be worthwhile. Moreover, the optimal level of output may be neither at point a nor point e, but where $MB = MC$.

Figure 2.4: A CEA as a CBA

Interestingly, we see right away a possible practical problem with a CEA. There is no guarantee that in a CEA one is comparing two cost-minimizing effect levels. Point b has a lower cost than point a, and point d is lower than e. So, strictly, one should be comparing the CM points b and d in the CEA.

If one does compare points a and e, and finds that the ratio of costs to effects (C_1/E_1') at point a is higher than the ratio (C_1/E_1'') at e, then, applying the logic of the CEA criterion, we would have to conclude that treatment 2 is more cost-effective than treatment 1. As we stressed in Chapter 1 this more effective treatment could, in fact, not be worthwhile (if the area under the MC at E_1'' is greater than the area under the MB curve). In addition, we can see from Figure 2.4 that even a socially beneficial outcome at E_1'' is not optimal, as the condition $MB = MC$ exists elsewhere (at intersection point c or point f, depending on which gives the higher total net-benefits).

2.4   APPLICATIONS

The first application relates to opportunity cost and tries to find the alternative uses of resources used in a surgical ward. The second study illustrates why the line separating a CM from a CEA is a very fine one. The study of the costs of ulcer treatment starts off as a CM, but an impasse is quickly reached. Cost-minimization is important in constructing long run cost curves to be used in a CBA. The account of costing a hospital stay for knee arthroplasty surgery in the third case study produces an estimate of two points on such a curve. The final application illustrates the classic CM exercise that tries to find the cost of an illness (AIDS).

2.4.1   The Opportunity Cost of a Surgical Ward

One of the first attempts to provide a precise analysis of possible foregone uses in order to estimate a resource's opportunity cost was by Harper (1979). When a particular treatment is being discontinued in a hospital, it is more realistic to assume that the resources freed up would be used for some other medical service, rather than left idle. Harper tried to identify and cost these alternative medical services.

Harper's first task was to define a comparable unit (numeraire) for any hospital treatment. He chose 100 bed days as this unit of work. Then he tried to find out how many procedures could be accommodated during a 100-bed day span. The five diagnostic groups he concentrated on were: acute appendicitis, peptic ulcer, varicose veins, inguinal hernia and carcinoma of the breast. Harper found (for a general surgical ward in Aberdeen in 1971) that if a ward stopped admitting 14 patients with acute appendicitis, then 100 bed days would become vacant. These freed resources could be used to admit 9 patients with peptic ulcer, 32 with varicose veins, 21 with inguinal hernias, or 6 with carcinoma of the breast. From there the analysis proceeds to calculate how many additional hospital services were associated with each of these five surgical treatments. The results are recorded in Table 2.6 below.

Table 2.6:   Reference requirements for 5 treatments (per 100 bed days)

	Acute appendicitis	Peptic ulcer	Varicose veins	Inguinal hernia	Carcinoma of breast
Theatre (min)	697	960	1717	1012	410
Drugs	3843	6231	2159	3747	2271
Ward care	467	537	311	327	413
Radiodiagnosis:					
Staff time (min)	170	110	150	450	500
Films and materials	15	29	12	20	56
Chemical pathology	136	238	41	80	82
Haematology	102	130	98	84	166
Bacteriology	183	168	30	119	56
Pathology	136	84	–	25	118
Blood transfusions	136	973	–	100	649
Physiotherapy	48	53	9	56	40
Electrocardiography	–	2	6	8	3
Emergency surcharge	17	12	–	4	4
No. of patients	13.6	8.9	31.9	21.1	5.7

Source: Harper (1979)

Once one knows the inputs necessary to treat the particular number of patients for each specified diagnostic group (i.e., one knows the production function), the final step to estimate costs is to apply cash values to the work units on the basis of the associated services just identified (i.e., one must price the inputs). Harper found that the mean costs per patient for the five treatments were: £106.9 for appendicitis, £203.1 for peptic ulcer, £64 for varicose veins, £73.5 for inguinal hernias, and £226.7 for carcinoma of the breast.

Note that the costs just estimated are for a particular disease and not for a particular procedure. Harper argues that information should be directed at the consultant level. For it is the consultant who (in the British system at that time), 'initiates most if not all health-care expenditures'. Thus

Harper's study can be viewed as an attempt to remedy one of the main drawbacks of health care evaluations practice (identified in section 1.4.3), that attention has been given to procedures, when health care expenditure decisions are made at a broader level (by consultants in the Harper context) and they need a wider range of evaluation information.

Harper's study of costs is complete in that it presents both the production function and the pricing of inputs. To use Harper's words, 'a hernia operation may be more expensive in Falkirk than in Birmingham either because available facilities are used inefficiently or because such facilities vary in cost'. He makes the point that 'the clinician is concerned only with using efficiently what is available to him and so requires only the non [cash] costed approach', which is his indirect reference to the production function part. But, to someone carrying out an economic evaluation, information on both parts of the costing exercise is required. One may get more physical output per input using method 1 than method 2. But, if the prices of inputs are so much lower with method 2, then this method may be better (cost-minimizing). The most economically efficient method need not be the most technologically efficient method as judged solely by the production function.

2.4.2   The Cost of Treating Ulcers

The output requirements for a CM are very stringent. When comparing treatments one must ensure that the various treatments have *identical* effects. In the study of alternative medications for the treatment of duodenal ulcer by Ashton (1991) related to New Zealand, she starts off using a CM, but quickly changes to a CEA. The main three medications for treating duodenal ulcers included in the study were: colloidal bismuth subcitrate (CBS), cimetidine and ranitidine.

A study of pharmaceutical products provides a good example of one of the strengths of using a CM. It is only the *difference* in costs of the treatments that one needs to estimate, not the total cost of each treatment. Hospital costs and physician costs, which constitute most of the costs of providing health care in the system as a whole, are clearly common to any kind of medication that is administered and cancel out when one tries to ascertain whether one type of medication is cheaper than another. In addition to these common costs, in the case of medications for treating duodenal ulcers, Ashton includes also non-pharmaceutical costs of initial treatment (such as the costs of the endoscopy which is used to diagnose duodenal ulcers), travel costs and time off by patients during the initial assessment.

Ashton includes in her sample only those patients whose ulcers healed successfully during the five-year period after initial treatment. Thus, one seems to have an unambiguous measure of effect to include in the CM. The treatment was either successful or not. In so far as side-effects exist (headaches, dizziness and diarrhea), Ashton stated that they can occur with all anti-ulcer medications. On the basis of this measure of effect, the second column of Table 2.7 records the cost per person treated for the three ulcer medications. CBS would be the cost-minimizing medication.

Table 2.7:   Costs per patient for ulcer treatment

Treatment	Cost per course of treatment (NZ$)	Present value of expected cost of treatment (NZ$)
Cimetidine	90.93	1025.89
Ranitidine	108.10	1407.29
CBS	60.27	605.46

Source: Ashton (1991)

The trouble with the specification of the effect of ulcer medication as a successful treatment outcome is that some patients were more successfully treated than others. Not everyone was cured right away. Relapse was possible, which necessitated further medical services up to the period when ultimate cure occurred. From a CM perspective, the relapses would be considered a complication that could be accommodated by measuring the extra costs caused by differential relapse rates of the three medications, in terms of physician salaries and patient waiting time and travel costs of further visits. The fact that these relapse costs were in the future would be recognized by discounting them to present value terms. Ashton used a 10% discount rate (which she said was the rate that was commonly applied to public projects in New Zealand).

However, it was not just the cost side that the differential relapse rates affected. CBS had a mean relapse rate in the first year of 50%, and it was 57% with ranitidine and 77% with cimetidine. The lower relapse rate of CBS meant that effects came earlier with CBS than the other medications. An earlier effect is more valuable than a later effect. Discounting future effects higher than current effects causes CBS to have larger effects than the alternatives. Allowing for differential effects converts Ashton's study from a CM into a CEA. The results of discounting effects and costs over the five-year period are shown in the second column of Table 2.7. CBS is the most cost-effective treatment as well as the cost-minimizing one.

One of the reasons why CBS was most cost-effective was due to the fact that having fewer relapses led to a reduction in the number of patient visits to the doctor, which lowered patient travel, waiting and consultation time. Ashton's study was one of the few that tried to quantify these elements. She estimated that on average it took 55 minutes to make an extra visit. The assumption was made that if a person was not making the visit, then three-quarters of the time they would be working at the average wage plus labor-related expenses. The rest of the time they would not be working and this would be valued at a quarter of the average wage. Thus, Ashton used the market wage rate as the basis for her measures of the opportunity cost of time. The cost of a physician visit was placed at NZ$10.66. For the 90% of the patients that traveled by car (for a journey that on average was 10 km), Ashton added on a further NZ$3.61 per visit to allow for travel costs.

The logic of why Ashton shifted from a CM to a CEA is clear. However, it does raise a practical issue concerning the choice of evaluation technique. Ashton's claim that it is solely differences in costs that one needs to quantify is strictly valid only if one uses (that is, she keeps to) a CM framework. In a CEA, common costs can affect the results. For example, say we have: $C_1 = \$4$ and $E_1 = 2$, while $C_2 = \$7$ and $E_2 = 3$, with a common cost equal to $5. Treatment 1 is cost minimizing both without the common cost ($4 < $7) and with it ($9 < $12). But, with a CEA analysis, treatment 1 is more cost-effective without the common cost ($4/2 < $7/3), yet treatment 2 is more cost-effective with the common cost ($12/3 < $9/2).

Our numerical example affected the results because the treatment that was initially the least cost-effective had a lower effect (as well as a higher cost). Thus, adding a common cost divided by a lower effect would raise its original ratio by more than a common cost divided by a larger effect. Fortunately, in the Ashton study, CBS was both cheaper and more effective than the other treatments, so the existence of common costs would not affect her results.

The other key issue related to Ashton's study concerns whether there is a bias in the results due to the selection of cases/patients included in the evaluation. The possibility of 'sample selection bias' is something one needs to check in any health care evaluation. Recall that because Ashton confined her study to patients whose ulcers had successfully healed (within five years), she was omitting those whose treatment failed. Ashton estimated that 10–30% of patients have ulcers that do not heal after initial and secondary treatment by medication (1 or 2% have complications that may lead to hospitalization with a chance of surgery).

Just like with the exclusion of common costs, it is the differential success rate across medications that decides whether any bias would affect the results. Ashton reports that the healing rates for CBS have been higher than for the other medications. The cost per person healed by CBA would therefore be even lower if the sample selection bias had not existed. The general conclusion is this. Unless a clinical trial takes places, it will often be the case that a biased sample will exist. However, the existence of a bias does not automatically invalidate the results of the evaluation. To invalidate the results one has to show that not only was the direction of the bias against alternatives that were given a low evaluation, but that the bias was also sizeable to possibly reverse the rankings of alternatives.

2.4.3   Hospital Costs of Total Knee Arthroplasty

The study by Stern et al., first utilized in section 2.1.3, sought to estimate how much savings would result from policy-induced changes in the hospital LOS. Hospitals in the US prior to 1982 were reimbursed by the government on a retrospective basis. Hospitals could decide how long a stay would be and what tests were appropriate and be reimbursed accordingly. After 1982, hospitals were paid prospectively, whereby a flat rate was paid per admission based on the expected average cost of a category of treatment (a diagnostic related group, or DRG). Any tests or length of stay in excess of the average would have to be paid for by the hospital. Clearly, under the new system, hospitals had a financial incentive to reduce the LOS.

The length of stay was of special interest to knee arthroplasty because this was such a high volume procedure where many of the patients were elderly and thus the government was the main payer (via Medicare). Between 1985 and 1993, the average LOS in the US fell from 13 days to 8 days. The issue was whether this reduction would decrease costs proportionately. In researching this topic, they provide an estimate of the long run marginal cost of a reduction in the LOS at a large (580-bed) urban medical center in Chicago between 1992 and 1994. As noted in the theory section, the LOS in 1992 was 8.7 days and this fell to 6.1 in 1994. Table 2.8, based on Table 3 of Stern et al., displays the categories of inputs and costs of knee arthroplasty in the two years.

The important point to observe in Table 2.8 is that, in practice, there is no simple separation of inputs into fixed and variable categories. Although in section 2.2.1 we simplified by assuming that operating room expenses were fixed costs, and nurses' expenses were variable costs, in actuality any input other than the prosthesis itself could be classified as both fixed and variable (to varying degrees). Interestingly, all of the inputs other than prosthesis and pharmacy had the majority of their expenses listed as fixed costs. For example, in 1992, 59.3% of total operating room expenditures were fixed and 40.7% were variable. Even nursing had most (i.e., 60.4%) of its expenses as fixed. This explains the main conclusion of Stern et al.'s paper. They found that any 'attempt at decreasing expenditures by reducing the length of stay only addresses the component of cost that occurs

Table 2.8:   *Inflation-controlled hospital costs for total knee arthroplasty*
              ($)

Cost	Variable		Fixed		Total	
	1992	1994	1992	1994	1992	1994
Operating room	3049	2970	4442	2739	7491	5709
Prosthesis	2440	2984	0	0	2440	2984
Nursing	1636	1311	2491	1837	4126	3148
Rehabilitation	471	409	534	507	1004	916
Radiology	128	61	232	109	359	170
Laboratory	290	448	547	492	837	940
Pharmacy	335	486	197	234	531	720
Miscellaneous	195	152	431	461	621	613
Total	8543	8821	8872	6379	17415	15200

Source: Stern et al. (1995)

after the patient leaves the operating room, which is at a time when the majority of costs have been incurred'.

An insight that Stern et al. bring to our attention concerning Table 2.8 is that one needs to check whether an input's costs are really fixed or not when making an evaluation. As they point out, 'by definition, the hospital's total fixed costs (rent, insurance, utilities, and administrative expenses) were invariant over the relevant range and, therefore, generally would not have changed'. In other words they are asking, what does it mean to state that fixed costs fell by \$2178 (\$8872 − \$6379) when *LOS* declined? Surely, 'fixed' costs are fixed? The answer is that it is true that saving operating room time may not really lead to a reduction in hospital expenses initially. But, if the reduction in *LOS* continues past some threshold level, as it did in the hospital in the case study, average *LOS* reductions eventually result 'in the closing of an inpatient unit with concurrent decrease in staffing'. In the long run potential savings become real savings.

We now turn to the estimate of the long run *MC* and *AC* implicit in Stern et al.'s work. The fall in *LOS* was 2.6 days. Table 2.8 reports that total costs decreased by \$2493 (\$8872 − \$6379). So the average *MC* over this range of reduction in the *LOS* was \$959 per day. The long run average cost for *Q* = 6.1 days was \$2491 (\$15 200/6.1) and it was \$2002 (\$17 415/8.7) for *Q* = 8.7. Thus, the falling cost per day with arthroplasty knee surgery as the *LOS* rises indicates that there are economies of scale.

The *AC* was more than double the *MC*. The difference between the *MC* and the *AC* highlights why estimating the *MC* is so important for making health care evaluations. As the *AC* for a *LOS* of 8.7 was $2002, it would seem that this would be the amount that would be saved by cutting back the *LOS* by a day. But the real saving would only be the *MC* of $959.

The relevance of the Stern et al. cost estimates for CBA depends on the nature of the 'project' one is trying to evaluate. If the project is an administrative/organizational change that focuses on the hospital LOS, then the loss of comfort, convenience and health outcomes that would accompany a shorter stay has to be compared with the $959 hospital cost savings. On the other hand, if the project is the arthroplasty knee surgery itself, then it is the costs of the total length of stay that one needs to ascertain. In this context the framework is one of CM. The procedure that requires a LOS of 8.7 days did cost $17415 in 1992, but now in 1994 it costs $15200. The 1994 input combinations are the cost-minimizing ones. As this is one of the main principles highlighted in this chapter, this point warrants further elaboration.

Say one intends to carry out a CBA of a total knee arthroplasty and one can estimate the benefits in monetary terms. The question is: what is the cost figure that one should be comparing with the benefits? The answer is that prior to undertaking the CBA one must undertake a CM study. On the basis of the Stern et al. work, the two candidates for the CM are the operating room-intensive production combination that uses 202 operating room minutes, and the less intensive combination that uses 182 operating minutes and more of the other inputs such as laboratory and pharmacy services. The former combination costs $17415 and the latter $15200. The less operating room-intensive combination is the cost minimization outcome. It is this cost of $15200 that the benefits need to exceed.

2.4.4 Lifetime Cost of HIV

In section 1.1.2 we mentioned that a frequent type of health care evaluation involved trying to estimate the entire cost of a disease (as if it could be eliminated). A useful way of thinking about such studies is to see them in the context of what would be saved if a disease or illness were prevented. Most communicable diseases are outside our control. But, when one considers the human immunodeficiency virus (HIV) that leads to acquired immunodeficiency syndrome (AIDS), an illness that is behavior related, then costing the disease to try to find the benefits of preventing AIDS makes sense.

In the context of costing a lifetime disease, the role of discounting is crucial. The long duration makes differences in discount rates all the more significant. A dollar of cost next year is worth 98 cents with *r* equal to 2% and is still worth 83 cents when *r* equals 20%. However, a dollar in 20 years' time is worth 67 cents using a 2% rate, but its value is only 3 cents at the 20% rate of discount.

In the study by Hurley et al. (1996) of the lifetime costs of HIV in Australia, they identified four phases of HIV that differ in the degree of severity of the disease (judged on the basis of a blood test related to the CD4 count). Phase 1 was when the person initially gets infected with the virus (called the 'seroconversion' stage) and this was expected to last seven years. Phase 2 lasted four years and phase 3 lasted 1.2 years. The final phase was when the person actually has AIDS. This phase was by far the most costly and was projected to last a maximum of five years. Table 2.9 (Table 2 of Hurley et al.) presents the mean lifetime costs of HIV at the four stages using a discount rate of 5%. Hospital beds and drugs were the two main components of lifetime cost, accounting for about 80% of the total.

Table 2.9:   Lifetime costs of HIV (in Australian $)

Service type	Lifetime cost, diagnosed at start of			
	Phase 1 (seroconversion)	Phase 2	Phase 3	Phase 4
Discounted to time of diagnosis				
Ambulatory care	8063	8720	7508	4727
Hospital bed days	23835	29705	41883	41430
Investigations and procedures	7476	6756	5436	4016
Drugs	45259	45695	36834	28599
Miscellaneous	3168	2322	1778	1293
Total	87800	93125	93333	79967
Discounted to time of seroconversion				
Ambulatory care	8063	6500	4229	2332
Hospital bed days	23835	22148	22148	20437
Investigations and procedures	7476	5039	3006	1981
Drugs	45259	34071	20232	14108
Miscellaneous	3168	1731	984	637
Total	87800	69489	50599	39495

Source: Hurley et al. (1996)

As we see in Table 2.9, the lifetime costs are dependent on: (1) whether one is doing the discounting to the first day of each phase or to the first day of phase 1; and (2) where in the lifecycle one begins the costing due to the timing of when the disease was first diagnosed. These two points, that the lifetime costs depend on the date when present value calculations are made, and the date at which the diagnosis is made, will be illustrated in turn.

1. The costs of the AIDS phase 4, if diagnosed at the start of phase 4, were $79 967 when discounted to the beginning of phase 4. This sum of $79 967 was worth only $39 495 if the present value calculation starts at the beginning of phase 1 rather than at the beginning of phase 4. This makes sense as phase 4 is over a decade later than phase 1 and any costs then must be worth much less.

2. The importance of the date of diagnosis, and its interaction with discounting, can be seen by focusing on the costs of phase 2. By themselves, the costs of phase 2 (when discounted to the beginning of phase 1) were $18 890 (being the difference between the lifetime costs of $69 489 at phase 2 and the lifetime costs of $50 599 at phase 3). It would then appear that $18 890 would be the sum that would have to be added to lifetime costs if detection took place earlier at the start of phase 2 rather than at the start of phase 3. This would clearly be the case if one is discounting in terms of the beginning of phase 1. But it would not be the case if one discounted at the diagnosis date. As one can see from Table 2.9, lifetime costs discounted to the start of phase 2 would be $93 125 and this was almost the same as the $93 333 when discounted to the start of phase 3. The reason for this result was that the costs of phases 3 and 4 would be discounted more heavily when started at phase 2 than at phase 3. This reduction in costs compensated for the increased costs of $18 890 brought about by incurring the costs of phase 2.

The main finding of Hurley et al. was that the lifetime cost of AIDS in Australia (when discounted to, and diagnosed at, the start of phase 1) was $87 800. This was lower than the $119 000 amount found by Hellinger (1993) for the US. (Note that Hurley et al. claimed that the Australian dollar was comparable in terms of purchasing power to the US dollar and therefore there is a one-to-one conversion between the two currencies.) However, the Hellinger figure was undiscounted. When discounted by Hurley et al., the Hellinger lifetime cost of HIV for the US was lower than the Australian estimate at $74 900. They therefore conclude that this, 'illustrates the importance of consistent discounting in comparing cost estimates in different studies'.

There are two aspects of the Hurley et al. study that reinforce important principles presented in this chapter. Both can be explained in terms of the key lifetime characteristic of HIV that the mean monthly costs were much higher for the terminal stages of the disease. Three months before death the cost was $8700. It was $11 700 two months before death and almost $16 000 in the final month, while the average over the AIDS phase was only $4 500 per month.

The first point to emphasize here is that one does not add 10% of the lifetime costs if a new drug is adopted that extends the lifespan of someone with HIV by a year (assuming 10 years was the lifespan before the change). Most of the costs come at the terminal stage and these would be unaffected by the drug (if one ignores the discounting issue that these costs would be pushed one year into the future and be lower because of this fact). Hence lifetime costs would only be minimally affected as one is effectively extending phase 1 when costs are the least. As with the hospital LOS costing problem previously analyzed, AC may not be a good guide to how costs are altered by marginal adjustments to the dimensions of treatment.

The other principle illustrated by the Hurley et al. study is the importance of identifying any sample selection bias when one considers a health care evaluation. Hurley et al. were surprised when they found that, after discounting, the US lifetime cost estimate was lower than the Australian amount, especially given the fact that overall the US spends twice as much per capita on health care than Australia. One explanation for the difference that they came up with concerned the samples included in the two studies. Hellinger may have underrepresented in his sample those at the terminal stage of AIDS where costs were the highest. The cost would then appear lower than the Hurley et al. estimate simply because they used a random sample for their study (which by chance included high cost patients), while Hellinger did not explicitly focus on including those who were in the last few months of AIDS.

2.5   FINAL SECTION

The problems, summary and looking ahead sections will now be presented.

2.5.1   Problems

A theme recurring throughout this book will be how best to provide care for those with severe mental illness. We introduce the subject by referring to the study of the costs of supplying the medication clozapine to treatment-resistant schizophrenics. The aim was to enable patients to move from a hospital to a community setting. If the medication is to be judged successful, hospital costs will have to go down more than outpatient treatment costs will go up.

The initial work on clozapine was carried out by Revicki et al. (1990). This research was criticized by a number of authors (see, for example, Frank (1991)). One criticism was that it ignored those patients who dropped out from the clozapine treatment regime. Because of this criticism, Meltzer et al. (1993) did a second study using the Revicki et al. data that tried to include the costs of those who dropped out. The data below (Table 2.10) comes from the Meltzer et al. study. A second criticism was that the clozapine research ignored discounting. The importance of allowing for sample selection bias and discounting were two main points stressed in this chapter. So we base our questions below on trying to calculate how these two points impacted the Revicki et al. work.

Table 2.10:   Costs of different treatments before and after treatment ($)

Type of patients	Cost before clozapine	Cost during clozapine treatment
Patients who continued		
Hospitalization	44810	2592
Outpatient treatment	8054	16875
Housing	8418	6142
Family burden	8710	231
Other costs	1789	65
Total costs	71779	25905
Patients who dropped out		
Hospitalization	93415	99995
Outpatient treatment	3158	3648
Housing	2116	2860
Family burden	1554	506
Other costs	10747	9208
Total costs	110990	116217

Source: Meltzer et al. (1993)

1. The study compares the costs before and after the treatment. Strictly, any comparison should be with and without treatment. To what extent does it matter that the Revicki study used the before and after perspectives?
2. Would the conclusion (based only on those who continued with treatment) that clozapine led to significant reductions in costs be altered if one includes the cost experience of those who dropped out?
3. The 'after' cost figures were based on experiences two years later. Would discounting make a difference to the conclusion that clozapine had significant cost reductions? (Hint: Frank (1991) suggested using a 2% rate for discounting in this particular study. Try also 5% and 10%. Use Table 2.4 to help you with your calculations.) Would it make a difference if the cost differences had related to a time period 10 years later rather than two years apart?

2.5.2   Summary

As a method of evaluation, CM is very limited, and in this chapter we pointed out a number of weaknesses in theory and in practice. However, the main thrust of this chapter is that CM should be viewed as a central step in any economic evaluation. CM is a necessary condition for ensuring that one chooses from alternatives that will lead to the most efficient outcome. Whether one is comparing treatment options by an E/C ratio, or by net benefits $B-C$, it is essential that the C be the lowest cost way of undertaking that treatment option. Thus, emphasis was given to explaining the mechanics of constructing short and long run cost curves.

The other fundamental evaluation principle established in this chapter was the importance of relying on marginal benefits and marginal costs as opposed to total benefits and costs. The total figures indicate whether a particular option level is worthwhile or not. But they will not tell one what is the best option level. Only seeking option levels where $MB = MC$ will give us that information. Focusing on marginal analysis points to looking at the whole range of outcomes that correspond to option levels. This helps to ensure that treatment options, although worthwhile at a given level, cannot be improved by alternative scales of operation.

'Cost' in economics is opportunity cost. It depends on the value of a resource in its next best alternative use. This cost is a function of time whether: (1) in an economic sense, where one distinguishes between situations where inputs are fixed (short run) from situations where they are freely variable (the long run); or (2) in a calendar sense, where a given monetary cost is worth less in the future than it is worth today. To put costs in different years on a comparable basis, one needs to find the discount factor, which is how much a dollar in the future is worth today. The discount factor depends on two variables: the discount rate and the length of the future time horizon. When all annual costs are made comparable in today's value terms, a process called discounting, the cost stream is called the present value of the costs.

The first application was devoted to costing a surgical ward. The opportunity cost of using a ward for 13 appendicitis patients was that one had to forgo patient care for those with other ailments. Specifically, 9 patients with peptic ulcer, 32 with varicose veins, 21 with inguinal hernias, or 6 with carcinoma of the breast could not be treated. These opportunity costs exist even if no monetary payments were required to secure the services of the 100-bed day ward. (Which one of the four alternative uses was 'next best', as required by the definition of opportunity cost, Harper did not say.)

The evaluation of treatments for peptic ulcer made clear how difficult it was for the main precondition for a CM to hold. A CM needs *all* the dimensions of output (quantity and quality) to be identical as between any two alternatives. Even when this may appear to be the case, the timing of output may vary and this will invalidate the comparison. Then the case study of hospital LOS for total knee arthroplasty highlighted the importance of distinguishing MC from AC. Cost savings estimated on the base of AC costs may be grossly inaccurate.

The final application of the chapter took a common type of CM evaluation, which tried to estimate the lifetime cost of a disease (in this case AIDS), and showed how such studies depended crucially on discounting future costs. It also highlighted the fact that, in order to compare the results of economic evaluations, one needs to ensure that there is no sample selection bias in any of the studies.

2.5.3 Looking Ahead

This chapter began our analysis of Part 1, dealing with CM, and this continues with the next three chapters. In this chapter we defined cost as opportunity cost and explored the logic of finding a treatment method that minimizes this cost. In the next chapter we examine the extent to which market prices can be used to measure opportunity costs. In subsequent chapters we broaden the perspective to cover costs that lie outside the market (external costs) and costs that are involved with financing the health care project (the excess burden of taxes). In this chapter we explained the logic of discounting. We leave till Chapter 7 the thorny issue of how to determine which interest rate to use to carry out the discounting.

3. Types of costs and their measurement

3.1 INTRODUCTION

We continue our analysis of costs within the context of CM and focus on how to measure these costs. We know that 'cost' means opportunity cost; but this cost comes in many forms, in particular, marginal, average, overhead, sunk and joint. It is MC cost that is most useful for evaluation purposes. However, often we have information only on AC. Worse still, we are usually faced with hospital or physician charges that may not even reflect AC. After presenting the main cost concepts, we examine the link between markets and costs. Market prices are often used to value resource inputs in health care. We shall see that only competitive market prices can be used for this valuation purpose. The next section examines in detail the relation between charges and costs, highlighting the use and misuse of the hospital cost-to-charge ratio. The applications cover the two main cost components in health care: hospital and physician services.

3.1.1 Marginal versus Average Cost

MC refers to the cost of one more or less unit, while AC looks at all the units produced and divides the total cost by the number of units. The basic problem with using AC is that some of the units produced in the past incur 'sunk costs', i.e., costs that cannot be recovered. Often a machine installed for one particular use may not be used for anything else. By definition its opportunity cost is zero (if it has no scrap value). If to produce the extra units the machine does not have to be replaced, then the cost of the machine is a sunk cost and should not form part of MC.

There are three considerations to help one think about whether sunk costs are involved:

1. Sunk costs are usually involved when capital expenditures for fixed assets take place.
2. Sunk costs exist when activities are done jointly (see below).
3. The longer the time horizon for making the evaluation, the less will be

the share of sunk costs. This is because, in the long run, all costs are variable (and hence marginal).

3.1.2 Overhead and Joint Costs

The term 'overhead cost' relates to resources that serve many different departments and programs, e.g., hospital administration, laundry, lighting, medical records, porters, etc. The patient does not pay for these services separately. Similarly, there are activities that serve more than one purpose simultaneously. The costs of these activities are called joint costs. These shared costs have to be allocated to individual programs in some way.

There are two main problems posed by overhead costs. First, economic theory suggests that we use the concept of MC. That is, what would be the change in total costs if the program under review did not exist. However, for overhead costs the principle breaks down. Consider two programs that have a joint cost. The MC of the joint activity for either program taken on its own would appear to be zero. But, together, the two programs jointly require all of the expenditure. In general, then, there needs to be some method of allocating the joint costs.

Dranove (1995) points out that administering drugs has the jointness/ overhead problem because often when nurses give the medication they monitor the patient's condition at the same time. He recommends that one should estimate the nurses' time required to do each task and not attribute both costs to the drug part of the treatment. Evidence of the simultaneity problem can be seen by the large coefficient of variation (the standard deviation divided by the mean) existing in reported studies of the costs of administering drugs. Administering the drugs is a reasonably standardized activity. Variation should not be large. But, in practice, the coefficients range between 0.5 and 1.0. Clearly, nurses are providing other tasks simultaneously with the drugs.

The second problem posed by overhead costs relates to the existence of scale economies. When costs are joint, one is able to produce output at little (or no) additional cost. With falling costs, firms have a constant incentive to increase the size of their operations. This ultimately leads to a situation where there is a single firm, called a 'monopoly'. As we explain in section 3.2.2, the price charged by a monopolist will be greater than its MC and thus could not be used to measure opportunity cost.

There are a number of methods for allocating the costs of service departments to health procedures ('production departments'). They are explained in many accountancy texts, e.g., Horngren (1982). All allocative methods of joint costs try to give more accurate estimates of the AC of particular treatments. But they do not deal with the marginal dimension of overhead costs. Here we will just outline the 'step-down' method and leave to the problems section the details of how to apply it in practice. This method is increasingly being used by hospitals in the United States. In fact, Horngren tells us, hospitals must use the step-down method to justify reimbursement from health care agencies.

The first stage of any allocation formula involves identifying the units of output of the service and medical departments to see how intensively the medical departments use the service departments. The unit of output for the service department is called the 'allocation basis'. For example, the allocation bases for a department such as administration would be the paid hours for the personnel and for laundry it would be pounds of laundry.

If there were just one service department (e.g., laundry) then the allocation of costs would be straightforward. Say there were two medical departments (orthopedics and radiology) and assume that of the total output of laundry (1000 pounds per week) orthopedics used 600 pounds and radiology used 400 pounds. If the hospital weekly expenditure on laundry were $4000 then this would be shared out 60/40 to orthopedics and radiology, resulting in a weekly laundry cost by orthopedics of $2400 and $1600 for radiology.

The complications arise when there is more than one service department and these departments interact. If both administration and laundering exist, and the administration department requires laundry services when the laundry department also uses administrative services, then there are a number of possible ways of accommodating the service and medical departments' interactions. The simplest method (called the 'direct method') involves ignoring the service department interactions. Cost allocation then follows the same method as if there were a single service department. At the other extreme is the most correct method that allows for all department interactions simultaneously and is called the 'reciprocal method'. In between is the step-down procedure that we are focusing on.

The step-down method allocates services in a prescribed sequence. The sequence begins with the department that renders service to the greatest number of other service departments (say it is administration). The sequence ends with the department that serves the least other service departments (laundry). Once a service department's costs have been allocated, no subsequent service department's costs are allocated back to it. Thus, in our four-department example, the administration department's output is shared out to laundry, orthopedics and radiology according to each department's use of administration. Next, laundry's output is shared out to the two medical departments; and finally the interaction between orthopedics and radiology is allowed for. In conclusion, the step-down method ignores self-use of a service and also the two-way interaction among service departments.

The final dimension to the overhead and joint costs problem relates to the idea of economies of scope. These exist when, as the output expands for one output, the AC of some other output falls. As we have just been discussing, many hospital department services are interrelated. So it is important to know how procedures that affect more than one hospital department impact on the total cost of all departments combined, rather than one department at a time. A test of economies of scope will be given in the applications section where, when one is considering closing down an emergency department, one wants to know how that would affect the costs for inpatient services.

3.1.3 Average Costing Using a *Per Diem*

AC is often measured on the basis of a *per diem* (per day) expense. This is obtained by dividing a hospital's total operating costs for the year by the annual number of patient days. The outcome is the average cost per patient day. To find the hospital costs associated with a program, all one needs to do is to multiply the average hospital stay of a patient involved with the program by the *per diem*. The obvious drawback of using *per diems* is that they are an AC and do not allow for the enormous patient variation that would be entailed in using MC. Also, *per diems* typically ignore capital costs.

A variation of the *per diem* method has been recommended by Hull et al. (1982). This involves dividing hospital costs into two categories: those related to the treatment under review, and those unrelated to the treatment. (Strictly, the distinction is between costs related to LOS and those that are not.) The costs unrelated to the treatment are called 'hotel costs'. The assumption made for these costs is that patients would use an average amount of these hotel costs. Hence the averaging process (*per diem* concept) is only applied to the second category.

In the study presented by Hull et al., the hotel costs were the operating costs (again, capital costs are ignored) unrelated to the special needs for patients receiving treatment for venous thromboembolism. The costs included room, food, laundry, maintenance, general laboratory services, etc. The hotel costs of the hospital (in Hamilton, Ontario) were $290 per patient, out of a total cost of $2209. The fact that hotel costs were a small share of the total patient costs is consistent with our finding in the total knee arthroplasty case study presented in the last chapter. Fixed costs do not get reduced as the length of stay declines. Only the hotel costs fall as the LOS is reduced.

3.2   COSTS AND MARKETS

So far we have not really distinguished an output Q from an effect E. Basically the two are the same, except that we can think of output as the final good (which gives the consumer satisfaction), while an effect may be an intermediary good (or a means to an end). Thus a lowering of the blood pressure may be an effect of medication that leads to a person eventually feeling better or having an improved probability of returning to work. Linked to this distinction is the idea that an output may be the result of a bundle of effects. An accurate diagnosis (one effect) may lead to an appropriate treatment that works quickly on the symptoms (a second effect) which then produces a cure (another effect). The cure may be marked by a cessation of treatment and then a summary medical bill. The patient may then see him/herself as receiving as an output the cure rather than the series of effects. But what is crucial in all this is that one thinks of an output as something for which an individual pays and hence a market exists.

3.2.1   Costs and Competitive Markets

A good starting point for measuring costs is to look to see how private markets value quantities. We consider a good such as bottles of aspirin. In equilibrium, competitive markets operate where demand equals supply. At this equilibrium point, output and price are jointly determined. Figure 3.1 shows market equilibrium with P_E the price and Q_E the quantity. The underlying principles behind demand and supply will now be explained.

Demand is the relationship between price and quantity on the consumer side. It shows what people are willing to pay at the margin for each level of output. The demand curve is drawn as a downward-sloping relation (from left to right) between price and quantity in Figure 3.1. This shape occurs because: (1) consumers organize their purchases so as to try to maximize their total satisfaction, and (2) the law of diminishing marginal utility applies. In order to maximize utility a consumer equates the price that they pay with their additional satisfaction (marginal utility MU):

$$P = MU \tag{3.1}$$

This rule follows the same logic as in Chapter 2, where $MB = MC$ maximized social net benefits; here we have $MB = MU$ and $P = MC$. This is why economists deduce consumer satisfaction from their WTP, i.e., the *price* that they are willing to pay. The law of diminishing marginal utility states that the more a person consumes of any good, the less is the additional

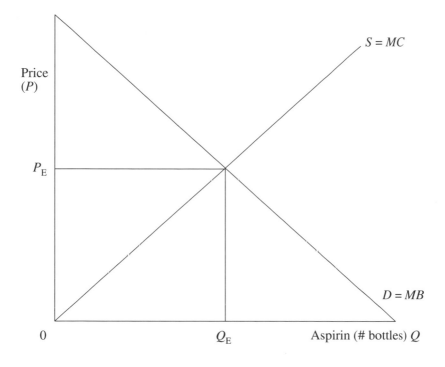

Note: A competitive market is in equilibrium where demand equals supply. With demand as a measure of *MB*, and supply measuring *MC*, market equilibrium brings about the equality of *MB* with *MC* that is necessary to maximize net benefits for a CBA. At equilibrium, the price that is required is determined as P_E and the quantity is Q_E.

Figure 3.1:   *A competitive market's demand and supply measures MB and MC*

satisfaction. So, if *MU* declines with *Q*, and *P* is equated with *MU*, then *P* must fall with *Q*, which is the demand curve relationship.

Supply is the relation between price and quantity on the producer side. In competitive markets the firm is a price taker. The individual firm is so small relative to the market that the price would be the same with or without the output of the firm. The price *P* is then fixed by the industry and the firm has to decide how much output to produce at that price. Firms are assumed to try to maximize their profits. This is achieved where the additional revenue, given by the fixed price, equals the additional costs *MC* of producing that output:

$$P = MC \qquad\qquad (3.2)$$

Once more this is the $MB = MC$ logic, with P the MB for the firm. If we assume decreasing returns to scale, i.e., rising costs as quantity rises (which is one possibility in the long run), then MC will be rising with Q and there will be an upward-sloping relation between P and Q for each individual firm that tries to maximize profits. The supply curve is the industry relation between P and Q, where the industry output is the sum of all the individual firms' outputs. As firm output responses are upward sloping, the industry supply curve will be upward sloping, as depicted in Figure 3.1.

The fact that competitive markets are in equilibrium where demand equals supply leads to the most desired outcome from a CBA point of view (the maximization of net benefits). This result, called the 'invisible hand' by economists, occurs because: equation (3.1) is satisfied by consumers following their own best interests, and equation (3.2) is satisfied by firms following their own best interests, which together implies $MB = MC$. In other words, the competitive price P is the 'go-between' linking producers and consumers in these two equations. When demand equals supply, MB and MC are brought into line, ensuring the social optimum.

This interpretation of how markets function explains why economists are so much in favor of competition. But, from an economic evaluation point of view, what is important is that if a competitive market exists, we have a simple way to measure MC. As we can see from Figure 3.1, the equilibrium market price P_E tells us the MC of using an additional unit of Q.

Underlying the market diagram, there is the equilibrium position for each individual firm. The competitive firm, being so small relative to the market that it becomes a price taker, faces a fixed price set by the market at P_E. The cost curve is assumed to be U-shaped. In the last chapter we saw that U-shaped cost curves would be expected in the short run. The implicit assumption behind U-shaped cost curves in the *long run* is that there is some resource owned by the firm that cannot be reproduced (such as entrepreneurial ability) and this causes something like the law of diminishing returns to apply. Figure 3.2 illustrates the price and AC for a typical firm in equilibrium. With perfect competition, firms only earn enough to cover their costs. (If $P > AC$ new firms enter the market and if $P < AC$ firms leave the market.) Thus quantity Q_E is the equilibrium output because at this quantity the market-determined price P_E equals AC.

At the equilibrium quantity Q_E, the firm produces at the lowest point of its AC curve. This is significant for two reasons: (1) The firm is producing output at the lowest cost possible and thus producing efficiently. (2) The AC is neither rising nor falling at its lowest point and therefore is equal to the MC (i.e., $AC = MC$ when AC is constant). This means that the market price P_E is not just a good measure of AC; it also indicates the MC as required by the CBA optimum condition that MB (the price) equals MC.

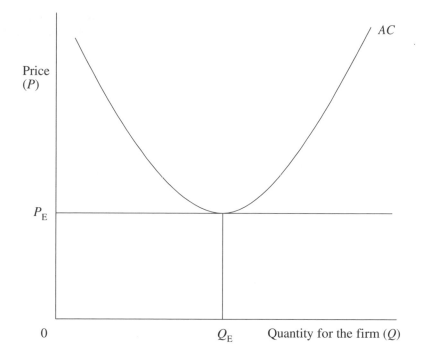

Note: The industry in perfect competition is in equilibrium when each firm just covers its costs. For the firm, this occurs where the price equals average costs *AC*. The price P_E is derived from the market equilibrium where demand equals supply. The firm produces a quantity Q_E at this price. At Q_E, the firm is producing at the lowest point of its *AC* curve. At the lowest point of the *AC* curve, $MC = AC$. So $P = AC$ also means $P = MC$.

Figure 3.2: A competitive firm produces at the lowest point of its AC

3.2.2 Costs and Non-competitive Markets

The invisible hand outcome is a result of competitive markets. The requirements for perfect competition are exacting: a large number of buyers and sellers, a homogeneous product, no barriers to entry or exit and perfect information. Unfortunately, other kinds of market may exist in health care. Culyer (1982) writes: 'The marketeer's economic ideal and the real world markets for health care do, of course, have something in common: the word "market".' Just like gardeners and lions have something in common; 'they both have mouths!' He adds: 'But that's about where the similarity ends. Indeed, when one compares real markets with their moral hazard, professional monopolies, insurance monopolies, agency relationships, public subsidies, consumer ignorances and misplaced enthusiasms' then the competitive model is not useful as a guide to what actually takes place in health care. Let us examine in detail the monopoly situation mentioned by Culyer.

A monopoly exists when there is a single producer in an industry. Unlike perfect competition, the firm is not a price taker. The firm's demand curve is the industry demand curve, which is downward sloping. This means that when the monopolist produces a lower output, the price will rise. Thus the monopolist has an incentive to restrict output in order to obtain the higher price and increase its profits. This is not possible under competition. There are so many other firms around which could sell the identical product at the market price and so no consumer would ever pay a higher price for it. Figure 3.3 illustrates what happens when a monopoly replaces a situation where competition previously existed.

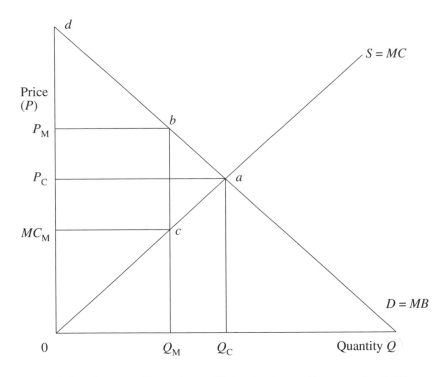

Note: Only at the competitive market equilibrium is price equal to marginal cost. If for any reason there is a distortion that holds back output to below equilibrium, then price and *MC* diverge. Price would not then be a good measure of *MC*.

Figure 3.3:   A monopolist's prices are greater than MC

By holding back output below competitive levels, $Q_M < Q_C$, the monopolist's price is greater than under competition, $P_M > P_C$. Consumers are worse off under monopoly. In cost–benefit terms, increasing output from the monopoly level Q_M to the competitive level Q_C would produce net benefits equal to the area *abc* (the difference between the area under the demand curve and the supply curve for the extra quantity $Q_M \, Q_C$).

The message that comes out of the monopoly model (or from any other situation whereby output is being restricted, e.g., because of sales taxes) is that the price charged is not a good measure of *MC*. In Figure 3.3 we can see that the monopoly price P_M overstates MC_M by the amount *bc*.

3.3 COSTS VERSUS CHARGES

In this section we are primarily discussing the extent to which hospital charges can be used to measure opportunity costs in a health care evaluation.

3.3.1 Distinguishing Costs and Charges

Finkler (1982) points out that there are two main reasons for thinking that charges would be a good proxy for costs. Most health organizations are non-profit, which means that costs cannot diverge from charges for too long. Also, in the fee-for-service system that used to predominate in health care delivery in the United States, insurance reimbursement was directly related to costs. However, costs are in essence very different from charges. Costs involve the resources consumed by providing the service, while charges often add to the costs a margin. The margin may be fixed across payees, in which case it would constitute a desire for profit. Or the margin may be set differently for different purchasers. In this case the variable margin exists to satisfy a designated pricing strategy, for example, to subsidize low-income users.

Nonetheless, there is a situation where charges are a good index of opportunity costs, and that is when it is the hospital that is paying (to suppliers), rather than receiving (from patients), the charges. In line with the analysis given in section 3.1.2, when hospitals purchase inputs in competitive markets there are no (fixed or variable) margins over costs to consider and the price paid for inputs would therefore accurately reflect costs.

Apart from this case, Finkler argues that charges would not be good measures of costs. As he says: 'Accounting costs differ from economic costs because by their very nature they tend to be average costs.' But accounting costs are not just any average costs. They are AC for those who pay their bills. Less than half of all patients must compensate for all of the debts, free service, community programs and disallowed costs. Charges must be set so that those who pay at the charge rate will make up any difference between total costs and reimbursement. Thus, the average charge is usually substantially above hospital measured costs.

On the other hand, charges that are paid by insurance companies may be too low. Charges are list prices and many purchasers get discounts from the list price. So cost based reimbursement may be below AC. One should not expect that there be a simple relation between costs and charges in health care. In the next sub-section we try to obtain some idea of orders of magnitude.

3.3.2 Cost-to-Charge Ratios

Many hospitals carry out their own internal accounting to try to estimate costs. They then calculate the ratio of these cost estimates to the charges that they set, called the cost-to-charge ratio, RCC. A good starting point to estimate costs would be to use a hospital's RCC to convert charge data into cost data. The question is, how accurate in general would be these cost estimates based on RCCs? Cost-to-charge ratios are based on AC related to hospital departments. Within the departments themselves, some inputs are more costly than others. To the extent that different patients use different combinations of inputs, the departmental averages may not be good measures of individual client costs.

Over 350 hospitals worldwide use a hospital cost accounting system (developed by Transition Systems, Inc.) that is more disaggregated than the departmental level. In this system, each item used is given a value that reflects its relative value compared to a department's baseline cost. The relative value units, RVUs, of each item used by a patient are summed and multiplied by the department's cost per RVU to obtain the cost of services used by the department. The patient's bill is then the sum of the departmental costs. This way of calculating patients' costs is considered much more reliable than relying on bills calculated just using the departmental cost-to-charge ratios. (The first set of problems in section 3.5.1 serve to illustrate how a patient's bill is calculated using the standard system based on departmental RCCs.)

Shwartz et al. (1995) carried out a study to quantify the extent to which cost-to-charge ratios were good approximations of 'true' costs using the disaggregated RVUs as the 'gold standard' (a phrase often found in health care to indicate best practice). In particular, there were three points of comparison between RCCs and RVUs that Shwartz et al. wanted to examine:

1. The extent to which RCCs that overestimate costs for some departments cancel out RCCs that underestimate costs for other departments, so that at the patient level the overall bill would be approximately correct;

2. The extent to which patient costs based on RCCs averaged over a sub-group of interest (a diagnostic related group, DRG) would be approximately correct; and
3. The extent to which cost estimates based on RCCs for a DRG in an individual hospital accurately reflect the same DRG average over a group of seven hospitals.

Table 3.1 displays their findings. The results are presented as ratios of RCCs to RVUs. If RCCs were accurate estimates of costs, the ratio would be equal to 1.00. The table gives an abbreviated version of Shwartz et al.'s distribution of ratios. The range within ±10% of 1.00 is highlighted.

Table 3.1: Percent of cases where RCC-estimated costs are within 10% of RVU-estimated costs

Unit of analysis	Ratio of RCC costs to RVU costs		
	<0.90	0.90 to <1.10	≥1.10
Patient level	19.1	50.9	29.9
DRG level, intrahospital	10.1	69.9	20.0
DRG level, hospital to group (departmental RCC)	8.7	76.4	14.0
DRG level, hospital to group (hospital RCC)	25.8	46.8	27.3

Source: Based on Shwartz et al. (1995)

The table shows that only a half of the estimates of patient average costs using RCCs would be within 10% of their RVU counterparts. At the DRG level, cost estimates using RCCs are much more accurate as about 70% are within 10%. The success rate rises to over three-quarters for DRGs at the hospital level (calculating a hospital DRG and comparing it with an average of seven other hospitals). If for any reason a departmental RCC is not known, and one uses a hospital-wide figure, the last row of the table tells us that this figure is not very accurate.

3.4 APPLICATIONS

In the last chapter we had a case study that estimated the cost of a service at a hospital for two levels of output. Statistical techniques exist for estimating costs for all levels and the first of our applications shows what one can do when more information is available. We know that cost estimates based on hospital RCCs are not very accurate. The second case study examines the extent to which resource allocation decisions would be distorted by using RCC data. Then we turn to studies that relate to physician costs. The third application deals with a new method for estimating resource costs for physicians and the last study tests whether physician bills can be used to measure costs accurately in a CBA.

3.4.1   Estimating Hospital Costs

We saw in section 2.3 that in order to achieve the most worthwhile outcome, one needs information on the entire range of the cost curve. But, if one knows that there are constant returns to scale for two treatment options one is comparing, then the results of a CM would not be output specific. Should there be economies or diseconomies of scale, MC and AC will diverge and the two types of cost need to be estimated separately.

Grannemann et al. (1986) analyzed a nationwide sample of non-federal, short-term, United States hospitals. They covered both inpatient and outpatient care (e.g., emergency department services, physical therapy visits and family planning services). Of interest was not only whether any type of service had economies of scale, but also whether there were economies of scope between two types of service. That is, if an emergency department were closed down, how would that impact on the cost for inpatient services?

For inpatient services they employed a two-dimensional measure of output that enabled them to distinguish the content of a hospital day from the average duration of a patient stay. Some hospitals would have intense stays of short duration, while other hospital stays had less intensity and longer durations. Both duration and intensity would be important in determining costs. To measure duration they used the number of days that patients stayed. To reflect intensity they used the number of discharges. The logic of this was explained in section 3.1.3, where a hospital stay was split up into two: a quantity of medical services (lab tests and surgical services) and daily services (routine nursing). The principle here is that the cost of a discharge, holding the daily services constant, would reflect the medical services that were given. The costs of daily services are the 'hotel costs' we identified earlier. The costs of these daily services are the product of the average length of stay times the cost per day. Thus the MC of a stay is:

$$MC_{stay} = MC_{discharge} + (LOS) \cdot MC_{day} \qquad (3.3)$$

Table 3.2 (Table 3 of Grannemann et al.) lists the MC for a seven-day acute inpatient care stay corresponding to three hospital sizes. 'Low' (approximately the 25th percentile), 'medium' (about 50th percentile) and 'high' (75th percentile) volumes are respectively 3000, 7000 and 13000 discharges annually. In terms of equation (3.3), they obtain the figure for medium stays, for example, by adding $880 to seven times $237. A reduction in *LOS* from seven to six days reduces *MC* by only 9% ($237/$2538). Economies of scale exist, but they are not large.

Table 3.2: Marginal cost of acute inpatient care ($)

Hospital volume	Cost per discharge	Cost per day	Cost per stay
Low	533	168	1706
Medium	880	237	2538
High	1064	231	2678

Source: Grannemann et al. (1986)

The interesting results were obtained for outpatient care. Grannemann et al. contrast the cost functions for emergency departments (EDs) with other outpatient departments (OPDs). The findings are reported in Table 3.3 (Grannemann et al.'s Table 4). Returns to scale can be measured by the ratio of the *AC* to the *MC*. Constant returns exist when the ratio is unity; increasing returns exist when the ratio is greater than unity; and decreasing returns is the case when *AC/MC* is less than unity. We see from the table that, at the output sample means, EDs have an *AC* of $201 with an *MC* of $123, forming an *AC/MC* = 1.63, and OPDs have a *AC* of $82 with an *MC* of $83, producing an *AC/MC* = 0.99. This means that EDs have increasing returns to scale (falling *AC*s) while OPDs have roughly constant returns to scale. Although EDs have economies of scale, they have diseconomies of scope between the emergency department and inpatient care. This can be seen in Table 3.3, where *MC*s and *AC*s rise as the level of inpatient days increases.

There are two main general messages from this case study. First, there could be a big difference in results if we look at the costs of an individual procedure in isolation, or as part of a group of procedures. Economies or diseconomies of scope may exist and this could cause the joint evaluation of procedures to be greater or less than individual procedures. Second, one needs to distinguish types of hospital services when deciding whether *AC*s are good proxies for *MC*s. Acute inpatient care and emergency department visits have scale economies and thus *AC*s overestimate *MC*s. But, for other outpatient care, constant returns exist and *AC*s accurately measure *MC*s.

Table 3.3: Per visit costs for hospital outpatient care by type of output ($)

| | Marginal cost | | Average cost | | *AC/MC* | |
	ED	OPD	ED	OPD	ED	OPD
At means	123	83	201	82	1.63	0.99
Level of inpatient days						
High	112	100	242	100	2.16	1.00
Medium	114	67	170	66	1.46	0.98
Low	69	33	89	33	1.29	0.97
Level of ED visits						
High	71	81	171	80	2.41	0.99
Medium	146	83	213	82	1.46	0.99
Low	225	181	252	79	1.12	0.98
Level of OPD visits						
High	121	84	206	82	1.71	0.98
Medium	124	82	199	81	1.60	0.99
Low	125	81	194	81	1.56	1.00

Source: Grannemann et al. (1986)

3.4.2 Costing and Evaluating DRG Categories

We saw in section 3.3.2 that RCCs produced cost estimates that often differed from their RVU counterparts that were considered more reliable. Schimmel et al. (1987) investigated whether these differences have any decision-making consequences. That is, would one wrongly approve or reject projects if one used the RCC cost estimates? If few mistakes were made, then one could save a lot of time and expense by not collecting RVUs.

Schimmel et al.'s decision-making criterion was the financial profit (revenues R minus costs C) generated by a hospital providing various diagnostic related groups. Financial profit is a flawed CBA criterion. Even if financial costs are considered to be good measures of opportunity costs, financial revenues may not be good guides to social benefits. A simple way to see the difference between using R instead of B, in a context where the demand curve is used to measure benefits, is to refer back to Figure 3.3. At the competitive level of output Q_C, benefits are given by the area under the demand curve, area $0Q_C ad$. Revenues are the product of price times quantity ($R = P.Q$). At Q_C, revenues are given by the rectangular area $0Q_C aP_C$. The difference between B and R is therefore the triangular area $P_C ad$.

The triangular area is called 'consumer surplus', being the difference between what consumers are willing to pay and what they actually have to pay. A major problem with financial evaluations is that they omit consumer surplus. Consumer surplus plays a very important role in CBA because it can be used to justify projects when for any reason prices cannot be levied or the optimal level of a price is zero. However, in this case study we are focusing on the reliability of cost estimates and so we can ignore differences in consumer surpluses among the DRG categories.

Schimmel et al. analyzed the profitability of each of the 25 highest volume DRGs at five hospitals scattered round the United States. On average, the difference between using cost estimates based on RVUs and RCCs was greater than $1000. More important than this average effect is the false signal that using wrong cost estimates would produce. In a financial context, one should close down a DRG that was making a loss and continue with a profitable DRG. If cost differences were such that otherwise profitable DRGs (judged by RCCs) were wrongly classified as financial failures (judged by RVUs), then decision-making would be distorted by the inappropriate cost estimates. Table 3.4 (Schimmel et al.'s Table 8.2) reports all the times a DRG category appeared profitable under one methodology and generated a loss under the alternative approach.

Table 3.4:   *DRGs that give different profitability outcomes using RVUs and RCCs*

Hospital	DRG category	RVU profit/case ($)	RCC profit/case ($)	RVU–RCC ($)
A	127: Heart failure	(321)	613	(934)
	138: Arrhythmia	(415)	743	(1,157)
	140: Angina pectoris	(47)	639	(686)
	143: Chest pain	(39)	568	(606)
	373: Vaginal delivery	14	(154)	168
B	127: Heart failure	62	(114)	175
	182: GI disorders	27	(28)	55
	209: Joint procedures	295	(342)	637
	355: Hysterectomy	16	(247)	263
	410: Heart failure	(199)	52	(251)
C	25: Seizure/headaches	(38)	1	(39)
	98: Bronchitis/asthma	(7)	40	(47)
	391: Normal newborn	(6)	22	(27)
D	87: Seizure/headaches	(755)	223	(978)
	391: Normal newborn	(45)	(119)	165
E	371: Cesarean section	(73)	7	(79)

Source: Schimmel et al. (1987)

Table 3.4 indicates that there would be numerous instances where resources would be misallocated if RCCs were used to estimate costs. The main sign of hope was that hospital E, the first one to adopt the RVU accounting system, had the lowest number of misclassified DRGs. This suggests that there is some 'learning by doing' taking place with cost estimates and that one can rely more on RCC data from institutions with established accounting systems, as they have had the time to align their charges with what are their real costs.

3.4.3   Resource Based Relative Value Scale

The competitive market analysis summarized in Figure 3.1 was used by Hsiao et al. (1988) as the model for determining what physicians' costs would be in the United States in the absence of market imperfections. Medicare (the government insurance policy for the elderly) reimbursed doctors using their 'reasonable and customary' charges. Many physicians believed that reimbursements on this basis undervalued cognitive services where evaluation was necessary and overpaid surgery and procedures. A new method for estimating the resource cost of physician services was devised called the 'Resource Based Relative Value' scale (RBRV or RBRVS). Hsiao et al.'s work was so influential that in 1992 their scale replaced the customary charge system for Medicare.

The logic behind the RBRV was articulated by Hsiao and Dunn (1991) as: 'In a competitive market, the long-run equilibrium price of a good should approximate the long-run average cost of its production. (We assume that the long run marginal cost approximately equals the long run average cost). The RBRVS we have developed is a method for approximating the average relative costs required to produce a range of physicians' services.'

The RBRV method is built around this formula for measuring the resource input for a physician service:

$$RBRV = TW\,(1 + RPC)(1 + AST) \qquad (3.4)$$

where TW is the total work input by the physician, RPC is an index of relative specialty cost, and AST is an index of amortized value for the opportunity cost of specialized training. TW includes work done preceding, during and after the service has been provided. It is mainly made up of the physician's time (and effort) expended in an activity.

A standard service is taken as the benchmark for each specialty and all other services in that specialty are ranked relative to it. For example, under general surgery, an uncomplicated inguinal hernia repair was assigned a value of 100. If a physician working on a lower anterior resection for rectal carcinoma judged this to be four times more difficult than doing the hernia operation, then the resection would be given a score of 400. This is the 'relative value' component of the RBRV and its role is similar to the baseline cost used to construct the RVU in the hospital cost accounting system (described in section 3.3.2). Estimates of *TW* were obtained from a questionnaire given to 3164 physicians and a reasonable consensus about the relative difficulty of various services was found. The *TW* then was given what we can call a 'mark-up', according to both the special equipment required in a specialty (via *RPC*) and the forgone income when physicians undertake additional years of specialty training rather than entering practice (via *AST*).

The RBRV figure derived for a service is in physical units. To express it in monetary terms a conversion factor had to be applied to it. Hsiao et al. used a conversion factor that would ensure 'budget neutrality'. That is, the total amount of all physician services times their RBRV values must approximate the total sum that was spent under Medicare using the old customary charge system in 1986.

Table 3.5 shows what difference would be made by using the RBRVs instead of the Medicare charges. Hsiao et al. listed 30 main services (and dealt with over 7000 services and procedures): see their Table 2. We cover four of these in our table. As with the analysis of RCCs in section 3.3.2, a ratio of unity is the benchmark. This time it is the RBRVs that provide the gold standard for the Medicare charges. Ratios less than one indicate services whose costs are underestimated by Medicare charges (and therefore would benefit from having RBRVs) and services with ratios greater than one have costs that are overestimated by Medicare charges (and thus would suffer a loss of revenues with RBRVs).

The results in the table support Hsiao et al.'s claim that office visits were paid less under the old Medicare system and that surgery and procedures were paid more. Certain specialties, like family practice and psychiatry, concentrate mainly on evaluative-type services and thus nearly all of their services are underestimated under Medicare (all their ratios are less than unity), while for other specialties (e.g., thoracic and cardiovascular surgery) most of their services have values greater than unity. The overall conclusion by Hsiao et al. was that using the RBRV scale to replace the previous system would increase the payments for evaluative and management services by 56%, while reducing invasive, imaging and laboratory services payments by 42%, 30% and 5% respectively.

Clearly, then, the RBRV scale gives a different estimate of costs than before. The issue is whether it gives a better estimate of costs. According to Hadley (1991), 'the formula for calculating RBRVS is inconsistent with the economic theory of cost in that it omits both the scale of production and the possible presence of economies (or diseconomies) of scope'. This criticism

Table 3.5:   Resource based relative values and Medicare charges

Procedure code	Service description	RBRVs ($)	Medicare charge ($)	Ratio of Medicare charge to RBRVS
	Dermatology			
90050	Office visit, limited service	38	25	0.66
90020	Office visit, comprehensive service	113	41	0.36
11900	Injection, intralesional	23	28	1.22
11642	Excision, malignant lesion	159	220	1.38
	Family practice			
90050	Office visit, limited service	49	21	0.43
90630	Initial consultation, complex service	283	86	0.30
45300	Proctosigmoidoscopy, diagnostic	118	53	0.45
90370	Subsequent care, skilled nursing	159	37	0.23
	Psychiatry			
90831	Telephone consultation	50	41	0.82
90862	Chemotherapy management	69	30	0.43
90844	Individual medical psychotherapy	94	75	0.80
90849	Multiple-family group psychotherapy	210	51	0.24
	Thoracic and cardiovascular surgery			
90020	Office visit, comprehensive service	213	64	0.30
32020	Tube thoracostomy with water seal	346	382	1.10
32480	Lobectomy, total or segmental	2148	2275	1.06
33512	Coronary artery bypass	2871	4662	1.62

Source: Hsiao et al. (1988)

follows because Hsiao et al. had assumed that (the long run) *AC* equaled *MC*, which implies constant returns to scale. However, this is really an empirical conjecture (that constant costs do not exist in physician markets) that is not related to theory, because economic theory can be used to explain any type of returns to scale (as we did in the last chapter). A criticism that does rely on economic theory is to point out that the RBRVS is simply an average of physician resource costs and is not necessarily the cost-minimizing amount for any given level of service.

Hadley's main contribution is to analyze the Hsiao et al. proposition that existing physician markets were distorted due to the existence of non-uniform insurance coverage that raises the demand for some services and not for others. Say evaluative-management (EM) services are not covered and procedures (PR) are covered by insurance. The higher demand for PR services will raise their prices relative to EM services. But, given the existence of competitive markets, the equilibrium position is characterized by $P = AC$ (as shown in Figure 3.2). So again, relative prices would reflect relative costs just as in the absence of insurance. As Hadley says: 'Insurance in and of itself does not make a competitive market non-competitive, even if it leads to higher quantities and higher fees.' It is the existence of non-competitive health care markets, with or without insurance, which brings costs and prices out of line.

With prices and costs out of line, how should one measure the value of physician services? In terms of Figure 3.3, where the level of services is Q_M, should one use the price P_M or the cost MC_M? The main criticism of the RBRVS raised by Hadley (and others) is that it just focuses on resource inputs and ignores the consumer satisfaction (WTP) of the services. Hadley argues: 'Viewing the problem as how to get value for money implies that Medicare should concentrate on what it gets as a result of a fee schedule, not on how physicians combine inputs to produce services.' Effectively, then, Hadley is recommending the use of the price that consumers are willing to pay, given by P_M.

There is a technical literature in economics that analyses how best to combine the consumer price and producer cost to estimate the social value of a good or service – for a summary see Brent (1996, ch. 6). But, there is a much simpler way of looking at matters. From a CM perspective, to measure costs, one has a dilemma whether to use the consumer price or what producers must receive to put a level of output on the market. However, from a CBA perspective, one plans to look at both the benefits and the costs of physician services. So one can use resource inputs to measure costs, just as with the RBRVS. In addition, one will be looking at the WTP of consumers when one turns to measuring the benefits. The demand for physician services is derived from the value of the services that they produce. Thus, when one tries to estimate the benefits of total knee arthroplasty (or any other intervention that follows from a physician performing a service) in terms of the WTP, one is valuing the service from the consumer's point of view.

3.4.4 The Social Value of Physician Services

Hsiao et al.'s RBRVS attempted to estimate the cost of certain physician services relative to other physician services, but it could not address the issue of whether the overall level of physician fees was too high or not. This was because it converted physical units to monetary units using a conversion factor that ensured that the government would pay out as much in physician salaries under the new system as it did under the old. It is widely believed that doctors are paid too much, as they are among the highest salary earners in most countries. Brent (1994) tried to test whether physician charges were good measures of the social value of their services. He focused on a plastic surgeon in a large northeastern, city hospital in the United States.

Drawing on the technical literature on social pricing in economics, Brent used a formula that expressed the gap between the price charged and the marginal cost as a function of how responsive consumers were to changes in price (called the 'price elasticity of demand', something we will be referring to a number of times). The social value would be closest to P and most above MC when consumers are least sensitive to price changes (elasticities are lowest). The logic of this rule is simple. Take the case where consumers are extremely responsive to price (and the elasticity is infinitely large). This case is illustrated by having a demand curve that is horizontal, as in Figure 3.2. The rule then would state that with the elasticity so high, the difference between P and MC should be very low. At the extreme, there would be no difference and hence $P = MC$. This result is exactly what we obtained intuitively with Figure 3.2. That is, under perfect competition, $P = MC$.

Apart from the elasticities, the social price depended on the importance of revenues to the government (called the 'marginal cost of public funds' and analyzed in depth in Chapter 5). Three values for this parameter were considered, corresponding to a low value, a best estimate and a high value.

The key part of the Brent study involved his measure of MC. Nearly all the bills charged by the plastic surgeon went to insurance companies (a mixture of public and private institutions). They would reimburse the physician according to their view of the true costs of the services. Thus, the amount received by the physician was used to measure MC and the bill charged by the physician corresponded to the price P. The objective of the study was to see how much of a dollar billed was judged to be costs by the insurance companies (i.e., how much of the variation in price was due to variations in costs).

Brent's sample consisted of 766 payments billed and received over the period 1986–88. Six main insurance companies were involved. Medicare was the public insurance carrier and the private insurance companies were: Group Health Insurance Plan (GHI), Health Improvement Plan of Greater New York (HIP), Blue Cross, Empire, and a number of health workers' unions (just denoted as 'union'). A seventh grouping was called 'joint' when two third-party payers were involved (one of them, almost always, was Medicare). Although only one physician was studied, it was third-party behavior that was being monitored (they decide how much to reimburse) and the insurance carriers included in the sample covered many thousands of individuals.

As with all the analyses of cost estimates in this chapter, we present the results in terms of a ratio that ideally would be equal to unity. The actual ratio we are considering here is roughly MC/P, and this equates to how much of a dollar billed is true cost. For example, if the physician bills \$1 and receives 50 cents from the insurance carrier then the ratio would equal

0.5. The ratios for each of the insurance carriers, and for the three values for the importance of public revenues, are given in Table 3.6 (based on Brent's Table 3). The best estimates in Table 3.6 reveal that, depending on the third party involved, between 41% and 58% of the price charged by the plastic surgeon reflects *MC*, i.e., between 42% and 59% of a physician's bill is not a part of costs. Brent's conclusion was that approximately a half of the amount charged by a physician should represent costs in a CBA.

Table 3.6: Estimates of the share of the physician's bill that counts as costs

Insurance carrier	Lower bound	Best estimate	Upper bound
Medicare	0.3659	0.4110	0.4501
GHI	0.4012	0.4475	0.4872
HIP	0.5281	0.5750	0.6135
Blue Cross	0.4861	0.5335	0.5729
Empire	0.4312	0.4782	0.5181
Union	0.5318	0.5786	0.6170
Joint	0.4963	0.5436	0.5829

Source: Brent (1994)

One last point is worth making. In a second study using the same data, Brent and Patel (1997) tried to test explicitly the basis of the belief by phys-icians that, prior to the RBRVS, cognitive services (like consultations) were under-compensated relative to surgery. Contrary to this belief, they found that per dollar billed, physicians were being reimbursed *more* for the con-sultations. It could be that the RBRVS would never have been devised if it were known that evaluative services were not underpriced under the old Medicare system.

3.5   FINAL SECTION

We continue with the problems, summary and looking ahead sections.

3.5.1   Problems

Two accounting concepts mentioned in this chapter, that were important ingredients in obtaining measures of economic costs, were cost-to-charge ratios and the step-down allocation method for estimating joint costs. The problems help one understand the details of these two accounting methods.

The first problem set requires one to use the RCC ratio to estimate actual costs. The data in Table 3.7 come from the Appendix of Weintraub et al. (1995). The second and third columns are filled in. The top part of the table assigns costs by a unit cost basis. For all other departments the RCC is used.

Table 3.7:   *Hypothetical translation of a patient's bill: charges to costs*

Description	Units	Unit cost ($)	Total cost ($)
Private room	7	347.64	
Intensive care	2	990.851	

	Charge ($)	Ratio	Cost ($)
Pharmacy	860.71	0.699677	
Medical or surgical supply	490.31	0.595271	
Laboratory	1853.90	0.500956	
Radiology	391.00	0.710770	
Nuclear medicine	586.00	0.806104	
Operating room	7987.24	0.627852	
Anesthesia	1404.00	0.830067	
Respiratory therapy	477.80	0.740606	
Physical therapy	235.41	0.621607	
Other emergency room	108.00	0.970334	
Pulmonary function	520.00	0.980776	
ECG	160.00	0.939473	
Total			

Source: Weintraub et al. (1995)

1(a) Calculate the costs for each department that correspond to the charges made.

1(b) Are charges overall a good measure of costs (i.e., compare the charge and cost totals)?

The second problem set, using data in Table 3.8, is based on Tables 1 and 2 of Finkler and involves applying the step-down method of allocating joint costs. The first and last columns have been filled in to help with the calculations.

2(a) Which service department affects more of the other departments? Start with this department and allocate its costs to the other three departments (i.e., fill in line 4 of the table).

Table 3.8: *Hypothetical use of cost centers ($)*

	Service sectors		Medical sectors		
	A	B	Lab	Surgery	Total
1. Direct dept cost	100	100	100	500	800
2. Relative use of A	0	70%	25%	5%	–
3. Relative use of B	0	0	20%	80%	–
4. Distribution of A	−100				0
5. Subtotal	0				800
6. Distribution of B	0				0
7. Total	0				800

Source: Based on Finkler (1982)

2(b) Find the cost allocation without the first service department (i.e., fill in line 5).

2(c) Make the cost allocation of the last service department (i.e., fill in lines 6 and 7).

3.5.2 Summary

For evaluation purposes, it is *MC* that one needs to compare with *MB*. Hence it is *MC* that one needs to minimize when making a CM comparison. The estimating problems we discussed in this chapter involved analyzing when *AC* could be used to measure *MC*, and when marginal adjustments were not possible because overhead/joint costs were involved. We also examined the non-economist's claim that 'you only get what you pay for' in the context of hospital and physician charges.

There is a mathematical relation between average cost and marginal cost that must hold. When *AC* is falling, *MC* is below *AC*; when *AC* is rising, *MC* is above *AC*; and when *AC* is constant, *MC* equals *AC*. This relation explains why the *MC* must go through the lowest point of the *AC* curve (as it is constant at that point). Thus when *P* = *AC* for a firm under pure competition, we have *P* = *MC*. So in the case of a U-shaped cost curve, as we had in Figure 3.2, price would be a good measure of *MC*. This result was the basis for the invisible hand property that economists point to when extolling the virtue of markets. At the practical level, this result also meant that *AC* = *MC*, so we could use average cost to estimate marginal cost. However, perfect competition is not likely to exist in health care.

The second situation when AC could be used to measure MC again uses the mathematical relation just cited. But this time instead of concentrating only on the lowest point of a U-shaped AC curve in perfect competition, one deals with an AC that is constant throughout its range. This is the constant returns to scale case. In this case, *at every level of output*, we have $AC = MC$. So estimating cost curves in health care is very important if we wish to establish generally whether AC can be used as a proxy for MC. Note that when one finds increasing returns to scale one has a strong reason to doubt whether pure competition exists. This is because in these circumstances firms would have an incentive to become large relative to the market in order to exploit the lower cost per unit that results from expanding output.

The other theme for the chapter was whether charges could be used to measure costs. Given that $P = MC$ would only result if there were perfect competition, and we thought that pure competition was unlikely in health care, we gave emphasis to the empirical work done on the link between costs and charges. Finkler warned that: 'The first rule of charges is to make the institution solvent.' So we should not be too surprised with our main finding that charges do not often measure economic costs accurately.

Cost estimates are more likely to be reliable if they are based on accounting systems that use relative value units. RVUs are more disaggregated than the departmental cost-to-charge ratios. RCCs are reasonable proxies for RVU costs when applied to a DRG category rather than at the patient level.

The applications started with an empirical analysis of hospital cost curves in the United States. The distinction drawn there was between costs that were related to specialist health care services, related to the number of discharges, and routine nursing care that depends on patient LOS. The length of stay component of costs was appropriate for using average costs on a *per diem* basis. These costs were also referred to as hotel costs. When the length of stay component of costs dominates the component related to discharges, then constant returns to scale can be expected. In this case, *per diems* may be good measures of costs, which is to say that AC can be used to measure MC. In the hospital cost study we saw that AC could be used for other outpatient care as these services were characterized by constant returns to scale. However, for acute inpatient care and emergency department visits, AC overestimates MC as economies of scale exist.

In the second application we explored the significance of the fact that RCCs were poor proxies for RVUs within a financial profitability criterion. In the absence of a social CBA, profitability is the main criterion for judging whether an activity would survive in a market economy like the United States. Within a profitability context, there were many instances where RCC cost estimates would give opposing recommendations for DRGs than the more accurate RVU estimates.

Relying on the perfect competition model, the third application analyzed the Resource Based Relative Value Scale as a method of measuring physician resource costs. The main difficulty with the RBRVS was that it just focused on the supply side and ignored WTP on the demand side. This was a weakness if one were to focus exclusively on costs, as one does in a CM framework. But, from a CBA perspective, the RBRVS could be used as a basis for estimating costs, as WTP is included when measuring MBs. In the final application, an analysis of the pricing by a plastic surgeon to a number of third-party insurance payers, the result was that only about a half of the physician's bill should be considered to be cost from a CBA perspective.

3.5.3 Looking Ahead

In this chapter perfect markets were center stage. Prices and costs are equal in these circumstances. In the next two chapters we show that P and MC may diverge even in perfect markets when external costs exist.

4. External costs

4.1 INTRODUCTION

We have just seen one reason why market prices may not reflect costs, that is, because markets may be imperfect. When external effects exist, even perfect market prices may be incorrect indicators of social value. The competitive market equilibrium output with external effects could be under or over the level that is most desirable. We first define an external effect and explain how this drives a wedge between private and social evaluations. We next look at the relation between external effects and markets. Then we accommodate situations where external effects vary over time. The theory and the applications focus on the external costs involved with alcohol related driving accidents and the external benefits of preventing contagious diseases.

4.1.1 Defining an Externality

External effects occur whenever someone other than the parties directly involved with a trade or transaction is affected. In the health care context, we can think of patients as the first party and the physicians and hospitals providing the care as the second party. Then third parties would be everyone else, i.e., the friends and families of the patients, other patients, other doctors and hospitals, and the rest of society.

In developing countries, a very important external effect of female education is that women can read labels on medications and thus take only the appropriate tablets. Infant mortality rates decline significantly when mothers have had just one year's education. External effects can be positive as in the education example (provide benefits) or negative (provide costs) as when toxic chemicals are released into the atmosphere when heavy industry takes place that causes pollution.

A standard definition of an externality in economics, attributed to Pigou (1920), involves an unpriced side-effect. Thus it is not an externality that my health depends on a pharmacist's behavior; because the medication the pharmacist provides is paid for by me (or by an insurance company). But, when I have to wait in line for my medications because there are a number of others who have presented prescriptions ahead of me, then my lost time in the pharmacy is an externality. One has to be a little careful when using the standard definition because, as we saw in the last chapter, prices may not always reflect all the costs even when they are charged.

The important ingredient in an externality is that there exist other people who have an interest in seeing that there is a different amount than the main parties directly involved choose to produce and consume: see Buchanan and Stubblebine (1962). So in our health care evaluations we have to add on, or subtract, amounts for the external effects, as we now explain.

4.1.2 Social Costs and Private Costs

As we are still discussing matters from the perspective of CM, we will emphasize the costs side. But all points made also apply to the benefits side, seeing that in a CM framework costs and benefits are symmetrical and they differ only by the sign attached to the amounts.

The costs affecting the main two parties to treatment can be classed as 'private costs'. All the costs that we covered in the last two chapters were of this nature. This includes the cost categories direct (medical) and intangible (pain and suffering) identified in Chapter 1. Indirect (non-medical) costs, covering forgone earnings, are in principle external costs as they relate to output that is forgone by the rest of society. But, the patient is thought to be incurring these costs and they are one of the main parties involved in the health treatment. So they are not really regarded as a third-party effect. The lost earnings of family members of the patient can though be thought of as being external costs.

In CBA, 'social costs' are the total costs incurred by all parties affected by the project or treatment. This means that social costs C_S are the sum of the private C_P and external costs C_E:

$$C_S = C_P + C_E \qquad (4.1)$$

Market economists are often uncomfortable using the word 'social' as it carries the connotation of 'socialism' with its regime of imposing government priorities over the preferences of private individuals. There should not, however, be any concern with the use of social costs in CBA because, as we stressed in Chapter 1, consumer sovereignty is one of the founding principles of the discipline. Individual preferences (through their WTP for resources, and their willingness to be compensated for giving up resources) are to count. The only nuance is that now we are considering the preferences of all individuals, not just those directly involved.

The main problems posed by external effects are empirical, not conceptual. How does one estimate the costs of those remotely connected to an activity (especially in the case of environmental costs)? Because of these problems, evaluators have to have some confidence not only that externalities exist, but also that they are quantitatively significant. Fortunately, in the health care field, we can be sure that externalities are clearly important. In some cases, as with alcohol treatment and vaccinations programs, they are the *primary* category of effect.

The main empirical problems involve the fact that we cannot rely solely on market valuations to guide our estimation even when perfect markets exist. We will explore these empirical problems in subsequent sections. Before we do this, we will outline an estimation technique that has been found to be useful in many different evaluation contexts, including the case of dealing with externalities.

4.1.3 Switching Values

There exists a very valuable evaluation technique that can be used whenever vital information is missing or considered unreliable. This technique involves finding the 'switching value' for a variable, i.e., the value for the variable that just makes one indifferent between undertaking the intervention and deciding against it. Thus, if the value were slightly different than this, one would *switch* from approval to rejection (or vice versa). The usefulness of the switching value is apparent whenever it comes up with values that are 'clearly' acceptable or unacceptable.

We can explain the basic idea underlying a switching value by reconsidering the very first criterion we presented in Chapter 1. Equation (1.1) stated the main CBA test as requiring: $B_1 > C_1$. Let B_1 be the unknown value that is considered too difficult to estimate and assume that one knows C_1. The switching value for B_1, denoted B_1^*, would be such that:

$$B_1^* = C_1 \qquad\qquad (4.2)$$

In terms of equation (4.2), the switching value for B_1 would be equal to C_1, for if it were any higher than this, the intervention would be worthwhile, and any value lower than this would mean the intervention should be rejected.

Say B_1 involved trying to place the value on a person's life that was going to be saved by a medical procedure (being supplied with an antidote for a poison). Many non-economists consider that trying to estimate B_1 is an impossible task. But, if the cost of the antidote were \$100 (that is, $C_1 =$ \$100), using equation (4.2) one would know that the switching value was \$100. Since almost everyone would agree that saving a person's life is worth at least \$100, then the intervention should take place *in this particular case*.

Thus even though you and I might not be able to agree that a life were worth $1 million, or $10 million, or an infinite value, we could still both agree that it was *at least* worth $100 and have a consensus that the antidote should be provided. Of course, if the antidote cost $5 million (in the range of possible dispute) then no agreement might be forthcoming. Knowing the switching value would not always ensure that difficult valuation decisions could be avoided.

A good illustration of how the switching value technique operates is in Musgrove (1992). One part of his study involved valuing the benefits of a vaccination for meningitis. He used a CM framework because he valued the benefits of avoiding meningitis by the treatment costs that would be avoided. With C_1 representing the cost of the vaccination and C_2 the treatment costs used to measure B_1, equation (1.1) becomes $C_1 < C_2$, which is the standard CM criterion given as equation (1.9). As no vaccination for meningitis was available, Musgrove understandably thought that its cost was hard to estimate. He therefore applied the switching value technique which, in the CM context with C_1 unknown, can be written:

$$C_1^* = C_2 \qquad (4.3)$$

For meningitis, treatment costs gave a value for C_2 equal to $0.27. So if a vaccine could be found with a cost of, say, $0.10, then the vaccination would be worthwhile; but one would not approve meningitis vaccinations if their cost were $1.00.

4.2 EXTERNAL COSTS AND MARKETS

As alcohol consumption and vaccinations constitute some of the clearest examples of externalities, we will explain the requisite principles and empirical difficulties in terms of these two areas of application.

4.2.1 Drinking and Driving

Irrespective of the view one takes about the value of alcohol from the consumer's perspective, there is no doubt that alcohol imposes large external costs due to the road accidents that drunken drivers cause. In 1980, almost half of the 51 000 fatal crashes in the US included alcohol-involved persons. In addition, those affected by alcohol contributed to about 20% of the 2.5 million crashes that resulted in injuries (these figures from Phelps (1988)).

The consumption of alcohol (say beer) can be analyzed in terms of standard demand and supply curves. The extra satisfaction to the drinker defines the demand curve and the forgone value of the resources used to produce the beer forms the supply curve. In the competitive market depicted in Figure 4.1, equilibrium is associated with a price P_C and a quantity Q_C.

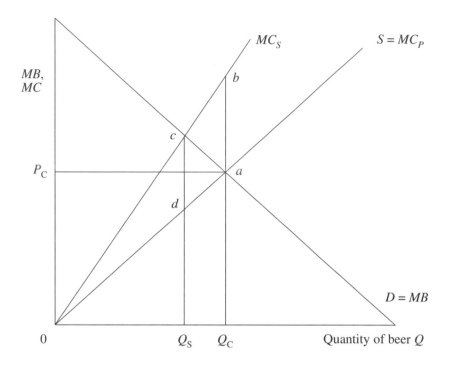

Note: The competitive equilibrium where demand equals supply leads to MB being equated with the private marginal cost MC_P. The social optimum, however, requires equating MB with the social marginal cost MC_S, which is the sum of MC_P and the external cost MC_E. The private market outcome produces too large an output when an external cost exists.

Figure 4.1:   *Competitive markets produce too little when a negative externality exists*

The social significance of the market equilibrium is different in the presence of externalities. The demand curve measures MB as before. But the supply curve relates to *private* marginal costs MC_P. When demand equals supply at point *a*, this brings about $MB = MC_P$. The consumption of beer is the quantity Q_C, which is greater than the socially optimal level Q_S which corresponds to the point *c* where $MB = MC_S$. The market equilibrium excludes external costs and this is why it leads to an over-consumption of beer.

The over-consumption of beer leads to there being a problem with the market price. P_C is too low. The market equilibrium brings about $P_C = MC_P$. In Figure 4.1, *ab* is the marginal external cost that corresponds to the output level Q_C. When marginal external costs are added to marginal private costs to form MC_S, the price resulting from $MB = MC_S$ would be given by point *c* at the output level Q_S. The logic of requiring a higher price is that, since external costs should be added to private costs, *MB* should also be higher to bring about the social optimum. The only way that *MB* can be higher is if quantity is cut back (seeing that *MB* slopes upward from right to left).

It is clear that we need to quantify external costs and then add them to private costs to estimate MC_S. What is not so obvious is that the external costs we need to know to establish the social optimum are not those that relate to the market output Q_C. It is the MC_E equal to *dc* that must be estimated, not that equal to *ab*.

Assuming that we can estimate MC_S along its entire curve, we can calculate in the usual way the net benefits of reducing the market output back to the socially optimal level. Moving from Q_C to Q_S produces a loss of benefits given by the area under the demand curve $Q_C ac Q_S$, and a cost saving equal to the area under the MC_S curve $Q_C bc Q_S$, resulting in a net benefit of area *abc*.

Up to this point in the book, we have interpreted a health care intervention to be a movement along the quantity axis. So in terms of Figure 4.1, an optimal policy involves moving from Q_C to Q_S. But an optimal policy can equivalently be thought to involve a movement along the vertical axis. If there were a price increase of *dc* added to the private marginal cost curve MC_C at Q_S (equal to the height $Q_S d$), then the combined marginal cost faced by consumers would be $Q_S c$. The equilibrium output at the higher price would be exactly equal to the socially optimal level of output.

The policy instrument that brings about the desired price increase necessary to achieve Q_S is an optimal commodity tax *t*. The optimal tax of *tdc* would then be said to 'internalize' the externality, in the sense that the cost *dc* would no longer be ignored by private consumers when deciding how much beer to consume. The first case study deals with this way of using taxes to achieve the optimal level of beer consumption.

4.2.2 Immunization Programs

We have previously remarked that, in a CBA, a cost is a negative benefit. The easiest way to understand this fact is to consider reversing an intervention or activity. That is, instead of doing something, one can think of *not* doing something. What was a benefit must now be regarded as a cost as one is giving up the benefit; and the cost of doing something is now a saving if one decides not to do it. With this reciprocal relationship in mind, we will analyze the external benefit case corresponding to the external cost case (discussed in section 4.2.1) in terms of the prevention of something (a disease).

A vaccination program thus has an external benefit by not allowing an external cost to materialize. The external cost of a disease is that, if it is contagious, one can pass it on to others. The external benefit of the vaccination is that one will not infect others. The private benefit is that the vaccine prevents the vaccinated person catching the disease.

An immunization program has two dimensions: should an immunization program take place and, if so, what percentage of the population will be immunized? (The difference between immunization and vaccination is that a vaccination will lead to immunization only if it is 100% effective.) According to Hannum (1997), most existing evaluations of vaccinations focus on the first dimension and ignore the second. This is unfortunate because an all-or-nothing decision is not necessarily compatible with finding the optimal level of output. Figure 4.2 (based on Hannum's Figure 3.2) can be used to explain why this is so.

Figure 4.2 shows the private and social benefits, and the costs, of increasing the proportion of the population (n) who receive vaccination. The private marginal benefits MB_P are the expected costs of treatment that are avoided. Private marginal costs MC_P entail the cost of the vaccine per person, which is assumed to be constant. Private equilibrium is where $MB_P = MC_P$ at point b. The vaccination rate chosen by a private market would be 40%. This rate $n = 0.4$ omits the external benefits to others who are protected without being vaccinated themselves. With this consideration, the social optimum would be at point c where $MB_S = MC$ (i.e., $MB_S = MC_S$), leading to a vaccination rate $n = 0.7$. The extent of under-vaccination by the private market would be the distance gh, equal to 0.3 in Hannum's example. The net benefits of increasing the vaccination rate to the social optimum are measured by the consumer surplus triangle abc.

When the literature evaluates vaccination programs, it focuses on a given (usually the current) extent of the program. If the benefits are greater than the costs for this given level, then the program is judged to be worthwhile. This is useful information. But, even if the existing program is worthwhile, it could still be too small *or* too large. We have dealt with the private equilibrium case and we know this leads to a level of vaccination that is below the optimum. So let us identify the over-provision situation.

Say, because there is large public concern with a disease, a vaccination program is implemented by the government that covers most of the population, i.e., $n = 0.9$ in Figure 4.2. Opponents of the program (those who have

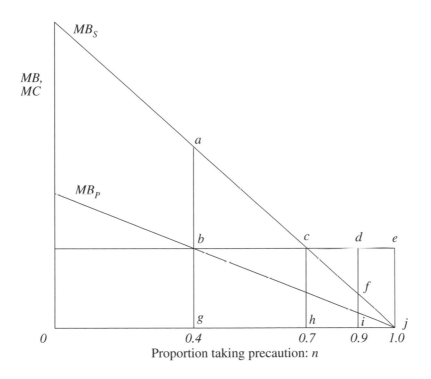

Note: A private market deciding how extensively to immunize would equate MB_P with MC and lead to equilibrium at point *b* with 40% of the population being vaccinated. The social optimum takes place at point *c* with a vaccination rate of 70%. The net benefit of increasing the vaccination rate to the socially optimal rate is given by the area *abc*. Note that the social optimum need not require a 100% vaccination rate.

Figure 4.2   100% vaccination may not be optimal

to pay for the program by paying higher taxes) require the government to justify the use of resources for vaccinations and this is to take place in the form of a CBA. This evaluation then shows benefits greater than costs. The government claims vindication for its policy. But this claim could be unwarranted. We can see from Figure 4.2 that $n = 0.9$ exceeds the optimum by the distance *hi*. At the immunization rate *i*, net benefits could be increased by the area *dcf* if a lower vaccination rate were adopted (the loss of benefits would be *hifc* and the cost saving would be *hidc*). Clearly, one can have 'too much of a good thing'.

This analysis can be extended easily to illuminate when complete eradication is worthwhile. Non-economists may express surprise if a policymaker balks at eliminating a disease completely. How can it not be desirable to rid the world of a disease? The answer is quite simple to explain for an economist. Eradication requires additional expenditures and these may not be worthwhile. In terms of Figure 4.2, being at point j (where $n = 1.0$) would involve a loss of net benefits equal to the area *ecj* relative to the optimum level of vaccinations h.

4.3   EXTERNAL COSTS OVER TIME

Health care evaluations need to consider not only different alternatives at the same point in time, but also the same program at different points in time. When variables change over time, we call the evaluation concerning these variables 'dynamic'. To help us analyze dynamic evaluations we will use the theory developed by Weimer (1987) to handle schistomiasis, a disease caused by a parasite (hosted by snails) contracted through skin contact with contaminated water.

4.3.1   Marginal Benefits and Costs in a Dynamic Context

The output variable that we will be considering is the 'prevalence' of the disease R, defined as the proportion of the population infected. (Note, in the epidemiological literature, 'incidence' is the number of new cases; 'prevalence' is what economists would call the stock of persons infected and incidence is the flow of infected persons.) The total population is growing over time. So, prevalence can fall because people are being successfully treated and there are fewer persons infected in a given sized population, or because the same number of infected people exist in a rising population. The health care interventions that we will be considering involve reductions in prevalence. Thus, $1 - R$ will be the variable whose scale is being altered.

   Weimer's analysis is in terms of a CM (over an infinite lifetime). The expenditures on controlling the disease are designated the 'costs' and the expenditures saved are then designated the 'benefits'. As usual, the optimal output will depend on a knowledge of the values of the MB and MC curves, and it is to the shape of these curves that we now turn our attention.

   It is assumed that MBs rise with prevalence (fall as prevalence is reduced) because initial cases are mild and more serious cases then follow. So it is the more serious cases that currently exist at the margin and it is these that one will be reducing first. The benefits of controlling the disease consist of the value of lost output from not being able to work. The degree of work disability depends on the extent of the aggregation of the parasite in the snail hosts. There is a high marginal benefit curve, MB_H, corresponding to a high level of aggregation, and hence high output loss, and a low marginal benefit curve, MB_L, when there is a low level of parasite aggregation and work loss.

The MCs depend on the type of control program implemented. There are two relevant control alternatives. The first (program 1) is to deal with the snails that host the parasite and the second (program 2) is to allow people to get infected, but treat them afterwards. For the time being, we will concentrate on the control program aimed at the snails. The marginal cost of limiting the area housing the snail population, MC_1, will be downward-sloping from left to right (with respect to prevalence reduction). It is instructive to consider why this is the case.

Public health interventions are the purest examples of effects external to markets because there are no private benefits and private costs to consider. No one has a direct interest in the existence of the snails. Here the external costs are the total costs ($MC_S = MC_E$). These external costs are indivisible with respect to the number of people infected. Which is to say that a snail that does not exist will not be able to infect *any* people, no matter how many people exist. So the more people that exist, at the extreme, there will be no extra cost in having them prevented from infection. This extreme case is called a 'pure public good' by economists, following Samuelson (1954). In practice, we recognize that there is more than one snail. So the more people we want protected, the more snails one needs to eliminate. MC_1 should be expected to be positive even though it falls with output.

The fact that MC_1 falls with output, i.e., we have 'economies of scale', leads to special problems for evaluating programs. The principle we have been emphasizing so far is that for an optimum level one needs to equate MB with MC. Strictly speaking (from the mathematics of optimization), this equality condition applies only for what we can call 'regular' problems. When we have economies of scale the situation becomes much more irregular. Figure 4.3 can be used to explain the complications.

In Figure 4.3, R_3 is the starting, current prevalence level. Prevalence reduction involves moving from left to right away from R_3. Let us begin our analysis using the high marginal benefit curve MB_H and try to match this with the marginal cost curve for the program controlling the snail population MC_1. It is immediately obvious that there is no point of intersection between the two curves, so no quantity for which $MB = MC$ holds. However, it is equally obvious how to proceed. In the Weimer analysis R_1 is taken to be the minimum level of prevalence that is feasible (one cannot eliminate every single snail that exists). If $MB > MC$ over the whole range of prevalence reduction, then one should go on trying to prevent infections as much as one can. So moving to R_1 would be the most beneficial output level (the difference between total benefits and total costs would be the greatest).

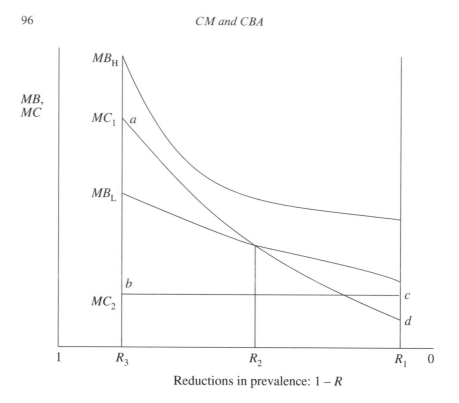

Note: The $MB = MC$ rule may fail when MCs fall with output. Current prevalence is at R_3 and the aim is to move to the right to achieve the lowest feasible rate R_1. With MB_H and MC_1, benefits always lie above costs and the optimum will be at R_1. Note that $MB > MC$ at the optimum. With MB_L and MC_1, the optimum will be either at R_3 or R_1, but not at R_2 where $MB = MC$.

Figure 4.3   *When MC falls, the MB = MC rule may fail to be socially optimal*

Now we consider the lower marginal benefit curve MB_L. This does have a point of intersection with MC_1. They meet at a prevalence level R_2 and this would seem to be the optimum level. The trouble with this case is that, if we just focus on MB and MC, we would never get involved with any prevention program in the first place. At R_3, $MB_L < MC_1$, so an initial program would not pass a CBA test. Moreover, once one starts a control program and moves to R_2, it is clear that one should not remain there because $MB_L > MC_1$ for all output levels to the right of R_2. Again, one should end up at R_1, *if one starts at all*. The need for this 'if statement' arises because R_1 itself may not be worthwhile. It is possible that total benefits (the area under the MB_L curve) may be less than total costs (the area under the MC_1 curve) at R_1.

There is a whole area of mathematics dealing with optimization and it is not our intention to cover this comprehensively in this chapter. The purpose of mentioning these complications is to ensure that one be aware of the importance of the practical CBA principle that underlay earlier chapters. That is, one should calculate benefits and costs at more than one output level to ensure that one is selecting the best use of our limited resources. We will now refine this practical principle.

What is important to understand about the results presented in Figure 4.3 is that, with only program 1 available, optimal prevalence will be at one end of the continuum or the other and not in between. With MB_H one must be at R_1. With MB_L, one could be at R_1 or R_3 depending on the size of the area under the MB curve relative to the area under the MC curve at R_1 and at R_3. Prevalence level R_2 will always be inferior to either R_1 or R_3. Economists call the outcome that places the optimum at one extreme or another (an all-or-nothing outcome) a 'corner solution'.

In light of the possibility that the outcome where $MB = MC$ might not be optimal, we should always ensure that the net benefit at this intersection point is not inferior to either doing nothing or pursuing the intervention to the maximum. That is, our practical principle (that one should consider other output alternatives) should be amended as follows. The health care evaluator should compare the net benefits of the fixed output level under review in a CM study with the net benefits for the zero and maximum output levels.

4.3.2 Prevention versus Cure

Weimer used his analysis to try to uncover the circumstances under which prevention is better than cure. Eliminating the snails (program 1) was the prevention program, while treating affected individuals with the disease (program 2) was the cure program. We wish to ascertain what difference adding the second option makes.

Since treatment is on an individual basis, there are no economies to others if one person gets treated. The marginal cost curve for treatment MC_2 would then be constant as prevalence changes. With MB_H the relevant benefit curve, the optimum output level would be the same (R_1) irrespective of the type of intervention used as $MB > MC$ for every level of prevalence reduction. The only issue is which control program to adopt. Program 2 would be the cost-minimizing option at R_1 as $C_2 < C_1$ for this level of R (area $R_3R_1cb < R_3Rda$). Cure (treatment) would be better than prevention.

With MB_L the relevant benefit curve, the previous indeterminacy disappears about whether R_3 or R_1 would be better when only program 1 was available. Cure (program 2) is not only cost-minimizing, it is also socially optimal, as the MB_L curve lies everywhere above MC_2. Thus, the optimum would take place at R_1.

4.4   APPLICATIONS

The first three case studies have all been referred to earlier when the theory sections were presented. They therefore complete the picture first sketched in sections 4.2 and 4.3. One of the studies included as part of the Hannum survey of immunization evaluations related to poliomyelitis vaccinations and the final application goes into the details of this study.

4.4.1   Taxes and the Social Cost of Drinking and Driving

We saw in section 4.2.1 that we could regard a tax on alcohol to be a health care intervention with a benefit and a cost. An optimal tax is the rate that would induce drinkers to cut back their consumption from the market equilibrium to the socially optimal level where $MB = MC_S$. In terms of Figure 4.1, a tax per unit equal to cd was the optimal rate.

The tax rate is determined by the magnitude of the external effect, the external marginal cost MC_E. This magnitude is difficult to quantify given that, in the case of drunken driving, lives are lost and people are reluctant to put a monetary value on a life. What Phelps (1988) did was present the information necessary to find the optimal tax, but the choice of tax rate was to be conditional on the value of a life that one is willing to accept.

Phelps used the consumer surplus loss from raising the consumer price due to the tax rate increase as his measure of the cost of raising the rate. This cost, at the optimum, corresponds to the area acd in Figure 4.1. The benefits are the number of lives no longer lost in accidents due to the alcohol consumption reduction induced by the tax rise. Table 4.1 shows the change in consumer surplus loss, the change in the number of lives saved, and the ratio of the two that forms the cost per life saved estimate. Two indicators of lives saved are shown. 'Total' refers to all lives lost by vehicle crashes caused by drunk drivers, and 'other' includes only the lives lost by other road users (i.e., it excludes the drunk drivers from the total). The other lives lost constitute the external cost category in this area of study.

Phelps' evaluation appears to be a CEA because he expresses his outcomes in terms of the cost of a life saved. But he is not really doing a CEA because he does not suggest that the tax rate leading to the lowest cost per life saved is the optimum tax. Instead, it is more useful to interpret the evaluation to be a CBA which compares the benefits, in the form of the price per life times the number of lives saved, with the (consumer surplus) cost. (This is the $B \equiv P.E$ specification of benefits first defined in Chapter 1). As Phelps leaves an estimate of the price per life unspecified, he is effectively employing the switching value technique for the value of a life. He is thus solving for the price per life in the equation:

$$(\text{price per life*}) \ (\text{number of lives}) = \text{consumer surplus cost} \quad (4.4)$$

The novelty is that he presents a series of switching values rather than a single estimate.

Using the switching value concept, we can summarize Phelps' results for finding the optimal tax as follows. If we ignore the drunken drivers' loss of lives, and adopt a switching value of $3 million per life, then the optimum tax rate would be about 35%. This is because, as Phelps says, 'at that level, the incremental consumer surplus loss (in the beer market) per life saved matches the incremental value of lives saved'. On the other hand, if one uses a switching value of $1 million, then the optimal tax is approximately 22% (i.e., in between tax rates 0.20 and 0.25, as $1 million is in between 0.93 and 1.44 in the second to last column of Table 4.1).

Table 4.1: Consequences of increased taxes in consumer surplus loss to drinkers and lives saved

Tax rate	Change in consumer surplus ΔCS ($ mill)	Change in lives saved $\Delta Other$	Change in lives saved $\Delta Total$	$\Delta CS/\Delta Other$ ($ mill per life)	$\Delta CS/\Delta Total$ ($ mill per life)
0.05	0.07	0.90	2.07	0.08	0.03
0.10	0.22	0.83	1.91	0.27	0.12
0.15	0.38	0.69	1.58	0.56	0.24
0.20	0.55	0.59	1.36	0.93	0.40
0.25	0.73	0.51	1.17	1.44	0.62
0.30	0.92	0.43	0.99	2.13	0.92
0.35	1.11	0.37	0.85	3.01	1.32
0.40	1.32	0.32	0.73	4.17	1.81
0.45	1.53	0.28	0.64	5.51	2.40
0.50	1.75	0.23	0.53	7.56	3.29
0.55	1.97	0.21	0.48	9.48	4.13
0.60	2.21	0.17	0.39	13.02	5.66
0.65	2.45	0.15	0.34	16.72	7.27

Source: Phelps (1988)

Having a series of switching values is useful only if one can find some way of justifiably excluding some part of the range of values. One way of doing this would be to point out that, since it is unlikely that a life saved would be worth only $30000 (or $80000 if we use the index omitting drunken drivers' lives), then it is not optimal to have *no* tax rate increase (at least a 5% rate increase is required).

Another noteworthy feature of the Phelps analysis is how it relates to the consumer sovereignty assumption that was identified in Chapter 1 to lie at the heart of CBA. In the current context, the issue raised by Phelps is whether to include the lives lost by the drunken drivers themselves as benefits of a tax rate increase. If one accepts consumer sovereignty, then a person who chooses to drink and drive should have considered the risk that this would cause to their own lives. In this case, their lost lives is not an externality to the driving and drinking decision, and therefore should not play a part in deciding what social adjustments need to be made to private decisions.

Phelps treats the consumer sovereignty issue as an information problem. Rather than rule out the drunken drivers' behavior as being irrational, which would directly violate the consumer sovereignty assumption, Phelps questions whether drunken drivers (mainly male youths) know the risks. His own research found that the average respondent in a survey of over 50 undergraduates judged the risk of fatality after 6+ drinks at 7.5 times a non-drinker, when in reality the increased risk was 100 fold. Because of this lack of information about risks by young drivers, Phelps puts most reliance on the last column results of Table 4.1 that relate to the total number of lives saved. On this basis, for whatever switching value one advocates, the optimal tax rate would be higher than using the other lost lives index.

4.4.2   Social Costs of Childhood Immunization

A key ingredient in Hannum's analysis of childhood vaccination programs is his identification of the prevailing vaccination rate as well as his estimation of the private and social rates. This step is important because, as we shall see, the prevailing rate was not equal to the private rate as one would expect. Identifying the prevailing rate enabled him to calculate the net benefits from moving from prevailing to social rates in addition to moving between private and social vaccination rates.

To find the private market equilibrium, Hannum used the probability of being infected *Prob* times the costs *C* that would be involved with the illness (treatment costs and forgone work output) to measure (expected) private benefits and the vaccination cost *V* to measure private costs. The $MB_p = MC$ condition therefore took the form:

$$Prob \,.\, C = V \tag{4.5}$$

Private MC were equal to social MC. So the only difference between a social and a private optimum is that the social benefits include the marginal external costs in addition to the private marginal benefits. The expression for MB_E took a very intuitive form. Those persons unvaccinated denoted by $(1 - n)$ with n, as before, the share of the population vaccinated benefit from some other person being newly vaccinated according to their changed probability of getting the disease $(\Delta Prob / \Delta n)$ that generates the illness loss C that they avoid. Hence Hannum used: $MB_E = (1 - n) (\Delta Prob / \Delta n) C$. The $MB_S = MC$ condition took the form:

$$Prob \,.\, C + (1 - n) (\Delta Prob / \Delta n) C = V \tag{4.6}$$

where the left-hand side of equation (4.6) represents $MB_P + MB_E$.

To apply his equation, Hannum used the data provided by a sample of the main childhood immunization CBAs that existed in the literature. To use these data, he had to convert all the studies onto a common basis. The main adjustments involved ensuring that all studies:

1. Included indirect as well as direct costs;
2. Began their calculations at year 1 when the vaccination decision was being made;
3. Converted outcomes to 1983 dollars using the medical care component of the CPI (consumer price index); and
4. Discounted benefits and costs at a 5% discount rate.

The results of Hannum's estimation are shown in Table 4.2 (his Table 4.1). The eight sets of estimates (related to six different studies) included in the table are by: Axnick et al. (1969), Koplan and Preblud (1982), Koplan et al. (1979), Hinman and Koplan (1984), White et al. (1985) and Weisbrod (1961). These eight sets of estimates are identified in the table by the order in which they have just been listed. Thus Axnick et al. (1969) is labeled Study 1 and Weisbrod (1961) is referred to as Study 8. White et al. (1985) supply three sets of estimates and these constitute Studies 5, 6 and 7. A 1% vaccination rate covers 1 million people. This means, for example, that the -4.073 figure for $(\Delta Prob / \Delta n)$, denoted by $(\Delta p / \Delta n)$ and related to Study 1 at the private optimum, indicates that an extra person vaccinated decreases the probability of another person catching the disease by -0.000004073.

The first set of net benefit figures shown in Table 4.2, comparing the private and social equilibrium positions, correspond to estimates of the triangle *abc* in Figure 4.2. Hannum estimated that (according to the particular

Table 4.2: Literature estimates of costs and benefits on a comparable basis

	Study 1 Measles 1963–67	Study 2 Mumps 1979	Study 3 Pertussis 1977–78	Study 4 Pertussis 1983	Study 5 Measles 1983	Study 6 Mumps 1983	Study 7 Rubella 1983	Study 8 Polio 1957
Private optimum								
Prob infected p	0.0781	0.0220	0.0026	0.0305	0.1945	0.0419	0.0025	0.0006
Illness cost C	128.77	101.51	934.34	984.15	199.38	139.48	2776.89	6099.21
$\Delta p/\Delta n$	−4.073	−1.479	−0.010	−0.091	−5.498	−1.679	−1.511	−0.026
Vaccinated rate n	0.910	0.739	0.586	1.000	0.857	0.842	0.860	0.584
Prevailing rate								
Prob infected p	0.34191	0.00531	0.00026	0.02890	0.00580	0.05660	0.00700	—
Illness cost C	130.52	101.37	1205.71	984.15	199.39	139.47	2768.20	—
$\Delta p/\Delta n$	−2.280	−1.557	−0.009	−0.085	−5.637	−1.588	−1.643	—
No. vaccinated n	0.825	0.750	0.900	0.900	0.860	0.833	0.857	—
Social optimum								
Prob infected p	0.00000	0.00000	0.00002	0.03050	0.00000	0.00000	0.00000	0.00000
Illness cost C	128.44	101.33	1907.79	1215.32	199.39	139.50	2781.53	6099.21
$\Delta p/\Delta n$	−5.390	−1.579	−0.001	−0.091	−5.669	−1.954	−1.529	−0.027
No. vaccinated n	0.926	0.753	0.064	1.000	0.861	0.864	0.862	0.604
Net benefits								
From private to social optimum	$2.599 m	$1.932 m	$6.993 m	$0.000 m	$2.419 m	$2.785 m	$3.393 m	$4.620 m
From prevailing to social optimum	$23.55 m	$0.446 m	$0.359 m	$7.884 m	$0.557 m	$3.983 m	$9.637 m	—

Source: Hannum (1997)

study data he was working with) area *abc* was equal to \$2.4–\$2.6 million for measles, \$1.9–\$2.8 million for mumps, \$0–\$7 million for pertussis, \$3.4 million for rubella, and \$4.6 million for polio.

Interestingly, the estimates comparing the current position with the socially optimal level of vaccinations give very different orders of magnitudes than the private–social comparison. Some estimates are greatly higher and some greatly lower. Clearly, the current and the private equilibrium positions are radically different.

When the private vaccination rate is less than the prevailing vaccination rate (as it is for Studies 1, 2, 3 and 5) this difference could be due to the existence of government policies promoting vaccinations. But, when the private rate exceeds the prevailing rate (as it does for Studies 4, 6 and 7), this probably indicates that private evaluations are defective and they either underestimate MB_P or overestimate MC_P. This supports Phelps' findings that information inadequacies sometimes vitiate the consumer sovereignty assumption on which CBA is based.

4.4.3 Controlling Schistomiasis

In our simplification of Weimer's analysis of the methods for controlling schistomiasis given in section 4.3, the choice was to do either program 1 (kill the snail hosts) or program 2 (treat those infected), but not both. In the actual Weimer study, he included multiple MC curves for each program conditional on levels of implementation of the other program. In this fuller analysis, one cannot easily represent graphically the mix of optimal programs, especially as they change over time. In which case it is simplest just to compare the time path of an optimal control program with the time path of the actual path of prevalence to see the extent to which current policies were optimal.

We present below Weimer's findings for Kunshan County in China, 1955–77, as Table 4.3 (his Table 1). He assumed a 1.4% per annum population growth and a snail host parasite density that led to a MB curve that was in between the MB_H and MB_L curves depicted in Figure 4.3. Both control programs were assumed to be fully used. For Kunshan County, the prevailing rate R_3 was set at 65.8% (cumulative infections of 310 000 for a population of 512 255) and the lowest feasible rate R_1 was put at 5.25%.

We can see in column 3 that the optimal control policy for schistomiasis conformed to the results predicted in section 4.3.1. In that section we explained that when MC is falling, we could expect a corner solution. The optimum is at one extreme or the other. However, in a dynamic analysis with controls that are jointly administered, the optimum path consists of bouncing around between the two extremes. Thus, in 1955 the optimum is

Table 4.3: Comparison of optimal and actual policies

(1) Year	(2) R actual (%)	(3) R optimal (%)	(4) T actual (1,000)	(5) T optimal (1,000)	(6) A actual (km²)	(7) A optimal (km²)	(8) C actual (mil Yuan)	(9) C optimal (mil Yuan)
1955	33	65.8	1	241	0	165	5.9	51.0
1956	41	35.1	9	130	1	69	8.8	19.3
1957	55	19.7	8	74	5	40	15.8	10.4
1958	54	12.0	136	45	26	31	22.4	7.0
1959	25	8.3	32	32	5	29	5.9	5.7
1960	22	6.6	68	26	8	28	6.9	5.2
1961	22	5.8	6	23	1	28	4.0	4.9
1962	29	5.5	6	22	1	28	5.7	4.8
1963	35	5.4	3	22	4	28	7.7	4.8
1964	62	5.4	8	22	5	28	22.8	4.8
1965	80	5.3	50	22	20	28	59.6	4.8
1966	47	5.3	60	23	60	28	21.5	4.9
1967	41	5.3	11	23	12	28	11.5	4.9
1968	46	5.2	30	23	18	28	15.3	4.9
1969	49	5.2	60	23	30	28	19.5	4.9
1970	48	5.2	140	23	118	28	32.5	4.9
1971	23	5.2	140	24	32	28	13.2	5.0
1972	14	5.2	49	24	18	28	6.3	5.0
1973	9	5.2	11	24	2	28	2.1	5.0
1974	7	5.2	13	25	5	28	2.2	5.0
1975	8	5.2	30	25	6	28	3.1	5.1
1976	4	5.2	10	25	7	28	1.9	5.1
1977	3	5.2	10	26	3	28	1.2	5.1

Source: Weimer (1987)

for the prevalence rate to be R_3 while, from 1968 onwards, the minimum rate R_1 should be realized.

Actual prevalence rates (column 2) differed greatly from the optimal rates (column 3) most of the time, but the two rates had converged by the end of the period. As a consequence, actual costs (column 8) were greater than the optimal level of costs (column 9) in all years but one between 1957 and 1972. The 1955 discounted present value of all the costs in column 8 was Y202 million, while under an optimal policy the costs would have been Y143 million.

Treatment (program 1) was actively pursued between 1958 and 1960; so much so that the number of people actually treated T (column 4) far exceeded the number that optimally should have been treated (column 5). This emphasis on program 1 was accompanied by a sub-optimal effort in terms of the preventative program 2 involving the area A in which snails were eliminated (see columns 6 and 7). Hence by 1963 (and up to 1970) the actual prevalence rate had risen back up above the initial level in 1955. In the early 1970s, prevention was to the fore and the snail area treated (column 7) was greatly expanded. Snail infested areas were cleared once and for all (thus diminishing chances of reinfestation) and this seems to be the reason why prevalence rates fell to below the postulated minimum.

The main conclusions reached by Weimer, based on the experience of Kunshan County, were these: (1) reducing prevalence to the minimum was desirable; and (2) the optimum combination of prevention and cure depended on the degree of aggregation of the parasites in the snails. The more highly aggregated the parasites, the greater the loss from forgone output. At high prevalence levels, with the parasites sparsely aggregated, the benefits of snail eradication are small. Hence treatment programs are more beneficial here. Eventually, prevalence levels fall so that snail eradication becomes worthwhile. The result is that prevention should come after cure! The logic of this result lies in the fact that a treated person can be reinfected if the disease is not completely eradicated. So, first one aims to reduce the level of the disease and then one acts to guard against reinfection. It is not efficient to lay down preventative groundwork before there is any reinfection to prevent.

4.4.4 External Costs of Poliomyelitis

Weisbrod's evaluation of polio was one of the studies (number 8) in the Hannum survey of the literature. But its importance lies in the fact that it was the pioneering CBA in the field and it laid down the blueprint that was followed by many of the subsequent studies.

Even the CBA criterion used by Weisbrod has special significance for a chapter devoted to evaluating external effects. Weisbrod evaluated the research expenditures devoted to developing a vaccine for polio. The benefits of the research B_R entailed finding a way for avoiding the treatment costs and forgone output that accompanies contracting the disease. The costs were not just the research expenditures C_R. They include also the costs of applying the research C_A assuming that it provided positive net-benefits. The application costs were the expected vaccination costs. The Weisbrod criterion for evaluating the polio research effort took the form:

$$B_R > C_R + C_A \qquad (4.7)$$

One way of thinking about the application costs is to consider them to be external costs to the research. Thus it is like there were two linked projects to be evaluated, i.e., doing the research and then applying it. The general principle for evaluations pertaining to joint projects is that, if they are inextricably linked, then they should be evaluated together, but not otherwise. Hiring an anesthetist is not an option one can avoid if one is paying for a surgeon. The cost of the anesthetist and the cost of the surgeon need to be combined to make up the cost of the operation. In the same way, there is no point in spending on research if one does not intend to apply it.

Using forgone earnings to measure the benefits of vaccinations is one feature of the Weisbrod analysis that many have emulated. But the way he included indirect costs has led to some confusion among those applying Weisbrod's methods. Weisbrod (1971, p. 531) deducted the lifetime expenditures on consumption from the forgone earnings when valuing a life that is saved by the vaccine because 'mortality involves the loss of a consumer as well as a producer'. This makes sense if one wishes to evaluate the loss of a life from the point of view of others. But, strictly, this is an external benefit that ignores the private benefits. Only in the case when private benefits are thought to be zero, as we observed in analyzing drunken driving, does subtracting consumption from lifetime earnings make sense. The point is that one does not really have a *choice* of two alternative methods for measuring indirect costs, as some evaluators believe. Lifetime earnings is the only method to use unless one particularly wants to isolate just the external effects.

Because there is no good reason to deduct lifetime consumption in the case of childhood immunization programs, Hannum added back consumption expenditures to make the polio study consistent with the rest of the literature. In addition, in line with the adjustments outlined earlier to bring all vaccination studies onto a common basis, Hannum altered Weisbrod's estimates by using a 5% discount rate (instead of 10%), using 1983 dollars rather than 1957 dollars, and converting costs to year 1 in which it is assumed that the vaccination decision is being made. The result of these adjustments is what appears in Table 4.2 for Study 8.

Apart from the way Hannum summarized Weisbrod's results, we can learn something from the way the original Weisbrod (1971) study was presented – see Table 4.4 below (which is derived from Weisbrod's Table 2 by focusing only on the 1930–80 time horizon and where actual research costs are equal to reported research costs). Weisbrod was the first to calculate the internal rate of return for a medical research program. The internal rate of return is that rate of discount for which the net present value equals zero. (In terms of equation (2.7), one is finding the value for r that makes the PV equal to zero when S is defined as net benefits.) For most purposes, showing the net benefits is the most useful way to view the outcome. The internal rate of return is the best index when there is a capital constraint: see Brent (1998), ch. 2.

Table 4.4. *Internal rates of return on polio research under a variety of assumptions*

Growth projection	Savings per case prevented	Vaccination costs ($ millions per year)		Rates of return (%)
		In 1957	After 1957	
I	Constant	350	9	8.4
I	Constant	625	19	0.4
II	Growing	350	0	13.4
II	Growing	625	0	7.9
III	Growing	350	9	11.7
III	Growing	625	19	4.5

Source: Weisbrod (1971)

Weisbrod includes more than one rate of return estimate in Table 4.4 because he recognized that forgone lifetime earnings due to mortality from polio can be expected to grow over time. He assumed that labor productivity increases at the rate of 3% per year and these are factored into the rates of return listed as II and III (estimates III are more pessimistic about the need for inoculating newborn babies after 1957). Estimates I assume no productivity growth. The use of productivity growth for indirect costs makes Weisbrod one of the first to carry out a dynamic health care CBA. Because Weisbrod puts most faith in a dynamic framework, he judges that although the rate of return for polio generally lies in the range 4–14%, his 'most likely' estimate was about 11–12%.

4.5 FINAL SECTION

We now present the problems, summary and looking ahead sections.

4.5.1 Problems

One technique for dealing with uncertainty about the reliability of estimates concerning crucial ingredients in an evaluation is to use the switching value method (outlined in section 4.1.3). An alternative approach is to
carry out a 'sensitivity analysis'. This involves raising or lowering the best
estimates of the key variables by some specified proportion (e.g., 10%
higher and lower) and seeing whether the evaluation criterion is affected by
(is 'sensitive' to) the alternative values. If the alternative values do not
change the desirability of the intervention, then one can proceed with the
recommendation based on the best estimates. However, if the alternative
values do affect the desirability of the intervention, then the recommendation based on the best estimates is to be considered provisional until one
obtains better estimates. The purpose of the problems is to illustrate how
to undertake a sensitivity analysis and to develop an understanding of the
link between carrying out a sensitivity analysis and using the switching
value technique.

The data for the problems come from a study by Siraprapasiri et al.
(1997) – see their Tables 1 and 2. They carried out a CBA of a vaccination
program in Thailand for Japanese encephalitis (JE), a mosquito-borne
arboviral disease. We focus only on the results of the 18-month program
and they are listed in Table 4.5.

Table 4.5: Sensitivity analysis for JE vaccination program in Thailand

(1)	(2)	(3)	(4)	(5)
Cost				
Unit cost of immunization	$2.16	$2.16	$2.16	$2.16
Population affected	900 000	900 000	900 000	900 000
Overall cost of program	$1 944 000	$1 944 000	$1 944 000	$1 944 000
Benefit				
Per case prevented	$72 922	$72 922	$72 922	$72 922
Number of cases prevented	123.700	82.375	41.321	24.793
Overall benefit of program	$9 020 451			
Net benefit of program	$7 076 451			

Source: Based on Siraprapasiri et al. (1997)

The second column of Table 4.5 records the costs, benefits and net benefits using the best estimates (see their Table 1). For our exercise, we regard the cost estimates as accurate and treat the benefits as problematic. In particular, we question whether the number of JE cases prevented is as high as the best estimate of 123.700. The three alternative values to be considered are 82.375, 41.321 and 24.793. The benefit per case ($72 922) is considered to be accurate. The overall benefit of the vaccination program is the product of the benefit per case times the number of cases.

1. Calculate the benefits and net benefits for each of the alternative benefit per case values (i.e., fill in columns 3–5).
2. Which of the alternative benefit per case values give the same recommendation as the best estimates?
3. Calculate the switching value for the benefit per case variable.
4. What then is the relationship between finding the switching value and carrying out a sensitivity analysis? (Hint: Compare your answers to questions 3 and 4.)

4.5.2 Summary

External effects are those costs or benefits related to persons or firms other than the main two parties to a trade or transaction. Private markets ignore external effects and hence their outputs can be either below or above the optimum level. Market prices would then not be good measures of social values. When external costs exist that affect others on an individual basis the external marginal costs MC_E will most likely rise with output. The optimum is where $MB_S = MC$. A tax equal to MC_E could internalize the externality and bring about the social optimum.

However, when external effects exist that affect others in an indivisible way (as when a person who gets vaccinated prevents spreading the disease to all persons unvaccinated), then the MC_E curve falls with output. The $MB = MC$ rule may fail to lead to optimal outcomes in these circumstances. We saw that the optimum could occur with $MB > MC$. In another case, the output where $MB = MC$ led to lower net benefits than at either very low or very high levels of output.

The rule of thumb that we suggested was that, when carrying out an evaluation, one should compare outcomes at the minimum and maximum levels of output as well as at the particular output level under review. One should then choose from among these output levels the one with the highest difference between total benefits and total costs.

Apart from the need to compare net benefits at different levels of output, we also saw the importance of comparing net benefits at different points of time, i.e., undertaking a dynamic evaluation. This is especially necessary when one is evaluating resource use that is affected by population growth, as was the case with vaccination and disease control programs. Evaluations at a single point of time fail to capture the element of change that is inherent in such programs.

The first case study illustrated the principle that it is not necessary to spend money in order for a viable program to be initiated. A tax could act as a signal to induce private individuals to produce less of the activity that generates the external cost (a subsidy could be used to promote activities that have external benefits). Just like projects that directly involve resource use, taxes that discourage drinking (and hence driving under the influence of alcohol) lead to benefits and costs. An optimal alcohol tax is one where the net benefits are greatest.

In the second application we saw that there is an optimum amount of an externality, which need not be zero. Childhood vaccinations do not have to be administered to everyone, even though it would be technically possible to eradicate the communicable disease. The optimum vaccination rate depended on the probability of getting the disease and how this probability fell with the number vaccinated. It also depended on the number of people who were left unvaccinated and the time and expense involved with getting vaccinated. Because these determinants varied by the childhood disease being considered, the optimum vaccination rate was different for different diseases.

In both the studies related to alcohol taxation and childhood immunization it was found that there was some doubt that individuals were the best judges of their own welfare. Information deficiencies led to behavior that questioned whether individuals were equating MB_P with MC_P.

Many times in connection with public policy decisions, outcomes are assumed rather than empirically tested. This is the case with the old health care adage that 'prevention is better than cure'. As was demonstrated in the analysis of the control programs for schistomiasis, cure was used in conjunction with prevention, and could optimally be implemented before prevention. There are no simple substitutes for actually carrying out a health care evaluation.

The applications closed with the pioneering immunization study by Weisbrod. This was one of the first studies to apply the human capital approach to measure the benefits of not being affected by communicable diseases. It stressed the need to check whether a project was inescapably linked to another. With linked projects, constituting a special kind of externality, a joint evaluation is required. Again one is using the principle that, in a social evaluation, one adds all the relevant benefits and subtracts all the relevant costs.

4.5.3 Looking Ahead

In this chapter we showed how taxes can be used to remedy the non-optimality of private outcomes when externalities exist. In the next chapter we explain how taxes that are used to finance health care projects can have a distortionary effect on outcomes for other markets subject to the taxes. Taxes therefore can cause externality problems as well as solve such problems.

5. Social cost of taxation

5.1 INTRODUCTION

There are two types of external costs. One type, just analyzed in the previous chapter, has to be estimated on a case-by-case basis. It is due to the fact that a market, irrespective of whether it is perfectly competitive or not, may fail to record the value of certain inputs. The other type, examined in this chapter, is independent of the particular health care expenditure being evaluated. The public sector is now assumed to be undertaking the health care expenditure. So tax revenues must be increased to finance it. Any cost involved with levying the taxes to pay for the public expenditure, over and above that entailed in the giving up of the revenues themselves, is an extra cost which needs to be included in an overall assessment of the health care expenditure.

The total cost of paying taxes is called the 'marginal cost of public funds' (MCF). This is related to both the utility loss of paying the tax revenue itself and the extra cost. Our first task is to explain what the MCF is and how it affects an evaluation of a health care expenditure. Then we examine how the extra cost comes into existence and what economic principles determine its size. From there we proceed to present actual estimates of the MCF. The applications emphasize what difference it makes to health care evaluations by including the MCF as a separate ingredient.

5.1.1 General Role of the MCF in CBA

The MCF affects the socially optimal output level just like any other negative externality. In the previous chapter (see Figure 4.1) we represented the externality as driving a wedge between private and social costs. There the wedge grew larger as the output of the good generating the externality (beer) increased. In the current context, we treat the externality as a constant amount that shifts up the production cost per unit. This is because, as pointed out in Chapter 1, the typical health care expenditure being evaluated is a small expansion of current activities and so, when its scale of operations alters, it does not affect the prices and costs of other goods and services. If the health care activity is on a small scale, the tax revenues required to finance it will also be a small addition to existing taxes. For simplicity, we also assume that the *MC* curve is constant.

Figure 5.1 illustrates how the MCF affects the decision as to how much to spend on an activity that promotes public health. Q_1 would be the optimum output if taxation were not needed (or imposed in such a way that it did not create distortions elsewhere). This is where $MB = MC$.

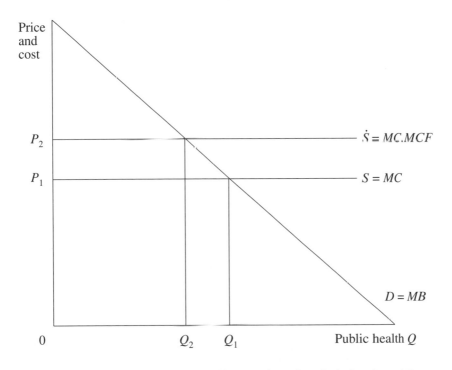

Note: If taxes could be raised neutrally (without causing a distortion), then the socially optimal level of output would be Q_1 as this is where the marginal benefit *MB* (given by the demand curve) equals the marginal cost *MC* (given by the competitive supply curve). With non-neutral taxes, costs have to be multiplied by a MCF figure that is greater than 1. Output of the public expenditure would have to be reduced to level Q_2, where the adjusted *MC* equals the *MB*.

Figure 5.1: *Modifying the MB = MC rule when taxes exist which cause a MCF*

Due to the need to finance the health project by taxation, the *MC* is to be multiplied by the MCF. The MCF is a factor greater than 1. This is because the MCF includes not just the loss of utility to pay for the tax (and a dollar of taxation can be thought to require a dollar's worth of loss of utility by the taxpayer), it also includes an extra loss of utility due to the tax distorting consumer choices on the taxed item (causing an output level that is different from that which gives most satisfaction). The additional cost is an *excess burden*. Since the MCF is a figure greater than 1, multiplying the *MC* by the MCF shifts upward the social cost curve that exists because of the existence of a tax elsewhere. $\dot{S}$ is the adjusted supply curve in Figure 5.1. Equating *MB* with *MC*. MCF leads to a lower optimal level of the public health output given as Q_2.

The implication is that if the MCF were 1.17, say, then the benefits of the government project at the margin would have to be 17% greater than the *MC* in order to be justified. Another way of expressing this differential is that, compared to a project undertaken by the private sector where there is no need to resort to taxation (and hence no excess burden to consider), the public project is required to have a 17% higher return.

This implication depends crucially on two assumptions. The first is that all of the costs are to be financed out of public sources of funds. This would be a valid assumption if one is considering a public health expenditure where it is difficult to charge user fees. On the other hand, if one were evaluating prescription medication that costs $10, and a prescription charge of $2 has to be paid by the patient in order for the pharmacist to complete the prescription, then the MCF should strictly only be applied to the $8 that the government (and not the patient) is paying. The role of user fees in the context of the MCF is highlighted in the privatization case study in the applications section.

Secondly, the MCF must be a number greater than 1 in order to require that the *MB* be greater than the *MC*. If the MCF were 0.83, the *MB* would then have to be 17% *lower* than the *MC* in order to be worthwhile. A MCF less than unity would be plausible if the government expenditure on health caused people's incomes to rise and they spent this increase on goods that are taxed. Then the government would require in taxes, net of what it receives later on, less than a dollar to pay for a dollar's worth of health expenditure costs now. However, the standard assumption in CBA is to assume that government expenditures are neutral with respect to earnings of tax revenues later on. In which case it follows that, in order to pay for a dollar's worth of financing on a particular public expenditure, an extra dollar needs to collected by the public sector overall. So the MCF will be a number greater than 1. Exactly how the value of the MCF comes out to be a number greater than 1 is explained in section 5.2.1.

5.1.2   Special Role for the MCF with Health Care Evaluations

As we have just seen, public expenditures financed by taxation require that one apply the MCF to the project-specific costs. Expenditure decisions therefore depend on the size of the MCF. What sorts of health care decisions are most likely to be affected by the existence of the MCF in the evaluation? Before we answer this question, we need to explain how cash payments to, or from, the private sector are incorporated in the CBA criterion when the MCF is also included.

When no public sector financing is involved, the basic CBA criterion is to require that net benefits $B - C$ be positive. The benefits are what consumers are willing to pay for the project. What they actually have to pay, by way of user fees and the like, can be called repayments or transfers (from the beneficiaries to those who pay the costs) and will be represented by the variable R. These repayments reduce the size of the gain to the beneficiaries to $B - R$. However, the repayments simultaneously reduce the loss to those who must pay for the costs so that the loss becomes $C - R$. The resulting criterion is that the difference between the benefits, net of the repayments, must be greater than the costs, net of the repayments. That is, the criterion is·

$$(B - R) - (C - R) > 0 \qquad (5.1)$$

Of course, if we remove the brackets from the expression in (5.1), we obtain: $B - C - R + R > 0$, which means that the Rs cancel out and we return to the original criterion that net benefits must be positive:

$$B - C > 0 \qquad (5.2)$$

The result is that the transfers do not at all affect the outcome of whether health care projects should be approved or not. This is the standard view of the role of transfers by practitioners in the health care evaluation field.

In the context of the above assumptions, the standard view is correct. The following example shows the logic of this approach to CBA. Say we are evaluating a surgical procedure that requires a five-day hospital stay. While in the hospital, the patient has lunch daily at a cost of $5 per meal. Should the weekly $35 costs of meals be included in the CBA criterion? The standard answer is no. The patient would have had the meals anyway, even if no hospital stay was involved. There is no new cost (or benefit) associated with the meals. If the patient were actually charged $35 for the meals, the outcome would not alter. There would be $35 more gain, and also $35 more cost, and the two sums would cancel out. The conclusion could not be otherwise because, whether one charged zero, $35, $50 or $100, the surgical procedure would still have the same benefits and costs even if the meals were not given in the hospital.

The only difference that R makes is in the distribution of the net benefits, not the size of the net benefits themselves. However, this distributional consideration may be something that is important in its own right and this is how the standard view can err. As mentioned in Chapter 1, efficiency may not be the sole social objective. In terms of distribution, there are two main dimensions. It may matter socially whether the patient making the transfer is rich or poor. This equity dimension we will be analyzing fully in Chapter 13 (building on Chapter 10). The second dimension to distribution is that related to the public versus the private sector. As we have already seen, if the public sector is involved with financing a project, any funds generate an excess burden. A dollar of funds involving the public sector will have a greater impact than a dollar of funds involving the private sector. Hence, the public sector funds attract a penalty if incurred (or a premium if earned) as measured by the MCF.

If we assume that health care expenditures undertaken by the public sector give net gains received by those in the private sector, while incurring net losses that require taxes and involve excess burdens, then criterion (5.1) needs to be amended to be:

$$(B - R) - \text{MCF} \, (C - R) > 0 \qquad\qquad (5.3)$$

Rearranging expression (5.3) we obtain:

$$B - (\text{MCF}) \, C + (\text{MCF} - 1) \, R > 0 \qquad\qquad (5.4)$$

When there are repayments, R attaches a positive sign because there is less of a need to use taxes, and thus less of an excess burden incurred (note that $\text{MCF} - 1$ is exactly the excess burden that is avoided per unit of R). If there are no repayments, the criterion in (5.4) reduces to:

$$B - (\text{MCF}) \, C > 0 \qquad\qquad (5.5)$$

This criterion, that is, $B > C.\text{MCF}$, is the test on which the analysis summarized by Figure 5.1 was based.

We are now in a position to answer our earlier question and identify three categories of health care expenditure where the MCF plays a crucial role. First, there are health expenditures that involve public cash transfers to private sector recipients. Secondly, the whole area of privatization (where the public sector sells or otherwise transfers ownership of an asset) is one where inter-sectorial financial changes take place. Thirdly, there are cases where costs are shifted from the public sector to the private sector, or from one tax jurisdiction to another, where a differential excess burden effect will ensue (the excess burden associated with one party paying is different from the excess burden associated with another party financing the expenditure).

5.2 ECONOMIC THEORY AND THE MCF

We start by showing diagrammatically how the excess burden of a tax arises and how it can be measured in a simple taxing situation.

5.2.1 The Excess Burden of a Tax

The tax that is being levied to finance the health care expenditure affects some other part of the economy outside of health care. In this section, we will assume that the tax being levied is an excise tax on cigarettes (an excise tax is one that is levied on just a few products and is not a general commodity tax like a sales tax). Let the tax rate be equivalent to $1 on each pack of cigarettes. We stick with the assumption of constant costs, equal to $2 per pack. Refer to Figure 5.2 below.

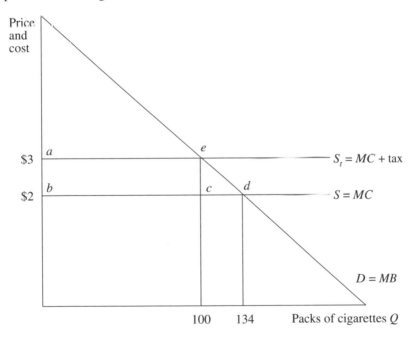

Note: The original equilibrium output would be at $Q = 134$ where *MB* equals *MC*. With an excise tax of a fixed amount per unit, that is, $1, the supply curve (which is assumed horizontal and equal to the constant MC) rises by the full amount of the tax. Output is reduced to level $Q = 100$, where the demand curve meets the new supply curve S_t. Tax revenues are the area *abce*. The excess burden is area *cde*. The MCF is the ratio given by the sum of the tax revenues plus the excess burden divided by the amount of the tax revenues, a ratio greater than 1.

Figure 5.2: Calculating the MCF when there are constant costs

Prior to the tax, producers must receive $2 per pack in order to put 134 packs onto the market. With the tax, they will put 134 packs onto the market only if the price rises to $3, for then they receive $3, give $1 to the government, and retain the required $2. But, now that consumers have to pay $3 per pack, they no longer are willing to buy 134 packs. So the quantity falls to 100. The new equilibrium is where 100 packs are sold at $3 each.

The MCF measures the loss of satisfaction per dollar of taxes paid by the consumer. Consumer satisfaction is measured by the area under the demand curve, which is also the *MB* curve. Figure 5.2 shows that, by output dropping from 134 to 100, consumers lose area *abde* in benefits. This area can be broken down into the rectangle *abce* and the triangle *cde*. The rectangle *abce* also measures the tax revenues collected (equal to the product of the tax rate times quantity sold). The triangle *cde* signifies the excess burden of the tax, i.e., the loss of satisfaction *in addition to* that reflected in paying for the tax. So the MCF is given as the ratio of the loss of total satisfaction *abde* to the tax revenues *abce*: MCF = *abde/abce*. Disaggregating the area *abde*, we get the equivalent measure: MCF = (*abce* + *cde*)/*abce* = 1 + *cde/abce*, where *cde/abce* is the marginal (per unit of extra tax) excess burden or MEB. Thus:

$$MCF = 1 + MEB \qquad (5.6)$$

Note that the MCF is written here as an expression greater than 1. This is because the ratio *abce/abce* reduces to 1. This looks like a mathematical necessity. But, more generally, the areas on the numerator and the denominator could differ. The area *abce* on the numerator always measures a part of the loss of utility from paying taxes. But the tax revenues collected on the denominator could be more than area *abce* if, for example, beneficiaries of the health care expenditure spend any additional income on taxed commodities that produce tax revenues elsewhere. In this case it is possible that the MCF could be less than 1. It is this case that is ruled out by the assumption of a revenue neutral public project.

Given the numbers indicated in Figure 5.2, we can quantify exactly the MCF. The area of the rectangle *abce* for the tax revenues is $100 (the height is the $1 tax per unit and the length is the quantity 100). The area of the triangle *cde* for the excess burden is $17 (being half the base of 34 and a height of $1). So MCF = $(100 + 17)/$100 = 1.17.

The logic of the MCF is now clear. A tax on some other market must be imposed in order to pay for the health care expenditure. Thus, for the optimum amount of the health care project to take place, some other market that incurs the tax is prevented from achieving its optimum. The net (of tax revenues) loss of satisfaction from this other market being below its optimum is the excess burden of the tax. It is this net loss that is the 17% extra cost of financing the health care expenditure.

5.2.2 Excess Burden and the Role of Elasticity

Let us repeat the analysis, but this time work with a different-shaped demand curve. Say the demand curve were vertical rather than the diagonal one depicted in Figure 5.2. What difference would it make to the size of the MCF? Figure 5.3 shows this special case.

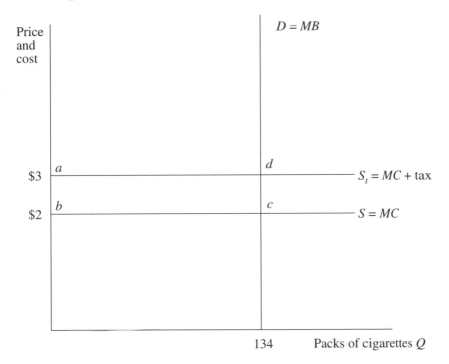

Note: When demand is completely unresponsive to changes in price, it can be drawn as a vertical straight line. The quantity of $Q = 134$ would be purchased both before and after the tax that shifts the supply curve upwards. Since output remains unchanged, there is no distortion to record from imposing the tax and the excess burden would be zero. With a zero excess burden, the MCF would be equal to 1.

Figure 5.3: Calculating the MCF when demand is perfectly inelastic

We can see immediately that there is no triangular area at all. The loss of utility from paying the tax is fully captured by the area of rectangle *abcd*, which is also the amount of tax revenues collected. With no triangular area, there is no excess burden, and the MCF = 1. Multiplying costs by unity does not affect their value, so the MCF concept would be irrelevant to the determination of health care expenditure decisions.

Obviously we need to explain what it means to have a vertical demand curve. Looking at the demand curve in Figure 5.3, we see that, irrespective of the price charged, the quantity demanded will be 134. Consumers here are completely non-responsive to changes in prices. Economists call the responsiveness of quantity demanded to changes in price the 'price elasticity of demand'. Changes in quantities and prices are recorded in percentage terms. So price elasticity, ε_p, is measured by:

$$\varepsilon_p = (\% \text{ change in quantity demanded})/(\% \text{ change in price}) \quad (5.7)$$

A vertical demand curve corresponds to the case where the % change in quantity demanded is zero no matter the % change in price. With the numerator of (5.7) zero, the measured elasticity of demand would also be zero.

The conclusion is that if the elasticity of demand is zero, then the excess burden is zero and the MCF would equal to unity. The general principle that follows from this conclusion is that the lower the elasticity of demand (the less responsive are consumers to changes in price), the less distortionary are taxes, and the less we need to be concerned about public sector financing in CBA. (We have dealt with the case of a commodity tax. But an excess burden is incurred with any type of tax (that is not lump sum such as a poll tax)).

5.3   ESTIMATES OF THE MCF

Our estimates of the MCF come from the US, where this concept is extensively analyzed and estimated. We report estimates for tax systems at both the federal and state levels.

5.3.1   US Federal MCF Estimates

Ballard et al. (1985) constructed a general equilibrium model of the US economy consisting of 19 producer goods industries, 15 consumer goods industries, and 12 consumer groups (distinguished by income). They envisaged the government spending on transfer payments, so there were no project benefits or costs. The only issue was the size of the marginal excess burden, MEB, associated with any R amounts – see MCF − 1 in criterion (5.4) above – and it is these MEB values that they attempted to estimate.

Their calculations were very sensitive to the elasticity assumptions used. Income that was not spent on consumption goods could be saved. They thus needed elasticities for saving as well as for the supply of labor to make their estimates. Four sets (pairs) of assumptions were used. Estimate 1 had both elasticities equal to zero. Estimates 2 and 3 kept one of the elasticities at zero, but had a positive value for the other. Estimate 4 had positive values for both elasticities (the savings elasticity was 0.4 and the labor supply elasticity was 0.15). Table 5.1 presents their MCF estimates for each of the four sets of estimates (and an average of the four sets which we have added in the last column).

Table 5.1:   *Estimates of the marginal cost of funds for the US federal government (* MCF_F *)*

Tax category	Estimate 1	Estimate 2	Estimate 3	Estimate 4	Average
All taxes	1.170	1.206	1.274	1.332	1.245
Property taxes	1.181	1.379	1.217	1.463	1.310
Sales taxes	1.035	1.026	1.119	1.115	1.074
Income taxes	1.163	1.179	1.282	1.314	1.235
Other taxes	1.134	1.138	1.241	1.255	1.192
Charges and miscellaneous	1.256	1.251	1.384	1.388	1.320

Source: Ballard et al. (1985)

Because they found values for the MCF that were of the order of 1.15 to 1.50, they concluded that excess burdens are significant for economies similar to the US. They argued therefore that CBA criteria adjusted for the MCF (as developed in this chapter) should be used to replace the simple positive net benefit requirement.

5.3.2 US State MCF Estimates

Brent (2003) derived estimates of US state MCFs from the Ballard et al. estimates of the federal taxes MCFs. The basic method involved finding the shares for each category of state taxation related to the groups of taxes for which there was a federal MCF estimate and weighting the federal MCF estimates by the state shares.

For example, Alaska received most (62.99%) of its state tax revenues from charges and miscellaneous. This category had a federal MCF estimate of 1.256 (according to Estimate 1 in Table 5.1). Multiplying 1.256 by 0.6299 produces a 0.7912 weighted MCF component due to this tax category. Property taxes for Alaska had a 2.36% share, income taxes had a 12.08%

share, and other taxes had a 22.58% share (there was no state sales tax). Multiplying each of these shares by the federal MCF estimates of 1.181, 1.163 and 1.134 respectively, we obtain state MCF components 0.0279 for property taxes, 0.1405 for income taxes and 0.2561 for other taxes. Adding these three components to the 0.7912 component for charges and miscellaneous, we obtain a MCF estimate for Alaska of 1.215.

Corresponding to each of the four sets of estimates in Table 5.1, an estimate was made of the state MCF using the tax shares as weights. For estimate set 2 for Alaska the MCF was 1.220, for set 3 it was 1.335, and for set 4 the MCF was 1.351. The average of the four estimates was 1.280. Similar calculations were made for all states. The average MCFs, and the state tax shares for the five categories of taxes, are shown in Table 5.2.

The states with the highest shares of property taxes have the highest MCFs and the states with the lowest sales tax shares have the lowest MCFs. Although all the state estimates seem to be quite close, if we ignore all the caveats and accept the earlier interpretation of how the MCF affects CBA decisions given in section 5.1.1, important differences do emerge. Publicly financed health care expenditure in Alaska has to be 28% higher than the same project financed by the private sector. But, in Nevada, the public project need be only 16% higher.

5.4   APPLICATIONS

The first case study looks at the MCF in the context of an aging population. The tax base changes over time and this means that the MCF will also vary over time. The other three applications focus on the role of the MCF in evaluations of the care of psychiatric patients. This area is one where public financial involvement is particularly high in terms of both the direct provision of the health services and the indirect assistance that is made in cash transfers.

5.4.1   MCF and Social Security Benefits

Wildasin (1992) made a calculation of the net benefits in the US of having future government transfer payments (social security benefits paid when one has retired) for the cohort of current workers who must pay taxes for it now. In the US, social security covers pensions and health insurance for the elderly (Medicare). Part of the costs was an estimate of the MCF caused by the income (payroll) taxes. Wildasin's study provides insights into the ingredients of the MCF and how it impacts outcomes in an important, general health policy setting.

Table 5.2: *Estimates of the marginal cost of funds for US state governments (MCF_S)*

State	Property taxes (%)	Sales taxes (%)	Income taxes (%)	Other taxes (%)	Charges and misc. (%)	Average MCF (%)
Alabama	1.69	19.26	25.08	25.79	28.20	1.218
Alaska	2.36	0.00	12.08	22.58	62.99	1.280
Arizona	3.82	36.68	22.17	18.19	19.14	1.187
Arkansas	0.22	29.10	28.97	21.01	20.70	1.196
California	4.03	25.63	42.03	11.27	17.03	1.206
Colorado	0.21	18.13	34.86	16.91	29.90	1.224
Connecticut	0.00	33.26	20.12	23.97	22.65	1.190
Delaware	0.00	0.00	33.91	31.85	34.25	1.251
District Columbia	25.98	15.67	27.77	12.56	18.03	1.239
Florida	1.66	48.76	4.63	24.47	20.48	1.164
Georgia	0.30	27.24	43.79	14.00	14.67	1.198
Hawaii	0.00	34.39	28.72	11.27	25.62	1.196
Idaho	0.01	26.85	32.41	19.05	21.68	1.202
Illinois	1.56	26.63	31.29	20.82	19.70	1.201
Indiana	0.04	33.35	28.78	14.11	23.72	1.195
Iowa	0.00	22.07	32.58	20.16	25.19	1.212
Kansas	0.96	25.60	33.11	19.60	20.74	1.204
Kentucky	5.44	20.18	27.46	24.87	22.05	1.215
Louisiana	0.45	20.84	16.29	25.74	36.68	1.222
Maine	1.36	24.61	31.78	17.96	24.29	1.209
Maryland	2.05	18.94	37.52	19.34	22.15	1.216
Massachusetts	0.01	18.07	47.49	13.10	21.33	1.218
Michigan	2.29	21.51	38.87	13.85	23.48	1.216
Minnesota	0.10	22.00	36.97	20.18	20.75	1.208
Mississippi	0.67	35.91	18.77	24.40	20.25	1.184
Missouri	0.19	30.46	33.32	16.85	19.18	1.195
Montana	3.36	0.00	29.51	33.91	33.22	1.252
Nebraska	0.20	24.06	27.20	19.63	28.92	1.212
Nevada	0.98	43.39	0.00	38.80	16.83	1.164
New Hampshire	0.90	0.00	17.21	37.93	43.96	1.257
New Jersey	0.18	22.56	30.06	22.26	24.94	1.210
New Mexico	0.01	25.54	13.58	21.18	39.70	1.218
New York	0.00	17.59	48.51	15.22	18.68	1.216
North Carolina	0.98	19.24	43.19	19.90	16.69	1.210
North Dakota	0.10	19.85	13.26	26.36	40.43	1.226
Ohio	0.09	24.04	31.87	19.91	24.09	1.208
Oklahoma	0.00	17.77	23.88	34.02	24.33	1.212
Oregon	0.01	0.00	48.03	17.93	34.04	1.256
Pennsylvania	0.93	25.78	26.68	26.30	20.32	1.200

Table 5.2 (cont.)

State	Property taxes (%)	Sales taxes (%)	Income taxes (%)	Other taxes (%)	Charges and misc. (%)	Average MCF (%)
Rhode Island	0.50	23.10	29.24	15.06	32.10	1.219
South Carolina	0.17	28.23	30.72	18.64	22.25	1.201
South Dakota	0.00	29.78	3.38	26.57	40.27	1.210
Tennessee	0.00	43.20	9.02	26.31	21.48	1.172
Texas	0.00	37.82	0.00	38.25	23.93	1.178
Utah	0.01	26.34	27.98	14.45	31.22	1.213
Vermont	0.04	13.76	26.04	25.82	34.34	1.231
Virginia	0.31	14.37	38.49	20.61	26.23	1.225
Washington	12.55	48.83	0.00	19.82	18.79	1.173
West Virginia	0.07	23.09	26.89	26.28	23.67	1.207
Wisconsin	1.69	23.07	36.95	16.57	21.72	1.210
Wyoming	7.30	13.86	0.00	31.73	47.11	1.244

Source: Brent (2003)

As the focus is on monetary effects, the evaluation is of transfer payments themselves, which we referred to in our earlier discussion as repayments R. However, the repayments are not symmetrical in terms of gains and losses, because the sum that is paid out when a person is retired may differ in value from the taxes that are paid now. As repayments are not symmetrical on both sides, criterion (5.1) which results in R canceling out to form $B - C > 0$, does not apply. Instead, we treat R as leading to separate values for benefits and costs. These values, relating as they do to transfer payments, are immediately expressed in monetary terms. The cost values relate to taxes paid. Since these taxes generate a MCF, the appropriate criterion for evaluating the cash benefits and costs is $B > C.MCF$, which is relation (5.5).

The cash benefits are received in the future when a person retires and so must be discounted at the rate r. The future is considered one period away from the current period when a person is working. (Essentially, Wildasin was using a two-period model for a worker aged 45 years with each period roughly 20 years.) For each dollar of social security, the benefit is simply: $B = \$1/(1 + r)$.

This benefit is less costly to current workers when more other workers are around to pay the income taxes and there are fewer retirees. Let n be the number of other young workers per person who retires. Then $(1 + n)$ is the total number of workers per retiree. Costs are inversely related to $(1 + n)$, seeing that, for a dollar of future benefit, the current cost for each worker paying taxes for the social security benefit is: $C = \$1/(1+n)$. For example, if there are four other workers for every retiree then $n = 4$. An individual worker has four others paying taxes on their incomes in addition to the tax that he or she is paying. So $1 + n = 5$ is the total number of people sharing the tax bill. Thus, for each dollar of social security benefits, an individual worker must pay $\$1/5$ (i.e., $\$0.20$ or 20 cents).

If we ignore the effect of the MCF, the result so far is that net benefits of a dollar's worth of social security financed by an income tax will be positive for a current worker if $1/(1+r) > 1/(1+n)$, i.e., if $r < n$. This would seem to be easily satisfied. But note two points. First, the rate of discount here is an intergenerational one covering a 20-year period. In this context, for example, a 5% annual interest rate makes $1 + r = 1.05$ and this compounded for 20 years becomes 2.65. The intergenerational r in this case would be 1.65 (as $1 + r = 2.65$). So r would probably be a number greater than 1 and not a small fraction. Second, the workers-to-retirees ratio n is not likely to be a constant over time. Fertility rates are falling in most industrialized countries. This factor, which eventually lowers the number of young workers, means that n will probably fall over time. So, even if for today's cohort of workers $r < n$, there may be a future cohort for which this inequality is reversed and net benefits of an extra dollar of social security would be negative.

Column (2) of Table 5.3 (which combines parts of Wildasin's Tables 1 and 2) shows the tax cost that existed in the US in 1985 and how it is likely to change over time using three alternative demographic and economic scenarios. Alternative I is 'optimistic', alternative III is 'pessimistic' and alternative II is in between. In all three scenarios, n falls over time, which means that the tax cost $1/(1+n)$ will rise.

Now let us consider the effect of incorporating the excess burden of taxation into the calculations of tax costs. An important way that there is an excess burden from wage taxes is that, by lowering the net wage, the effective price of leisure is reduced. So one can expect that the labor supply will be reduced. That is, people will work less (e.g., fewer hours). The less people work, the less will be wage earnings and so the tax rate necessary to pay for any level of benefits will rise, causing the tax cost to rise. This distortionary impact on leisure of changes in net wages is quantified (as in the Ballard et al. study) by the elasticity of supply of labor.

Wildasin makes the point that for an activity like social security, where the benefits are cash transfers, it does not make any sense to adopt the standard assumption that government expenditures will be revenue neutral. The incomes of workers will initially rise due to the cash benefits. The workers can afford to buy more leisure and work less, which is to say that they will choose to earn less subsequent income. When taxable income falls,

Table 5.3:   *Net benefits of a permanent $1 increase in social security*
             (1985–2060)

Year	Tax cost $1/(1+n)$	Tax cost with MCF (Case 1)	Net benefit (Case 1)	Tax cost with MCF (Case 2)	Net benefit (Case 2)
(1)	(2)	(3)	(4)	(5)	(6)
1985	0.200	0.210	0.220	0.270	0.15
Alternative I					
2000	0.207	0.220	0.230	0.270	0.17
2025	0.308	0.330	0.100	0.430	0.01
2050	0.314	0.340	0.090	0.430	0.01
2060	0.313	0.340	0.090	0.430	0.01
Alternative II					
2000	0.214	0.230	0.210	0.290	0.15
2025	0.339	0.370	0.030	0.370	−0.13
2050	0.393	0.440	−0.050	0.630	−0.29
2060	0.411	0.460	−0.080	0.670	−0.34
Alternative III					
2000	0.219	0.240	0.190	0.310	0.11
2025	0.376	0.430	−0.110	0.730	−0.51
2050	0.514	0.630	−0.450	1.950	−2.38
2060	0.577	0.740	−0.620	3.550	−4.79

Source: Wildasin (1992)

tax revenues will fall. So the labor supply distortion per unit of revenue (which is the MCF in the Wildasin model) will go up when the revenues fall.

Columns (3) and (5) in Table 5.3 show the effect on the tax cost to finance $1 of future benefits of both the labor supply distortion and the loss of revenues due to the income effect. Wildasin combined alternative estimates for the labor supply elasticity (0.07 and 0.27) with alternative estimates of the decrease in tax revenues per dollar of social security benefits (−0.20 and −0.17). (Case 1 pairs 0.07 with −0.20; while case 2 pairs 0.27 with −0.17.)

Wildasin does not present his MCF estimates explicitly. But we can deduce the estimates from columns (3) or (5), which relate to MCF.C, and column (2) in Table 5.3, which records C on its own. For example, in 1985, if we multiply the unadjusted cost of 0.200 in column (2) by 1.05 we get the MCF adjusted cost of 0.210 in column (4). So the lower bound (case 1) MCF estimate is 1.05. The upper bound MCF estimate (case 2) is 1.35, i.e., the 0.200 in column (2) multiplied by 1.35 leads to the 0.270 figure in column (5). Over time the MCF estimates rise dramatically, so much so that in 2060, the lower bound for the MCF is 1.28 and the upper bound is 6.15.

The result, i.e., the net benefits of a permanent (every year) increase by $1 in social security benefits for the two cases, is shown in columns (4) and (6) of Table 5.3. The discount rate applied to the benefits was 3% per annum. In either case, after 2025, the net benefit of social security for current workers becomes negative.

5.4.2 MCF and Privatization of Psychiatric Hospitals

Denote by subscript 1 effects related to private sector production and subscript 2 effects related to public sector production. Privatization, by definition, involves replacing public production by private production. So privatization will entail the private sector producing something that generates benefits B_2 and costs C_2 at the expense of the public sector no longer producing something that generates benefits B_1 and costs C_1.

Apart from this, privatization usually entails some repayment effect R. The most obvious and primary repayment effect is derived from the government selling the assets that enabled it to produce. The sum R goes to the public sector while the private sector gives up the R. Less obvious, but in some privatization schemes just as important, is the transfer of the consumer cash revenues from one sector to the other. Whether the public sector gains or loses these revenues depends on whether the previous consumers were private or public and whether the new consumers are going to be private or public. As we have seen in section 5.1.2, R going from, or to, the public sector has a different social impact from that associated with private sector R changes. The MCF must be attached to the R changes involving the public sector. Essentially, then, criterion (5.3) is the appropriate criterion, except that there are two versions, one for each sector (the public sector before the privatization and the private sector after the change).

In Brent's (2000a) study of the privatization of non-federal general hospitals (NFGHs in the US, he found that new hospitals (or new psychiatric wards) were set up to care for the mental patients that previously were being treated by state hospitals. No sale of public assets was involved in the process. Repayment effects R came about because, prior to privatization, the public hospitals had both private and government clients and this was projected to continue after privatization. There were two revenue flows that needed the MCF term attached to them: the revenues that used to go to the public sector from the private clients, and the funds that the government now pays to the private sector to care for public clients.

In the US, the private sector producing psychiatric care consisted of two groups: the for-profit hospitals and the nonprofit organizations. The for-profit hospitals were assumed to maximize profits for their private clients, so revenues could be greater than costs; while the nonprofit hospitals dealing with private clients, seeking to break even, would equate revenues with costs. Both private sector groups were assumed to be paid for public clients according to the costs incurred.

The basic data on the NFGHs appears in Table 5.4. We can see that the nonprofit sector in 1990 produced the most quantity (the number of episodes adjusted both for hospital length of stay and the quality of care as reflected by the medical staff–patient ratio). The cost per unit was lower for the public hospitals than in the private for-profit hospitals, but the nonprofit hospitals had the lowest cost of all.

Table 5.4:   *The data on prices, quantities and costs for non-federal general hospitals (1990)*

	Public	Private for-profit	Private nonprofit
Quantity sold to government	70 549	23 563	193 016
Quantity sold to private clients	22 047	18 264	154 329
Cost per unit ($)	8497	8660	7953
Price to government ($)	8497	8660	7953
Price to private clients ($)	8497	10 659	7953

Source: Brent (2000a)

Benefits are not shown in this table. They were measured by Brent in the standard way by the areas under (client) demand curves. The price data gave points on the relevant demand curves by assuming that: (a) client demand curves were linear, and (b) the quantities that the public sector sold to the private and public clients before privatization would be the quantities that would be sold to the two types of clients after the privatization. Revenues can be obtained from the data in Table 5.4 by multiplying price times quantity. The cost estimates were obtained by assuming that constant costs prevailed in all sectors. The MCF estimate was 1.245. This is the average of the four estimates for all US taxes given by Ballard et al. (See the first row and the last column of Table 5.1.)

The net benefits are shown in Table 5.5. The main finding was that privatization was economically worthwhile only for certain kinds of clients and particular forms of organization. Revenues effects, and hence the role of the MCF, were decisive in all cases.

Without the excess burden effect being included (the second column of the table) privatization would be beneficial only if production were transferred

Table 5.5: *Net benefits of privatization of non-federal general hospitals in the US*

Privatization change	Net benefits with MCF = 1	Net benefits with MCF = 1.245
Public to for-profit		
Sales to public sector	−$8 million	+$89 million
Sales to private sector	−$7 million	−$53 million
Total	−$15 million	+$36 million
Public to nonprofit		
Sales to public sector	+$71 million	−$158 million
Sales to private sector	+$48 million	+$2 million
Total	+$119 million	−$156 million

Source: Based on Brent (2000a)

to the nonprofit sector. This sector had the lowest costs and this was the main factor in the result. Also, the for-profit sector charged higher prices, which lowered quantities and hence their benefits. With the excess burden effect (the third column), the results were reversed. Privatization via for-profit NFGHs was worthwhile, while reassigning ownership had negative net benefits. Crucial here was the fact that the nonprofits produced on such a larger scale than other organizational forms. The government would have had to increase its sales greatly to nonprofit hospitals after privatization (the lower costs, and hence prices, increase the quantity demanded). The extra revenues that this entails, when weighted by the MCF, produced the adverse result.

5.4.3 MCF and Community Psychiatric Care

The process of deinstitutionalization of state mental hospitals in the US, whereby patients are moved from public hospitals to community care, has similarities with privatization. But, even though the care was transferred to private organizations with deinstitutionalization, the finance of the care was retained by the public sector. The main difference was that while patients were in state hospitals all of the funds came at the expense of state funds. However, when the care switched to the community (any type of institution other than the state hospitals) the costs were shared roughly 50–50 between the state and federal governments.

Altering the source of funds would not seem to be important, for as Grob (1994) states: 'Efforts to shift costs moreover make little sense from an economic vantage point; an expenditure is an expenditure irrespective of the origins of the funds.' However, we have seen in this chapter that the source does matter, particularly if public funds are involved. The special circumstance posed by deinstitutionalization was that, rather than considering public versus private funding, one now is dealing with one government source being substituted for an alternative government source of finance. Section 5.3.1 revealed that state MCFs can be different from the federal MCF as they rely on a different tax mix (and hence alternative average excess burdens).

The underlying criterion is still $B - (MCF)\ C$ as given in Equation (5.5). This now needs to be adapted by identifying the government entity responsible for the taxation. So $B - (MCF_F)\ C_F$ is the criterion when the federal government is involved and $B - (MCF_S)\ C_S$ when a state government does the financing.

The cost-shifting application we will be referring to relates to data collected by Dickey (1995) of cost and outcomes of mental health provision in three regions of Massachusetts, viz., Boston, central and western. Each region had different shares of state hospital and community care. Each region thus constituted different systems of care as defined by varying degrees of deinstitutionalization. The central region relied most on state institutions and 46.3% of total costs were attributable to psychiatric inpatient care. The western region was more community based and only 12.6% of its costs were taken up by state hospital care. The Boston system was in between the other two regions and had 24.5% of its costs going to state inpatient hospital care.

Brent (2000b) used the Dickey data to evaluate the three Massachusetts systems. Outcomes were judged to be the same in all regions, so benefits did not figure in the comparison. The evaluation reduced to a (weighted) CM, with $(MCF_S)\ C_S$ being the state hospital costs and $(MCF_F)\ C_F$ being the federally financed community care costs. As each region had a mix of hospital and community care, the two tax jurisdiction costs had to be summed, which made the total cost in a region: $(MCF_S)\ C_S + (MCF_F)\ C_F$. It was this total weighted cost that needed to be minimized.

All the community costs were covered by the Medicaid program (in the US, Medicare is the public insurance program for the elderly and Medicaid is the public insurance program for low income patients). The Medicaid funded costs were: psychiatric inpatient costs at a general hospital, psychiatric costs of outpatients, and general medical expenses. The state costs consisted only of the psychiatric inpatient costs. Table 5.6 gives the per patient costs for each of the regions in unweighted and weighted forms.

In unweighted terms (with the MCF = 1 at both the state and federal levels), the central region had the highest costs. The state funded cost was $8415 and the non-state, Medicaid, cost was $9742. Since the Medicaid costs were shared equally by the state and federal governments, the state allocation of the total cost was $13 286 (i.e., $8415 + $4871). The federal

Table 5.6: Weighted costs of systems of psychiatric care in Massachusetts

Cost source	Boston	Central	Western
Unweighted costs			
State funded	$3421	$8415	$1762
Medicaid	$10542	$9742	$12235
Total costs (all sources)	$13963	$18157	$13997
State allocation of total costs: C_S	$8692	$13286	$7880
Federal allocation of total costs: C_F	$5271	$4871	$6118
Total costs (all sources)	$13963	$18157	$13997
Weighted costs			
$(MCF_S)\, C_S + (MCF_F)\, C_F$	$17149	$22247	$17215

Source: Brent (2000b)

government's allocation was the remaining $4871 (the half of the $9742 that it had to pay). Boston had the lowest costs, $34 below the western region.

For the weighted costs, the estimates $MCF_F = 1.245$ (the average for all taxes in Table 5.1) and $MCF_F = 1.218$ (the average for Massachusetts in Table 5.2) were used. Boston continued to have the lowest costs and central the highest. The edge that Boston had over the western region almost exactly doubled from $34 to $66. In percentage terms these differences are extremely small. But, with a total population of some 16000 clients in Massachusetts, the per client increases due to cost shifting between the state and federal government would amount to over a half a million dollar extra differential in favor of Boston (i.e., 16000 times $32).

It is quite clear from this case study that, for Massachusetts, community care does not equate with transferring care from public to private funding. So, if we now turn our attention from cost shifting to possible public/private sector cost differences, we see that allowing for the excess burden of state and federal taxes has raised costs dramatically. For Boston, for example, its unweighted costs of $13963 balloon to $17149 with MCF considerations. This is a 22.8% difference. There is scope for private institutions in Boston to have a sizeable cost advantage in the provision of psychiatric care.

5.4.4 MCF and Case Management Programs

A question that is often raised in the context of mental health programs is whether to include maintenance costs (food, housing, clothing, transportation, etc.) as part of the evaluation. The literature includes examples where all of the maintenance costs are treated as costs – see Rice (1992) – as well as examples where none of the maintenance costs are considered relevant, as in Clark et al. (1994).

Maintenance costs are center-stage in attempts to move patients out of inpatient psychiatric care because the main objective itself is to bring about independent living in the community. Some of these maintenance costs are financed privately by the families of the patients and the rest come from government sources. Jerrell and Hu (1989) carried out a detailed cost-effectiveness analysis of three case management programs in California designed to substitute community costs (what they called 'support costs') for inpatient hospital costs (what they called 'intensive costs'). The support costs consisted of medical, legal, family and other.

A case management program in this context refers to interventions that: (1) integrate all the medical and supportive services that psychiatric patients would require in the community, and (2) ensure continuity of care. The three case management programs considered differed greatly in the level of support they provided for the patients. The three programs were:

1. A Program for Assertive Community Treatment (PACT) that had a multidisciplinary team who met daily to report on their cases. The average caseload was 15–20 to 1. Most services were provided outside of the office setting;
2. A 'Clinical Team' program that had mainly social workers who acted as generalists. The caseloads were high, varying from 35 per therapist to 40–45 when the patient was thought stabilized. Teams met weekly and services were provided primarily in a clinic/office setting; and
3. An 'Intensive Broker' program whereby the case managers provided the link (i.e., were brokers) between the clients and the services they required. What made the program 'intensive' was the fact that the staff provided a relationship with the patients and helped with socialization, unlike most broker models that supplied linkage-only services. Case managers were para-professionals, operating largely in field-based settings, meeting weekly with their clinical supervisors, and having caseloads of 18 to 1.

The data in the Jerrell and Hu study were converted by Brent (2000b) into a cost–benefit framework by using the standard CM assumption that a benefit was a negative cost. The benefits then of the case management programs were the inpatient hospital costs that were avoided by incurring the community costs (including the case management costs).

The issue then was how to treat all the transfers associated with the case management programs. Brent split the transfers into two: private (R_P) and public (R_G). The private transfers (e.g., family costs) can initially be assumed to have no net impact when the beneficiaries and the donors are considered to be the same group (the family). The public transfers were treated differently according to the beneficiaries and financers. The public source of the finances meant that the MCF would be applied. So $1 of public transfers were assigned a cost of $ (MCF)1.

The recipients of the public transfer were the psychiatric patients. $1 of their income was judged to have a social value greater than $1 because their income (if any) was way below the average and they were regarded as a socially deserving group. As will be explained fully in Chapter 13, the premium given to the income of the beneficiaries (the patients) can be captured in a CBA by a money income distribution weight a_m, which typically has a value greater than 1. The benefit of $1 transferred to the patients then became $ (a_m)1. The net social impact of each dollar transferred was determined by the difference: a_m − MCF. Brent derived a value of 2.28 as the distribution weight and he chose a MCF = 1.3 (the upper limit of the Californian MCFs whose average was given in Table 5.2 as 1.206). The public transfers therefore had a *positive* impact of 0.98 per dollar transferred, i.e., a dollar transferred amounted almost exactly to a dollar of benefits.

The resulting costs, benefits and revenues of the three case management programs are presented in Table 5.7. The top part of the table has all the CBA ingredients separately. The unweighted net benefits correspond to a traditional CBA where all transfers are ignored (and so are distributional issues and the excess burden caused by public funding). The PACT program was clearly the most beneficial (it was also the most cost-effective program in the Jerrell and Hu study).

In order that we can appreciate the independent and joint impacts of the MCF and the distribution weight, three versions of the weighted net benefits are given in Table 5.7 (based on Brent's Table 2 and weight set 3 of Table 3 – see section 13.4.1 below). Note that the distribution weight, when it applies, is not only attached to the public transfers; it also magnifies the benefits (the sums spent on the programs are on behalf of the patients). Similarly, the MCF attaches to the (government financed) costs as well as to the public transfers.

With just the MCF included, the absolute size of the numbers is smaller than for the unweighted amounts. This is because the MCF is attached to the costs, making weighted costs larger – along the lines of criterion (5.5) – and hence the net benefits are lower. When the distribution weight is applied, the benefits are multiplied by 2.28. Benefit magnitudes dominate cost magnitudes, so the absolute size of the net benefits more than doubles. When both the MCF and distribution weights are incorporated, amounts still double the unweighted values due to the larger size of the distribution weight compared to the MCF figure.

Table 5.7:　Evaluation of case management programs

CBA category	Intensive broker	Clinical team	PACT adaption
Benefits: B	14560	15157	16437
Costs: C	2326	2670	2769
Private transfers: R_P	−45	−123	−141
Public transfers: R_G	295	248	616
Unweighted net benefits: $B - C$	12200	12487	13668
Weighted net benefits:			
With MCF = 1.3	11448	11612	$12653
With distribution weight of 2.28	31248	32205	$35496
With MCF = 1.3 and distribution weight of 2.28	30462	31331	$34481

Source:　Based on Brent (2002b)

No matter how the absolute numbers are transformed, the result is that the relative sizes of the net benefits are not altered. The PACT program is the most beneficial irrespective of which weighting scheme is adopted. This is simply because the PACT program has the highest gross benefits *B*, as well as the highest net benefits, and so it has the most weighted benefits.

This study also uncovered an additional dimension of transfers. Apart from the excess burden and income distribution effects of transfers, there is a third way that transfers impact an economic evaluation. This is via a 'productivity' effect. The transfers themselves cause benefits and costs to be different. For the various case management programs, the transfers were a necessary ingredient to obtain the hospital cost savings. In fact, a dollar of public funds R_G transferred had a higher correlation with declining hospital costs than even the expenditures on case management programs. Typically, for each $1 of R_G, the hospital (intensive) costs, which form the benefits, fell by $1.60.

5.5　FINAL SECTION

We close with the problems, summary and looking ahead sections.

5.5.1　Problems

In the theory section we explained how the excess burden and the MCF depended on the size of the elasticities. There is a second factor that is important that we have so far ignored, that public finance specialists emphasize. The neglected factor is the size of the tax rate itself. Typically, see for example, Browning and Browning (1987), where an equation is derived that quantifies the effect of the tax rate. Instead, in the following problems, we will establish the importance of the tax rate effect by re-examining the Wildasin case study, which provided implicit estimates of the MCF that varied with the tax rate.

Table 5.8 is based on a subset of the information in Table 5.3. The focus is just on population projections using alternative III and the case 2 set of assumptions. In column (2) of Table 5.8, the tax costs of Table 5.3 are reproduced and relabeled 'tax rates'. This is because the tax cost is per dollar transferred and so is the equivalent of a tax rate. Column (3) of Table 5.8 is derived from Table 5.3 by dividing its column (5) by column (2). Recall in the discussion of Table 5.3 that one column is C and the other is $C.MCF$; so dividing the latter by the former would derive an estimate of the MCF. Column (4) of Table 5.8 has to be filled in as one of the problems.

Table 5.8: The relation between the excess burden and the level of the tax rate

Year	Tax rate	MCF	Marginal excess burden
(1)	(2)	(3)	(4)
2000	0.219	1.416	
2025	0.376	1.941	
2050	0.514	3.794	
2060	0.577	6.153	

Source: Based on Table 5.3

1. Calculate the marginal (additional) excess burden per dollar transferred from the MCF figures for each tax rate in column (3) and insert them as column 4.
2. How would you summarize the relation between the tax rates and the marginal excess burdens? (For example, as the tax rate changes, does the marginal excess burden increase proportionally, less than proportionally, or more than proportionally?)
3. On the basis of your answer to question 2, would it always then be valid to draw a fixed difference between the MC.MCF and the S curves (like that in Figure 5.1) as the scale of a health care intervention expands and additional tax finance is required?

4. On the basis of your answers to questions 2 and 3, examine the appropriateness of assuming a fixed MCF to apply to extra funds required to finance each of these health care evaluations: (a) buying 10 more wheelchairs for a hospital; and (b) providing universal health insurance for all citizens.

5.5.2 Summary

Typically, health care evaluations, and health economics journals, have ignored the role played by the MCF in making economic evaluations. Presumably the view was that the MCF was a public finance topic and thus not applicable to health economics. In this chapter we have argued that the excess burden of the tax revenues used to finance a health care project was just a particular type of negative externality. Since including externalities makes economic evaluations more comprehensive and responsive to all the consequences that individuals care about and value, there is no good reason to ignore this consideration just because it is attached to non-health effects. In order for the effects of a health expenditure to exist at all, resources must be withdrawn from other activities. In the process of withdrawing inputs from elsewhere, consumers have to forgo more satisfaction than is directly reflected in the tax revenues passed over. This extra satisfaction forgone is the excess burden of financing the tax and this, when added to the revenue effect, amounts to the MCF. The main determinant of the size of the MCF is the elasticity of demand.

Of course, not all health care projects are financed by public funds and it is only for these types of expenditures that a non-unitary MCF is required. The public sector is obviously involved when it undertakes the health services itself, i.e., public ownership. Hence when public ownership is transferred (privatized) the MCF must be attached both to funds gained as well as given up by the public sector.

A second way that public funds are involved is where the private sector carries out the production, but cash transfers are required to ensure that the scale of private operations are not too low from a social perspective. Cash transfers are not directly resource effects. But they usually will entail distribution effects, whether between the private and public sectors, or between rich and poor groups. The MCF is required for the first type of distributive effect and this chapter has focused primarily on this aspect. Distribution weights are required for the second type of effect and the last case study introduced this particular dimension to the evaluation process (to be developed further in later chapters).

The implicit assumption used in economic evaluations is that the finance for a new health care expenditure would be from the same set of taxes that generated past government expenditures. So we referred to a comprehensive study of MCFs for US federal taxes by Ballard et al., and took the average of these estimates to give us an idea of the magnitude of the MCF. Since different states have different tax mixes, a state's MCF is simply a weighted average of the federal tax MCFs, where the weights are the state tax shares coming from the various federal tax categories.

The applications stayed within the confines of the CM approach by dealing with cases where benefits were the same across alternatives, or where benefits were ignored, or where benefits were regarded as negative costs. The applications illustrated the many different ways that transfers could impact an economic evaluation. These case studies added an alternative justification for why the MCF should be included in health care evaluations. That is, they showed that including MCFs made a difference to the desirability of certain health care projects. Some types of hospital privatization were judged worthwhile only when the MCF was set equal to 1; while future social security transfers changed from being worthwhile to being undesirable when a MCF that rose over time was incorporated.

5.5.3 Looking Ahead

With this chapter, we have completed the examination of the cost side of evaluations. From here we proceed to a consideration of the consequences. The next part covers CEA.

PART III

CEA and CBA

6. Fundamentals of cost-effectiveness analysis

6.1 INTRODUCTION

Here we start with the first of two chapters on CEA, focusing on the basic principles. Unlike a CM, which only deals with costs, a CEA includes effects as well as costs. The two are related by forming a cost-to-effects ratio. What to include in this ratio is the first topic under discussion. Then we present the underlying CEA decision-making model and illustrate how cost-effectiveness calculations are to be made and interpreted. Because of the inherent shortcomings of CEA, we quickly turn attention to ways of converting CEA into CBA. The case studies are primarily devoted to showing how these conversion methods have been put into practice.

6.1.1 CEA as an Approach to Evaluation

Unlike a CM study, a CEA looks at both the consequences (effects) and costs of a procedure. A CEA looks at the amount of cost per unit of effect: C/E. One can now compare across (some) programs. Moreover, one can allow for the fact that different programs achieve their objectives to different degrees. Thus, for instance, the cost per case detected can be used to make comparisons of screening programs for different diseases. If one screening program can detect more cases than another, this is allowed for in the comparison. For CM one must have a given/fixed level of output.

On the other hand, there is a fundamental problem with a cost-effectiveness (and cost–utility) outcome. It can state whether one procedure can achieve a given objective (effect) with fewer resources than another procedure. But a CEA cannot ascertain whether using even the best procedure is itself socially worthwhile. Moreover, it cannot compare programs that involve different kinds of effect.

6.1.2 Which Costs to Include?

From a CBA perspective, the question as to which costs to include is easy to answer. *All* costs should be included. Also, the criterion depends on the size of net benefits $B - C$. So whether an item is classed as a negative C or a positive B does not matter. The difference $B - C$ would be the same figure irrespective how it was treated. Not so with a CEA. Which costs to include is not always agreed upon. And whether an effect (e.g., the reduction in custodial care brought about from an intervention) is regarded as a positive consequence on the denominator of the C/E ratio, or is treated as a cost saving and hence deducted from the numerator of the ratio, makes a big difference to the value of the ratio.

As we shall see, behind the CEA model is the requirement of a fixed budget constraint. The trouble is that the budget amount is typically fixed in terms of health care expenditures only. So non health care costs are often ignored. For example, indirect cost may be paid for by the patients and not be a part of the total C that is fixed for the agency making the decisions. Ignoring non health costs is consistent with trying to maximize the effect for a given agency budget; but it need not lead to the most socially worthwhile programs being adopted.

Weinstein and Stason (1977) include in C the costs of treating diseases that would not have been treated if the person had died, e.g., treating hypertension extends people's lives, and thereby leads to the possibility that they will have to be treated subsequently for cancer. Drummond et al. (1987, p. 80) argue that, on the whole, these costs should not be included. They give two reasons: (1) Economic evaluations usually assume 'all other things are held constant', and therefore other aspects would continue as before; and (2) The decision whether to treat someone for cancer is, in principle, a separate one, from the decision whether to treat someone for hypertension (and should be decided on its own merits).

Point (2) contains the implication that if one treatment depends crucially on the existence of another, then the two treatments should be combined into one package for evaluation. Drummond et al. give as an example the case where if one prevents the birth of a child with Down's syndrome, it is likely that the mother will want to have a replacement pregnancy. The abortion and the replacement decisions would thus be so inter-related that the costs and effects of both events should be combined. Moreover, in the context of hypertension, as Gold et al. (1996) point out, while one can exclude future cancer treatment, one should not exclude future hypertension related disease costs and savings (due to the treatment of strokes and myocardial infarctions) and treating the adverse side-effects of hypertension treatment.

The one general principle for non-related treatments is that if one includes the effects on other medical treatments on the cost side, one should include them also on the benefit side.

6.1.3   Which Effects to Include?

An effect must be defined in terms of a description of the course of an illness without intervention. It is not always obvious that an intervention has an effect, if there is no change over what would have otherwise occurred. The first step for a CEA is to establish that an effect does exist. Otherwise there is no point in implementing a program efficiently if it is ineffective. The existence of a prior, controlled, clinical trial would therefore seem to be a prerequisite for any CEA. The only reservation is that it is important to show that *in the actual circumstances where the intervention is likely to take place* that positive effects are forthcoming. One should not try to control for everything other than the medical treatments. Differences in individual and socio-economic characteristics need to be allowed for in establishing effectiveness.

The consequence can be an input (frequency that medication is taken) or a final output (year of life gained). In general, it is more useful to deal with final effects. For an input, one should be able to demonstrate the link between the input and a final effect. Or, the input should have value in itself. For example, defining the effect as the ability to detect the existence of a disease can provide reassurance to both the doctor and patient. Note that both CEA studies covered in this chapter are of the input effect kind.

To be able to use CEA, programs must either have a main objective in common (e.g., lowering blood pressure by a specified amount) or have many objectives achieved to the same extent (e.g., two surgical procedures for the treatment of a particular complaint that have similar chances of complications and recurrence). In the second case, the exercise is really one of CM. The method falls down when different effects are relevant to varying degrees (though we present an application which shows how that drawback can be overcome), for one has to choose only one effect to use on the denominator of the C/E ratio.

6.2   BASIC PRINCIPLES OF CEA

We cover principles that apply to both the theory and the practice of CEA.

6.2.1   Basic Cost-Effectiveness Model

Weinstein (1995) gives a very clear statement about the underlying logic of the cost-effective approach to medical decision-making. The analysis starts as follows. One is considering a menu of programs, where i identifies a typical program and is numbered from 1 to N. All programs are assumed to be divisible with constant returns to scale. The programs are not repeatable (or else one can just keep on doing one program over and over again if that one is the most cost-effective). All programs on the list must be feasible, such that if one is adopted, that does not preclude another being adopted later on (thus, for example, one program cannot be an alternative drug for a drug treating the same condition in another program). The decision-maker selects an effect E that s/he is trying to maximize given a fixed budget cost C. One calculates all the programs C_i that make up the budget cost C and one also measures each program effect E_i. If an E_i is negative, one simply deletes it from the list.

From this starting point, one proceeds to rank order (from lowest to highest) all the cost-effectiveness ratios C_i/E_i. Programs are selected from the top of the list and working downwards until the entire budget has been exhausted. The set of programs so identified provide the most total effect for the budget. To illustrate the method, we will take Weinstein's (1995) hypothetical example (Box 5.2), and add a column for the cumulative cost, to form our Table 6.1.

Table 6.1:   Hypothetical example of the cost-effectiveness paradigm

Program	Effect	Cost ($)	C/E ratio ($)	Cumulative cost ($)
A	500	1 000 000	2000	1 000 000
B	500	2 000 000	4000	3 000 000
C	200	1 200 000	6000	4 200 000
D	250	2 000 000	8000	6 200 000
E	100	1 200 000	12000	7 400 000
F	50	800 000	16000	8 200 000
G	100	1 800 000	18000	10 000 000
H	100	2 200 000	22000	12 200 000
I	150	4 500 000	30000	16 700 000
J	100	5 000 000	50000	21 700 000

Source: Based on Weinstein (1995)

Say the budget available is $10 million. Program A is affordable and is the most cost-effective, so it must be chosen (if any one is chosen). Working down the list, we choose B and C and continue down to G, which corresponds to a $10 million cumulative cost. Program H would exceed the budget, so cannot be selected. By choosing programs A to G, the total effect obtained is 1700. This is the most effect that the $10 million can buy.

Although, as we have emphasized a number of times already, CEA cannot tell us whether any of the A to G programs are socially worthwhile in absolute terms, Weinstein makes the important point that we are now at least in a position to identify better and worse programs in relative terms. Program H's cost of $18000 per effect is the benchmark or 'cutoff' ratio in this process. It tells us that if any new program wants to be adopted instead of any of the A to H, it must at least be able to lead to an effect that costs less than $18000. If a new program costs $19000 per effect, the money is best left in program G; while if the cost per effect of the new program is $17000 it can then replace project G. In this case, if G were worthwhile, then the new program would be even more worthwhile.

What happens if the programs are mutually exclusive (e.g., different treatments for the same condition are being considered, as with alternative drugs for dealing with hypertension) since this means that one program would be used at the expense of another, and thus not all programs are feasible? Weinstein points out that in these cases one needs to adjust the basic framework given above and turn from average cost-effectiveness ratios to *incremental* cost-effectiveness ratios $\Delta C/\Delta E$. An incremental cost-effectiveness ratio for any two programs 1 and 2 can be defined as:

$$\frac{\Delta C}{\Delta E} = \frac{C_2 - C_1}{E_2 - E_1} \tag{6.1}$$

where ΔC is the incremental cost and ΔE is the incremental effect.

To see how this ratio is used in the context of mutually exclusive programs, we refer to Weinstein's Box 5.3, and add columns for average and incremental cost-effectiveness ratios, which become our Table 6.2.

Table 6.2: *Hypothetical example of the cost-effectiveness paradigm with competing choices*

Program	Effect	Cost ($)	C/E ratio ($)	$\Delta C/\Delta E$ ratio ($)
K_0	0	0	—	—
K_1	10	50000	5000	5000
K_2	15	150000	10000	20000

Source: Based on Weinstein (1995)

The idea here is that we are adding to the list of J programs in Table 6.1 a possible new program K. There are three competing alternative candidates for this new spot. All three are identified by a subscript in Table 6.2 because only one of them can be chosen. Program K_0 is the no-program option and this is why it has zero effect and zero cost. (Note that having no program will not always involve zero costs and effects because illnesses sometimes improve on their own and untreated illnesses can still incur non-medical costs.) The incremental cost-effectiveness ratio for K_1 is calculated relative to the no-program alternative and the ratio for K_2 is calculated relative to program K_1.

The key assumption is that the funds to finance the new program must come out of the original budget of $10 million. So program G is the one that would have to be sacrificed in order to allow the new program to be adopted. With a cost-effective ratio of $18000 for program G, this is the benchmark as before. But this is now to relate to incremental ratios and not average ratios. That is, any new project must produce a unit effect at an incremental cost lower than $18000 in order to replace program G.

The decision-making process is as follows. Program K_1 is considered first. With an incremental cost-effectiveness ratio of $5000, it is well under $18000 and so can be approved instead of program G. Now we consider program K_2. On the basis of the average ratio of $10000, it would seem to be more cost-effective than G. But this ignores the fact that K_1 has replaced G. Relative to K_1, that is, on the basis of its incremental ratio, it costs $20000 per effect. This amount exceeds the critical value of $18000 and so K_2 does not justify approval. The end result is that the $50000 to produce 10 units of E by K_1 is used to replace the $50000 that previously produced approximately 3 units of E in program G (this is where the assumption of program divisibility comes in) for a net gain of 7 units of E.

6.2.2   Calculating and Interpreting Cost-Effectiveness Ratios

To complement and reinforce the theoretical model just outlined, we will use a case study to help identify some of the practical considerations involved with CEA. We revisit the hypertension study by Logan et al. (1981) that we first presented in section 1.4.4. In Chapter 1 we compared the study relative to what a CBA would entail. Here we focus on what general principles we can learn from it as a CEA.

Recall that Logan et al. compared two methods of providing hypertension treatment. The standard treatment (RC, for regular care) is by physicians at their office. The alternative (WS, for worksite) program is to treat a person by a nurse at a person's worksite. Effects were measured in terms of the annual blood pressure reduction from treatment, that is, mm Hg reduction. In Table 6.3 we present some differences from the data in Table 1.2. (The 'total costs' of Table 1.2 are called 'treatment costs' in Table 6.3. We now add screening costs and consider alternative levels of effect. Table 6.3 combines material in Logan et al.'s Tables 4 and 6.)

Table 6.3:   Cost and effect per patient for worksite care and regular care

Variable	Worksite care (WS)	Regular care (RC)	WS – RC
Cost			
Treatment costs	$242.86	$211.34	$31.52
Treatment and screening costs	$465.86	$434.34	$31.52
Effect (mm Hg)	12.10	6.50	5.60
Cost-effectiveness ratio			
With treatment costs only	$20.07	$32.51	$5.63
With treatment costs and screening costs	$38.50	$66.82	$5.63
Effect with no treatment	7.10	1.50	5.60
Cost-effectiveness ratio			
With treatment costs only	$34.20	$140.89	$5.63
With treatment costs and screening costs	$65.61	$289.56	$5.63

Source: Logan et al. (1981)

The table shows that the WS program was the more effective, and the more cost-effective (the C/E ratio was lower). This result can also be shown graphically with *C* on the vertical axis and *E* on the horizontal axis – see Figure 6.1 below (based on Logan et al.'s Figure 2), which maps out the relations ignoring the screening costs. The program with the lowest slope is the one that is most cost-effective. As the line joining 0 to WS has a lower slope than that joining 0 to RC, this confirms the superiority of the WS program.

It turns out that if one did include the screening costs, and worked with the most comprehensive measure of costs, then the slopes of the two alternatives would be unaffected. So the relative cost-effectiveness would be unaltered. Ignoring some categories of costs does not always bias the results, especially when the excluded costs are the same for all alternatives.

In any CEA, the 'no program' alternative should explicitly be considered. The no-program alternative could greatly affect the C/E ratios. In the hypertension example, Logan et al. recognized that in their study persons who were not treated, but had an increased awareness of the condition, tended to have a 5 mm Hg reduction after a year without any expenditure. As a consequence the net effects of the two programs would be different (5 mm Hg lower) by considering the no-program alternative, as shown by the second set of estimates of effect ('effect with no treatment') in Table 6.3. With the lower level of effect, the cost per effect (ignoring screening costs) for the WS program rises from $20.07 to $34.20, and it rises for the RC program from

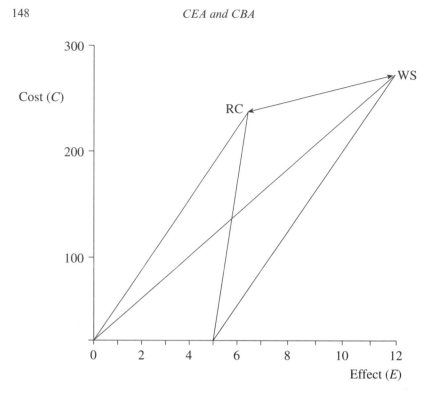

Note: Lines ending with RC indicate the regular care program and lines ending with WS denote the worksite alternative. Different lines can be drawn according to the values of the no-program alternative. If this alternative program has zero effects and zero costs, then the lines emanate from the origin. When there would have been a 5-unit effect even without the program, lines start from 5 on the horizontal axis. The (average) cost-effectiveness ratios are represented by the slopes of the line. A flatter line is a more cost-effective alternative. The slope of the arrowed line linking RC to WS shows the incremental cost-effectiveness ratio. This slope must be compared to the benchmark ratio.

Figure 6.1:   Average and incremental cost-effectiveness ratios

$32.51 to $140.89. While the C/E ratios are altered, the relative rankings are not. The line linking 5 units of effect to WS in Figure 6.1 is still lower than the line joining 5 to RC, leaving the WS program as the more cost-effective.

By now, the significance of the WS − RC difference in Tables 1.2 and 6.3 should be clear. This difference leads to the construction of the incremental cost-effectiveness ratio. Note that only one of these treatment sites can be used. With mutually exclusive programs, as Weinstein emphasized above, incremental cost-effectiveness ratios are the relevant ratios to use. Thus, the issue for decision-making is whether it is worthwhile to pay $5.63 per mm Hg reduction for extra treatment and screening with the WS program, rather than go along with the $66.82 cost of the standard RC program. The incremental C/E ratio is shown as the slope of the arrowed line in Figure 6.1 joining RC to WS. It is interesting to see that, in this case, considering the no-treatment program alternative does greatly affect the individual C/E ratios, but does not affect at all the incremental C/E ratio.

Of course, we do not know whether it is worthwhile to pay $5.63 for a mm Hg reduction in blood pressure. Nor do we know in the Logan et al. study that a fixed budget was being applied to the hypertension programs. Without knowledge of the size of the budget, we do not know whether the extra $31.52 of costs for the WS program would be available. Without such a guarantee that extra funds are available, it may not matter that the WS program was more cost-effective. The RC program could be the only afford-able program and hence the only one that can be implemented.

6.3 METHODS FOR CONVERTING A CEA INTO A CBA

Because of the fundamental problems with CEA just mentioned, we devote the next section to trying to find ways to convert CEAs into CBAs.

6.3.1 Using the Utility of Income as the Cut-Off Ratio

Garber and Phelps (1997) constructed a two-period, utility maximizing model to try to find the cut-off ratio to determine when a particular cost-effectiveness ratio is worth investing in. Utility stems from income. The cost of a health program is the loss of income, and hence utility, that one sacri-fices in the first period by devoting funds to the program. The benefit of the program is that, in the second period, the probability of surviving increases. This produces more years of income and correspondingly more utility. At the optimum, the extra cost will equal the extra benefit. From this equality, the cut-off ratio can be deduced. The details are as follows.

The starting point is the optimum condition that $MB = MC$. The extra cost MC is in terms of an additional loss of utility in the first period ΔU_0, where Δ stands for 'change in', U is utility, and 0 indicates the first period. This addi-tional loss of utility comes about via changes in first period income. We can represent this process simply by multiplying and dividing by the change in first period income, ΔY_0, to obtain the expression: $MC = (\Delta U_0 / \Delta Y_0) \Delta Y_0$. Since the term in the bracket is the marginal utility of first period income $MU(Y_0)$, and ΔY_0 is the cost of the program ΔC, we end up with:

$$MC = MU(Y_0) \Delta C \qquad (6.2)$$

Garber and Phelps (1997) define MB as the additional utility gained in the second period or ΔU_1, where 1 indicates the second period. Again, utility comes from income obtained in the second period $U(Y_1)$. The effect of the program is not, however, to raise that annual income directly. So, ΔY_1 does not alter, and neither will there be a change in utility from second period income $MU(Y_1)$. Rather the effect is to increase the probability of living longer in the second period. Thus, the program increases the number of years that utility is earned from annual income. The number of years is measured in quality adjusted terms, i.e., a QALY, as introduced in Chapter 1 (and covered in detail in Part IV of the book). So ΔQALY is the increase in the number of years that income is obtained. This means that ΔQALY times $U(Y_1)$ is the extra utility from the increased number of years that utility is obtained from income, and this measures ΔU_1. With ΔE defined by ΔQALY, we have:

$$MB = U(Y_1)\,\Delta E \qquad\qquad (6.3)$$

Substituting for (6.2) and (6.3) into the optimal condition requiring $MB = MC$, and rearranging, we derive the result:

$$\frac{\Delta C}{\Delta E} = \frac{U(Y_1)}{MU(Y_0)} \qquad\qquad (6.4)$$

Thus, the cut-off ratio given by the Garber and Phelps' model involves the cost-effectiveness ratio being equal to the ratio of the utility of income in the second period relative to the marginal utility from income in the first period. This ratio depends on 'the preference structure of consumers' and relies on the concept of the marginal WTP for a program, that is, 'the amount an individual would pay to reduce a risk of death'. (Note that this concept will be examined in detail in Chapter 12.)

To use the Garber and Phelps method, one needs to formulate an operational representation of an individual utility function for income. In general, such a function will vary with the age of an individual and the degree of risk aversion. How Garber and Phelps formulate their utility of income function is explained as an application (see section 6.4.2).

6.3.2   Using the MCF as the Cut-Off Ratio

Brent (2002) proposed a general method for valuing (putting a price on) effects by using the concept of the marginal cost of public funds (the MCF). The MCF provides the 'missing link' between CBA and CEA because it is this that records the social opportunity cost of the dollar from which one is trying to get the most effectiveness.

Brent's method can be deduced simply from the cost–benefit criterion which recognized the excess burden of taxes. This criterion was expressed in equation (5.5): $B-(\text{MCF})C>0$. The version of this criterion that we need to use is in terms of a *change* in benefits and costs, replacing B by ΔB, and C by ΔC. Changes are required because one is considering altering programs until one reaches the highest (weighted) net benefits. At the optimum, the change in benefits must equal the weighted change in costs. Criterion (5.5) can be transformed into:

$$\Delta B=(\text{MCF})\,\Delta C \qquad (6.5)$$

In Chapter 1 we explained that we could decompose benefits by considering them to be the product of a monetary price of an effect P and the quantity of an effect E: $B\equiv P.E$. In terms of changes, this definition would be $\Delta B\equiv P.\,\Delta E$. Substituting for ΔB in (6.5) we obtain:

$$P.\,\Delta E=(\text{MCF})\,\Delta C \qquad (6.6)$$

Dividing both sides of equation (6.6) by ΔE, we end up with:

$$P=\text{MCF}\left(\frac{\Delta C}{\Delta E}\right) \qquad (6.7)$$

Equation (6.7) tells us that to value an effect in monetary terms one simply multiplies the cost-effectiveness ratio of the last program that fits into the budget by the MCF. Thus, if one gets an effect for $100 by utilizing our budget most effectively, and each dollar we need to pay for the effect comes at the expense of 1.20 of total satisfaction, then the value of that effect that proceeds from that optimizing process must be $120.

The main difference between this method and the one devised by Garber and Phelps is that Brent is using the supply price (the opportunity cost of resources) while Garber and Phelps are using the demand price (what consumers are willing to pay for the resources). Recall from the analysis of competitive markets in Chapter 2 that, at the equilibrium quantity, what consumers are willing to pay is equal to what the producers must receive to give up their resources. So, in theory, one can use either the demand price or the supply price at the optimum to value the resources. The MCF is involved as part of the supply price because, as shown in Figure 5.1, the supply curve in the presence of an excess burden due to the public financing of a program consists of MC times MCF.

6.3.3   The Revealed Preference Approach

A very general approach to deriving estimates of the key ingredients of an economic evaluation is to impute them from past decision-maker behavior using statistical means. The outcomes of the past decisions are known. If we assume that these decisions were determined by the ingredients that we are interested in (and measures of these ingredients are available), then there is an empirical link between the decisions and the ingredients. The decision-maker is said to have acted 'as if' the ingredients were important. The coefficients attached to the ingredients indicate their relative importance; in other words, their relative values are revealed by these coefficients.

To illustrate how the approach works, we will consider two measurement exercises. In the first, one is trying to measure an overall effect and in the second, one is trying to value an effect in dollar terms. We start with the measurement of an overall effect, focusing on the effect of an alcohol treatment program (see Brent (1998b)).

Alcohol leads to many disruptive personal and social side-effects. For example, heavy drinking leads to individuals losing their jobs and causing fatalities in driving accidents. An effective alcohol treatment program would lead to reductions in those adverse behavioral responses. These reductions relate to a number of different effects. How can one combine them to form an overall index of improvement?

In the case of alcohol, the key element in the measure of improvement was taken to be a reduction in the beer Q–F (quantity–frequency) index which we will identify as E_1. All other treatment effects were eventually to be expressed in terms of E_1. A second effect was the number of times a person was drunk, denoted by E_2. How the second variable was expressed in terms of the first can be explained as follows.

A decision-maker is to decide on the basis of a set of changes in effects (from before treatment to after treatment) whether there was sufficient overall improvement to be able to conclude that the treatment program had been effective. This decision we represent as D (where $D=1$ means that the program was effective and $D=0$ means that the program was not effective). D is the dependent variable in the statistical relationship. The independent variables are the set of effects (E_1, E_2, etc.). The complete equation (called a 'regression equation') for the two-effect case looks like:

$$D = a_0 + a_1 E_1 + a_2 E_2 \qquad (6.8)$$

where the a coefficients are fixed numbers and these are estimated by statistical means (on the basis of their being the 'best fit' or their being the 'most likely' estimates).

The meaning of the coefficients is that they show the effect on the dependent variable of a unit change in an independent variable. Thus, we have $a_1 = \Delta D / \Delta E_1$ and $a_2 = \Delta D / \Delta E_2$. The ratio of the coefficients gives the 'rate of exchange' between the effects:

$$a_1 / a_2 = (\Delta D / \Delta E_1) / (\Delta D / \Delta E_2) = \Delta E_2 / \Delta E_1 \qquad (6.9)$$

That is, the ratio of the coefficients shows how much a change in one effect is equivalent to a change in the other effect (according to the judgment of the decision-maker). So, if $a_1 = 1.0000$ and $a_2 = 6.8425$, then one unit of drinking measured by the Q–F index is equivalent to 0.1461 times being drunk. In this way, different units of effects can be made commensurate and combined into a single measure of effect.

The method just described used independent variables that were different categories of the same measure, i.e., an effect. The technique also applies when the independent variables are expressed in completely different measurement units. Say one variable is an effect, but the other is a cost or benefit variable measured in dollars. This second illustration of the method is interesting because it shows how effects can be measured in monetary terms.

Assume that the two independent variables consist of one effect E_1 and one monetary outcome variable Y, that is, changes in income. Income gained is a benefit and income lost is a cost. Again there is assumed to be a social decision-maker who chooses to approve or reject projects according to these two variables. The regression equation appears as:

$$D = a_0 + a_1 E_1 + a_2 Y \qquad (6.10)$$

where, as before, D is the decision which judges alcohol program effectiveness, and E_1 is changes in drinking, but the a_2 coefficient is now attached to the income variable. The regression coefficients are $a_1 = \Delta D / \Delta E_1$ and $a_2 = \Delta D / \Delta Y$. This time the ratio of the coefficients gives the rate of exchange between the effect and income:

$$a_1 / a_2 = (\Delta D / \Delta E_1) / (\Delta D / \Delta Y) = \Delta Y / \Delta E_1 \qquad (6.11)$$

The ratio of the coefficients shows how much a change in drinking is equivalent to a change in income. If $a_1 = 1.0000$ and $a_2 = 0.0485$, then one 1 unit of drinking measured by the Q–F index is equivalent to \$20.61. With $P = \$20.61$, one multiplies each unit of drinking reduction by this price to measure the benefits of the treatment program along the lines: $B = P \cdot E_1$. With the effect measured in dollars, it is now commensurable with costs and a CBA of an alcohol treatment program can be undertaken.

6.4   APPLICATIONS

We start with a CEA classic and proceed to applications of the three methods presented in section 6.3 for converting a CEA into a CBA.

6.4.1   A CEA of Deep-Vein Thrombosis

A perennial problem in medicine is whether it is better for a physician to make a diagnosis or whether it should be left to some 'objective' test. This was the focus of the Hull et al. (1981) study of testing patients with symptomatic deep-vein thrombosis. The effect was defined in terms of the number of patients correctly identified.

At the time, there were three main methods of diagnosis: clinical diagnosis, venography and impedance pletthysmography and leg scanning (IPG). These methods can be used on their own or in combination. Until the prior decade, clinical diagnosis was the most common method. Subsequently, venography became the standard method, but it is invasive and can cause pain and other side-effects. IPG is a non-invasive method. The fact that the three methods could have different detection rates makes this a suitable example of CEA rather than CM.

Because clinical examination was the starting point for all 516 patients, the cost of clinical examinations was not included in the analysis. Hull et al. made separate calculations for the US (New England) and Canada (Hamilton District). We present only the figures for the US. The cost of each diagnostic method was the direct cost of administering the diagnostic test plus the treatment associated with a positive test. The part of the treatment costs that involved hospitalization was measured as 'hotel' costs (as explained in Chapter 3). The total cost and number of correct diagnoses are shown in Table 6.4 (based on Hull et al.'s Tables 1 and 2, and Drummond et al.'s (1987) Table 3.1).

We can see in Table 6.4 that the average C/E ratio of \$3003 for IPG plus outpatient venography differs greatly from the \$4781 incremental ratio over IPG alone. The incremental ratio is the correct one because, compared to using IPG alone, one would be incurring an additional \$282 064 to detect an extra 59 cases correctly.

One advantage of using an incremental CEA can readily be seen from these results. Clinical diagnosis, which used to be the most preferred procedure, is completely dominated by diagnosis method 2. Effects are the same, but costs are higher with clinical diagnosis. In this case, there is no point in considering this diagnosis test further – it should be replaced by a more cost-effective procedure. Using the incremental approach makes this point explicit. For the incremental cost-effectiveness ratio for method 2 over 1 is infinite.

Table 6.4:   *Total costs and results of the alternative strategies to diagnose deep-vein thrombosis*

	Cost ($)	No. of correct diagnoses	Cost per correct diagnosis ($)
Diagnostic approach			
1. IPG alone	321 488	142	2264
2. IPG plus outpatient venography if IPG negative	603 522	201	3003
3. Clinical diagnosis	986 508	201	4908
Incremental analysis			
Method 2 – Method 1	282 064	59	4781
Method 3 – Method 2	382 956	0	Infinite

Source: Based on Hull et al. (1981)

The meaning of the incremental ratio is interesting in this study. Usually the increment is a difference between two programs. In this study, procedures were applied in an additive way. Hence, the incremental program 2 minus 1 was an actual program in its own right, i.e., the venography technique. Hence, the Hull et al. study highlights the fact that cost-effectiveness studies can be used to ascertain the cheapest order in which to apply screening techniques.

Another point that comes out of the Hull et al. study (and the Logan et al. paper) is that when one uses an input measure like the number of cases detected, one is effectively defining the effects contemporaneously with the costs. Thus, one does not need to use discounting on either the cost or the effect sides. This will not normally be the case, as we shall see in the next chapter.

6.4.2   An Estimate of the Cut-Off Ratio for a Hypothetical Serious Disease

Recall from section 6.3.1 that the cut-off ratio given by the Garber and Phelps model involves the cost-effectiveness ratio being equal to the ratio of the utility of income in the second period $U(Y_1)$ relative to the marginal utility from income in the first period $MU(Y_0)$. To use their method, then, one needs to specify both utility components.

Garber and Phelps assume a general functional form for the utility function and allow its particular shape to emerge by varying various parameters. The utility function they use has the form: $U(Y) = \beta (1 - e^{-\gamma Y})$, where β is a fixed parameter, e is the Napier constant 2.718 (the base of the natural logarithm system), and γ is a parameter measuring an individual's aversion to risk. The corresponding marginal utility of income function is: $MU(Y) = -\gamma \beta e^{-\gamma Y}$. The value for Y that appears as an exponent in both $U(Y)$ and $MU(Y)$ is the median *per capita* income in the USA of $18000 in 1989. (The values for β and γ used in the utility functions were not separately reported in the article.)

To help understand the essentials of what is being assumed, consider a simpler version of the marginal utility of income function. Set $\gamma = 1$ and $\beta = -1$ in the Garber and Phelps formulation. Then the marginal utility of income curve is represented by a standard exponential function of income Y of the form: $MU(Y) = e^{-Y}$. This curve is depicted in Figure 6.2 below.

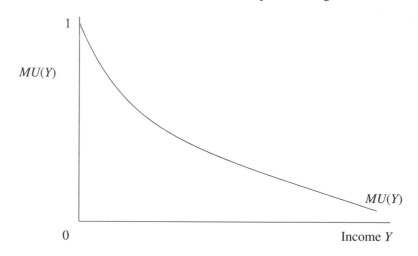

Note: The exponential function of the form e-^{Y} starts at 1 and declines smoothly until it approximates the horizontal axis when Y equals infinity. Its declining slope illustrates the principle of the diminishing marginal utility of income.

Figure 6.2:   *The exponential function depicting the diminishing marginal utility of income*

This curve starts with a $MU(Y)$ value of 1 and declines smoothly over the range of positive values of Y. The role of other variables (such as the risk aversion parameter) is to alter either the height of the curve or its slope. The falling slope signifies the assumption of diminishing marginal utility of income, i.e., the more (less) income one has, the less (more) one values additions to that income. Thus, the more one spends on health care in the first period, the less net income one has, and the higher will be $MU(Y)$ in that period. As $MU(Y_0)$ is on the denominator of equation (6.4), the higher its value the lower will be the cut-off cost-effectiveness ratio.

Garber and Phelps envisage the health program being for a very serious illness, such as cancer, where the probability of dying could be reduced by as much as 0.3. For such an illness, and on the basis of the utility function (and other assumptions), they construct estimates of: (1) the optimal cost-effectiveness ratio, and (2) the optimal amount of spending. Table 6.5 below (their Table 4) shows how these two estimates vary with the discount rate and the age of a person. The discount rates used are 0%, 2%, 5% and 10%. The table uses the discount factor $\delta = 1/(1+r)$ to express these four interest rates. (It is a two-period model, with discounting related to the second period only, so equation (2.6) with $t = 1$ produces the appropriate formula.) The figures relate to males. Estimates for females are similar, except that they are smaller because women have lower probabilities of dying and hence have less scope for reducing probabilities.

Table 6.5:   *Optimal spending and CE ratio: men, income = $18000*

Age	$\delta = 1$		$\delta = 0.98$		$\delta = 0.95$		$\delta = 0.91$	
	Spending ($)	CE ($)	Spending ($)	CE ($)	Spending ($)	CE ($)	Spending ($)	CE ($)
30	780	34560	320	35890	0	36870	0	36870
40	1000	33930	620	35020	150	36410	0	36870
50	1140	33520	850	34340	480	35430	0	36870
60	2000	31210	1780	31790	1480	32600	1060	33760
70	2260	30540	2110	30930	1900	31470	1590	32290

Source: Garber and Phelps (1997)

There are two main results of using the model that are illustrated in Table 6.5. First, optimal spending levels increase rapidly with age. This is because when one is young there is such a small probability of dying that a program designed to lower that probability would not lead to many extra years of life. Older people have higher probabilities of dying and hence more scope for lowering these probabilities. Second, the optimal cost-effectiveness ratio falls with increasing health spending. The reason is due to the diminishing marginal utility of income property pointed out earlier. That is, as health spending increases, net income declines, and the marginal utility of income rises, lowering the cut-off ratio.

Table 6.5 also shows that, although optimal spending does depend on the discount rate, the optimal cut-off rate is not sensitive to changes in the discount rate. The cut-off rates range from $30 540 to $36 800. In fact, the lowest value in any of the Garber and Phelps tables is $29 530 (and $36 800 is the largest). So the estimates cluster in a small range and can be called 'robust'. Seeing that the estimates shown in Table 6.5 were based on an income figure of $18 000, the authors concluded that the 'cutoff should be about double the annual income'.

6.4.3   Valuing State Expenditures on Mental Health Inpatient Episodes

Brent applied his MCF method to try to find an implicit US federal government valuation of state hospital expenditures on inpatient psychiatric care. The idea was that each state's expenditures would be treated as a potential federal program. With a fixed federal budget, one is trying to find out which of the state's expenditures one should approve on the basis of their cost-effectiveness ratios, in the form of the cost per episode.

The setting then is exactly like that envisaged by Weinstein in his description of the basic cost-effectiveness model as outlined in section 6.1.2. Following the CEA method, all the state cost per episode figures were estimated and the states were ranked in ascending order on this basis. Table 6.6 shows the state rankings, and the state total and cumulative cost figures for 1990. Wisconsin is the most cost-effective with a cost per episode of $1799. Pennsylvania is the least cost-effective with an episode cost of $43 000. To finance all 50 state expenditures (and Washington DC), the budget would need to be $7 billion.

The MCF method for valuing an effect was given in equation (6.7). It involves multiplying the cut-off cost-effectiveness ratio by the MCF. Since a federal government valuation was involved, Brent used the Ballard et al. (1995) estimate of the average MCF of taxes raised at the federal level, which was shown to be 1.246 in Table 5.1 (when rounded up). The cut-off ratio to be used would depend on the budget available.

Say the federally approved budget for psychiatric hospitals was $1 billion. This would be sufficient to fund the first 13 state expenditures, i.e., from Wisconsin to the District of Columbia. The cut-off ratio would be a cost of $8361 per episode. Multiplying this by 1.246 produces a valuation of $10 418. Or, if $4 billion were made available, Virginia would be the state where any new funds would be spent, at a cost of $15 817 per episode. Multiplying $15 817 by 1.246 produces a valuation of $19 708.

The logic of the method then is that the amount of the budget allocation would imply the valuation of an episode. Thus, if $4 billion were approved by the federal government to be spent on inpatient psychiatric care, this would only be the case if policy-makers valued an episode at $19 708, because that is the amount that the government values $15 817 of taxpayer funds.

Table 6.6:   Federal evaluation of state psychiatric hospital care

State	Cost per episode ($)	State total cost ($)	Cumulative cost ($)
Wisconsin	1799	47375450	47375450
Nevada	2478	27191268	74566718
Montana	3771	16825881	91392599
Missouri	4118	131517096	222909695
North Dakota	4628	12434779	235344474
South Dakota	5195	8056779	243401253
West Virginia	6743	18474860	261876113
Iowa	6761	40284997	302161111
New Mexico	6876	18698000	320859111
Nebraska	7310	35935334	356794445
Tennessee	7572	95141799	451936244
Texas	7753	249043665	700979909
District Columbia	8139	98113214	799093123
Georgia	8361	248813620	1047906743
Delaware	8441	24495200	1072401943
Kentucky	8514	63394461	1135796404
South Carolina	9107	113740450	1249536854
New Hampshire	9418	31597396	1281134250
Oklahoma	9476	60065841	1341200091
Illinois	10848	219694700	1560894791
North Carolina	11257	172413557	1733308348
Mississippi	11271	67076191	1800384539
Colorado	12029	75241733	1875626272
Wyoming	12160	12038754	1887665026
Kansas	13229	71952505	1959617531
Idaho	13412	10139200	1969756731
Oregon	14210	67623840	2037380571
New York	14221	1590298169	3627678740
Hawaii	14620	15336070	3643014810
Ohio	15497	257164288	3900179098
Virginia	15817	193906717	4094085815
Alaska	15965	15198350	4109284165
Louisiana	16669	73292879	4182577044
Minnesota	17520	103417839	4285994883
Maryland	17587	209461981	4495456854
Washington	18398	106101345	4601558209
Maine	19079	51016133	4652574342
Vermont	19222	10130069	4662704411
Indiana	19734	100680880	4763385291
New Jersey	19894	274222000	5037607291
Arkansas	22241	44260368	5081867659

Table 6.6 (cont.)

State	Cost per episode ($)	State total cost ($)	Cumulative cost ($)
Michigan	23050	368458825	5450326484
Alabama	23362	111202492	5561528976
Arizona	24224	30716067	5592245043
Massachusetts	26252	180638209	5772883252
Utah	29783	17869896	5790753148
Connecticut	30080	140806509	5931559657
Rhode Island	31329	23339773	5954899430
Florida	33408	213144114	6168043544
California	39626	395391000	6563434544
Pennsylvania	43772	451421000	7014855544

Source: Brent (2002)

6.4.4 Measuring the Effects and Benefits of Alcohol Treatment Programs

Including the no-treatment alternative in an evaluation is especially relevant to the case of alcohol treatment programs because its effects are so controversial. People *do* pass through treatment programs with positive effects in terms of reduced drinking. The problem is, according to one estimate by Fingarette (1988, p. 72), about one third of all heavy drinkers exhibit natural improvement. So drinking reductions observed after treatment programs have been completed may reflect this natural improvement rather than the effects of the program *per se*. As Vaillant (1983, p. 285) says, 'treatment as we currently understand it does not seem more effective than natural healing processes'.

It is in the context where difficult judgments about value parameters must be made (as with determining income distributional weights), or where key technical variables must be estimated for which the current state of knowledge is incomplete (as with the case of alcohol treatment effectiveness), that the revealed preference approach is especially useful in helping to make economic evaluations. Brent (1998b) used this approach in two ways in his study of alcohol treatment programs: (1) to derive measures of effects, as well as (2) trying to value these effects in monetary terms in order to convert them into measures of benefits.

A sample was taken of 1689 program effectiveness judgments from the National Alcoholism Program Information System (NAPIS) tapes for the period 1977–81. The first issue was whether one could uncover the basis (the determinants) of these judgments. That is, could one find out exactly why some individuals had outcomes that the evaluator thought constituted an effective treatment while other individual outcomes were classed as ineffective? Many different types of effect (behavioral improvements from entry into a program compared to six months later) existed in the data set. The effects that were unlikely to have occurred by chance (were 'statistically significant') are listed in column (1) of Table 6.7 (which combines Brent's Tables 3 and 4).

Table 6.7: Determinants of decisions concerning alcohol treatment effectiveness

Change in behavioral variable	Usual units	Impact in usual units	Impact in standard units	Monetary value per unit
(1)	(2)	(3)	(4)	(5)
Beer consumption	Beer Q–F index	0.001422	1.0000	$20.61
Times drunk	No. per month	0.009730	6.8425	$141.02
Times missed meal	No. per month	0.004082	2.8706	$59.16
Drinking on the job	Category change	0.104061	73.1793	$1508.12
Non-driving arrests	Category change	0.081281	57.1596	$1226.75
Income	Dollars per month	0.000069	0.0485	$1.00

Source: Brent (1998b)

Column (3) shows the impact of a usual unit of a category on effectiveness (being the coefficients of a regression equation). For purpose of direct comparison, these coefficients are all expressed in column (4) in terms of a common unit, i.e., units of the beer Q–F index. Thus, for example, with the first coefficient 0.001422 rescaled to be 1.0000, the number of times drunk's coefficient of 0.009730 (being 6.8425 larger than 0.001422) becomes rescaled as 6.8425. As explained in the discussion of equation (6.9), this also means that a beer Q–F unit is equivalent to 0.1462 days of drinking on the job (being the reciprocal of 6.8425).

The key to the second issue, how to value the effects in monetary units, lies in the units that the effect of the income variable had. It was in dollar terms. By relating its coefficient to the coefficient of any other effect, one can find equivalent impacts on the decision-maker and hence equivalent changes in units, along the lines of equation (6.11). Consider the impact of the effect involving the number of times a person was drunk. Each occasion that this was reduced, the impact on the decision-maker amounted to 6.8425 standard units. A dollar's worth of extra monthly income earned had an impact on the decision-maker of 0.0485 standard units. Since the reduction in being drunk had a 141.02 times larger impact, it follows that a unit reduction in being drunk must be worth 141.02 times more than a $1 rise in income. Of course, 141.02 times a dollar is simply $141.02. This equivalence and those for all the other effects are shown in column (5).

The usefulness of Table 6.7 for making economic evaluations is immediately apparent. Say one wishes to compare the cost-effectiveness of program 1, where the main effect is a reduction in the Q–F index, with another program 2, where the effect is a reduction in the number of times a person becomes drunk. A standard CEA cannot make the comparison because the units are different. However, if every time a person is drunk is multiplied by 6.8425, both programs have effects in equivalent Q–F units and their ratios relative to costs would be comparable. Alternatively, either program could be evaluated as a CBA. Every unit in program 1 can be multiplied by a price of $20.61 and every unit in program 2 can be multiplied by a price of $141.02 to form the benefits of the programs. Costs can now be deducted and the overall worth of the programs determined.

6.5   FINAL SECTION

We continue with the problems, summary and looking ahead sections.

6.5.1   Problems

Doubilet et al. (1986) surveyed a number of CEAs and found that the phrase 'cost-effective' was very loosely applied in medical publications. They claim that, 'communication would be improved with less frequent and more precise use of this term'. The following questions each work with a different interpretation of the term that Doubilet et al. suggest and explore their implications if they are used as an evaluation criterion. The data in Table 6.8 (their Table 1) relate to the costs and effects of alternative intervals of screening for cervical cancer using Pap smear tests.

1.   Assume that cost-effective means 'saving costs'. Would any screening take place? Why or why not?
2.   Next, define cost-effective as meaning 'effective'. Which screening intervals would pass this test?
3.   Frequently the implied meaning of 'cost-effective' in medical applications is that there is 'cost saving, with an equal (or better) health outcome'. Why would it be impossible to compare any pair of screening strategies using this definition?
4.   Lastly, take cost-effective to mean 'having an additional effect worth

Table 6.8: *Effects and costs of screening for cervical cancer using the Pap smear*

Interval between Pap smears (years)	Increase in life expectancy (days)	Program cost ($)
1	67.08	315.10
2	64.55	149.39
3	61.56	95.61
4	58.00	69.65
5	53.99	54.54

Source: Doubilet et al. (1986)

the additional cost'. How does the choice of screening strategy depend on the amount of money one is willing to pay for each additional year of life?

6.5.2 Summary

A marginal analysis looks to see how much extra costs would be involved with an extension of a particular program. An incremental analysis looks to see how much extra costs would be involved with satisfying extra output by switching to some alternative program. It is with incremental analyses that CEA is most concerned.

The underlying CEA model requires a fixed budget constraint. Then programs are ranked in ascending order, and approved, until the budget is exhausted. The C/E ratio of the last program approved provides the benchmark for a possible new program. The incremental ratio of the new program must be lower than the benchmark in order to replace the last program previously approved. In order to calculate the incremental ratio for the new program, it is important that the no-program alternative be considered. This alternative need not involve zero costs and effects.

CEA is problematic when there is no set budget constraint or if there are multiple effects that are generated by the program to degrees different from the alternatives. Also, even when one does ensure that the least costly alternative is approved, there is no guarantee that this alternative is socially worthwhile. So, in both the theory and the applications sections we concentrated on possible methods for converting CEAs into CBAs.

One can use a method that focuses on the demand side and works with marginal utilities. Or one can use a method that operates on the supply side that relies on the MCF to record the opportunity cost of the dollar generating the effects. Finally we introduced a general approach to estimation that measured the revealed preferences of decision-makers. To use this approach all one needs is information on program evaluator decisions and measured patient outcomes. Revealed preference values are not necessarily the 'correct' values. But they are values based on actual experience that help firm up one's convictions about what are the correct values. If past values are thought to be too low or too high for any reason, one at least knows a starting value from which to begin setting new parameter estimates and ensuring that one is at least moving in the right direction towards correct values.

6.5.3   Looking Ahead

This chapter established the fundamentals of CEA. There are some technical issues that we did not cover. We mentioned that discounting was not an issue when effects are measured by inputs, as this usually meant that costs and effects were considered in current year terms. But we did not discuss in general whether effects being in different units from costs led to problems for discounting. Nor did we deal with the problem of how to allow for sampling error involved with generating average cost and effect estimates. These two issues form the subject matter of the next chapter.

7. Further issues of cost-effectiveness analysis

7.1 INTRODUCTION

Although economists are unanimous in adopting discounting for costs, there is no such widespread agreement in the health care field for discounting effects. If costs are discounted and effects are left undiscounted, obviously C/E ratios would be radically altered. Even when discounting of effects is accepted, not everyone agrees that the discount rate on effects should be the same as that used for costs. The second section addresses these issues. From there we proceed to a second main theme, i.e., how do CEAs need to be conducted and interpreted when the values that we use for C and E are average ones that may come from a sample with a large amount of sampling variation? Our first task is to cover some background issues concerning these two themes.

7.1.1   When is Discounting Especially Needed?

Discounting is particularly important for screening or preventative programs for which the costs are immediate, but the health effects are in the future. Otherwise, as Viscusi (1995) points out, discounting is important when health effects are cumulative (diet or exercise programs) and/or occur with a lag (cigarette smoking). Any major surgery has long-term effects that require discounting. Environmental effects affect future generations (e.g., Taxol used in treatment for cancer comes from the bark of Pacific Yew trees and thus the stock of these trees gets depleted when the Taxol drug is manufactured). Drug companies must invest years in research and supervised testing of drugs before being able to market them.

7.1.2   Uncertainty and Economic Evaluations

In our prior discussion of the Logan et al. (1981) study of hypertension and the worksite treatment program (see Tables 1.2 and 6.3), we reported the total cost of treatment for the WS program as \$242.86 per patient, being the sum of health system costs of $197.36 and patient costs of $45.50. Although these numbers were used to form the cost-effectiveness ratios appearing in the study, a prior table in Logan et al. reported these figures slightly differently. The health system costs were listed as $197.36 ± 4.99, and the patients' costs as $45.50 ± 3.23. The meaning of these ± adjustments is that the costs should really be considered to be a range of values, that is, *an interval estimate*, rather than a particular value, *a point estimate*. The interval estimates translate into $192.37–$202.35 for health system costs and $42.27–$48.73 for patient costs.

Interval estimates are possible whenever data on individual persons or cases are available. Once one recognizes the existence of sampling variation that generates these confidence intervals, cost-effectiveness ratios now are not so simple to interpret. Differences may have occurred by chance (be statistically insignificant) and thus may not indicate more cost-effective interventions.

7.2   DISCOUNTING IN CEA

7.2.1   The Rate of Discount and Economic Theory

In the health care field one usually uses market prices to value effects. Why not use the market rate of interest as the discount rate? There are two types of reason: there are capital market imperfections (e.g., taxes and regulation) that greatly impact market interest rates; and individual decision-making limitations. Here we will expand on the second type of reason and then deal with the first type.

Usually, one can assume that individuals are the best judges of their own welfare. But Pigou (1920) has argued that, for inter-temporal choices, the individual suffers from myopia, i.e., the individual has a 'defective telescopic faculty'. There are three main reasons why individuals could be considered to be myopic:

1. Individuals may be irrational. They are irrational because they do not have sufficient experience in making such long-range planning choices.
2. Individuals do not have sufficient information. In order to make sensible inter-temporal choices they need to compare lifetime income with lifetime consumption.
3. Individuals die, even though societies do not. Mortality rates give lower bounds to an individualistic discount rate (sometimes called the 'pure' time preference rate).

If one finds these myopia arguments unconvincing, or dismisses them as they imply following decision-making rules that would be undemocratic, one still faces numerous practical problems in using market interest rates. People who save the funds receive as interest a rate that is very different from the rates that investors can earn by using the funds. Capital and income taxes drive a wedge between the two rates. So there is not just one market rate of interest to consider even if one confines attention to riskless rates of interest. One could try to take an average of all the investor and savings rates. But what should be done when savings rates (after allowing for inflation) turn out in many years to be negative?

The biggest problem with trying to use actual interest rates is, even if there were just one rate observed in financial markets, that rate would not be a private market rate of interest reflecting demand and supply. In modern economies, the largest saver and investor in private capital markets is the government itself. Interest rates therefore reflect government macro economic and monetary policy. For example, domestic interest rates determine rates of inflation, private real investment and foreign capital flows. Governments intervene with interest rates to try to influence all these considerations.

The concept that indicates what part of a dollar society is willing to give up tomorrow in order to have the use of that dollar today is called the 'social time preference rate' (STPR). This is the primary concept for fixing the discount rate because it records project impacts that occur at different time periods. Rates of return that the private sector gives up in order to provide funds for the government are important when assessing the value of a dollar's worth of capital relative to a dollar's worth of consumption. However, these rates of return do not directly record inter-temporal preferences, which is the information that we are seeking. The STPR concept is wider than that of an individual's time preference rate. It can include factors that many individuals ignore, such as a concern for future generations.

We will now explain how the STPR is usually constructed. The language is in terms of valuing income at different time periods. But the key aspect is that these valuations relate to units that are in dollar terms. In a CEA, costs are in monetary units. So we initially designate the STPR as the discount rate for costs, denoted as i_C.

There are two factors to be incorporated into the STPR. Future generations will be richer than the current generation due to a probable positive growth rate of per capita income g. Because of this, society would (if it were concerned with intergenerational equity) value $1's worth of future income less than $1's worth of income today (since today's people are less well off). Define by η society's aversion to income inequality, where $\eta = 0$ reflects no aversion and $\eta = \infty$ signifies maximum aversion to inequality. The extent to which future generations will be richer (given by g) and the extent to which we downgrade a \$1's worth of income by the rich relative to the poor (given by η) are the two ingredients in the STPR. The discount rate can be determined by multiplying these two factors as follows:

$$i_C = \eta.g \qquad (7.1)$$

So if h were fixed at 2, and g was found to be 3%, the STPR would be 6%. How to estimate η will be discussed in Chapter 13. Typically, following the lead of Squire and van der Tak (1975), who devised a methodology for economic evaluation for World Bank projects, η is set equal to unity. So the main determinant of the STPR is the growth rate of the economy.

A discount rate for effects, i.e., i_E can be derived in a similar fashion to that for costs: see Brent (1993). CEAs often use mortality as a measure of effect in terms of the impact of an intervention on a person's life expectancy (see the last case study in this chapter). How society values an extra year in the future relative to a year today can be called the 'life expectancy discount rate' (LEDR).

Just like the high likelihood that society in the future will be richer than today's in terms of income, one can expect that future generations will also live longer than today's generation and thus be 'richer' in terms of time (the number of years of life available). The LEDR will depend on how many extra years future generations have and the rate to which extra years are devalued. Define by λ the growth rate of life expectancy and denote by α society's aversion to inequality of life expectancies. Then the LEDR will be determined by the product:

$$i_E = \alpha.\lambda \qquad (7.2)$$

Brent argues for a value of $\alpha = 1$ on the grounds of intergenerational equity, which leaves the growth rate of life expectancies as the main determinant of the LEDR.

7.2.2 Discounting of Benefits in Cost-Effectiveness Studies

Should benefits be discounted as well as costs? The fundamental reason for discounting non-monetary benefits as well as monetary costs is one of consistency. There are a number of aspects to this consistency requirement. Some aspects relate to logical consistency, and others relate to consistency of choice.

Logical consistency

When costs and benefits are both in monetary terms, everyone agrees that one discounts the benefits as well as the costs. If one discounted only the costs, one would make irrational decisions. For example, if the discount rate were 10% and the investment choice involved giving up $110 next year in order to get $105 next year, not discounting the benefits would mean accepting the investment even though one is losing $5 by doing so. The investment would be accepted because the present value of the $110 costs would be $100, which is 5 less than the (undiscounted) benefits of $105. Given this, why should matters be different just because effects are in non-monetary terms?

Actually, people *do* argue that matters are different when effects are in non-monetary terms. But these are not good arguments. (1) It is claimed that, unlike with the cost side where people do trade resources over time, health effects cannot be traded. This is wrong because a person *is* often able to trade off non-monetary activities today for health in the future by, for example, abstaining from smoking. (2) It is claimed that, unlike with the cost side where society discounts because future generations are richer than today's generation, health effects by not being in dollar terms are not affected by the future generations being richer. This is wrong on two grounds. If future generations are richer they can spend more on health than today's generation. Moreover, future generations will probably be healthier because of technological advances in medicine. The point is that if one is concerned with the distribution of income over time (seeing that the future generation will be richer) one should (on logical consistency grounds) also be concerned with the distribution of health over time (seeing that future generations will also be healthier).

Weinstein and Stason (1977) argue that, aside from intergenerational fairness, health effects should be discounted like dollar costs. The reason is that effects (what they call 'non-monetary benefits') are being valued relative to the dollar costs. If dollar costs are discounted, then health effects need to be discounted in order to preserve the desired relation between costs and effects. To see this, assume that costs are discounted at 5%, and consider two programs A and A3. Consult Table 7.1 below.

Programs A and A3 have the same monetary cost today, but A has effects 40 years in the future, while A3 has 1/7 of these effects today. Consider these equivalencies:

1. A is equivalent to A1, seeing that costs are discounted, and the present value of $70000 in Year 40 at 5% is $10000.
2. A1 is equivalent to A2, if one assumes that life years are valued the same in relation to costs no matter the year one is in.

Table 7.1:   *Programs with varying timing of costs and benefits*

Program	Dollar cost	Non-monetary benefit
A	$10000 now	1 year of life expectancy in Year 40
A1	$70000 in Year 40	1 year of life expectancy in Year 40
A2	$70000 now	1 year of life expectancy now
A3	$10000 now	1/7th year of life expectancy now

Source: Weinstein and Stason (1977)

3. A2 is equivalent to A3, seeing that both costs and effects in A2 have merely been divided by 7 to form A3.
4. Thus, A is equivalent to A3.

Note that A3 is just A with the benefits discounted at 5%. So, when one assumes a constancy between the value of a unit of effects with that of a dollar of costs over time, one is effectively requiring that benefits be discounted as well as costs (seeing that costs are being discounted).

Unfortunately, the assumption that one keeps constancy between the value of a unit of effect with that of a dollar of costs over time is quite a strong assumption. Van Hout (1998) has shown that to make A1 equivalent to A2 one is effectively assuming $i_C = i_E$. This is easy to understand from the specifications of these two rates given by equations (7.1) and (7.2). Ignoring the inequality aversion parameters (or simply setting both equal to 1), we see that both rates are determined by their respective growth rates. So say today society holds that 1 unit of effect is equivalent to 1 dollar of cost. This relation will hold in 40 years' time only if one is as wealthy in terms of income as one is in terms of life years. For this to happen, the growth rate of income must have equaled the growth rate in life years. And from the specification of the two discount rates, this means that $i_C = i_E$.

What remains of this consistency argument is that, if one assumes that the discount rate for effects is equal to the discount rate for costs, and the discount rate for costs is positive, then one must also discount effects at a positive rate.

Consistency of choice
Keeler and Cretin (1983) point out that the whole decision-making process could break down completely when benefits are not discounted. This occurs whenever it is possible to delay programs and achieve the same total of undiscounted benefits and costs. A good example of this situation is presented by the authors. Say there is a program to implement a healthy diet among school age children. When the program is delayed a year, the program will apply to

a different population. But, viewed from the perspective of the cohort served by each program, the costs and benefits will have the same time profile.

The problem is this. By delaying the program one year, total benefits (which are undiscounted) would be unaffected. But costs come later in the delayed program. So, the cost-effectiveness ratio of a delayed program is always greater than if the program were implemented today. As a consequence, no program would ever be implemented. One would always be waiting till next year. Thus Keeler and Cretin say that, *not* to discount the benefits would in these circumstances have 'a paralyzing effect on the decision-maker'. To see this clearly, consider Table 7.2. Total effects are 500 whether the program is delayed or not. Since costs are discounted, their timing is important. If the discount rate is 5%, the present value of the costs when the program is implemented today is 295, and when delayed 1 year is 281. The C/E ratio falls from 0.59 to 0.56 by delaying the program 1 year.

Table 7.2: *Programs with a delayed timing of costs and effects*

Program	Costs ($)			Effects		
	Now	Year 1	Year 2	Now	Year 1	Year 2
Implemented today	200	100	0	300	200	0
Delayed 1 year	0	200	100	0	300	200

Source: Created by the author relating to Keeler and Cretin (1983)

Van Hout also questions this consistency argument. He notes that in the Keeler and Cretin analysis the program stops after the second year. This is why in Table 7.2 there are no effects and costs in the second year if the program were implemented today. He shows that if one has recurring effects and costs, and if the basis of comparison is to implement the program, call it A, over some other existing program, call it B, then the discounted C/E ratio for A over B is exactly the same as for comparing doing A over implementing A next year. However, even in van Hout's analysis, he has the C/E ratio lower for implementing A next year over B (relative to doing A now over B). So waiting a year still dominates. Only if the choice is politically or administratively restricted to A versus B, and excludes waiting a year versus B, would the Keeler and Cretin paradox disappear.

7.2.3 Should Effects be Discounted at the Same Rate as Costs?

Weinstein and Stason's analysis also indicates when effects and costs should be discounted at different rates. Recall that the argument for discounting effects arose because (in Table 7.1) it was assumed that the opportunities for purchasing health benefits do not change over time. Thus, if $70000 could buy one year of life expectancy in Year 40, under A1, then this should also be true now, under A2. If it is expected that medical technology will change in the future so that it becomes cheaper to save a year of life, then A2 would be less valuable than A1. Effects would then have to be discounted higher than costs (effects being more abundant in the future). The opposite is also true. If it becomes technologically more expensive to save lives in the future, the discount rate for effects would be lower. This would also be true if society values lives higher in the future and is willing to pay more than $70000 for one year of life.

A useful way of thinking about this issue is to consider Viscusi's (1995, p. 130) argument that when productivity increases (by a rate g), then the discount rate should be the regular rate r minus the productivity rate g. This is like saying that the higher productivity in the future changes the technical possibilities of converting dollars into lives saved. The only difference is that Viscusi sees it as a demand effect (higher productivity raises income, and higher income raises the demand for health proportionally when the income elasticity for health is unity as he estimated) while with Weinstein and Stason this would be more a supply side (technological) effect.

If for any reason one wishes to discount effects *lower* than costs, one runs into a version of Keeler and Cretin's problem stated earlier. Delaying any program with positive effects lowers the C/E ratio. If one can delay the program long enough (and not affect total effects), one can ensure that the C/E ratio is lower than for the best program initiated now. The best current program could only be initiated provided that there were sufficient funds to cover the program after setting aside funds to finance the delayed programs with a lower C/E ratio. Even so, we would have the inconsistency that current programs would be put to a more stringent test than for future programs.

The overall conclusion of this section is that effects should be discounted, and at the same rate (or higher) than the rate on costs.

7.2.4 Recommended Discount Rates

Drummond et al. (1987, p. 52) present these criteria for choosing the discount rate, and setting the range for a sensitivity analysis:

1. They should be consistent with economic theory (2% to 10%).
2. They should include any government recommended rates (5%, 7%, 10%).
3. They should include rates that have been used in other published studies to which you wish to compare results.

4. They should be consistent with 'current practice' (5% often has been
    used in papers in the *New England Journal of Medicine*).

More recently, a US government panel was set up to come up with recommendations concerning the appropriate use of CEA in health (which we
will cover in more detail in the next chapter). The book that summarized
the panel's findings, by Gold et al. (1996), argued for a single discount rate
to be used for both costs and effects. Although 5% was the rate most often
used in CEAs, 3% is the discount rate that they recommended (with 5%
being the main alternative rate used in a sensitivity analysis). They chose
3% for a number of reasons, the main one being that they wanted to
measure the time preference rate and used for this the observed (net of
inflation) rate on riskless, long-term securities. They recommended that
rates in the range 0% to 7% be used in sensitivity analyses. 'The lower bound
provides the social decision maker with insights into the effects of discounting by showing what happens in its absence; the upper bound represents a
reasonable (if not liberal) ceiling on the real consumption rate of interest
in current markets.'

7.3 SAMPLING ERROR AND UNCERTAINTY ABOUT ESTIMATES

First we look at sampling error for a single variable, i.e., costs, and then
look at sampling error when both costs and effects are involved.

7.3.1 Sampling Error and Statistical Theory

We begin the analysis by summarizing basic statistical theory regarding distributions of values for a single variable (refer to any introductory text,
such as Weiers (1998)). Any variable's distribution of values can be summarized by two measures: first, a measure of central tendency, and second
a measure of dispersion around that central tendency. We will focus on the
average (mean) as the measure of central tendency and the *variance* as a
measure of dispersion. To calculate the mean for a variable X, denoted $\bar{X}$,
one sums all the values X_i and divides by the number of observations N:

$$\text{Mean: } \bar{X} = X = \frac{\sum X_i}{N} \tag{7.3}$$

The variance is defined as the average of the squared residuals (deviations
of a value from the mean):

$$\text{Variance:} \frac{\sum (X_i - \bar{X})_2}{N-1} \qquad (7.4)$$

Note that in samples (for statistical reasons) the average of the squared deviations for the variance divides the sum by $N-1$ (and not just N as with the mean). In order to express the measure of dispersion in units that are comparable to the mean, statisticians often replace the variance by its square root, called the *standard deviation*:

$$\text{Standard deviation} = \sqrt{} \ (\text{Variance}) \qquad (7.5)$$

Table 7.3 gives a simple illustration of how the summary measures are calculated for two interventions, the experimental and the control, for a pair of three-person groups. For convenience the individuals are ranked from lowest cost to highest cost. From Table 7.3, one can see why the residuals need to be squared in equation (7.2). The sum of deviations from the mean (as shown in column 3) is always equal to zero. Its value would be the same no matter the shape of the distribution. Table 7.3 shows that the experimental group has the lower average costs, but it also has the higher dispersion. What this means is that, although the experimental treatment seems to have lower costs, there is a great deal more uncertainty about this result. Perhaps

Table 7.3:   Programs with costs that vary by individuals

Program	Costs per person ($) (C_i)	Residual $(C_i - \bar{C})$	Residual squared $(C_i - \bar{C})^2$
Control			
Person 1	100	−120	14440
Person 2	200	−20	400
Person 3	360	140	19600
Total	660	0	34440
Mean $\bar{C}$	220		
Standard deviation	131		
Experimental			
Person 1	40	−160	25600
Person 2	100	−100	10000
Person 3	460	260	67600
Total	600	0	103200
Mean $\bar{C}$	200		
Standard deviation	227		

Source: Created by the author

there are more people like person 3 around, whose costs of $460 are over twice the average.

The way that information about the dispersion is factored into judgments about the average is through the concept of a *confidence interval* around the mean. An interval is just a range of consecutive values. What makes an interval for a mean a confidence interval is that one has to be able to tell the probability that the mean lies within that range. For example, one may know that there is a 95% probability that the mean is within this range. Obviously, the greater the probability, the less uncertainty one has about a particular mean's true value. The confidence interval is determined by:

$$\text{Confidence interval for the mean: } \overline{X} \pm Z \text{ (standard error)} \quad (7.6)$$

where Z is a number, typically between 1 and 3, and the *standard error* can often be assumed to be equal to the standard deviation divided by the square root of the sample size:

$$\text{Standard error: Standard deviation}/\sqrt{N} \quad (7.7)$$

The sample size is on the denominator because, the larger the sample we take, the more reliable will be the estimate from the sample and the narrower the confidence interval.

The number Z is determined by two considerations: (1) the error that one is willing to accept and (2) the assumed shape of the distribution of values for likely values for X. If one is willing to accept a 5% chance of accepting a wrong value for the mean (one has 95% confidence in the value of an estimate), and if the distribution of mean values is assumed to be what statisticians call 'normal' (i.e., a bell-shaped, symmetric curve), then the corresponding Z value (now properly called a 'Z-score') would be 1.96.

For Z values of 1.96, with means and standard deviations as in Table 7.3, and a sample size of $N=3$ (which means that its square root is 1.73), the confidence interval for costs for the experimental group would be $200 \pm 1.96\,(131.21)$ or between $-$57 and $457. With such a wide interval, the mean of $200 is very unreliable, as the value could with 95% confidence even be as high as $457 (or even negative which is not economically possible). One would not have much confidence that the experimental group had costs $20 less than the control group. (If one used the appropriate statistical formula, one could find the exact probability of observing no difference in the two sample means (the answer is around 90%; it is very probable).)

Before leaving this section, we can use the confidence interval concept to define precisely the statement made in the last chapter (in the context of regression coefficients in Table 6.7) that some estimates were unlikely to have occurred by chance, i.e., were 'statistically significant'. If one forms a 95% confidence interval around finding a zero estimate, say the range is from -20 to $+20$, and one actually comes up with an estimate of 25, then one can say with 95% certainty that the estimate of 25 is unlikely to have been 0. The value 25 is not in the confidence interval around zero and this is what makes this particular estimate *statistically, significantly different from zero*.

7.3.2   Sampling Error and Cost-Effectiveness Ratios

We have just seen that a costs estimate may have a confidence interval around it indicating a range of uncertainty about its precise value. The same logic applies to any estimate of effects. It will also have a confidence interval around its mean value. This means that when we try to form the ratio C/E we will come up with a whole set of alternatives to the average estimate $\overline{C}/\overline{E}$ which was the outcome measure we were dealing with in the last chapter.

Following O'Brien et al. (1994), let us call the lower and upper bounds of a costs confidence interval C_U and C_L, respectively, and the lower and upper bounds of an effects confidence interval E_U and E_L respectively. Then the extreme bounds for the cost-effective ratio can be formed from the extreme values of the two intervals as follows: the highest value for the ratio would pair the highest costs estimate C_U with the lowest effects estimate E_L to form C_U/E_L; and the lowest value for the ratio would pair the lowest costs estimate C_L with the highest effects estimate E_U to form C_L/E_U. The result is that there is now a range of ratios for any intervention in which $\overline{C}/\overline{E}$ lies, from C_L/E_U to C_U/E_L.

In the same way as for the average ratio for a single intervention, one can construct the lower and upper bounds for the incremental cost-effectiveness ratio for the outcomes of an experimental group T over a control group C. The incremental ratio for costs and effects would be defined as: $\Delta C/\Delta E = (C_T - C_C)/(E_T - E_C)$. Using this definition, the incremental ratio for average costs and effects would be: $\Delta \overline{C}/\Delta \overline{E}$; the lower bound ratio would be $\Delta C^L/\Delta E^U$; and the upper bound ratio would be $\Delta C^L/\Delta E^U$. Figure 7.1, based on O'Brien et al.'s Figure 2, depicts these three ratios graphically.

The result of there being sampling variation is that the incremental cost-effectiveness ratio is unlikely to be a single, unique value. The average ratio given as the slope of 0b in Figure 7.1 is just one possibility. The ratio could be, plausibly, any value between the slope of 0a and 0c. This means that, even if one does come up with the result that the average ratio is lower than the cut-off ratio that emerges from the marginal program in a past cost-effectiveness allocation, the upper ratio may not be lower. Uncertainty in estimation leads to outcome indecisiveness.

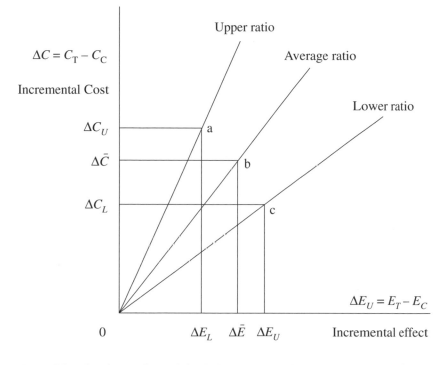

Note: When there is sampling variation in both costs and effects, there is not just a single, average ratio $\Delta\bar{C}/\Delta\bar{E}$ to consider. One can combine the lower bound value for the difference in costs with an upper bound value for the difference in effects to obtain a lower bound for the incremental ratio. Alternatively, one can pair the upper bound value for the difference in costs with a lower bound value for the difference in effects to produce an upper bound for the incremental ratio. The diagram shows that the incremental cost-effectiveness ratio could be any value between the slope of the line 0a and the slope of line 0c. The average ratio given as the slope of line 0b is just one possibility.

Figure 7.1:   *Incremental cost-effectiveness ratios with sampling variation in costs and effects*

It is important to understand that the lower and upper bounds for the ratios represented in Figure 7.1 need not have the same probability associated with them as the bounds for a particular probability confidence interval applied to incremental costs or effects separately. For example, if the lower bound of a 95% confidence interval for incremental costs is combined with the upper bound of a 95% confidence interval for incremental effects, the ratio of these two values that forms the lower bound ratio for the incremental cost-effectiveness ratio need not be the least value for a 95% confidence interval for ratios. In particular, as O'Brien et al. emphasize, if the two distributions are independent, then the probability of being at the lower bound of both the costs and effects distribution at the same time would be less than 5%. More generally, one should expect that costs and effects would be related and thus it is the joint probability that one needs to estimate.

This distinction between joint and separate distributions of costs and effects helps explain Siegel et al.'s (1996) point that the average of each person's C/E ratio is not in general the same as $\overline{C}/\overline{E}$. Some simple numbers demonstrate this. If three individuals' costs are $3, $4 and $6 and their respective effects are 1, 2 and 6, then the average of the individual C/E ratios (i.e., $3, $2 and $1) is $2; while the average of the costs (i.e., $2) divided by the average of the effects (i.e., 3) is only $0.67.

The question then arises as to which measure should be used, the average of the individual ratios or the ratio of the averages. Once again, the answer is straightforward if one takes the societal perspective for evaluation that we have been advocating all along. In this context it is the total effects that we get from the fixed budget that is important. Thus, by using the ratio of the averages, one would be maximizing the effects per dollar invested. In terms of the numbers assumed in the previous paragraph, the budget of $6 would 'buy' 9 effects. This is the most that the $6 could obtain. The average is $6/9, or $0.67 per effect, which is exactly the ratio of the averages $2/3.

However, Siegel et al. argue that the individual C/E ratios may be the preferred measure for those who are responsible for most of the costs (the patients), for those who act as their agents (their physicians), or for those concerned with the efficient production of health (the cost-producing provider). When the focus is on individual ratios, then the relationship between individual effects and individual costs needs to be allowed for in the estimation of the confidence intervals associated with the average cost-effectiveness ratio. Although it is not possible to estimate directly the variance of any ratio, such as C/E, several recent contributions in the literature have suggested indirect statistical methods of estimating confidence intervals for individual ratios (that use approximations or rely on transformations) and have applied their methods to actual data (see, for example, Gardiner et al. (1995), Willan and O'Brien (1996), and Lasker et al. (1997)).

7.4   APPLICATIONS

7.4.1   Individual Discount Rates in the Choice of Industry of Employment

Moore and Viscusi (1988) adopted the revealed preference approach to find estimates of the implicit discount rates that individuals used when deciding which industry to work in. Certain industries are riskier to work in than others. Individuals are willing to work in these industries only if they are compensated for the additional risk by having higher wages. The impact of the risk depends on how many years of life the individual has remaining once this has been discounted. The risk from working in an industry is thus measured by:

$$\text{Expected Life Years Lost} = (\text{Death Risk}) \times (\text{Discounted Remaining Life Years})$$

Say a worker has 20 years of life remaining. If the discount rate the individual uses is 5%, then this would equate to a present value of 12.6 years (assuming continuous discounting). With a 1 in 20000 probability of dying due to the riskiness of the job, the expected life years lost would be 0.00063, or 5.5 hours. The object was to see how large a wage increase the worker would demand in order to compensate for forgoing these 5.5 hours of life. The estimating equation thus took the form:

$$\text{Wage rate} = \alpha_1 \,(\text{Expected Life Years Lost}) + \alpha_2 \,(\text{Other Variables}) \quad (7.8)$$

In the measure of lifetime exposure to job risk (expected life years lost) the discount rate was used to convert the life remaining to present value terms. Moore and Viscusi used a technique that allowed the discount rate to be calculated as part of the estimation process for the wage equation. The results are recorded in Table 7.4. We have listed the weighted estimates for the statistically significant variables in their Table III.

Table 7.4: *Wage equation estimates*

Independent variable	Coefficient estimate	Standard error
Discount rate	0.122	0.043
Expected life years lost	17.732	5.880
Sex (female or not)	−0.273	0.068
College degree	0.123	0.062
Firm size	0.000049	0.000019
Blue-collar occupation	−0.148	0.043
Union status	0.145	0.042
Expected annuity	−0.0024	0.0008
Lost workday accident rate	0.058	0.014
Lost workday accident rate X replacement rate	−0.055	0.013

Source: Based on Moore and Viscusi (1988)

The dependent variable is the net of tax wage rate expressed in logarithms. This means that the regression coefficients can be interpreted in terms of percentages. Thus the discount rate estimate is 12.2%. The lifetime exposure to risk was significantly different from zero (at the 95% confidence level). The 'other variables' in equation (7.8) were: sex (females get 27% lower wages); education (those with a college degree earn 12% more); firm size (larger firms pay more); type of job (blue-collar workers get paid 13% less); membership in a union (there is a 14% premium on being in a union); death benefits (those with death insurance get lower wages); and accident risk is important in addition to death risk.

To aid the discussion of the discount rate estimate, let us first construct the 95% confidence interval for it. The standard error is 4.3%. From equation (7.6) with $Z = 1.96$, we get the range 12.2% ± 8.4%, or between 3.8% and 21%. Moore and Viscusi state that: 'The percent confidence interval for rates of discount is restricted to generally plausible values.' Based on this interval, they find that one can reject both extreme positions, that workers do not discount (zero is not in the interval estimate) or are myopic (have infinite discount rates).

From the point of view of the discount rate theory developed in this chapter, it is interesting how Moore and Viscusi interpret the test of whether $i_C = i_E$. They interpret it to be a test of worker rationality. They take the 12% estimate and add the 6% US rate of inflation to obtain a *nominal* estimate of the rate of discount of 18%. (Note that in CBA one has a choice of how one does the calculations. One can either deal with benefits, costs and discount rates in nominal terms, or convert all of them into real terms.) They argue: 'This discount rate is above the 9 percent nominal rate for new home mortgages in 1976, but equal to the 18 percent rate of interest charged in most states by credit card companies. Our estimated rate of time preference is thus consistent with a hypothesis of rationality of workers' intertemporal trade-offs.'

On the basis of this study, one might be able to conclude that individuals do behave as if $i_C = i_E$ and so a single rate of discount can be used to discount effects and costs.

7.4.2 Country Estimates of Social Discount Rates

Brent (1993) provided estimates of equations (7.1) and (7.2) for a large number of countries. We can thus obtain an idea of the relative magnitudes for i_C and i_E when they are calculated from a social perspective. For both discount rates the value parameters (η and α) were set equal to unity. The discount rates were then determined by the growth rates of national income (for i_C) and life expectancies (for i_E). Table 7.5 gives the estimates of the two rates

Table 7.5: *Estimates of social discount rates for the period 1965–89 (%)*

Country	Based on income growth i_C	Based on life expectancies i_E	Difference $i_C - i_E$
Ethiopia	−0.1	0.5	−0.6
Tanzania	−0.1	0.5	−0.6
Somalia	0.3	0.9	−0.6
Bangladesh	0.4	0.6	−0.2
Malawi	1.0	0.9	0.1
Nepal	0.6	1.0	−0.4
Chad	−1.2	1.0	−2.2
Burundi	3.6	0.5	3.1
Sierra Leone	0.2	0.5	−0.3
Madagascar	−1.9	0.6	−2.5
Nigeria	0.2	0.9	−0.7
Uganda	−2.8	0.3	−3.1
Zaire	−2.0	0.8	−2.8
Mali	1.7	1.0	0.7
Niger	−2.4	0.8	−3.2
Burkina Faso	1.4	0.9	0.5
Rwanda	1.2	0.4	0.8
India	1.8	1.1	0.7
China	5.7	0.8	4.9
Haiti	0.3	0.8	−0.5
Kenya	2.0	0.9	1.1
Pakistan	2.5	0.7	1.8
Benin	−0.1	0.8	−0.9
Central African Rep.	−0.5	0.9	−1.4
Ghana	−1.5	0.6	−2.1
Togo	0.0	1.0	−1.0
Zambia	−2.0	0.8	−2.8
Sri Lanka	3.0	0.4	2.6
Lesotho	5.0	0.6	4.4
Indonesia	4.4	1.4	3.0
Mauritania	−0.5	0.9	−1.4
Bolivia	−0.8	0.8	−1.6
Egypt	4.2	0.8	3.4
Senegal	−0.7	0.7	−1.4
Zimbabwe	1.2	1.2	0.0
Philippines	1.6	0.6	1.0
Côte d'Ivoire	0.8	1.0	−0.2
Dominican Rep.	2.5	0.7	1.8
Morocco	2.3	0.9	1.4
Papua New Guinea	0.2	0.9	−0.7

Table 7.5 (cont.)

Country	Based on income growth i_C	Based on life expectancies i_E	Difference $i_C - i_E$
Honduras	0.6	1.1	−0.5
Guatemala	0.9	1.0	−0.1
Congo, People's Rep.	3.3	0.9	2.4
Syria	3.1	0.9	2.2
Cameroon	3.2	0.9	2.3
Peru	−0.2	0.8	−1.0
Ecuador	3.0	0.7	2.3
Paraguay	3.0	0.1	2.9
El Salvador	−0.4	0.6	−1.0
Columbia	2.3	0.7	1.6
Thailand	4.2	0.7	3.5
Jamaica	−1.3	0.4	−1.7
Tunisia	3.3	1.1	2.2
Turkey	2.6	0.9	1.7
Botswana	8.5	1.4	7.1
Panama	1.6	0.5	1.1
Chile	0.3	0.8	−0.5
Costa Rica	1.4	0.6	0.8
Mauritius	3.0	0.6	2.4
Mexico	3.0	0.6	2.4
Argentina	−0.1	0.3	−0.4
Malaysia	4.0	0.8	3.2
Algeria	2.5	1.1	1.4
Venezuela	−1.0	0.4	−1.4
South Africa	0.8	0.7	0.1
Brazil	3.5	0.6	2.9
Uruguay	1.2	0.2	1.0
Yugoslavia	3.2	0.4	2.8
Gabon	0.9	0.9	0.0
Iran	0.5	0.8	−0.3
Trinidad and Tobago	0.4	0.4	0.0
Portugal	3.0	0.6	2.4
Korea Rep.	7.0	0.9	6.1
Oman	6.4	1.6	4.8
Libya	−3.0	0.9	−3.9
Greece	2.9	0.3	2.6
Saudi Arabia	2.6	1.1	1.5
Ireland	2.1	0.2	1.9
Spain	2.4	0.3	2.1

Table 7.5 (cont.)

Country	Based on income growth i_C	Based on life expectancies i_E	Difference $i_C - i_E$
Israel	2.7	0.2	2.5
Hong Kong	6.3	0.6	5.7
Singapore	7.0	0.5	6.5
New Zealand	0.8	0.2	0.6
Australia	1.7	0.3	1.4
United Kingdom	2.0	0.3	1.7
Italy	3.0	0.3	2.7
Netherlands	1.8	0.2	1.6
Kuwait	−4.0	0.7	−4.7
Austria	2.9	0.3	2.6
France	2.3	0.3	2.0
Canada	4.0	0.3	3.7
Germany	2.4	0.3	2.1
Denmark	1.8	0.1	1.7
United States	1.6	0.3	1.3
Sweden	1.3	0.2	1.1
Finland	3.2	0.3	2.9
Norway	3.4	0.2	3.2
Japan	4.3	0.4	3.9
Switzerland	1.4	0.3	1.1

Source: Based on Brent (1993)

over the period 1965–89 for a sample of 99 countries (all the countries in Brent's Tables 1–3 for which estimates of both rates existed) listed in ascending order of their 1989 *per capita* income. To aid comparison, we have also included the difference between the two rates in the last column of the table.

The average country estimate for i_C shown in Table 7.5 is 1.7%, and the average estimate for i_E is 0.7%. So the cost discount rate was on average 1 percentage point greater than the effects discount rate. As the standard error was only 0.2256, the difference was statistically significant at very high confidence levels (using a paired, two-sample test). We can therefore reject the view that the two rates are the same. The average difference of 1 percentage point looks small. But, for individual countries the differences are large, being as high as 7.1 percentage points for Botswana and −4.7 percentage points for Kuwait.

Interestingly, for 34 countries the effects discount rate is actually higher than the cost discount rate. The main contributing factor for this is the *negative* cost discount rate observed for some countries, 19 in all. Negative discount rates do not make much economic sense, except for the fact that many individuals have positive savings even when real savings rates are negative.

Every one of the 99 countries had a positive effects discount rate. So if one insists on using a single social discount rate, and one wants that rate to be positive, then the effects discount rate would be the better choice for discounting purposes. However, for no country would that rate be as high as 3% as recommended by the US government panel.

7.4.3   A CEA of Medications for Individuals with Schizophrenia

Schizophrenia is a mental illness where the patient has hallucinations and/or delusions. Nowadays, many patients with serious mental illness can be treated with medications and do not always have to be housed as an inpatient in a specialist psychiatric hospital. C. Siegel et al. (1996) used data related to the Stabilized Response Treatment Intervention (SRTI) trial to illustrate their ideas and methods concerning the role of sampling error in estimating and interpreting cost-effectiveness ratios.

The SRTI trial consisted of four medications (each identified by a letter by Siegel et al.) for a target population of schizophrenia patients with a history of nonresponse to conventional antipsychotics. The four medications were:

Q: An experimental treatment for general use as an antipsychotic agent;
R: A long-acting form of a widely used conventional drug for mental illness that is administered once a month;
S: An atypical medication that was highly effective for this population, but it was expensive and required weekly blood tests to monitor serious side-effects; and
T: An atypical medication that was less expensive than S, but also less effective.

Since the plan was to get the patients to function properly in the community, and different medications would vary in their effectiveness and thus require different levels of medical and social support, the expenses for the support services were added to the costs of the medicines to obtain the measure of costs. The patients were discharged into the community and monitored for a period of two years. There were three measures of effectiveness:

E_1:   Average number of months in which the level of psychiatric symptoms was less than 50% of the baseline value;

E_2: Average number of months residing in the community; and
E_3: Average number of months in which the patient worked.

In the previous chapter we explained an empirical method (based on the revealed preferences of policy decision-makers) for combining different measures of effectiveness into a single outcome. An alternative approach is to construct the relative importance (weights) of the alternative effectiveness measures using judgment. This second approach was the one adopted by Siegel et al. The overall measure of effectiveness, denoted E_4, was equal to $0.25E_1 + 0.25E_2 + 0.50E_3$. The values of 'the weights were determined by a consensus group process involving clinicians and treatment recipients and reflected the opinion that successful integration back into the work force was a much more significant therapeutic accomplishment'. Hence E_3 had twice the weight of the other two measures in forming E_4. We just label the effectiveness measure E.

Siegel et al. constructed a 95% confidence interval for the cost-effectiveness ratio of each medication (using a transformation of the ratio based on Fieller's theorem). $\bar{E}$ and $\bar{C}$ were positively related, so their intervals for the ratios would not have been the same as for intervals based on $\bar{E}$ and $\bar{C}$ taken separately. The results (using our notation) appear in Table 7.6 below (their Table 5). Note that they present their ratios in inverse form ($\bar{E}/\bar{C}$ instead of $\bar{C}/\bar{E}$). So the most cost-effective alternative is the one with the *highest* ratio, not the lowest.

Table 7.6: *Estimates and 95% lower and upper confidence limits for $\bar{E}/\bar{C}$ in the SRTI trial*

Parameter	Intervention			
	Q	R	S	T
$\bar{E}$	10.05	17.70	10.85	8.20
$\bar{C}$	21.30	20.90	31.60	28.50
$\bar{E}/\bar{C}$	0.472	0.664	0.343	0.288
95% lower limit	0.376	0.562	0.275	0.208
95% upper limit	0.565	0.751	0.406	0.360

Source: C. Siegel et al. (1996)

As with any CEA, there are two stages in finding the preferred alternative. First, one removes alternatives that are dominated by alternatives already under consideration. A dominated alternative is one that has *both* higher costs and lower effects. Then, from the remaining, non-dominated alternatives, one chooses the most cost-effective one.

In the first stage, medication T can be eliminated as it is dominated by alternative R. Siegel et al. used information on sample variation to eliminate T and did not just rely on the point estimates which show that T has average costs that are 7.60 units higher (measured in logs) and average effects that are 5.5 units lower. From among Q, R and S, R is the most cost-effective. The 95% confidence interval for R lies above those for the other two medications. Thus, even if one takes the lower bound ratio of 0.562 for R, it would be greater than the upper bound ratio for S (i.e., 0.406), and basically the same as the upper bound ratio for Q (i.e., 0.565).

7.4.4   A CEA of the Implantable Cardioverter Defibrillator

Each year, millions of people around the world die suddenly and most of these deaths are caused by heart rhythm irregularities (arrhythmias). One way to make the heart rhythm more effective is to use a defibrillator, a device that applies a strong electrical shock to the heart. One reason why these devices are not in more widespread use is that they are expensive. Gardiner et al. (1995) applied their methods for the analysis of stochastic cost-effective ratios to an evaluation of an implantable cardioverter defibrillator (ICD). There was no randomized clinical trial to assess mortality in subjects without ICD. So they constructed a hypothetical electro-physiology-guided drug therapy (EP) to act as the comparison intervention.

Costs included Medicare charges, physician fees and local drug charges. For ICD they assumed a four-year life for batteries. Cost estimates were based on the literature and expert opinion. The measure of effect was the number of years of survival. People who died in the first eight days were excluded from the ICD group, and those who died in the first 30 days left out from the EP group. This exclusion was to account for operative mortality. On average, those in the ICG group lived longer (3.78 years longer versus an extra 2.06 years), but costs were higher ($123 039 for ICG and $79 413 for EP). The average C/E for ICG was $38 000 and it was $32 581 for EP.

We have just seen in the previous application confidence intervals for average ratios. Here we just focus on the incremental cost-effectiveness ratios in the Gardiner et al. study. The ratios are shown in Table 7.7 with and without discounting (at 5%). Confidence intervals for the ratios were obtained by approximating the variance of the ratios by a variance of differences.

The interesting finding is that the confidence intervals are not symmetric about the mean as they usually are. With discounting, the lower bound estimate is $2179 below the mean, while the upper bound estimate is $3555

Table 7.7:   Confidence intervals (CI) for incremental cost-effectiveness ratios, ICD vs EP

Discount (%/year)	Cost-effectiveness ratio ($/year)	
	Estimate	95% CI
0	22 680	20 940–25 455
5	25 420	23 241–28 975

Source: Based on Gardiner et al. (1995)

above the mean. Cost differences that are lower (and effects differences that are higher) are more likely to be considered statistically significant than cost differences that are higher (and effects differences that are lower). It is worth mentioning that the confidence intervals presented by Siegel et al. in Table 7.6 were also asymmetric. But the asymmetry was less pronounced and, in that case, the lower bound estimates were *further* from the mean than the upper bound estimates.

Gardiner et al. did not explain why they used 5% as the discount rate. Although the interventions added only 2–3 years to a person's life expectancy, this occurs at the *end* of one's lifetime. Thus discounting begins further in the future and not just over the next couple of years. With effects being discounted over a number of years, and the main item of costs (the surgery) occurring in the current period, the effect of discounting was to raise the incremental cost-effectiveness ratio by 12%. One should not get the impression that if one discounts both effects and costs, and discounts at the same rate, then this therefore implies that discounting will turn out to be neutral over time.

We have already identified the role a benchmark ratio has in CEA. It is the ratio that has the highest cost per effect of all those adopted from a given budget. If a new program has a lower ratio, then it should replace the existing program. The health care evaluation literature, as we shall see in the next chapter, uses an alternative benchmark criterion. One looks at ratios in other evaluations and compares them to the results of the particular intervention being evaluated. If the current study comes up with an intervention that has a ratio that is lower than those in the other programs, then the particular intervention must be 'better' than elsewhere and thus worthy of consideration.

In most CEAs, the effect is specific, like a reduction in blood pressure. There may not be any other interventions with ratios that can be compared. In the Gardiner et al. study they used a life expectancy/life duration measure of effect. Many interventions affect mortality and this allowed them to use the results of the evaluations for other interventions as a benchmark. Their conclusion was: 'In health-care cost-effectiveness research, in terms of dollars expended for each life-year saved, values in the range of several hundred thousand are considered good, tens of thousand moderate, and hundreds of thousands attractive. The ICD therefore measures favorably against EP.'

We will examine the role of comparing CEA evaluation results in the next chapter. At this stage we just repeat our familiar CEA warning that a 'better', or more 'favorable', intervention does not necessarily mean that it is socially worthwhile.

7.5   FINAL SECTION

We close with the problems, summary and looking ahead sections.

7.5.1   Problems

The problems aim to reinforce the reader's understanding of statistical significance and confidence intervals while also introducing a further consideration into discounting. Cairns and Van Der Pol (1997) carried out a survey to find individual (implicit) discount rates: 'Respondents were asked what future level of benefit would lead them to be indifferent between a specified benefit to be received 1 year in the future and the delayed more distant benefit.' The length of the delay for future benefit was varied for different individuals, between 2 and 19 years. Thus, for example, if a person said they would be indifferent between having \$100 next year and \$144 three years from now, then the individual's implicit discount rate, denoted by r, would be 20% (seeing that 0.694, or 100/144, was the implied discount factor).

The individual discount rates from the survey then became the dependent variable in a statistical analysis of the determinants of the rates. The estimating equation was roughly of the form:

$$r = \alpha_1 \text{ (Years of Delay)} + \alpha_2 \text{ (Other Variables)}$$

One of the regressions estimated α_1 to be equal to -0.0152 with a standard error of 0.00097.

1.   Assuming that individuals use a constant rate of discounting, what would be the expected size of the coefficient α_1? (Hint: The number of years of delay is just the variable t in formula (2.6) and r in this formula is the same (constant) in each year.)

2. Construct a 95% confidence interval for the coefficient attached to the years of delay. Does this interval include zero? On the basis of your answer to this question, is the expectation given in your answer to question 1 supported by the data in Cairns and Van Der Pol's study?
3. Could (with 95% probability) the sign of the true value of α_1 be positive or negative? On the basis of your answer, does the study imply increasing or decreasing 'timing aversion' (aversion to having future benefits) as opposed to a constant aversion?

7.5.2 Summary

Uncertainty in economic evaluations in health care has been handled in two main ways. When one is unsure about the precise value of a price or cost, or the magnitude of an input or output, one can use statistical means for dealing with the problem that makes use of information about sampling variation. When one is uncomfortable about setting the size of a value judgment parameter, such as the social discount rate or a distributional weight, one can vary parameter values via a sensitivity analysis. Constructing a C/E ratio relies on estimation from data and so is an example of how the first type of uncertainty is handled. The US government panel set up to establish guidelines on CEA proposed a discount rate of 3% and suggested that sensitivity analyses use rates in the range 0% to 7%. The discount rate guidelines therefore illustrate the second way of dealing with uncertainty.

However, this chapter also used the first approach to deal with estimating discount rates because many economists believe that social values should be determined by individual values. Individual values are often implicit in the choices that they make. Data on choices can then be used to uncover the value parameters. Hence individual intertemporal choices were examined in the context of setting discount rates.

While utilizing individual preferences is central to CBA, and will be relied on for most of this book, for intertemporal choices there is some hesitancy in accepting consumer sovereignty. Myopia exists in theory, and in practice individuals often are revealed to use double-digit discount rates. Moreover, how can one rely solely on individual valuations when some of the affected individuals (those in future generations) have not been born yet? So we concentrated more on social formulations which try to estimate how much richer (or healthier) future generations will be and then make adjustments for society's aversion to income (or health) inequality. Single-digit estimates for the discount rate come from these methods and they thus fit in much better with the recommended US guidelines than the estimates revealed by individual behavior.

The whole issue of discounting in a CEA is more complicated than for a CBA because the costs and the effects that form the ratios are in different units. There are in principle two rates to consider: one for costs and one for effects. There are a number of inconsistency problems if two different rates are used, especially when the rate for effects is set equal to zero. So recommended practice is to use a single rate. But which one should be used? Our case studies threw some light on this issue because we showed that if one used individual valuations, the two rates were estimated to be the same; while if we use social valuations, there was a statistically significant difference between them. The cost discount rate was higher. However, the cost discount rate was not always positive and so, perhaps, the effects discount rate makes the most economic sense. Estimates in the range 0% to 2% were low even by the standards of the US panel guidelines that recommended a rate of 3%.

In this chapter we also consolidated our understanding of 'statistically significant differences'. One C/E ratio may be lower than another and thus be different. But this difference could have occurred by chance. We obtain the notion of chance by accepting a particular probability of making an error, say it is 5%. Then we have 95% confidence that we have not made an error. Typically, with 95% confidence, averages lie within a band of around ± 2 standard errors. The size of the standard error is related to the dispersion/variation of observations in the sample from which the averages were calculated. So if the confidence interval for the difference in ratios includes zero, then it is likely that the difference was due to sampling error and a product of chance. If the confidence interval does not cover zero then we say that the difference is statistically significant.

Incorporating confidence intervals into the analysis of C/E ratios is somewhat recent because finding the standard error for a ratio is more complicated than that for variables considered separately. Advances in statistical methodology have made the problem more tractable. We have seen that the confidence intervals may not be symmetrical. But, whatever their shape, they can be applied in the standard way to establish significance.

7.5.3   Looking Ahead

One fundamental drawback of CEA is the limited basis for comparing evaluations of different interventions. There is thus a need for a comprehensive measure of effects. A QALY is such a measure and this is the unit used in a CUA, which we will be analyzing next. Once one has a comprehensive measure of effects, a whole new set of issues arises, such as interpersonal comparisons of effects. Is a poor person's QALY, or an elderly person's QALY, worth the same as for everyone else? These and other issues we will be addressing in the next part.

PART IV

CUA and CBA

8. Fundamentals of cost–utility analysis

8.1 INTRODUCTION

In this chapter a general measure of effect is discussed, that is, a QALY. With this more general measure, it is now possible to compare across health care programs. We focus on how CUA widens the sphere of influence of CEA analysis and leave till the next chapter the technical details of how QALYs can be estimated. We compare and contrast CUA with both CEA (in the first section) and CBA (in the third section). In between these comparisons of evaluation methods, we explain how lists of CUA, called 'league tables' are, and should be, constructed. We also look at a US panel's guidelines for making CUA studies comparable. We then outline a comprehensive actual CUA exercise – the Oregon plan – that tried to establish health care priorities in an explicit policy-making setting. The case studies concentrate on how comparisons are made in CUA in order to determine when a cost-per-QALY is worthwhile.

8.1.1 CUA versus CEA

A cost–utility analysis can be viewed as a CEA analysis that has output measured in only one kind of dimension: a quality adjusted life year (QALY). The quality adjustment weight is a utility value (usually between 1 and 0), which can be measured, estimated, or taken from past studies.

The CUA approach was developed as a response to the human capital approach to evaluation, which valued lives according to their expected lifetime earnings. The first use of a QALY was apparently by Klarman et al. (1968). Kaplan and Bush (1982) prefer the term a 'well year' to a QALY because it emphasizes the link of the index to health conditions. A well year is a year free of dysfunction, symptoms, and health related problems.

Drummond et al. (1987) provide a set of guidelines for when to use a CUA and when to use a CEA:

1. A CUA should be used when: quality of life is the main concern (e.g., with arthritis, which does not affect mortality); both mortality and morbidity are involved (e.g., with estrogen therapy, which eliminates discomfort, but increases mortality due to uterine bleeding); programs that have a wide range of outcomes (e.g., with pneumonia vaccines, which prevent the disease, but leave some patients with swelling and fever, and others with temporary paralysis); and programs are to be compared with others that have already been evaluated using CUA.
2. A CEA analysis should be used when: there is a single index of quality of life; outcomes have equal effectiveness; and there is evidence only of the intermediate, and not the final, effectiveness of a treatment.

8.1.2   CUA as a Generally Comparable CEA

The use of a specific measure of effect in a CEA analysis (e.g., diastolic blood pressure) is not suitable for comparisons across different disease groups. Nor is it of use for assessing the side-effects of a treatment (e.g., treatments for hypertension cause gastric irritation). A CEA analysis is therefore not able to show an overall assessment of a treatment. On the other hand, a CUA combines morbidity and mortality into a single index, the QALY. All programs are comparable in that they share the common goal of improving health status.

8.1.3   Cost–Utility League Tables

Since CUA uses a common unit of measure for programs, it allows comparisons across *all* health care programs. In the classical setting for a CEA study outlined in Chapter 6, there would be a budget constraint and thus a benchmark ratio for new programs to try to match. But CUA is often applied when the budget constraint is implicit. There would not be then an obvious project that one could identify as being liable to be replaced. In this context, the plan would be to see how much current programs cost for a QALY, and to judge the particular program one is analyzing on the basis of these norms. For examples of cost per QALY outcomes, consider the summary of CUA results provided by Torrance and Feeny (1989), which is our Table 8.1 (and their Table 2).

Torrance and Feeny's QALY league table can be used to locate comparable programs. The program under consideration may have a cost per QALY that falls into one of three categories:

1. It may be lower than ratios for well-accepted programs (such as neonatal intensive care) and thus should be approved;

Table 8.1: *Comparative cost–utility results for selected programs*

Program	Reported cost/ QALY gained in US $ (year)	Adjusted cost/ QALY gained in US $ (1983)
PKU screening	<0 (1970)	<0
Postpartum anti-D	<0 (1977)	<0
Antepartum anti-D	1220 (1983)	1220
Coronary artery bypass surgery for left main coronary artery disease	3500 (1981)	4220
Neo-natal intensive care, 1000–1499g	2800 (1978)	4500
T4 (thyroid) screening	3600 (1977)	6300
Treatment of severe hypertension (diastolic ≥ 105 mm Hg) in males age 40	4850 (1976)	9400
Treatment of mild hypertension (diastolic 95–104 mm Hg) in males age 40	9800 (1976)	19 100
Estrogen therapy for postmenopausal symptoms in women without a prior hysterectomy	18 160 (1979)	27 000
Neo-natal intensive care, 500–999g	19 600 (1978)	31 800
Coronary bypass for single vessel disease with moderately severe angina	30 000 (1981)	36 300
School tuberculin testing program	13 000 (1968)	43 700
Continuous ambulatory peritoneal dialysis	35 100 (1980)	47 100
Hospital hemodialysis	40 200 (1980)	54 000

Source: Torrance and Feeny (1989)

2. It may be higher than controversial programs (such as renal dialysis) and thus should be regarded as unacceptable; or
3. It may lie somewhere in between.

As an alternative to looking at particular examples in Torrance and Feeny's league table, one can consider broad generalizations from the table.

For example, we can use Kaplan and Bush's (1982) rule of thumb. Kaplan and Bush argue that standard marginal economic analysis should apply when making comparisons. If the dollar cost per QALY is considered socially efficient for one program, then programs with similar cost/utility ratios are also justifiable. On the basis of their experience, they suggest as a guideline that $20000 per QALY should be the cut-off ratio for programs. Programs that cost less than this (and they claim that most programs analyzed are in this category) are cost-effective by current standards. Between $20000 and $100000 programs are to be judged justifiable, but possibly controversial. Programs that cost more than $100000 are questionable by current standards. They chose the $20000 figure because many current expenditures in tertiary medical care are approved with costs less than this amount. Human capital and WTP decisions also agree with this figure (they claim!).

Weinstein (1995) points out that $20000 is close to *per capita* GDP and this could have been one of the reasons they used this cut-off value (i.e., using the human capital approach, $20000 is what people could earn on average if they lived and worked an extra life year). This is in sharp contrast to the Garber and Phelps (1997) utility-maximizing approach presented in Chapter 6 where, on the basis of an income figure of $18000, the authors recommended that the cut-off should be about *double* the annual income.

8.2   BASIC PRINCIPLES OF CUA

In this section we explain how QALYs should be measured and give an illustrative example of how a QALY was measured in the Oregon plan in the US. The Oregon plan is an important example of the CUA method being used for assigning health care priorities and this plan is then explained in detail.

8.2.1   The US CEA Panel Recommendations

The Panel on Cost-Effectiveness in Health and Medicine was convened by the US Public Health Service in order to come up with recommendations to improve the comparability and quality of CEA studies. Their work was published as three articles in the *Journal of the American Medical Association* (*JAMA*) (see Russell et al. (1996), Weinstein et al. (1996) and Siegel et al. (1996)) and the full report appeared as a book by Gold et al. (1996). There were 13 scientists and scholars with expertise in CEA on the panel. They met 11 times during a two and a half year period.

The over-riding consideration of the panel was to try to standardize CEA practice. It was from this viewpoint that they suggested using the

QALY as the measure of an effect. Only a QALY enables consistent practice to take place 'across conditions and interventions – prevention, therapeutic, rehabilitative, and public health'.

The cornerstone of the panel's recommendations is for each study to include a 'reference case' *in addition to* the type of analysis that the researcher is most interested in undertaking and presenting. This provides maximum flexibility as it enables researchers to zero-in on a particular area for assessment yet also enables others to compare results. The reference case should have the following ingredients (in addition to using QALYs to measure effects):

1. The perspective should be from that of society as a whole. So 'all important impacts on human health and on resources must be included somewhere, either in the numerator or in the denominator'.
2. 'To avoid double counting, monetary values for lost life-years should not be imputed in CEA and should not be included in the numerator of the C/E ratio.'
3. The utilities that are used to weight the life years should be based on 'community preferences, rather than those of patients, providers, or investigators'.
4. The discount rate used should be 3%; and rates of 5%, and between 0 and 7% used in sensitivity analyses (as noted in the previous chapter).
5. The C/E ratios should be incremental, 'comparing each intervention with the next most effective option'.
6. 'Transfer payments (such as cash transfers from taxpayers to welfare recipients)' just redistribute resources from one individual to another and so 'cancel out from the social perspective' (in sharp contrast to the approach outlined in Chapter 5!).
7. Patient time should be handled as follows: (a) time spent seeking health care or undergoing intervention should be valued in monetary terms and included into the numerator of a C/E ratio; and (b) time spent sick is part of the health outcome and measured in the denominator of the C/E ratio.
8. Effectiveness (comparing the course of the health problem with and without treatment) must be demonstrated.

Apart from these main recommendations they also suggested that: market prices ordinarily be used to measure costs (especially wage rates to measure the opportunity cost of labor); sensitivity analyses be employed to allow for uncertainty and for distributional effects; and there be a standardization of the reporting of reference case results, e.g., total costs, effects, incremental ratios, method used to estimate utilities, excluding dominated options (where both the costs are higher and the effects are lower), and so on.

8.2.2 Calculating a QALY

Eddy (1991a) explains how to calculate a QALY using Kaplan and Anderson's Quality of Well-Being (QWB) Scale. The scale defines 24 health or functional states, ranging from perfect health to death. Examples of QWB states are: loss of consciousness, such as seizure, fainting, or coma; general tiredness, weakness, or weight loss; and spells of feeling upset, being depressed, or of crying.

The net effect of a service is the difference between the QWB with treatment (QWB_{Rx}) and the QWB_{No} without treatment multiplied by the duration of that service:

$$\text{Net effect of a service} = (QWB_{Rx} - QWB_{No})\ \text{Duration} \qquad (8.1)$$

The QWB of each of the treat/no treat alternatives is given by the product of the utility weight W_i of being in any state i times the probability P_i of being in that state. So:

$$QWB_{Rx} = \Sigma_i P_{i,Rx} \cdot W_i \quad \text{and} \quad QWB_{No} = \Sigma_i P_{i,No} \cdot W_i \qquad (8.2)$$

The incremental ratio of costs to effects (which Eddy calls the 'Cost–Benefit Ratio') is therefore defined as:

$$\Delta C/\Delta QALY = \text{Cost of Service}/(\Sigma_i P_{i,Rx} \cdot W_i - \Sigma_i P_{i,No} \cdot W_i)\ \text{Duration} \qquad (8.3)$$

Eddy took the case of acute appendicitis/appendectomy for his illustration. There were thought to be relevant four potential outcomes or QWB states. These four states, and their utility weights, were:

1. Complete cure of the condition with no residual symptoms ($W_i = 1$);
2. Survival with symptoms of abdominal pain, i.e., 6th QWB state ($W_i = 0.747$);
3. Survival with symptoms such as vomiting, fever and chills, i.e., 8th QWB state ($W_i = 0.630$); and
4. Death ($W_i = 0$).

The probability of death was judged to be 0.99 if the appendicitis was untreated and only 0.01 if treated. Of the 99% who survive with treatment,

97% were thought to be in the complete cure state, with 1% in each of the other states with symptoms (but alive). A typical patient with appendicitis was a young adult in the age range 19 through 35. So, if treated, the benefits were assumed to last 47 years. Table 8.2 (which combines Eddy's Tables 1 and 2) summarizes the ingredients into the calculations of the QWB.

Table 8.2:   Calculations of QWB with and without treatment

Outcome	Probability X Weight	Score
Without treatment		
Death	0.99 X 0	0
No adverse outcome	0.01 X 1	0.01
Sum across all outcomes		0.01
With treatment		
Death	0.01 X 0	0
QWB state 6	0.01 X 0.747	0.00747
QWB state 8	0.01 X 0.630	0.0063
No adverse outcome	0.97 X 1	0.97
Sum across all outcomes		0.98377

Source: Eddy (1991a)

The table shows that QWB_{Rx} was 0.984 and QWB_{No} was 0.01, which made the difference $QWB_{Rx} - QWB_{No} = 0.974$. With an expected duration of 47 years, the net effect of the service was 45.778. The cost of appendicitis from Oregon's Medicaid records was $5744. The resulting $C/QALY$ ratio was around $125 (Eddy's figure was $122). This was the priority score for appendicitis. On a list of 1600 services (with a range of $1.5 to $2 782 350), appendicitis' priority score placed this service with a ranking of 397.

8.2.3   Using CUA to Set Priorities

The decision-making set-up for a CUA is exactly the same in structure as that for a CEA. Recall from Chapter 6 that one: measures costs and effects (QALYs), forms cost-effectiveness ratios, ranks feasible projects from lowest to highest, and works down the list by approving all projects until the fixed budget is exhausted. In Chapter 6 we used the hypothetical figures devised by Weinstein (1995). In this section we outline an actual budget-exhausting exercise as carried out by the Oregon Health Service Commission (HSC).

As pointed out previously, Medicaid is a joint, federal/state government financed health insurance program in the US for those with low incomes.

In Oregon, their way of running the Medicaid program was interpreted as one of rationing. Only those families with incomes up to the 67th percentile of the federal poverty level were eligible for the Medically Needy Program. In 1989 legislation was enacted to increase access such that those with up to 100% of the federal poverty level would be eligible. It was estimated that an additional 116000 families would now get coverage. With a fixed budget allocation, this increased access could only be achieved by limiting the number of health services the state would cover.

In August 1989 the Governor set up an 11-member HSC. As described by Klevit et al. (1991) in a progress report of the commission, they were told to report: 'a list of health services ranked by priority from the most important to the least important, representing the comparative benefits of each service to the entire population to be served'. The plan was that the legislature would then determine at what point on the list a line would be drawn below which services could not be funded unless additional resources could be found.

The HSC chose the Kaplan and Anderson QWB scale as the method to calculate the relative benefits. Klevit et al. summarize the scale as: 'it measures how an individual functions independently and how he/she feels normally and during illness.' The utilities were based on a random telephone survey of 1001 Oregon citizens, supplemented by surveys of people in special categories, e.g., bedridden or chronically depressed. The preliminary results of systematically using the CUA methodology were made public on May 2, 1990. The top 10 on the list of the approximately 1600 services, according to Klevit et al., are presented as the first set of results recorded in Table 8.3.

Table 8.3:   Top 10 priorities of the Oregon HSC initially and subsequently

Rank	Initially (Klevit et al. (1991))	Subsequently (Kaplan (1995))
1	Bacterial meningitis	Medical treatment of bacterial pneumonia
2	Phenylketonuria	Medical treatment of tuberculosis
3	Non-Hodgkin's lymphoma	Medical or surgical treatment of peritonitis
4	Septicemia	Removal of foreign bodies (from larynx etc.)
5	Meningococcemia	Appendectomy
6	Disseminated candidiasis	Repair of ruptured intestine
7	Salmonellosis	Repair of hernia with obstruction/gangrene
8	Wilms' tumor	Medical therapy for croup syndrome
9	Other bacterial infections	Medical therapy for acute orbital cellulites
10	Autoimmune hemolytic anemia	Surgery for ectopic pregnancy

Source: Created by the author from the identified sources

Once the initial list was made public, this gave the opponents of the Oregon plan the opportunity to criticize and ridicule the whole process. Alleged 'aberrations' (clinical inconsistencies) in the ranking were identified. For example, Hadorn (1991) cites as glaring anomalies placing dental caps for pulp exposure higher than surgery for ectopic pregnancy, and ranking splints for temporomandibular joints higher than appendectomies for appendicitis.

In response to these criticisms, the HSC abandoned the use of the utility weights and dropped all reference to costs. They came up with a new list of priorities based on their own subjective judgments. Kaplan (1995) characterized the new scheme as placing interventions in three basic categories: essential, very important, and valuable to certain individuals. In the first category were cases (such as appendectomies) where problems were severe and treatable yet possibly fatal if untreated. Here treatment prevents death and there is full recovery. The second category consists of cases (such as hip replacements) involving acute, nonfatal, one-time treatments that lead to increases in the quality of life. In the lowest category were cases (such as treatments at the end stage of cancer) where interventions were known to be ineffective. The revised top 10 of 709 newly constituted condition–treatment pairs (as listed by Kaplan) appear as the second set of rankings in Table 8.3.

To implement the amended priority list, Oregon needed a waiver (exemption from existing rules) from the US Department of Health and Human Services. In August 1992, Oregon's application was turned down because it was judged to violate the Americans with Disabilities Act of 1990.

The merits of the charge of discrimination against the disabled will be discussed in Chapter 10, and an assessment of the initial and subsequent rankings is given as a case study later in this chapter. Here we make a few remarks that will try to put the Oregon exercise into a wider context as an economic evaluation.

There are very few examples where basic evaluation principles are at the forefront of actual health care decision-making. The Oregon plan is one major instance where the economic evaluation process was taken seriously, even if it was ultimately abandoned. It was a great learning experience for society as to the strengths of systematically evaluating options within a consistent framework. Economic principles were publicly debated even if they were not yet fully understood.

We reported earlier the guidelines of a US panel on CUA. They recommended that community preferences be used to obtain the estimates of the utility weights when forming the QALYs. The Oregon plan was clearly consistent with this directive. But, put into a democratic setting, community preferences are very much linked to voting mechanisms. One should not then be surprised to see that a ranking based on economic evaluation principles becomes transformed into a much more political, and a much less cohesive, ranking scheme.

8.3   CUA VERSUS CBA

In this section we rely on the analysis by Pauly (1995). The two methods will be compared by examining the extent to which they lead to different decisions. When differences in rankings are found, the criterion for deciding between the two evaluation methods will be the expected outcome for an individual who is uncertain as to his/her individual situation prior to being faced with a large set of alternative circumstances that may occur. This is called a 'constitutional' decision-making context by Buchanan and Tullock (1962). In this 'veil of ignorance', the individual will be fair to everyone in the hope of being fair to him/herself.

8.3.1   Fixed Budget Constraint

With a fixed budget constraint, one assumes that one or more programs are socially desirable, as this was why the funds were allocated in the first place. CUA then does not need to worry about obtaining an implicit price for a QALY. Its task is to choose the most cost-effective ones until the budget is exhausted. The issue is whether the programs chosen under CUA would be the same as with CBA. The version of CBA that is relevant here is the one that ranks programs by their C/B ratios and chooses from lowest to highest until the budget is spent. Pauly identifies three separate cases:

1. *Unidimensional effects with identical preferences and incomes*: Here the ranking by CUA and CBA would be the same. This is because when one aggregates QALYs, a common value is given to them no matter who gets them. This corresponds to the assumption of a single price P applied to each effect, as envisaged in moving from equation (1.4) to (1.5) in section 1.2.2. So if treatment 1 had a higher benefit–cost ratio than treatment 2 (i.e., $PE_1/C_1 > PE_2/C_2$) then treatment 1 would also be more cost-effective (i.e., $C_1/E_1 < C_2/E_1$).
2. *Unidimensional effects, common incomes, but different preferences*: Now it matters whether the persons who get the QALYs are the ones who are willing to pay the most for them. If there is no correlation between WTP and who gets the most QALYs per head, then on average there should be no difference between CUA and CBA rankings. But, if there were a positive correlation, then a CBA would rank higher programs

that give more QALYs to those with the highest WTP. The CUA rankings would not change as equal weight is given to all QALYs (in the traditional approach). CBA would be the preferred method because, with the fixed budget, QALYs in one period could be obtained only by sacrificing QALYs in other periods. The individual would like to have the QALYs when they have the highest value and CBA would guarantee this. CUA gives equal weight and would be indifferent to when the QALYs are obtained.

3. *Unidimensional effects, common preferences, but different incomes*: Assuming good health is a normal good, the higher one's income, the higher one's WTP for a QALY. Thus, income differences mean that, like case 2 just analyzed, QALYs and WTP will be positively related, and so CBA will be the preferred method. This is the constitutional decision-making advantage of CBA. If individuals do not know what their lifetime income is going to be, they would prefer that they spend less on health when their incomes are low so that they can spend more on other goods. When their incomes are high they can spend more on health. CUA measures of effects do not depend on income and so would not discriminate the two periods.

But, if in the constitutional stage one is risk averse and not risk neutral as assumed above, CBA may not be preferred. When there is diminishing marginal utility of income (the individual is risk averse), one gains from having QALYs when one could not otherwise afford them. Thus, by giving equal weights to QALYs, more QALYs would be given when states of the world are adverse than would be forthcoming from a CBA (where one would cut back QALYs when incomes are low). So a CUA, by giving more QALYs in the low-income states, provides a sort of income in-kind insurance. The more imperfect are social insurance instruments, the more important will be this advantage of a CUA.

To summarize, the smaller the variance in tastes, the lower the distribution of income, the greater the risk aversion, and the more imperfect other social instruments for insuring against adverse states, the more a CUA is a valid evaluation method.

8.3.2 Variable Budget Constraint

CBA is clearly preferable in these circumstances. There are two main reasons:

1. CUA cannot, by itself, decide what is socially desirable. That is, one does not know how low the C/E ratio must become in order to approve

the program. To solve this problem, some critical ratio must be estimated. No matter the way this is estimated, Pauly considers that the
monetary value will be somewhat arbitrary. As he says, 'the product of
a precise number and an arbitrary number is still arbitrary'. He thus
thinks that there is a lot of misspent energy in a QALY (i.e., by trying
to get a precise value for a QALY) and then using an implicit monetary
value, when CBA derives the monetary value more precisely.

2.   CUA is not very useful when there are multidimensional effects. CEA
     must choose just one effect as its main one. CUA can combine survival
     and quality of life effects, but (as we shall see in the next chapter) it
     must do this by imposing many restrictions on the form of the utility
     function. In CBA, all effects are included automatically, and one can
     ask, if need be, for an evaluation of the project itself, something a CUA
     cannot do.

8.4   APPLICATIONS

We start with a CUA classic that we use to highlight the central weakness
of CUA from a CBA perspective. Since the rationale for moving from CEA
to CUA is to be able to make comparisons across programs, the second
application analyses the usefulness of CUA league tables covering a large
number of interventions. Then we examine the Oregon plan, which is a
study of how CUA principles were applied in an actual decision-making
context. Finally we look at general CUA comparability from the perspective of a particular intervention.

8.4.1   CUA of Neo-Natal Intensive Care

Here we examine in greater detail the neo-natal intensive care case study by
Boyle et al. (1983) first presented as the base for the problems in Chapter 1.
As explained in section 1.5.1, the provision of neo-natal intensive care
involves spending large sums early in order to increase a baby's future survival chances. Boyle et al. targeted infants whose birth weight was less than
1500 g because intensive care was most effective for this group (in terms of
mortality). They sub-divided the group into two: birth weights between
1000 and 1499g and those between 500 and 999g. The lower weight sub-
group contains the more serious cases.

   A methodology for valuing a QALY for those in the neo-natal intensive
care program was specially devised by Torrance et al. (1982). Boyle et al.
obtained measures of utilities to form the QALY by reference to a method
that we will be explaining in the next chapter. The estimates of utility came

from a study of the preferences of 148 parents of school children in Hamilton-Wentworth County, Ontario. Parents rated some chronic dys-functional states in children as worse than death. So the scale used was 1 to −0.39 (rather than the usual 1 to 0). Note that, on aggregate, the value of one year of life saved by neonatal intensive care was estimated to be 0.75 of a healthy year. So there must have been a lot of sample variation and a con-fidence interval around the mean estimates should have been presented.

The results that we report in Table 8.4 below relate to the sub-groups given separately (based on Boyle et al.'s Table 4). We highlight only the cal-culations related to costs and consequences projected over the infant's life-time (i.e., 'to death'). All categories are on an incremental basis (relative to the before treatment period). The main difference from our earlier presen-tation of the results is that all the cost figures are now discounted (at a rate of 5%).

Table 8.4:   Measures of economic evaluation of neo-natal intensive care by birth weight

Period: To death (projected)	1000–1499 g	500–999 g
1. Cost/life year gained	2900	9300
2. Cost/QALY gained	3200	22400
3. Net economic benefit (loss)/live birth	(2600)	(16100)
4. Net economic cost/life year gained	900	7300
5. Net economic cost/QALY gained	1000	17500

Source: Based on Boyle et al. (1983)

What needs explaining in the table are the 'net' figures. In all cases these are the costs net of the projected lifetime earnings. These net figures have a natural interpretation in terms of line 3, as these reflect the CBA outcome using the human capital approach (i.e., B − C). In a CEA or CUA context, on lines 4 and 5 respectively, the net figures are problematic.

Boyle et al. interpret their net figures to represent a 'cost recovery' per-spective. That is, the future earnings can, in principle, be used to finance the current costs of treatment and, in this sense, indicate the ability of the inter-vention to self-finance. For a CBA, this interpretation would be valid when-ever the costs and benefits both affect the same group. User fees for a service (e.g., prescription charges) paid by the patients would be an example.

In terms of a CUA (or a CEA) the interpretation of earnings as negative costs highlights the issue first raised in section 6.1.2 that ratios can greatly be affected by how components are classified while differences are not. In

Chapter 6 the point was made that having a component on the numerator and simultaneously on the denominator will greatly affect the size of the ratio. The problem then with the Boyle et al. interpretation is that they subtract earnings from the numerator, but don't include them somehow on the denominator as an effect. (Note that this is precisely the situation that ingredient 2 of the recommendations by the US panel on CEA was designed to rule out (see section 8.2.1)).

At a minimum there is a practical problem. Should one take the cost per QALY from line 2 of the table or from line 5? A CUA perspective cannot give an unequivocal answer. Again, the answer is very clear from a CBA standpoint. If the numerator part of the ratio that forms line 5 is the net benefits, then dividing by the number of QALYs produces the net benefits per unit. If the average net-benefits curve were constant, line 5 could be a good proxy for total net benefits in line 3; while line 2 would be even more remote by excluding the earnings.

A comparison of lines 2 and 5 with line 3 reveals that neither lines 2 nor 5 are, in fact, good proxies for net benefits. Net benefits are negative, while lines 2 and 5 are positive. This is one of the most important findings presented in this text because it supports the central proposition that only a CBA can tell whether a treatment is worthwhile. It does not matter if neo-natal intensive care is a more cost-effective way of generating a QALY than others typically undertaken. The benefits are not greater than the costs and this means that it should not be approved. Of course, this particular CBA finding is based on the human capital approach. But the point is that even a CBA using WTP to measure benefits could also decide that neo-natal intensive care is not worthwhile.

It is interesting to focus on why exactly the CBA figures in Table 8.4 result in a negative outcome, while the net benefits in Table 1.5 were positive. The cause of the outcome difference is that in Table 8.4 the costs and earnings are discounted at a rate of 5%, while in the earlier table the figures are undiscounted. Boyle et al. undertook a sensitivity analysis for the discount rate and found that the switching value for the 1000–1499 g sub-group was 3.5%. So strictly, if one accepts the guidelines presented in the previous chapter that 3% be the discount rate, then a CBA would actually approve neo-natal intensive care. But, for the lower birth weight group, no positive discount rate would produce positive net benefits and the divergence between CBA and CUA remains.

8.4.2 Assessment of CUA League Tables

Drummond et al. (1993) analyzed a recent league table of 21 health care interventions in the UK constructed by Maynard (1991) to see whether the existence of the table does 'more harm than good'. An abridged version of his Table 2 is reproduced as Table 8.5 below. It is almost inevitable that someone reading the table will look to see what is high in the table and conclude that this must be in some sense better than a lower ranked intervention. Drummond et al. looked at the methodologies underlying the studies to see how misleading are these rankings and how their defects can be minimized.

There were six source studies for the table and the years of analysis ranged from 1982 to 1989 (all estimates being converted to 1990 prices). The abbreviations are as follows (column by column): 'na' is not applicable and U is unknown; L is literature source, X is 'guesstimates', M (related to utility values) is non-standard methodology, C is clinician values, R is Rosser matrix, and P is patient values; A_0 is average C/QALY compared with do-nothing, A_1 is average C/QALY compared with minimum intervention, and M is marginal C/QALY of expanding to a new treatment group; S means the C/QALY originate from the author, S_1 means the C/QALY are calculated by the authors using data from other research, and Q means the C/QALY are quoted from elsewhere.

Drummond et al. used the table to highlight four methodological areas and to see how homogenous were these studies across those areas. The four areas were:

1. *Discount rates*: This was the most consistently applied methodological feature. Most studies discount (when necessary) and apply the same 5% rate to both costs and effects. This can largely be explained by the fact that these were UK studies and the Treasury recommended that rate over that period. There were three studies that did not use discounting, two of them ranked in the top four of the table. As the prevention of death was involved and this has consequences over one's lifetime, the omission of discounting was a major cause of non-comparability.
2. *Utility values*: There were many different methods used to measure the utility values for health states in the table. Obviously, the use of different methods is going to reduce the comparability of the estimates greatly. The most frequently used method was to refer to the utilities in a study by Kind et al. (1982) that developed the 'Rosser matrix'. Drummond et al. conjectured that a North American version of the table would probably have even greater lack of comparability because more extensive basic research into utility measurement takes place there and researchers develop their own approaches.
3. *Range of costs and consequences*: In all but two of the studies (ranked 3rd and 17th on the list) only direct costs were included. Most included only direct benefits. Only one of the sources, related to GP (general

Table 8.5: Some extracts of cost for QALYs for competing treatments

Treatment	C/Q £1990	Discount rate Cost	Discount rate Benefits	Utility values	Average/ marginal	Data source
Cholesterol testing and diet therapy only (all adults, aged 40–69)	220	5%	5%	L=X	A_0	S_1
Neurosurgical intervention for head injury	240	na	0%	M+C	A_0	S
GP advice to stop smoking	270	na	5%	X	A_0	Q
Neurosurgical intervention for subarachnoid haemorrhage	490	na	0%	M+C	A_0	S
Anti-hypertensive therapy to prevent stroke (age 45–64)	940	U	5%	X	A_0	S
Pacemaker implantation	1100	5%	5%	R+C	A_1	S
Hip replacement	1180	5%	5%	R+L	A_1	S_1
Valve replacement for aortic stenosis	1140	5%	5%	R+C	A_1	S
Cholesterol testing and treatment	1480	5%	5%	L=X	A_0	S
CABG (lmv disease, severe angina)	2090	5%	5%	R+C	A_1	S
Kidney transplant	4710	5%	5%	R+L	$A_1 = A_0$	S_1
Breast cancer screening	5780	5%	5%	R+L	A_0	S_1
Heart transplantation	7840	5%	5%	R+L	A_1	S_1
Cholesterol testing and treatment (increm.) of all adults aged 25–39	14150	5%	5%	L=X	M	S_1
Home haemodialysis	17260	5%	5%	R+L	$A_1 = A_0$	S_1

CABG (lvd, moderate angina)	18830	5%	5%	R+C	A_1	S
CAPD	19870	U	U	U	U	U
Hospital haemodialysis	21970	5%	5%	R+L	$A_1=A_0$	S_1
Erythropoietin treatm. for anaemia in dialysis patients (assuring a 10% reduction in mortality)	54380	na	na	R+(L=P)	A_1	S
Neurosurgical intervention for malignant intracranial tumours	107780	na	0%	M+C	A_0	S
Erythropoietin treatm. for anaemia in dialysis patients (assuming no increase in survival)	126290	na	na	R+(L=P)	A_1	S

Source: Drummond et al. (1993)

practitioner, i.e., family doctor) advice to stop smoking, included patients' time as part of the costs. The ranking of this intervention was biased downward because of this more comprehensive approach to costing.

4. *Comparison program*: The six sources used different comparison programs when forming their incremental ratios. Drummond (1990) showed that, in a CUA study of AZT (zidovudine) for people with AIDS, an extra year of life could be saved for £8000 if some basic level of care was given. Since the basic level of care can cost as much as £30000, whether one assumes no or minimum care without the intervention can make an enormous difference to calculated C/E ratios (especially when what constitutes a 'minimum' program differs across studies).

8.4.3   A CEA of the Oregon Plan

David Eddy has provided a comprehensive assessment of the Oregon plan in a series of papers in the *Journal of the American Medical Association* (*JAMA*). Here we feature two of them: Eddy (1991a, 1991b).

Eddy's assessment of the Oregon plan is based on the fundamental principle that the plan was devised to achieve. That is, the aim was to decrease coverage for some who have Medicaid in order to free up resources to increase the numbers who can now receive Medicaid. In this light, the initial exercise of ranking by C/E ratios was the correct one rather than the second ranking that is based on perceived effectiveness that ignores costs. The question then is not whether providing one person with dental caps is more beneficial than treating one person for ectopic pregnancy. Rather the appropriate comparison is between treating 105 patients with dental caps at $38 each versus treating one person with surgery for ectopic pregnancy at $4015. On this basis, many of the perceived inconsistencies in the initial Oregon rankings that identified the top 587 services as basic and 122 services as being uncovered would disappear.

Table 8.6 summarizes the changes brought about by the Oregon plan in a form that Eddy calls a 'balance sheet'. This splits the changes into three components: the number of gainers and losers; the size of the gains and losses in terms of the number of services provided; and the costs to the government (both federal and state). Since the plan was viewed as a 'demonstration project', it was expected that Oregon employees and consumers would eventually pay all the government costs.

The gainers and losers are assigned to three groups. Group 1 consists of those who are currently covered by Medicaid. They get 587 services with the plan when they used to get 709 (strictly, they lose 122 but gain 7 new

Table 8.6: *Balance sheet of expected effect of demonstration program on*
number of people covered, services covered and financial costs

	Current	Proposed	Change
People covered, no.			
Group 1	200 000	200 000	0
Group 2	0	120 000	+120 000
Group 3	0	330 000	+330 000
Total			+450 000
Services covered, no.			
Group 1	709	587	−122
Group 2	0	587	+587
Group 3	0	587	+587
5-year costs ($ million)			
Federal government (Medicaid)	3806	3915.6	+109.6
State government (Medicaid)	2236	2331	+95.0
Total			+204.6

Source: Based on Eddy (1991b)

services, so the net loss is actually 115 and not 122). Group 2 comprises those with low enough incomes to be below the federal poverty line, but who currently do not qualify for Medicaid in Oregon. They will get 587 services with the plan. Lastly, there is group 3 comprising those who are not poor and therefore not eligible for Medicaid, but are privately uninsured. Most in this category will get coverage under the plan via a mandate that was part of the overall legislation that required employers to provide coverage. They will receive the same set of services (587) as groups 1 and 2.

The table shows that the net result is a gain of 587 services for the 450 000 people in groups 2 and 3 as against a loss of 122 services for the 200 000 people in group 1. Hence whether the plan is judged to have positive effects or not depends on the desirability of the services and the value assigned to the number of people in the three groups.

Eddy presents a worse case scenario for estimating whether the plan produces positive effects or not. If the Oregon plan's attempt to form priorities was a failure, then the 709 services on their list could have been thought to be assigned at random. Then the value of a service gained would be as likely to have the same value as a service lost. With this assumption that each service has (probably) the same value, the determining factors then become how many people are gaining and losing, and how many services are involved.

The unit of account (called the numeraire by economists) is a 'person-service unit', i.e., one person getting a single service. The total PSUs at a point of time is the product of the number of persons multiplied by the quantity of services that they receive. Ignoring group 3 entirely (as a starting point), Eddy then calculates PSUs before and after the plan. The gain to group 2 is 70 440 000 PSUs (120 000 times 587) and the loss to group 1 is 24 400 000 PSUs (200 000 times 122). The net result is an effect of +460 040 000 PSUs.

The previous calculation was carried out in the context of gains and losses for a single distributional grouping, i.e., the poor, as both groups 1 and 2 relate to Medicaid eligibility. So +460 040 000 PSUs is the effect if one weights a person in group 1 the same as a person in group 2. Eddy pointed out that, although group 2 were poor, the losing group 1 were poorer as most of them were on Welfare (specifically, they were single mothers who were recipients of Aid to Families With Dependent Children, AFDC). He therefore proceeded to make a refined calculation that included a distribution dimension related to those on AFDC and the rest of those affected. This new calculation relied on ideas from earlier chapters, viz., 'switching values' first discussed in Chapter 4 and distributional weights mentioned in Chapter 5.

From before, we know that group 1 would lose 24 400 000 PSUs. If we aggregate groups 2 and 3, then we have 450 000 in the non-AFDC group. They receive 587 services each, which amounts to 264 150 000 PSUs. This is over 10 times as large as the PSUs of those in the losing group. Thus the weight on a PSU to someone in the non-AFDC group would have to be less than one-tenth of someone in group 1 (an extreme assumption considering that groups 2 and 3 are both disadvantaged) for the overall effects not to have been positive.

The conclusion so far is that the change in effect is most likely to be highly positive. The next issue is whether this increase in effect is worth more than the extra costs. After the demonstration project is over, i.e., after the five-year trial period, the savings from excluding services should match the extra expenditures for adding new Medicaid recipients, at least from the government's point of view. In the long run therefore there will be positive benefits at zero extra costs. What remains to be evaluated is the five-year $109.6 million cost to the federal government of having the demonstration project. Eddy used a revealed preference, CEA argument to justify these expenditures.

Without the plan, the government would have paid approximately $3850 million to cover 709 services for 200 000 people in group 1 for five years, which amounts to 709 services for 1 million person-years, or 709 million person-services in total. Dividing $3850 million by 709 million results in a cost per PSU of $5.36. The government was willing to pay this price. If one again just focuses on group's 2 gain of services and compares this with group 1's loss, the cost per PSU for five years of the Oregon plan was only around $0.60 (i.e., 309 million PSUs gained over five years minus 122 million PSUs lost, i.e., 187 million net, divided into $109.6 million = 0.59). This is much less than the $5.36 benchmark for services without the plan. The plan was therefore cost-effective for the fixed budget of $109.6 million.

8.4.4 CUA of Total Hip Arthroplasty

Chang et al. (1996) carried out a CUA of total hip arthroplasty (THA) for those with hip osteoarthritis who were significantly functionally limited. This third stage (class III) of the disease was before total dependency (class IV) where costly custodial care was needed. Pain was implicitly allowed for because this is a major determinant of functional outcomes with arthritis, and limited functioning would be associated with a lower utility of a life year.

To evaluate THAs it is very important to study the life-cycle of the disease. Osteoarthritis is a degenerative disease and not to operate will be costly as the patient will require the assistance of other people for day-to-day existence. Also many complications can occur with the surgery (other than death) through the need to repeat the operation if the primary one was not successful. Infections can also occur, as can aseptic failure (recurrent dislocation, prosthesis breakage, or loosening). Probabilities of occurrence have to be estimated and the costs of each eventuality must be assessed when they do occur. All this made it sensible for Chang et al. to provide separate analyses in four age categories: age 60, age 70, age 80, and ages 85 and older. There were eight evaluations in all, excluding sensitivity analyses, as (white) male and female patients were distinguished for each of the age categories. Special emphasis was given to the two extremes: 60-year-old women and men 85 and over.

Apart from the risk of operative death (covering on average 1.59 operations per patient), the main effect of THAs is to increase quality of life rather than to alter life expectancies. Using the standard gamble technique (to be explained in the next chapter) Chang et al. set a utility value for a life year at 0.5 in the third stage of osteoarthritis and 0.3 in the fourth stage to which a patient would progress without the operation. This differential in utility weights was sufficient to generate (relative to a patient without THA) an extra 6.88 QALYs for a 60-year-old woman and 2.00 QALYs for a man 85 and over. Corresponding to these incremental QALYs, there would be a *saving* in lifetime costs for 50-year-old women and an *increase* in lifetime costs of around $9100 for the oldest male group.

Table 8.7 (their Table 8) presents the resulting CUA calculations for the two limiting THA cases and compares them with other expensive, but widely accepted, technologies that extend life, especially coronary artery bypass surgery and renal dialysis. Again the assumption is that if these alternatives are accepted and THAs are more cost-effective than these alternatives, then THAs should also be accepted.

Table 8.7:   Cost-effectiveness ratio estimates of THA and other procedures

Procedure	Additional cost (1991 US prices)
1. THA (lifetime estimate): 60-year-old white woman	Cost saving
≥85-year-old white man	6100/QALY
2. Low-dose zidovudine therapy for asymptomatic HIV infection – continuous effect	7800/ LY
3. Coronary artery bypass, left main disease plus angina	8100/QALY
4. THA (first 3 years following surgery)	8700/QALY
5. Hydrochlorothiazide for hypertension	24900/LY
6. Screening mammography, women ≥50 years	20000–50000/LY
7. Coronary artery bypass, two vessel disease plus angina	87400/QALY
8. Renal dialysis, in-center benefit, men	59400–68300/LY
9. Low-dose zidovudine therapy for asymptomatic HIV infection – one-time effect	83600/ LY
10. Cholestyramine for high cholesterol	91200/LY
11. Captopril for hypertension	98100/LY
12. Autologous blood donations for elective THA	218800/QALY
13. Screening mammography, women <50 years	220400/LY

Source: Chang et al. (1996)

As we can see from Table 8.7, THAs were more cost-effective than coronary artery bypass and renal dialysis. However, Chang et al. did not document whether all the analyses listed in the league table were, in fact, comparable. Let us go through each of the four areas specified by Drummond et al. (1993) from section 8.4.2 regarding comparability:

1.   Chang et al. used a 3% discount rate, which is in line with the US panel guidelines, but lower than the 5% norm used prior to 1991. Chang et al. did not mention the discount rates used in the other studies. Since some (e.g., number 11 on the list) were carried out in the 1980s, it would be very unlikely that the same discount rates were used.

2.   Chang et al. used the standard gamble technique. This is best practice if one has faith in a patient's ability to assign probabilities to uncertain

events. But most CUAs do not use this method. So again it is unlikely that those other studies on the list would have used the same methodology to assign utilities.

3. Only direct costs were covered by Chang et al. in their study. One cannot be sure what costing methods were used by the other studies as nothing was stated about this. While most studies *do* actually include only direct costs, this is not a consolation, as alternative health interventions involve differing amounts of indirect costs. So some ratios would be more incomplete than others from a social perspective. It is not the case that all ratios would then be equally proportionately distorted.

4. The comparison program for making the marginal calculations for THAs was not to do nothing, as custodial care would be required for those progressing to stage IV of the osteoarthritis disease. The costs of having this custodial care in the absence of surgery were very expensive (equal to $38 499 a lifetime for the 60-year-old women group). It is on this basis that the incremental costs could turn out to be negative and the CUA result for THAs be cost saving for women. As with the AZT study for AIDS mentioned by Drummond et al., the costs of minimum care for THAs were widely different from no care. One needs to know (but is not told) for each of the other studies included in Table 8.7 which ones used the minimum and which used the no care alternatives.

Two final remarks are in order. On the face of it, the fact that THAs are cost saving for women (line 1) seems to contradict the claim that only a CBA can tell whether an intervention is worthwhile. For clearly, according to the CUA result these THAs must be approved. However, such results are not really exceptions, because the context is really one of cost minimization that is a special case of CBA. Any situation where effects are held constant is a CM exercise; and any time when benefits are constant and costs reduced, a CBA would approve of it.

One of the criticisms of the Oregon plan that Eddy (1991b) did think was valid was that there was an overly broad definition of 'services'. Categories should be selected such that everyone who receives a particular service should have the same expected benefits and costs. Table 8.7 illustrates the wisdom of this advice. THA is not a homogenous service. For most women THAs are cost saving, while for males this is not the case. Women live longer and so there are more years for the hip replacement to contribute quality of life. Similarly, while THAs (line 1) may be more cost-effective than AZT (line 3) if one considers lifetime effects, this will not be the case if one just estimates the first three years after surgery (line 4). Linked to this point about the breadth of definition of services is the need to disaggregate services into self-contained procedures so that they can be evaluated separately.

Providing blood for one's own hip surgery may be recommended by the surgeon, but that does not mean that this procedure is really necessary and cost-effective. Line 12 shows that the cost per QALY is very high for these blood donations.

8.5   FINAL SECTION

We end with the problems, summary and looking ahead sections.

8.5.1   Problems

In Gerard and Mooney's (1993) discussion of the pitfalls of using QALY league tables, they emphasize the importance of identifying the exact opportunity cost involved with accepting a new health care intervention. The problems probe this issue in the context of 'importing' league tables from another country (but not focusing on exchange rate issues). As a preliminary to the problems, review the league tables listed in Tables 8.1, 8.5 and 8.7, but now assume (heroically) that none of the differences in each of the tables is due to methodological differences.

1. What are the similarities and dissimilarities in the relative QALY rankings for health interventions in the UK and US?
2. Concentrate on the US rankings as presented in Table 8.1.
    (a) If there is a budget constraint of $20000, what is the opportunity cost of introducing a new health care intervention?
    (b) If there is no specified budget constraint, what is the opportunity cost of introducing a new health care intervention? Could the opportunity cost be an income assistance program for the poor?
3. Concentrate on the UK rankings as presented in Table 8.5.
    (a) If there is a budget constraint of £8000, what is the opportunity cost of introducing a new health care intervention?
    (b) If there is no specified budget constraint, what is the opportunity cost of introducing a new health care intervention? Could the opportunity cost be an assisted housing program?
4. How would you account for any of the differences in rankings between the US and the UK?

8.5.2   Summary

By specifying an effect in terms of a QALY, one has a common basis for, in principle, comparing any type of health treatment because all consequences must involve an impact in terms of either the quantity or quality of life (or both). A CUA, like any kind of CEA, works best when there is a budget constraint. The ratio for the last ranked project on the list is the benchmark for a potential new project. In a CEA, when there is no explicit budget constraint, the evaluation process comes to a halt. But in a CUA used in this no-budget context, progress still can be made, by either comparing the potential project's cost-per-QALY with the ratio of some well-accepted intervention or seeing if the ratio is less than a suggested absolute amount, where less than $20000-per-QALY is acceptable and greater than $100000 is questionable.

Of course, there is no point in making numerical comparisons if the methodologies used are widely different. In this chapter we provided: (a) a check-list by Drummond et al. (1993) as to what components to look for when comparing methodologies; and (b) a set of guidelines by a US panel seeking to establish methodological comparability. The check-list covered establishing: what discount rate(s) was (were) used; what method was used to estimate the utilities; whether only direct costs were measured; and what was the base from which incremental ratios were calculated (no care or minimum care). The guidelines were built around creating a reference case (in addition to the particular one the authors thought was most useful for their original purposes) that standardizes the ingredients and therefore can make any study's results comparable. The reference case should, *inter alia*, have a social perspective, use a 3% discount rate, and be on an incremental (minimal care) basis.

When comparing rankings based on CUA relative to those based on CBA and the WTP approach, one needs to know whether or not a fixed budget constraint is in place. Without a budget constraint being specified, CBA is more efficient. When a CUA is concerned with a unidimensional treatment, and people have identical preferences and incomes, then a CUA would give the same rankings as a CBA.

The Oregon Medicaid plan was one of the few occasions when an economic evaluation was comprehensively employed in making a real world decision. Even though the formal CUA analysis was ultimately abandoned, the original formal rankings did set the stage for what took place and were instrumental in what transpired. The need to cut services in order to free up resources to expand health care provision to those without insurance is one of the most crucial public policy issues in the US at this time. In one form or another, an Oregon-type plan will have to be developed and implemented in a number of US states.

On almost everyone's list of benchmark CUA interventions that takes place, and is acceptable, is neo-natal intensive care. So one of the featured applications involved this case study. Surprisingly we found that neo-natal care, when evaluated as a CBA using the human capital approach, was not actually worthwhile even though it was accepted. To be sure to come up with a worthwhile intervention, a CUA could require that the project be cost saving (as we saw for hip replacements for 60-year-old women). But this would still be within the domain of CBA. So the conclusion that only a CBA can detect worthwhile projects still holds.

8.5.3   Looking Ahead

Central to CUA is the measurement of the utility value of a life year. The main methods for estimating these utilities will be explained in the next chapter. The Oregon plan was ultimately rejected by the political process because it was thought to discriminate against QALYs accruing to the disabled. This claim of discrimination makes little economic sense. As Kaplan (1995) points out, having a low utility does not mean that one's concerns are given a low importance. There is no point in trying to improve the quality of life of persons with unity utilities. So disabled persons having low utilities would have much to gain from treatments that raise their quality of life. Nonetheless, the whole issue of equity in CUA is worth discussing in depth and this examination takes place in Chapter 10.

9. Measuring utilities in cost–utility analysis

9.1 INTRODUCTION

The number of QALYs associated with any health state can be expressed as the product of the number of years T (for time) in that state and the average quality of a year in that state, which will be denoted as $\bar{U}$, i.e., QALYs $= \bar{U}.T$. We will (unlike some of the literature) use the term *quality* interchangeably with *utility* and *value*. This chapter is devoted to explaining, comparing and contrasting the three main methods for deriving estimates for $\bar{U}$. By a method we mean the type of question asked to a person to extract his/her preferences and the way this gets recorded as a number (usually) between 0 and 1. We will not be referring to alternative statistical estimation techniques as different methods. The three methods covered are: the category rating scale (RS), the standard gamble (SG), and the time trade-off model (TTO). We make comparisons in terms of both theory and practice. Before explaining each method in detail, and then presenting the applications, we cover some background issues.

9.1.1 Measurement Stages

In order to measure utilities for a particular study, there are four stages that need to be recognized:

1. The first stage involves identifying the relevant health states. For example, in a study of kidney transplants, there were four health outcomes, viz.: kidney transplant, hospital dialysis, home dialysis, and death.
2. The second stage involves providing descriptions of the health states identified. In order to extract people's preferences, they need to know what is involved. As the duration of a health state is an important determinant of a utility value, we examine this dimension separately in this introductory section.
3. Then the selection of the subjects to be interviewed needs to be made.

Whose values to include is a controversial issue, and we also examine
this controversy below.
4.   Finally, a measurement instrument must be used. As stated above, the
     three main methods we will be analyzing are RS, SG and TTO.

9.1.2   Duration as a Separate Consideration

Torrance et al.'s (1972) pioneering paper on the TTO method argues that
one must always consider explicitly the length of time one is in a health
state. A highly confining state's utility is a decreasing function of time;
while an inconvenient, but less confining, state's utility is an increasing
function of time. Hence, patients prefer bed confinement for a short duration, but prefer being hooked up to a kidney dialysis machine for the longer
duration.

As an illustration of the importance of duration, refer to Table 9.1
which shows how the general public and patients valued time spent on
kidney dialysis (artificially removing waste from the blood). The results
are based on Sackette and Torrance's (1978) Table 4. We see that, for both
groups, the utility values decline with duration. The implication of these
results is that, although it is still possible to represent QALYs by $\bar{U}.T$, one
needs to be aware that the averages $\bar{U}$ are really functions of the T.
Averages for patients treated over long durations would not be good
measures of averages for patients treated over short durations (and vice
versa).

Table 9.1:   *Utility values using TTO for patients versus general public by*
duration

Health state and duration	General public	Dialysis patients	Percent difference	Probability that the difference is due to chance
Hospital dialysis				
3 months	0.62	0.81	31%	0.01
8 years	0.56	0.59	5%	Not significant
Life	0.32	0.53	62%	0.01
Home dialysis				
8 years	0.65	0.72	11%	Not significant
Life	0.39	0.56	44%	0.06

Source: Sackette and Torrance (1978)

9.1.3   Whose Utility Values to Use

We will discuss the issue of whose utility values to use from two perspectives. First we consider the choices that the CUA literature has analyzed and then we put the issue into a CBA context.

1. From a CUA perspective, whose preferences to use is basically a choice between interviewing the general public or those with the disease. Drummond et al. (1987) argue that for *social* decisions, an informed member of the general public (or community representative) should provide the values. This position, as we saw in the last chapter, was exactly the same as the one taken by the US panel on CEA who wished to standardize evaluations. The argument was that, by always using community preferences, one can best compare results across diseases. Different diseases affect different patients (males/females, young/old, etc.); but that would not matter if one does not intend to use the patient preferences.

    Even if one accepts that the general public's preferences are the most relevant, there is still a problem as to how to ensure that they are well informed. The question then becomes, can healthy people appreciate all the nuisances of living with a disease just from a verbal description? If not, then patient preferences may have to be used as patients are clearly well informed. As recognized by the US CEA panel (see Weinstein et al. (1996)): 'Use of patient preferences to value health states is acceptable only when adequate information is unavailable regarding community preferences.'

    On the other hand, patients have an incentive to exaggerate the disutility of their condition in the hope that more resources will be allocated to their disease if the QALYs gained from treating their disease appear greater. Actually, the US panel was concerned with the reverse case, as one of the reasons why the US panel opted for community preferences over patient preferences was 'because of the possibility that those with disabilities assign higher scores to their health states' – see Russell et al. (1996). In either case, it is an important empirical matter whether patients and the general public value health states the same. The Sackette and Torrance results reported in Table 9.1 for the RS method also have a bearing on this issue. Patients on kidney dialysis valued utilities up to 62% higher than members of the general public and this difference was highly significant. Note that patients here did *not* have higher disutilities than for the general public and so did not appear to be responding strategically.

    As an alternative to choosing between patients and the general public one could possibly use medical professionals as agents of the patients. Having an agent represent a client is a standard way of making decisions when information is not equally available to parties in a transaction (i.e., there is 'asymmetric information'). The choice now is between doctors and nurses. Nurses often deal with patients on a daily basis and may know the patients' personal preferences better; while doctors would have a better understanding of diseases and treatments.

Churchill et al. (1987) also measured utilities for patients with kidney problems, this time related to end-stage renal disease. They used both the RS and TTO methods. The RS results are what we are interested in here as the RS method was applied to patients, nurses and nephrologists (kidney specialists). Treatments for this disease included transplantation and the two kinds of dialysis, i.e., hemodialysis (relying on a machine) and peritoneal dialysis (relying on the patient's abdominal wall) in various settings (hospital, self-care and home). Table 9.2 (their Table 3) shows that for the RS method nurse valuations were much closer to patient preferences than were the doctor values. Nurses were the more representative agents.

Table 9.2: Mean time trade-off and visual analogue scores

	Time trade-off	Patient visual analogue	Nephrologist visual analogue	Nurse visual analogue
Hospital hemodialysis	0.43	0.77	0.55	0.62
Home/self-hemodialysis	0.49	0.75	0.66	0.74
Continuous ambulatory peritoneal dialysis	0.56	0.79	0.65	0.72
Transplant	0.84	0.86	0.69	0.81

Source: Churchill et al. (1987)

On the other hand, Kaplan (1995) disputes the claim that different groups provide widely different values. He reports studies where ethnicity, being a patient or not, and location were not different on average. He suggests that everyone would agree that it is better to live free of pain. Nonetheless, we have to conclude that there is no consensus in the CUA literature as to whose preferences to use.

2.   From a CBA perspective, the question as to whose utility values to use is easy to answer. Assuming consumer sovereignty, the people who are affected are the ones who should be consulted. If patients have higher valuations than the general public then so be it. The problem with the

CUA literature is that it is seeking to find the *one* person or group whose values are to count. The general public may be the best representative of society as a whole from this perspective. But a CBA takes the inputs and outputs and finds *all* those who are affected and applies the valuations of each affected party to each input and output. So patients are to be consulted about pain and suffering. Family members are to be consulted about time taken to visit and care for patients. And the consumers who must give up resources are the ones to be consulted about paying the taxes to provide for the treatment resources. To repeat what was emphasized in Chapter 1, a social CBA measures the evaluations of all parties affected by a particular intervention. CBA assumes that individuals are the best judges of their own welfare. When this is violated by a lack of information, then methods other than WTP may be employed. But, if consumer sovereignty holds, then it is consumer preferences that should be used to make a health care evaluation.

9.1.4 Statistical Accuracy of the Methods

Torrance (1976) tested the accuracy of the three methods that we will be discussing. One aspect of accuracy is the reliability/consistency of the results obtained by a method. That is, can the results be replicated by:

1. Asking a similar question in the original questionnaire ('internal consistency')? or
2. Asking the same question at a later date?

The correlation between the original utility estimate and the similar question estimate was 0.77 for both SG and TTO. A correlation of 1.00 would be the highest correlation value (for a positive association) and zero would be the lowest. Torrance (p. 132) calls these figures 'respectable'. The correlation coefficient between the original estimate and those one year later were: 0.53 for SG, 0.62 for TTO, and 0.49 for RS. Drummond et al. (1987, p. 118) call these figures 'poor for all techniques'.

Another aspect of accuracy is 'precision', i.e., how large an individual estimate is relative to its standard error. A 95% confidence interval for an estimate would be given by the estimate plus-or-minus about twice the standard error (assuming a normal distribution – see equation (7.6)). The standard error for SG was 0.125, and for TTO was 0.135. Thus, if the estimated utility were 0.60, the 95% confidence interval for SG would be 0.35–0.85, and 0.33–0.87 for TTO. These ranges are wide. However, for health care applications, it is the mean of the individual estimates that is important. The standard error of the mean is the standard deviation of the estimate divided by the square root of the size of the sample – recall equation (7.7). Thus, the precision of the mean can always be reduced by increasing the size of the sample.

According to Churchill et al. (1987), two criteria that any utility method must satisfy are to be 'reliable' (i.e., reproducible) and 'valid' (i.e., measure what it purports to measure). These authors tested the extent to which these two criteria were satisfied for the TTO method as applied to end-stage renal disease. Part of their results was previously reported in Table 9.2. To test for reliability, Churchill et al. measured TTOs on two occasions, four weeks apart, and estimated the correlation between the utility measures. The correlations were estimated separately for each type of treatment (called 'intra-class correlation') and overall. The correlations between time 1 and time 2 are reported in Table 9.3 (their Table 2). The correlation coefficients were greater than 0.75 for all treatment modalities except home and self-care hemodialysis. The overall correlation was 0.81 and highly significantly different from zero (and not statistically different from 1).

Table 9.3:   Intra-class correlation using time trade-off

Hospital hemodialysis	Home and self-care hemodialysis	Continuous ambulatory peritoneal dialysis	Transplant	All
0.87	0.50	0.79	0.86	0.81

Source: Churchill et al. (1987)

To test whether the TTO method estimated what it purports to, Churchill et al. used the concept of 'construct validity', i.e., whether the method provides estimates between treatment groups in line with *a priori* prediction. We remarked in the last chapter (when discussing the Oregon plan) that it was inconsistent to use the economic evaluation approach backwards and judge a method by the result rather than the other way round. But, in the context of a particular disease (rather than a whole range), it does not seem unreasonable to argue that the quality of life is better if a person can be treated at home rather than in a hospital (or does not need constant treatment). So it may make sense to expect that a valid utility method should produce a value that was highest for transplanted patients and lowest for hospital hemodialysis patients, with the other treatment modalities having values in between.

The construct validity of the TTO and RS methods for kidney disease is confirmed by the results reported in Table 9.2. Transplant utilities were highest and hospital hemodialysis values were lowest irrespective of the method or group involved. Churchill et al. interpreted the fact that the RS method used a smaller portion of the scale as a sign that the TTO method was a more discriminating measurement instrument.

9.2 MAIN MEASUREMENT SOURCES

Torrance (1986), in his survey of methods for measuring utilities, identifies three main sources that evaluators can use for fixing the utility values. Analysts can estimate the utilities by judgment, they can look at values in the literature, or they can measure the values themselves. We explain each method in turn.

9.2.1 Judgment by the Analyst

A central proponent of the use of personal judgment by the analyst is Weinstein. In the hypertension study by Stason and Weinstein (1977) they adjusted life years saved by 1% for any medical side-effects that treatment might impose. The meaning of this adjustment is that patients would give up 1% of their life expectancy (i.e. 3.5 days each year) to avoid the side-effects of the treatment. They report that the C/E ratios (based on QALYs) were very sensitive to the adjustments made for the side-effects. If instead of 1% the figure of 2% were to be used for the side-effects, the cost-effectiveness ratio would rise on average by 5%.

Weinstein (1980) in his study of estrogen use in postmenopausal women, again makes the 1% adjustment for the benefit that the treatment gives in removing the symptoms of menopause. However, for the fact that estrogen leads to a lower chance of hip fracture (as it retards bone loss), Weinstein made a 5% adjustment for the pain that is avoided. Weinstein uses a different approach for another quality of life effect involved with the use of estrogen. Rather than apply a percentage, he deals with units of a QALY directly. That is, to allow for patient anxiety (as estrogen increases the chances of endometrial cancer and the need for a hysterectomy) there is a one-year QALY reduction to the effects.

Because the use of estrogen led to a very small increase in life expectancy (reduced chances of dying from hip fractures were almost matched by the increased chances of dying from endometrial cancer), judgments over quality of life issues could outweigh issues over the length of life.

Weinstein recognizes that the use of personal judgments by the analyst is inherently a subjective process. But, in his applied work, he shows that it would be irresponsible to try to avoid making some judgments. To guard against bias, Weinstein recommends that sensitivity analysis be incorporated in any study that uses personal judgments.

9.2.2   Reference to the Literature

This is the simplest approach. If, for example, one is studying mastectomy for breast cancer, one could refer to the 0.48 QALYs obtained by Sackette and Torrance (1978) using the TTO technique. But, in order to work towards the ideal of the US panel on cost-effectiveness (who recommended incorporating a 'Reference Case' methodology in order to achieve greater comparability), it is useful to consider a more general framework.

We now explain the Rosser matrix 'R' that we referred to in the last chapter when we presented Drummond et al.'s (1993) cost per QALY league table. Twelve of the 21 treatments listed in Table 8.5 used the 'R' method to derive their utility estimates. The matrix consists of all (ordered) pairs that correspond to a two-dimensional listing of health states according to what Rosser and Kind (1978) call 'objective disability' and 'subjective distress'.

There were eight levels of disability specified in terms of how one can function in society; at work; shopping; and at home with and without assistance. Associated with each of these disability levels there could be four levels of distress that involved various degrees of exposure to pain and types of medication for dealing with the pain. The eight categories of disability as they defined them were:

1.   No disability.
2.   Slight social disability.
3.   Severe social disability and/or slight impairment of performance at work. Able to do all housework except very heavy tasks.
4.   Choice of work or performance at work severely limited. Housewives and old people able to do light housework only but able to go out shopping.
5.   Unable to undertake any paid employment. Unable to continue any education. Old people confined to home except for escorted outings and short walks and unable to do shopping. Housewives able only to perform a few simple tasks.
6.   Confined to chair or to wheelchair or able to move around in the home only with support from an assistant.
7.   Confined to bed.
8.   Unconscious.

The four levels of distress were:

1.   No distress.
2.   Mild.

3. Moderate.
4. Severe.

Table 9.4 below (which is based on French et al.'s Table 2) contains the median utility estimates for each of the pairs of disability and distress states for 70 persons interviewed by Rosser and Kind. Potentially, as there were eight disability categories and four distress levels, there could be 32 pairs. But, seeing that disability state 8 is 'unconscious', distress levels would not be applicable (NA) for any of the three levels other than 'none'. So there are 29 health states listed in the table.

Table 9.4: The Rosser and Kind index of health status

	1: No distress	2: Mild	3: Moderate	4: Severe
Disability state 1	1.000	0.995	0.990	0.967
2	0.990	0.986	0.973	0.932
3	0.980	0.972	0.956	0.912
4	0.964	0.956	0.942	0.870
5	0.946	0.935	0.900	0.700
6	0.875	0.845	0.680	0.000
7	0.677	0.564	0.000	−1.486
8	−1.028	NA	NA	NA

Source: Based on French et al. (1996)

We can see from the table that it is the mix of distress and disability that is important and not just the disability level. Thus, it is better to be more restricted with mild distress at pair (3,2) than to be less restricted with severe stress at pair (1,4), that is, one has a utility level of 0.972 rather than 0.967.

French et al. (1996) used the Rosser and Kind index to estimate a QALY for time with hepatitis B (one of six main diseases that illegal drug users typically contract). They used this index because it avoided counter-intuitive rankings by asking respondents to reconsider their rankings in light of their implications for health care allocations, in terms of what interventions would be funded and how many people could be treated. A typical interview by Rosser and Kind took between 1.5 and 4 hours.

French et al. assumed that a moderately acute case of hepatitis B was equivalent to a (3,3) pair in the Rosser and Kind set of health states. We can see from Table 9.4 that the utility value for this health state is 0.956. Any part of a life year with this disease (estimated to be two months for an illegal drug user) would decrease utility by 0.044 relative to a state of no disease (which has a utility value of 1).

9.2.3   The Analyst Measuring the Utilities

Preferences can be measured using any of the three methods RS, SG and TTO. These three methods will be explained in detail in the next section. Here we give an overview to these methods by applying three alternative interpretations to a resulting pair of utility measures obtained for two different health states (see also Nord (1992)'s Table 3).

Say we are considering how to interpret an outcome where state A gets assigned a utility score of 40 and state B was judged to have a value of 80. Three possible interpretations would be:

1. Rating scale: On a scale of 0 to 100, with 0 the worst possible health state and 100 the best possible health state, 'I think that state A is 40 points higher than the lowest health state and state B is 40 points higher than state B'. (In terms of the Rosser and Kind index, one would say that state A was half as good as state B.)
2. Standard gamble: 'I think it is just as good to gamble with a chance of 0.4 of getting well immediately and a chance of 0.6 of dying immediately as to live in state A with certainty.' (Similarly for state B.)
3. Time trade-off: 'I think it is just as good to live 0.4 year being healthy as living 1 year in state A.' (Similarly for state B.)

9.3   MAIN MEASUREMENT METHODS

When applying a particular method to a specified health state, it matters whether the state one is considering is considered worse than dead or not. So the measurement instruments make separate provision for these two cases.

9.3.1   Category Rating Scale (RS)

This is the simplest technique that has the lowest cost to administer. It involves referring to a line on a page with the best health state at one end, and the worst state at the other end. The person is asked to place all the other health states in between, pointing out that the spaces between the placements correspond to differences in preferences. Usually the end states are being healthy and being dead.

When being dead is the worst state, this can be given a zero value, and being healthy a unity value. When a 'feeling thermometer' is used, the healthy state is given a value of 100. Say there are three (intermediate) health states A, B and C, and the person ranks A>B>C. The person is then asked to place the three in line with each other. Assume that the placing is A = 80, B = 52 and C = 35. This simply relates to the unit interval by dividing by 100. So the utilities would be A = 0.80, B = 0.52 and C = 0.35.

Now assume that health state C was judged to be worse than dead. Being dead, health state D, might then be given a value of 0.40. Clearly state C must have a negative value. To allow for this, all states are converted by the formula: $U(x) = (x - d)/(1 - d)$, where d is the value attached to being dead and x is the value of any other health state. Using this formula we get:

$$U(A) = (0.80 - 0.40)/(1 - 0.40) = 0.4/0.6 = 0.67$$
$$U(B) = (0.52 - 0.40)/(1 - 0.40) = 0.12/0.6 = 0.20$$
$$U(C) = (0.35 - 0.40)/(1 - 0.40) = -0.05/0.6 = -0.08$$

9.3.2 Standard Gamble (SG)

SG is an inherently costly (time consuming) method that can only be handled with an interview. First, set the utility of being healthy, $\bar{U}(H)$, as unity and the utility of being dead, $\bar{U}(D)$, as zero. All other health states (than the extreme states) are to occur with certainty. They are considered in pairwise comparisons between the particular health state and a gamble consisting of the extreme states. The healthy state is to occur with probability Π, while the dead state occurs with probability $1 - \Pi$. The variable that a person chooses is the probability Π in the gamble. That is, a person is asked for the value for Π that would make the person indifferent between having the particular health state and accepting the gamble.

Again, assume A > B > C. Say that the person cannot decide between (is indifferent to) having state A for sure and accepting an 80% chance of being healthy and a 20% chance of dying. The person is then accepting $\Pi = 0.8$. This translates into a utility value as follows. The person has chosen: $\bar{U}(A) = 0.8\,\bar{U}(H) + 0.2\,\bar{U}(D)$. Because of the fact that we set $\bar{U}(H) = 1$ and $\bar{U}(D) = 0$, it means $\bar{U}(A) = 0.8$. This is, of course, the probability that was assigned in the gamble. So, the setting of Π and the setting of $\bar{U}(A)$ is one and the same process. With B being worse than A, the person *should* (if s/he were rational) accept a lower probability of being healthy in order to be indifferent between it and the gamble. $\bar{U}(B)$ would be this lower probability value. And so on for option C.

When the states are temporary, state D does not apply. The worst state, C, replaces D in the formula. One then uses for the gamble, $\Pi\bar{U}(H) + (1 - \Pi)\,\bar{U}(C)$. Since $\bar{U}(C) > 0$ (it is preferred to being dead), the utility of a particular state is no longer just Π. But it is easy to calculate. For example, if in choosing between A and the gamble, the person selects $\Pi = 0.55$, and with $U(C) = 0.4$, then $U(A) = 0.55(1) + 0.45(0.4) = 0.73$. How does one find $U(C)$ in the first place? By comparing it with a standard gamble including H and D. One needs to follow a sequential path with the alternatives, starting with the worst one.

The standard gamble is the same as the Von Neumann and Morgenstern (1944) method for measuring utilities under uncertainty. It is for this reason that SG is regarded as best practice, i.e., the 'gold standard'. What this basically means here is that the SG method fits in best with economic theory. However, this method requires logical consistency and there are a number of axioms that have to be satisfied. More precisely, $\Pi \ \bar{U}(H) + (1 - \Pi) \ \bar{U}(D)$ is the *expected utility*. The axioms of the expected utility theorem must therefore hold for the method to be valid. (The three axioms are: that preferences exist and are transitive; independence; and continuity of preferences.) Unfortunately, according to a number of studies (and also Starmer's (2000) recent survey), there are a large number of empirical violations of the axioms. So the *potential* theoretical superiority of the SG method should not be decisive. How techniques function in practice is going to be the focal point in the applications.

In order to appreciate the case studies, and the final application in particular, we need to understand that when one uses the expected utility equation $\Pi \ \bar{U}(H) + (1 - \Pi) \ \bar{U}(D)$, one is assuming that a person is *risk neutral*. In fact, this is how one defines risk neutrality in economics. For example, if one is indifferent between having \$1 for sure and accepting a 50/50 chance of receiving \$2 or having nothing, then one is risk neutral. If people are not neutral as to risk, or find it difficult even thinking about dying, then the SG would not be the best in practice.

9.3.3   Time Trade-Off (TTO)

This is basically a simpler version of the SG method that was formulated by Torrance et al. (1972). Again a pairwise comparison is used, but this time probabilities are absent, i.e., one is dealing with certainties in each comparison one is making. One is comparing being in a particular state A (say, living with arthritis) for the rest of one's life t with being fully healthy for a specified number of years x. As the utility of being healthy is greater than the utility of being with arthritis, i.e., $\bar{U}(H) > \bar{U}(A)$, one would only consider the comparison if the number of years with full health were shorter than the period with arthritis, i.e., $x < t$.

The question then is, how much shorter would the time in full health have to be for one to have the *same* lifetime utility in the healthy state as in the disease state? In other words, how much time x would one 'trade off' of time with the higher health state to equate in utility terms with a lifetime *t* with arthritis? The utility of the two lifetimes would be equal only if:

$$x \cdot \bar{U}(\text{H}) = t \cdot \bar{U}(\text{A}) \qquad (9.1)$$

As before, the utility of being in full health is set equal to unity. With $\bar{U}(\text{H}) = 1$ in equation (9.1), we have $x = t \cdot \bar{U}(\text{A})$, or: $\bar{U}(\text{A}) = x/t$. So as *t* is known, one determines the utility value $\bar{U}(\text{A})$ as soon as one specifies the time period *x*. Say a person has a remaining life expectancy of 40 years and s/he has arthritis. This sets *t* = 40. The person is asked whether this state is preferable to living 20 more years, but healthy. If the person is indifferent, then *x* = 20 is the chosen value. The utility of a year with arthritis would be 0.5 (i.e., 20/40).

The above method applies to permanent states, such as having arthritis for the rest of one's life. For temporary states, one follows a similar approach to that used in SG. One particular temporary state (say, B) is to be evaluated relative to a worse other temporary state (say, C). Time *x* is varied until the person is indifferent between time in state B and the time *t* in state C. The utility value would now be: $\bar{U}(\text{B}) = 1 - [1 - \bar{U}(\text{C})](x/t)$, with $\bar{U}(\text{C})$ being estimated previously by reference to a permanent state.

There is a version of the TTO method, first devised by Mehrez and Gafni (1989), called the *Healthy-Years Equivalent* (HYE) that has generated a large recent debate (see Ried (1998) or Morrison (1997)). The HYE calculates the utility value in two steps, where each step involves a gamble. The first step involves a SG comparison between A for a given time period and a risky gamble between a successful health state with a probability Π and a failure health state with a probability 1 − Π. This SG may or may not be the same as the SG that we described earlier, because: (a) the specification of state A may be say, arthritis, but it need not be for a time period that is one's remaining life *t* = 40, and (b) the success state need not be fully healthy and the failure state dead. The second step then asks one to find a length of time, that occurs with certainty *with the best possible health state*, that is equivalent to the gamble with the stated probability Π expressed in step 1.

It is the conversion of the Π to an equivalent length of time with certainty that suggests that the two methods HYE and TTO are similar. Because the HYE may use health states other than H or D in the SG, one can concur with Ried (1998) that HYE is a 'generalized time trade-off method'. However, the HYE approach is really just a hybrid method as it uses the SG to come up with a TTO. If one chooses the TTO method precisely because one wishes to avoid using the probabilities that are fundamental to the SG method, it is difficult to understand why one would use the HYE approach.

9.4   APPLICATIONS

Many empirical studies find that the TTO method is the most appropriate instrument for measuring utilities. The case studies illustrate the many ways that the TTO method is shown to be superior. We begin by comparing all three methods, first against each other, and second against a direct measure of preferences (i.e., rankings). Then the TTO method is contrasted with the SG approach for quantifying the quality of life associated with vision loss. The final study measures utilities for persons who are high-risk takers.

9.4.1   Survey of Utility Estimates

Nord (1992) gave an overview of a number of studies that estimated utilities using the three main methods. He summarized the differences obtained by using each instrument for the same health state and then attempted to explain why these differences existed. Table 9.5 (his Table 1) presents the results of his review.

We can see from Table 9.5 that (apart from the Richardson study) the RS estimates are typically much lower than for SG and TTO. The SG values are often the highest, being much greater than the TTO values in two studies and approximately equal to the TTO values in the other two studies. Nord attempted to explain the differences found in values by the various methods in terms of: (1) *what* was being asked in a question, and (2) *how* it was asked.

1.   What was being asked in the SG and the TTO methods was a trade-off (between certainty in SG and lifespan in TTO), while for RS people were asked to apply a numerical scale directly to a clinical condition. Since people do not have much experience in directly assigning numbers to conditions, while they often make trade-off decisions, Nord argues that there is no reason to think that RS estimates would be close to the values obtained by the other two methods. To account for the higher values found for SG than for TTO, Nord points out that the SG approach may be affected by people's aversion to risk, while TTO valuations may be affected by time-preference. People may show a reluctance to 'gambling with their own health' and thus give high value to outcomes that are determined with certainty, which is what determines values in a SG. The more life years one has, the more one would be willing to trade-off lifespan for better health, which is what determines values in a TTO.
2.   A fundamental consideration regarding how questions are asked is the benchmark (or 'anchor') that one is using to express one's preferences.

Table 9.5: Selected results from comparative valuation studies

Author	N	Kind of subjects	SG	RS	TTO	State
Torrance (1976)	43	Students	0.75	0.61	0.76	Not indicated
			0.73	0.58	0.70	
			0.60	0.44	0.63	
			0.44	0.26	0.38	
Bombardier et al. (1982)	52	Health care personnel	0.85	0.65	0.78	Walking stick
		Patients	0.81	0.47	0.58	Walking frame
		Family	0.64	0.29	0.41	Needs supervision when walking
			0.55	0.18	0.28	Needs one assistant for walking
			0.38	0.08	0.11	Needs two assistants
Llewellyn-Thomas et al. (1984)	64	Patients	0.92	0.74		Tired. Sleepless
			0.84	0.68		Unable to work. Some pain
			0.75	0.53		Limited walking
						Unable to work. Tired
			0.66	0.47		In house. Unable to work. Vomiting
			0.30	0.30		In bed in hospital. Needs help with self-care. Trouble remembering
Read et al. (1984)	60	Doctors	0.90	0.72	0.83	Moderate angina
			0.71	0.35	0.53	Severe angina
Richardson et al. (1989)	46	Health care personnel	0.86	0.75	0.80	Breast cancer:
						Removed breast unconcerned
			0.44	0.48	0.41	Removed breast. Stiff arm. Tired
						Anxious. Difficulties with sex
						Cancer spread. Constant pain
			0.19	0.24	0.16	Tired. Expecting not to live long

Source: Nord (1992)

As Nord remarks, 'everything is relative'. A state that is compared to being in full health will score badly, but the same state will score highly when compared to being dead. In Kaplan et al. (1979), one benchmark was a state halfway between being completely well and dead. Clearly if one regarded this as 'half-dead' then this would be a very serious condition, and other states would be valued highly relative to this. On the other hand, Rosser and Kind in measuring utilities for their index had a reference state that people judged to be 200 times better than death. It is not surprising that other states were not as highly valued relative to this state.

9.4.2   Comparison of Methods with a Direct Measure of Preferences

We have just seen in the Nord study (which is consistent with findings in other research, such as Horberger et al. (1992)) that SG weights are higher than TTO weights, which are in turn higher than RS weights. Weights that differ systematically by method are a problem because an intervention that is marginally rejected if the TTO method is used to estimate weights could be judged worthwhile if SG weights had been used. The logical question to ask now is which method is in some sense 'best'. Bleichrodt and Johannesson (1997) attempted to answer this question empirically by comparing how well each of the weights obtained by the three main methods correlated with a direct measure of individual preferences as contained in explicit rankings of health states.

The starting point to use in any method is to provide a respondent with a description of the health state they are going to value. That is, to be able to extract an individual's preferences that person needs to know what is involved. The reference state used in Bleichrodt and Johannesson's study we will call state E (they call it state D, but in this chapter we attached the label 'death' to state D) and this corresponds to commonly occurring types of back pain and rheumatism.

State E was one of 625 possible states, each one being a combination of four attributes that have five levels (i.e., $(5)(5)(5)(5) = 625$). The four attributes were: the ability to do general daily activities (at home and at work); the capacity for self-care (eating, washing, dressing); the ability to perform types of leisure activities; and the extent of pain and other health complaints. For each attribute, level 1 was the least restrictive or painful, and level 5 was the worst. State E had the particular description:

General daily activities   Unable to perform some tasks at home and/or at work.
Self-care   Able to perform all self-care activities albeit with some difficulties.

Leisure activities   Unable to participate in many types of leisure activity.
Pain and/or other complaints   Often moderate to severe pain and/or other
    complaints.

State E was evaluated by everyone on the assumption that it was to last
for 30 years. For this duration, each individual was asked to put a utility
value on state E using each of the three methods. The sample consisted of
172 students, 80 from the Stockholm School of Economics (the Swedish
sample) and 92 from Erasmus University Rotterdam (the Dutch sample).
Table 9.6 below (their Table 5) records the mean utility scores. Any differences between scores in the two sub-samples were not statistically significant. As one would expect, SG values are higher than TTO values, which
are higher than RS values (all differences were significant at the 1% level).

Table 9.6:   Mean SG, TTO and RS quality weights for health state E

Method	Dutch sample	Swedish sample	Total sample
RS	0.3867	0.4274	0.4056
TTO	0.5958	0.5575	0.5780
SG	0.6786	0.6620	0.6709

Source: Bleichrodt and Johannesson (1997)

Prior to eliciting these utility scores, respondents were asked to rank
seven 'profiles'. A profile consists of the health state E, in conjunction with
alternative durations in the two extreme health states, H and D. The total
time in the three health states for each profile is always 20 years. The seven
profiles are listed in Table 9.7 (their Table 3). The ranking of these seven
profiles by each of the 172 respondents forms the *direct* measure of preferences.

The next step in the analysis was to convert the utility scores obtained by
each of the three methods for state E into a ranking of the seven profiles so
that they can be compared with the rankings that constitute the direct
measures of utilities. By their design of the experiment, as soon as one fixes
a value for state E one has an implied ranking for each of the profiles.

To illustrate the process, let us assume that a respondent for any of the
three methods came up with a 0.5 utility weight for state E. Profile 1 would
produce an estimate of 10 QALYs for the 20-year period, i.e., 20 years
valued at 0.5 per year = 10 years. Profile 2 would produce 18 years valued
at 1 each per year, plus 2 years with each year valued at zero, for a total of
18 QALYs. Since 18 QALYs are greater than 10 QALYs, profile 2 would

Table 9.7:   *The seven health profiles included in the experiment*

Number profile	Years in full health	Years in E	Years dead
1	0	20	0
2	18	0	2
3	16	0	4
4	14	0	6
5	12	0	8
6	8	8	4
7	6	11	3

Source: Bleichrodt and Johannesson (1997)

(should) be ranked higher than profile 1 on the basis of that 0.5 utility weight for state E. Similarly, one can produce a total QALYs and thus a ranking for each of the seven profiles.

The ranking for all seven profiles that correspond to the weight 0.5 is given in column 2 of Table 9.8 (their Table 4). In that column we see that the 18 QALYs of profile 2 would give that profile the highest ranking (1), while the 10 years of profile 1 give that profile the lowest ranking (7). For different utility values for state E, there would be different QALY totals for each of the profiles and thus alternative rankings.

Table 9.8:   *Implied rankings of the seven health profiles for different quality weights*

Number profile	Weight =0.5 rank	Weight =0.6 rank	Weight =0.7 rank	Weight =0.8 rank	Weight =0.9 rank	Weight =1.0 rank
1	7	6	3	2	1	1
2	1	1	1	1	1	2
3	2	2	2	2	3	4
4	3	3	3	6	6	6
5	4	6	7	7	7	7
6	4	4	6	5	5	4
7	6	5	5	4	4	3

Source: Bleichrodt and Johannesson (1997)

Table 9.8 shows the rankings for utility values for state E that are between 0.5 and 1.0. Only if individuals would not at all trade off quantity of life for quality of life (i.e., if utility for state E were given a unit value) would profile 2 not be ranked above profile 1. All the rankings in Table 9.8 assume that there is zero discounting.

The final step in the analysis is to find the strength of the relationship between the direct rankings and the indirect rankings that were implied by the utility values elicited from respondents. As there were three different estimates of utility for each respondent, according to each of the three methods, there are three sets of implicit rankings to compare with the direct rankings. The object is to see which of the three methods produced indirect rankings that were most strongly related to the direct rankings.

The Spearman rank correlation coefficient r_S was used to measure the strength of the relationship between the direct and indirect rankings. Rankings are measured on an ordinal scale, which means that profiles can be judged higher or lower, but the differences between rankings are not comparable (i.e., a rank of 1 is higher than a rank of 2; but we cannot say by how much 1 is higher than 2). r_S was devised to measure the association between variables measured on an ordinal scale. r_S has an upper bound of $+1$ and a lower bound of -1. A positive r_S means that a higher ranking by one measure would be associated with a higher ranking by the other measure. The test then is to find out which utility measure has the highest average r_S relating direct and indirect rankings. Table 9.9 (their Table 6) presents the resulting correlations that are all positive.

Table 9.9:   *Mean Spearman rank correlation coefficients between the direct rankings and the predicted rankings of RS, TTO and SG*

Comparison	Dutch sample	Swedish sample	Total sample
RS – direct	0.7208	0.7932	0.7545
TTO – direct	0.8194	0.8669	0.8415
SG – direct	0.6891	0.7684	0.7259

Source: Bleichrodt and Johannesson (1997)

TTO was the method that produced indirect rankings that had the highest correlation with the direct rankings. r_S was equal to 0.8415 in the full sample for the TTO. This correlation was significantly different from the 0.7545 correlation for RS and the 0.7259 correlation for SG (in both cases at the 1% significance level).

The results in Table 9.9 are for the case where there is no discounting. As was emphasized by Nord earlier (and is inherent in the notion of time preference when evaluating utility in *time* units), we would expect that discounting would affect most the valuations from the TTO method, and this is indeed what was found by Bleichrodt and Johannesson. Using a 5% discount rate in each of the three methods produced new indirect rankings that lowered the correlation coefficient for the TTO method from 0.8415 to 0.8162, lowered the correlation for RS from 0.7545 to 0.7401, and *raised* the correlation of SG from 0.7259 to 0.7752 in the total sample. TTO still had the strongest relation to the direct rankings, but this time the difference in the correlations was only significant at the 5% level relative to RS and at the 10% level relative to SG.

9.4.3   Utilities of Vision Acuity

The standard way that eye doctors (ophthalmologists) measure quality is in terms of vision acuity (sharpness). The most widely used test is the Snellen classification which is expressed in units such as 20/20, 20/30, 20/40, etc. (where 20/20 is best). This system can also be expressed in decimals, e.g. 20/20 = 1 and 20/40 = 0.5. When vision gets very blurry, the measures switch to verbal categories CF (counting fingers), HM (hand motion) and worst of all, NLP (no light perception).

Brown (1999) was aware that doctors and patients regard vision quality differently. He took the individualistic position that patient preferences should count when making health evaluations. A common way of measuring patient preferences regarding vision is to use an instrument based on people's ability to function. In the version that he used for 325 of his patients, Brown asked 22 questions, such as whether people have difficulty reading small print, recognizing people across the room at 20 feet, or are frustrated by their vision. The results are recorded in the second column of Table 9.10 below (which combines his Tables II and VI) and they relate to vision acuity in the better-seeing eye, which is recorded in column 1. Comparing the results in the first and second columns, we see that patient values were very similar to the doctor valuations. Patient scores declined in line with each reduction in physician-assessed vision acuity.

Brown recognized that this correspondence between patient function results and doctor vision scores was not helpful if one wanted to compare utilities across programs not related to ophthalmic disease. So he turned to the CUA measures SG and TTO to see which of the two methods corresponds better with the patient function values. The result, as we can see by comparing columns 3 and 4 with column 2 in Table 9.10, is that although both CUA measures fall in line with decreases in the patient function scores, the size of the declines are more commensurate for the TTO method. Thus, for example, moving down from the best vision (20/20) to the lowest vision category (HM–NLP) leads to a reduction from 91.5 to

Table 9.10:   *Results for visual function and utility values according to visual acuity*

(1) Visual acuity	(2) Function result	(3) Time trade-off	(4) Standard gamble
20/20	91.5	0.92	0.96
20/25	88.3	0.87	0.92
20/30	83.0	0.84	0.91
20/40	78.6	0.80	0.89
20/50	72.0	0.77	0.83
20/70	60.1	0.74	0.80
20/100	46.7	0.67	0.82
20/200	43.6	0.66	0.80
20/300	35.6	0.63	0.78
20/400	31.6	0.54	0.59
CF	26.3	0.52	0.65
HM–NLP	15.4	0.35	0.49

Source: Based on Brown (1999)

15.4 with the function score; the reduction was from 0.92 to 0.35 with TTO, but only from 0.96 to 0.49 with the SG method.

Brown's study provides a deeper understanding of what it means to say that one method is easier for respondents to answer than another. Of the original 350 persons contacted, 25 were unwilling to answer the questions posed in the questionnaire. Non-respondents are obviously one category of person for which a utility method does not work. But in addition, Brown reports numbers who were unwilling to make the kind of judgments required by a particular estimation method. Table 9.11 (Brown's Table 6) shows the numbers and percentages of people in various sight categories that *were* willing to make the necessary trade-offs (time in the case of TTO and risk of immediate death in the case of SG).

Start with the last row of Table 9.11, which relates to those with the sharpest vision in the better seeing eye. For those with 20/20 and 20/25 vision, 35 of the 81 would be willing to make a time trade-off to improve their vision in the worse eye using the TTO method, which meant that 46 were unwilling to make such a trade-off. With the SG method, only 32 of the 81 were willing to risk death in order to improve their vision in the worse eye, with a corresponding 49 unwilling to accept any risk of death. For this sight category, then, the majority of people were not willing to give up either time or risk for vision improvement.

Table 9.11: Patients willing to trade time for improved vision (TTO method) and risk immediate death for improved vision (SG method)

Vision	TTO method	SG method
CF–NLP	16/18 (89%)	14/18 (78%)
20/200–20/400	36/38 (95%)	26/38 (67%)
20/70–20/100	47/60 (43%)	37/60 (62%)
20/30–20/50	77/128 (60%)	62/128 (47%)
20/20–20/25	35/81 (43%)	32/81 (40%)

Source: Based on Brown (1999)

As we move up in Table 9.11, and cover deteriorating vision categories, we see that the number willing to trade off time and risk increases, which means that the two utility measures become more meaningful. When we reach the top row, for the categories with the worst vision (CF and NLP), only two people were unwilling to make the kinds of trade-off required by the TTO method.

Overall, the number unwilling to make the required trade-off was 114 for the TTO method and 154 for the SG method. So the TTO method was more operational than the SG method. In total (adding the 25 who refused to answer the question to 114 who were unwilling to make the required time trade-off) there were 139 out of the original 350 who did not respond in a manner required by the TTO method. The total non-responding and non-responsive for the SG method was 179 – over half.

9.4.4   Utilities of HIV Infection

Bayoumi and Redelmeier (1999) were aware that most studies found that SG estimates were higher than those using the TTO method, and RS utilities produced the lowest estimates. However, in their study of the quality of life for those affected with HIV infection, while they confirmed the low RS results, they found that SG and TTO utilities were basically the same. This was true irrespective of which disease stage HIV patients were classified. The three stages identified were: symptomatic HIV with no AIDS Defining Illnesses (ADI); minor ADI, such as pneumonia and TB; and major ADI, including wasting syndrome and toxoplasmosis (disease from a parasite hosted by cats). Table 9.12 below records the findings (their Table 2).

Table 9.12: **Ratings of standardized health states**

Elicitation method	Symptomatic HIV	Minor ADI	Major ADI
Standard gamble			
Mean	0.80	0.65	0.42
Median	0.90	0.75	0.40
Range	0.05–1.00	0.00–1.00	0.00–1.00
Time trade-off			
Mean	0.81	0.65	0.44
Median	0.96	0.75	0.50
Range	0.004–1.00	0.00–1.00	0.00–1.00
Visual analog			
Mean	0.70	0.46	0.25
Median	0.70	0.49	0.21
Range	0.32–0.95	0.00–0.81	0.00–0.70

Source: Bayoumi and Redelmeier (1999)

Bayoumi and Redelmeier gave a number of explanations of why they thought the TTO and SG results were so similar in the case of HIV when SG utilities for other diseases are normally found to be higher. They remarked that it is a dislike for gambling that is supposed to account for the inflated SG scores. However, they gave four reasons why they thought things would be different for a HIV group:

1. HIV patients are more likely to be willing to take risks than other groups.
2. Once HIV has been contracted, they are more likely to be willing to take risks due to their being accustomed to the stresses of living with a terminal disease.
3. The hypothetical SG scenario may have been so attractive that it prompted risk-seeking attitudes (specifically, the wording of the question included a possible cure that would restore the 'best possible health', that was 'easy to take and would require only a single administration', while if death occurred it would be 'painless').
4. Given that the life span is so limited in the group, HIV patients may be more reluctant to give up even small amounts of life as required by the TTO method. So TTO scores may be higher than for other diseases and lifted up to the SG levels.

TTO and SG scores were found to be similar whether one used means or medians as measures of central tendency. But it was the measures of dispersion, the ranges, that most concerned Bayoumi and Redelmeier.

With both the SG and TTO methods, the scores varied from 0 to 1, and thus spanned the entire scale of possible scores. This range was observed for many people rating the same health state using the two different methods. This led the authors to conclude that so much individual variation means that: 'Economic methods provide imprecise estimates of the quality of life associated with HIV.'

The existence of such a wide range of values does make it difficult to find statistically significant differences in method outcomes. A sensitivity analysis that has to use the extremes 0 and 1 would not be very useful as no values are being excluded. However, this does not mean that the main methods are inherently flawed or that conclusions about the number of QALYs related to this disease cannot be obtained. It simply reflects the reality that some of the complications with AIDS can be extreme. It is not so surprising that people's reactions also should be extreme. But it does mean that, for HIV, one should avoid taking utility averages and multiplying average life expectancies by this value to obtain the total number of QALYs. Instead, one should multiply individual utility estimates by individual life expectancies and sum these to obtain the total number of QALYs.

9.5   FINAL SECTION

We present in turn the problems, summary and looking ahead sections.

9.5.1   Problems

The intention is to review one's understanding of the role of duration in utility estimation. Refer back to Nord's summary of utility estimates listed in Table 9.5. Nord revealed that for the RS method, the specified durations were indefinite in Llewellyn-Thomas et al. (1984), five and ten years in Read et al. (1984) and three months in Torrance (1976).

1. To what extent can differences in specified duration account for the differences in utility estimates found in various studies?
2. The QWB method devised by Kaplan and associates (referred to in Chapter 8 and used for the Oregon plan) measured the net effect of a service as the difference between the QWB with treatment (QWB_{Rx}) and the QWB_{No} without treatment multiplied by the duration of that service – see equation (8.1):

$$\text{Net effect of a service} = (QWB_{Rx} - QWB_{No}) \text{ Duration}$$

where the QWB of each of the treat/no treat alternatives was given by the product of the utility weight W_i of being in any state i times the probability P_i of being in that state.

(a) On the basis of equation (8.1), compare the way that duration is allowed for in the QWB method relative to how duration is thought to be factored in according to the Torrance TTO method.

(b) The utility of being in a health state at a point in time in the QWB method is, in practice, the utility of being in a health state for a *single day*. Given this specification of duration, how would you expect the size of utility estimates in the QWB to relate to the utility estimates in the rest of the literature listed in Table 9.5?

9.5.2 Summary

This chapter reviewed the three main methods by which utilities can be measured to obtain a QALY. A category rating scale was the simplest method and this involves comparing a health state with being dead (having a value of zero) and being fully healthy (having a value of unity). A value equal to 0.5 corresponds to being half way between dead and fully healthy. SG was the most complex method. This involved comparing being in a particular health state with certainty and accepting a 'lottery' which has a probability Π of being fully healthy and a probability $1 - \Pi$ of being dead. The lottery choice is the uncertain effect of undertaking treatment as this could be fully successful or fully unsuccessful. The probability that would just equate the two choices turns out to be the value of living in the particular health state. In between the two methods in terms of sophistication is the time trade-off method. This requires one to specify how many life years in a particular health state one would give up in order to live a shorter, but fully healthy, life.

The methods were compared in three ways. The first was in terms of their correspondence with mainstream economic theory. The SG method was the best method on this basis, as using the expected utility criterion is a fundamental way that economists deal with decision-making under uncertainty. Unfortunately, many of the axioms on which expected utility rests are not supported by empirical evidence.

The second way that we compared methods was statistical. We only just touched on a few aspects in a voluminous literature, such as replicability, precision and validity. Typically the SG results are used as the benchmark and then one sees how well the results of the other methods measure up. Many studies have found that the highest utility values are obtained using the SG method, followed by the TTO estimates with the RS values being the lowest. Given these *systematic* differences by method, one is forced to choose amongst them. If one cannot just assume *a priori* that the SG is the best method, one needs an alternative way of assessing the methods.

The third way that we compared methods was to see how well the methods estimate utilities in practice. On this basis the TTO method is often the best. The TTO method is simpler conceptually than SG as it does not require respondents to deal with probabilities and this translates into it being simpler operationally. The RS is easiest to apply, but perhaps easiest to lead to impressionistic responses. When a direct measure of people's preferences in the form of rankings was the benchmark, we saw that the TTO estimates supplied the closest approximation.

What was especially revealing from the vision acuity case study was that both the SG and TTO methods require individuals to make trade-offs that they may not be willing to make. That is, for an eyesight improvement someone in a SG must be able to accept some risk of dying and in a TTO be able to accept giving up years of life. However, this does not mean that these techniques cannot be used. It implies only that some treatments do not yield positive utility *changes*. One must not assume that utilities are continuous functions of each level in a health state.

The HIV case study challenged conventional thinking about the relative size of SG and TTO utility estimates. The utilities found for the SG method were the same as for the TTO method (and not higher). This finding goes to the heart of the logic of the SG approach, which is based on comparing the expected utilities of health states. Using expected utility as the criterion assumes risk neutrality. If people are risk-takers, which is typical of the HIV population, then the SG method is clearly going to give different results than for other populations.

It is standard practice when estimating QALYs to obtain a duration in a health state and multiply this by an average utility value. But one must be careful with using averages. One needs to ensure that duration has explicitly been specified in the question trying to elicit the preferences. When a condition restricts activities, a longer duration usually attaches a lower value than for a shorter duration. Moreover, as we saw in the case study related to the HIV virus, averages may not be representative when the range is so large that elicited utilities include both extremes, 0 and 1.

9.5.3 Looking Ahead

The three methods that we analyzed in this chapter are appropriate for a clinical decision-making setting, where a doctor and a patient are trying to determine the best course of treatment for an individual. We need to explore now whether estimation methods should be different in a social decision-making context. In particular, we need to decide whether people who have more QALYs than others, by that very fact alone, should have their QALYs weighted lower when summing QALYs for society as a whole.

10. Cost–utility analysis and equity

10.1 INTRODUCTION

The QALYs that have been constructed so far have been built on the assumption that everyone's QALYs are valued the same. In this chapter we analyze why and how to value individual or group QALYs differently. A major way that unequally weighted QALYs were introduced into CUA was via outcomes measured in terms of Disability Adjusted Life Years (DALYs). We cover DALYs in section 10.2 after we have clarified the meaning of equity and the role of QALY weights. DALYs give different weights to different age groups. Section 10.3 discusses the general issue of QALYs and age discrimination (ageism). DALYs rely on a different instrument for measuring utilities, that is, the person trade-off (PTO) method. The case for and against the PTO method in CUA is presented in section 10.4. The applications cover evaluations based on DALYs and the estimation of weights using the PTO method.

10.1.1 Equity in CUA

Assuming costs are the same, Wagstaff (1991) associates the situation where person 1 gains more QALYs from treatment than person 2 as signifying that person 1 has a greater *capacity to benefit* from treatment. If one defines equity as requiring that people who 'need' treatment get treatment, then capacity to benefit is not sufficient for equity. For Wagstaff, following Williams (1974), interprets someone 'needing treatment' as meaning that the treatment is required to reach some socially desired improvement in health. Persons dying from thirst in the desert can be said to need water if the water would keep them alive *and* others agree that they ought to have it. So in addition to someone having the capacity to benefit from treatment, one also has to know the extent to which society regards the health improvements as *desirable*. 'In order to establish needs, society has to decide how the health improvements of one person are to be weighed against those of the other.' Thus, the requirement is for weighted QALYs.

Equity, or fairness, in economics is often defined in terms of two interrelated criteria. First there is *horizontal* equity, which is the requirement that people in equal circumstances should be treated equally. For CUA this principle could be interpreted as follows. If I would get 1/4 QALY from a broken leg being reset, and you would get 1/4 QALY from medication for a severely strained ankle, then caring for each of our bouts with immobility should have the same social value. The second criterion is *vertical* equity, which requires people in unequal circumstances to be treated unequally. It is from this equity viewpoint that unequal QALY weights derive their justification. If I have 20 QALYs from treatment and you gain only 2 QALYs, then my QALY circumstances are different from yours. So each one of my QALYs should not have the same social value as each one of your QALYs.

10.1.2   The Role of QALY Weights

The standard approach in CUA is to strive on the effects side for QALY maximization. In this approach a QALY is given an equal weight. This is irrespective of (1) the age, sex or income of the person gaining the QALY, and (2) how many QALYs a person will get. Equity (a concern for distribution) can be brought into CUA and CBA by applying non-unity weights to the consequences.

In CUA, for two individuals (or groups) 1 and 2, with 1 having more QALYs than 2, one can depict QALY maximization as trying to obtain the largest amount of total QALYs:

$$\text{Total QALYs} = \text{QALY}_1 + \text{QALY}_2 \qquad (10.1)$$

More generally, one can write total QALYs as a weighted sum of the individual QALYs:

$$\text{Weighted total QALYs} = a_1\,\text{QALY}_1 + a_2\,\text{QALY}_2 \qquad (10.2)$$

where the weights a_1 and a_2 record the relative QALY weights for the two persons. We can call attempts to secure highest totals on the basis of equation (10.2) *weighted* QALY maximization.

QALY maximization based on (10.1) is just the special case of the general formulation (10.2) where $a_1 = a_2 = 1$. If one tries to ignore equity issues in CBA or CUA one is implicitly assuming equal, unity weights. Why is assuming a weight of 1 more scientific than assuming non-unity weights? Since one cannot avoid making value judgments when doing economic evaluations, it is better to do the weighting explicitly rather than implicitly.

It is important to understand that a weighted QALY criterion incorporates a concern for *both* efficiency (the size of QALYs) and equity (how the number of QALYs is distributed across the population). It does not focus on just one of the two objectives. For example, if one wants to pursue equity only, in the form of equal health for all, then this would prevent treatments that provide additional QALYs for solely one person. This would be in violation of equation (10.2), which would show an overall increase irrespective of whether it was person 1 or 2 who is to gain.

10.1.3   Determining the QALY Weights

Distribution weights can be derived in two main ways. One can obtain estimates empirically by surveying individual preferences in social settings. The PTO method fits into this approach. Alternatively, the evaluator can determine the weights '*a priori*' by specifying in advance what the weights should be on the basis of economic reasoning. The DALY method would come under this heading.

Wagstaff presented a version of the *a priori* approach that is similar to the one that has been used for income distribution weights that we will be covering in Chapter 13. We will use his framework to help organize the analysis that takes place in this chapter. For the weights in equation (10.2), he suggests using a constant elasticity function (that looks like the relation in Figure 6.2) that takes the generic form:

$$a_i = \alpha_i \, (QALY_i)^{-\tau} \tag{10.3}$$

where the parameter α_i is a social preference related to some characteristic of individual or group i, and the parameter τ reflects society's aversion to inequality of health (the distribution of QALYs).

The characteristics parameters could be different because, for example, individuals or groups were of different ages. Wagstaff calls the case where characteristics are not important, i.e., $\alpha_1 = \alpha_2$, an 'anonymity principle'. The parameter τ exists to compensate for the fact that person 1 has more QALYs than person 2. If this distribution difference does not matter then $\tau = 0$. A value of $\tau = 1$ implies that if person 1 has twice as many QALYs person 2, then each QALY gained by person 1 would be valued by society as equal to ½ QALY, and each QALY gained by person 2 would contribute a total of 2 QALYs.

The situation where all QALYs are weighted equally, $a_1 = a_2$, therefore corresponds to the special case where $\alpha_1 = \alpha_2$ and $\tau = 0$. In this chapter we examine separately the two situations bringing about unequal weights, where $a_1 \neq a_2$. That is, we examine when we might have $\alpha_1 \neq \alpha_2$ (basically due to age differences) and also when we might have $\tau \neq 0$ (due to differences in individual quantities of QALYs). DALYs give different weights according to age, so we begin our analysis of distribution weights with this outcome measure.

10.2 DALYs

The DALY approach, as explained in Murray and Lopez (1996) and Murray and Acharya (1997), was developed to be the measurement unit to quantify the burden of disease in countries around the world. One can think of a DALY as a negative QALY. Instead of an intervention gaining a QALY, if one does not intervene one endures a DALY. We explain its rationale, show how DALYs are estimated and present the implications of their use as a global measurement of disease.

10.2.1 DALYs and Equity

Murray and Acharya use the notions of vertical and horizontal equity to justify their construction of DALYs. They were particularly concerned with the fact that, in practice, horizontal equity would not be applied, and one would therefore end up weighting each person's QALYs differently. Every disease affects someone differently in certain respects. Even when the same disease affects the same gender and age group, the duration, intensity and location will vary. As they say, 'At the limit, if all possible information is used, every health outcome is unique and thus the "like as like" principle has no meaning.' So they suggest the following ethical principle: All non-health characteristics of an individual other than age and sex should be ignored. Weights due to characteristics (the α_i) are restricted only to these two causes. It is important to note that, in line with all of the CUA literature, the income of a person or group is to play *no* part in deciding health care priorities. The reasons for the two exceptions, gender and age, will now be explained.

1. A person who dies prior to their life expectancy has lost years of life. Murray and Acharya used as a person's life expectancy an ideal benchmark, i.e., the maximum lifespan that any country now obtains. Females in Japan have a life expectancy at birth of 82.5 years and this is the highest in the world. On the other hand, males in Japan are expected to live 80 years, which is 2.5 years less. The 2.5 years' difference is interpreted to be biological in nature and not behavioral. Although there is approximately a seven-year gender difference in life expectancies in the OECD, 4.5 years of that difference is due to 'differences in the use of tobacco and alcohol, occupational exposures and a tendency for males to adopt riskier lifestyles. The norm for male survival should not reflect these differences in risk factors which in the future may be modifiable through public health action.'

    The logic of the whole exercise is therefore this. Take, for example, a male who dies at 40 due to TB in one of the Pacific Islands (Tokelau

Island), where male life expectancy is 65 years (and female life expectancy is 70 years). The disease has caused an initial loss of 25 years $(65-40)$ plus the 15 years' differential $(80-65)$ due to living in Tokelau Island and not Japan, for a total of 40 lost life years $(80-40)$. A female dying at 40 from TB on the same island would have lost 42.5 years $(82.5-40)$ by not living a full life in the health environment of Japan. The 2.5 years' gender difference was due to biological factors and could not have been obtained by a male living a full life in Japan. Interestingly, though, if Japan were not the benchmark, the gender difference would have been 5 years and not 2.5 years in the context of Tokelau Island. In any case, the gender difference is basically because females generate more years of life expectancy. So there are more DALYs and one is not really valuing a female health output more than a male health output.

2.   Murray and Acharya utilize age weights mainly because they recognize that some individuals or groups (such as parents of young children) play a critical role in the well being of others. There is thus an interdependence among individuals that needs to be incorporated formally into the outcome measure. It is in the middle years when most people look after the young and elderly. So the middle years should get the most weight.

   Although it is the middle years when people also contribute most to the economy (their earnings peak then) this consideration is *not* why age weights are used in DALYs. Recall that income differences are by design excluded and it is not the case that the rich contribute more to the welfare of others than the poor. This rationale should be borne in mind when the DALY approach is summarized (for example, by Peabody et al. (1999)) as explicitly valuing 'economic productivity'. It is not the human capital approach that DALYs are trying to reintroduce. Rather one can say that one gets more *total* DALYs per person from saving this group from disease. That is, the prime age person gets DALYs and dependants thereby (indirectly) also get DALYs. There is thus a sort of 'multiplier' effect with the middle age group.

10.2.2   Measuring a DALY

A DALY, just like a QALY, combines mortality with morbidity to form a single outcome. Mortality is recorded by life years as usual, but with the difference that it is the ideal of 82.5 or 80 years that is the benchmark depending on gender. Morbidity for a DALY translates into 'disability' and this is to be measured by a particular utility method, the PTO. The other element in a DALY that is not in a QALY is the age weights. The discount rate used was 3%, which, as we saw, was the recommended rate in CUA. The PTO estimates, and the age weights, used in DALYs will now be presented.

Disabilities were classed into seven categories. The PTO questions asked were of the form 'would you as decision-maker prefer to purchase, through a health intervention, 1 year of life for 1000 perfectly healthy individuals or 2000 blind individuals?'. The utility measures obtained from an international consensus meeting on disability weights (convened by the WHO) are shown in Table 10.1 (Murray and Acharya's Table 1).

Table 10.1: *Revised disability classes for the Global Burden Disease Study based on the results of the PTO protocol used at the Geneva meeting on disability weight*

Disability class	Severity weight	Indicator conditions
1	0.00–0.02	Vitiligo on face, weight-for-height less than 2 SDs
2	0.02–0.12	Watery diarrhea, severe sore throat, severe anemia
3	0.12–0.24	Radius fracture in a stiff cast, infertility, erectile dysfunction, Rheumatoid arthritis, angina
4	0.24–0.36	Below-the-knee amputation, deafness
5	0.36–0.50	Rectovaginal fistula, mild mental retardation, Down's syndrome
6	0.50–0.70	Unipolar major depression, blindness, paraplegia
7	0.70–1.00	Active psychosis, dementia, severe migraine, quadriplegia

Source: Murray and Acharya (1997)

DALYs as conceived by Murray and Acharya are to have age weights that have a humped shape over a person's lifetime, with the weights being highest in the middle years, and lowest for the young and old. (The equation is: $0.1658 \, x \, e^{-0.04x}$, where x is age.) Babies at birth have a zero weight, 5-year-olds have a 0.678 weight, and the weight reaches 1.525 at the age of 25. The weights fall continuously after the age of 25, but at a slow rate of decline. Thus a person aged 40 has a weight of 1.339, a person aged 60 has a weight of 0.902, and a person aged 80 has a weight of 0.541.

We can understand how the age weights work out in practice by considering the way that age weights interact with life expectancy and discounting in a DALY study of sleeping sickness in Uganda by Politi et al. (1995) as shown in Table 10.2.

Table 10.2:   DALY losses by age at death in Uganda

Age at death	Average loss of DALYs
0–9 years	35
10–19 years	37
20–29 years	33
30–39 years	27
40–49 years	20
50+ years	10

Source: Created by the author based on Politi et al. (1995)

In Uganda, it is the teenagers (and preteens) who look after others the most and whose deaths would cause the largest DALY loss.

10.2.3   Measuring the Global Burden of a Disease

The World Bank (1993) used the DALY measure to compare the impact of various diseases around the world. Instead of just focusing on mortality they wanted to broaden concern to include morbidity as well. Table 10.3 below shows that judged by mortality, non-communicable diseases have the most impact, while from a DALY perspective, communicable diseases cause most harm. So, compared to death classifications, DALY classification schemes give more weight to diseases that predominately affect children and young adults and diseases that cause disability, but not death. Peabody et al. point out that two broad classes of problems that have been under-recognized, and cause disability without affecting one's life expectancy, are nutritional deficiency and psychiatric problems. These two classes have significantly more importance in the DALYs than the mortality rankings.

Table 10.3:   Comparison of DALYs versus deaths in demographically developing countries by categories of disease

Category of disease	DALYs (%)	Deaths (%)
Communicable maternal, and perinatal diseases	47.6	39.98
Non-communicable diseases	43.4	52.02
Injuries	10.0	8.00

Source: World Bank (1993)

The distinction between communicable and non-communicable diseases has an age dimension because the elderly are more likely to be affected by non-communicable diseases, in contrast to the young. So as populations age, non-communicable diseases will cause a majority of the world's death and disability – projected to be 73% of all deaths by 2020.

However, Gwatkin et al. (1999) argue that this picture painted by the World Bank's global disease study distorts the position from the poor's perspective. One should not necessarily base plans for future health care interventions based on average DALYs. Communicable diseases were much more important for the poor. As is evident from Table 10.4, which relates to 1990, the poor (those with the lowest 20% *per capita* income) were almost six times as likely to be affected by communicable diseases than the rich (those with the highest 20% *per capita* income). One must not forget therefore that the young are also the poor (roughly 40% of the poor and around 20% of the rich are under 15 years of age) and for this group non-communicable diseases are of limited importance.

Table 10.4: Comparison of DALYs versus deaths by income grouping

Category of disease	DALYs (%)	Deaths (%)
Communicable maternal, and perinatal diseases		
Poorest 20%	64	59
World average	44	34
Richest 20%	11	8
Non-communicable diseases		
Poorest 20%	23	32
World average	41	56
Richest 20%	76	85
Injuries		
Poorest 20%	13	9
World average	15	10
Richest 20%	13	7

Source: Constructed by the author based on Gwatkin et al. (1999)

10.3 QALYs AND AGEISM

Some have argued that treating QALYs as equal no matter who receives them is egalitarian. Others argue that this process is 'ageist'. We have just seen that DALYs base their weights on age. Is this ageist? To help understand the issues, we will consider age as an equity factor and then combine equity and efficiency.

10.3.1   Age and Equity

Let us consider various individual lifetime profiles as conceived and analyzed by Tsuchiya (2000). There is a young person (for simplicity called 'she') and an elderly person (called 'he') each with a given life expectancy at birth who, due to a health care intervention, have a specified number of years of life remaining. Each individual is competing for a life-saving treatment, without which they will shortly die. The choice is whether to save his QALYs or her QALYs. Utilities of life years are valued the same (equal to 1) irrespective of age. Table 10.5 summarizes various sets of assumptions (cases).

Table 10.5:   Life expectancies at birth and after intervention (remaining years)

Case	Younger person (she)			Older person (he)		
	Age now	Life expectancy at birth	Remaining years	Age now	Life expectancy at birth	Remaining years
1	30	75	45	70	75	5
2	30	35	5	70	75	5
3	30	35	5	75	85	10

Source: Created by the author based on Tsuchiya (2000)

In case 1, there is an intervention that averts a life threatening disease that restores people's life expectancies. The older person has fewer years of his life expectancy remaining and so he would accrue fewer QALYs than she would. Maximization of QALYs would record her 45 years as being greater than his 5 years and so would choose to save her, not him.

QALY maximization in case 1 is not necessarily ageist. As Tsuchiya points out, 'to live is to age, passing through alternative ages one by one: a 30-year-old today will be (unless he/she dies prematurely) aged 70 in 40 years' time'. So one switches from an inter-personal comparison (her versus him) to an intra-personal comparison (the same person at different stages in his/her life). In 40 years' time, when she becomes 70, she will have fewer years left than a future 30-year-old and then it will be her turn to let the younger person have the treatment. In this way, everyone is treated equally over his or her expected lifetime.

In case 2, both he and she have 5 more years to live, even though she is younger than he. This is due to the fact that she (due to a disability or some other reason) has a lower life expectancy. On what basis would one give higher weight to her 5 years than his 5 years? Harris (1985) came up with the argument that someone may have had a 'fair innings' and therefore is less deserving than someone who has not had a fair innings. Williams (1997) then suggested using unequal QALY weights based on the fair innings argument. If the fair innings were judged to be 75 years, then neither person would have had a fair innings and one would not be able to decide between them. But, if the fair innings were set equal to 70 years, he had had a fair innings and her 5 remaining life years would be given preference.

In the original version of the fair innings argument, any years after the threshold would be given zero weight. So, for case 3, even though he has 10 more years and she has just 5 more years, only her years would count with a 75-year threshold and she would be given preferential treatment. This is equivalent to valuing *lives* equally (no matter how long they are expected to last) and not valuing QALYs equally. This version of the fair innings argument would give *no* guidance if both persons were below or above the threshold.

When one excludes a specification of a threshold number of years for a fair innings, one is in the domain of the 'relative fair innings argument'. The older person always has lived longer and so has had a longer innings than the younger person. From this perspective the younger person nearly always deserves priority no matter how many years remaining either person has. So in cases 2–3 she is chosen.

The exception is case 1, where her remaining years of life are greater than his current age. If he died now, and she was saved, she would end up having had more years of life, that is, had a longer innings. In this case the relative fair innings argument would give no guidance as to whom to save.

10.3.2 Age in the Context of Efficiency and Equity

Up to now we have been considering situations where one is deciding between giving either full (unit) weights or zero weights to remaining years. The more general situation would be where one gives importance to not only a fair innings, but also to how many extra years of gain there are. This means that one accepts the existence of a trade-off between equity and efficiency.

The DALY formulation implies such a trade-off. In a DALY, disability or loss of life affecting the middle-aged group is more socially harmful on efficiency grounds. As we saw, weights start at zero for newborns, rise rapidly and peak at 25 and thereafter fall off gradually, but never reach zero. This implies that, with DALYs, providing she is older than 25 years, a weight to her years will always be greater than for his years. Thus, she will be given preference when the remaining number of years are the same as in case 2. When he has more remaining years, which is case 3, the outcome will depend on the precise weights chosen and the exact number of years. At some number of years, her greater weight will be off-set by his greater number of years. At this point (age) his life would be the one that would be saved.

From the perspective of an individual's life cycle, it is clear that the use of age weights in DALYs is not ageist. Just as with the Tsuchiya defense of giving priority to the younger person in case 1 (who argued that when she eventually gets to 70 she will have to give way to the younger person), one can argue that everyone gets a turn at being middle aged. Young people *will be* middle aged in the future, and then given priority; while the elderly *were* middle aged in the past, and would have been given priority at that stage of their life. To use Murray and Acharya's words: 'Age, however, does not discriminate between the lives of different individuals but simply differentiates periods of the life cycle for a cohort.'

10.4   THE PERSON TRADE-OFF

This method was first developed by Patrick et al. (1973), who called it an 'equivalence of numbers technique'. Nord (1992) was the first to call it the person trade-off. We first give the rationale for the PTO approach and then analyze how its components combine to produce the overall PTO outcome.

10.4.1   Rationale for the PTO

As we explained earlier, the maximization of unweighted QALYs effectively defines 'need' as the capacity to benefit. If need is defined in terms of ill health (those in the worst health states are those in most need of treatment) then the pre-treatment health state is the most important criterion for deciding priorities. If need is defined in terms of final health status then post-treatment health status is more important. So there is a conflict between efficiency (defined in terms of health gains) and equity (in terms of pre- and post-health status). The PTO approach (unlike the RS, SG and TTO methods) combines valuations of health *levels* with valuations of health levels' *change* and so addresses the equity issue in utility measurement. It thus can be regarded as the most appropriate instrument for making social decisions.

The PTO method asks someone to identify the *number of people X* in one health project *A* that they would need to treat to make them indifferent to treating a *given number* Y in another health project B. So X is the unknown and this depends on the prior specifications for Y, A and B.

The identification of projects A and B has to make clear what outcomes are expected to follow from treatment. For example, Nord (1995) in one version of his survey stated that one project would increase the capacity of people who were moving with difficulty at home, needing assistance in stairs and outdoors, to become able to have no problems walking. The other project helped improve people from being able to sit (but needing assistance on stairs) to become able to move about without difficulty (but still having difficulty on stairs and outdoors).

What is essential to the PTO method is the social context. People are being asked to evaluate situations that affect other people and not themselves, which was the perspective used in the utility methods presented in the last chapter. That this is a crucial difference can be seen immediately from the Dolan and Green (1998) study. 25 out of 28 respondents preferred one treatment to another using the PTO method, even though they had just valued the treatments equally using the RS and TTO methods. This group judged that it was better to give treatment to those with a less severe state to start with, while Nord (1993) found that those initially in a worse state were favored. But, in either case, the initial position was considered and it was not just the number of QALYs evaluated from a personal perspective that was important when the PTO was applied.

The PTO way of thinking was influential in CUA studies previously cited even when it was not the actual method used to obtain the utility estimates. When Rosser and Kind (1978) wanted to ensure that respondents fully understood the implications of their initially stated preferences for the overall allocation of health resources, they were informed about the impact of their values in terms of *how many persons* would, and would not, receive various treatments. Also, when Eddy (1991c) wanted to make the point that cost should be considered when evaluating treatments, he also expressed it in terms of numbers. Recall that he stressed that the issue was not whether 1 dental cap was worth the same as 1 ectopic pregnancy, but whether 105 persons having dental gaps was worth the same as treating 1 person with ectopic pregnancy when these two alternatives cost the same in total.

On the other hand, Dolan (1998) points out that the PTO weights combine at least four things simultaneously:

1. The severity of the pre-intervention health state for projects A and B;
2. The severity of the post-intervention health state for projects A and B;
3. The health gain as a result of intervening (difference between pre- and post- states for projects A and B); and
4. The number of persons treated Y.

Dolan suggests that combining all four aspects could lead to 'cognitive overload' and thus reduce the validity of responses. He endorses a framework such as that represented in (10.3) where the weights would be specified separately. He then goes on to argue that methods like the PTO make it 'impossible to disentangle the relative contributions of potentially numerous efficiency and equity considerations'. However, as we shall see in the next section and in the applications, one can ask different and simpler questions in a PTO (for example make projects *A* and *B* the same) and thus decompose a PTO into its constituent parts.

Decomposing the PTO

Ubel et al. (1998) compare results for a PTO and a RS on the same set of respondents. As usual, they find that PTO estimates are higher than RS magnitudes. They considered three main reasons why the two instruments give different values. First, PTOs ask people to think about how conditions affect people other than themselves. Second, PTOs ask people to think about the benefits of treatments; and third, people are asked to choose among patients with different conditions. They then sought to establish which of these three reasons was the most important in practice by isolating one component at a time.

They analyzed treatments for a knee condition and headaches. We will just concentrate on the knee example, where the initial health state description was, 'You have a leg condition that prevents you from engaging in athletic activity and frequently causes your knee to give out on you when you walk. In addition, your knee aches for approximately one hour every day, to the point where it is hard to concentrate. The rest of the time you are able to function normally.' A value of zero is equivalent to being dead and unity is perfect health.

Their main method involved expanding the scope of the questions typically asked in a RS study. There were three versions of the RS:

1. *RS–self survey*. The initial version states that the knee condition affects *you* and wants to know how you value this health state.
2. *RS–other survey*. The initial description in this option was changed such that the knee condition affects *people* (and therefore not necessarily you).
3. *RS–other/cure survey*. In this version the description replaced the words 'the knee condition' with the 'benefit of curing the condition' that affects people. Zero now means no benefit from the knee treatment and 100 means equivalent to saving a person's life.

The PTO question (for the case without a budget constraint and called 'PTO–comparison') was: 'How many people would have to be cured of the knee condition to equal the benefit of curing ten (10) people of an acutely fatal disease?'. Responses stating '100 people' as an answer have the utility of the knee improvement recorded as 0.1 (i.e., 10/100), implying that the utility of the untreated knee state had to have been 0.9 (i.e., $1 - 10/100$) in order for the health state *after* treatment to be valued at 1.

Table 10.6, part of Ubel et al.'s Table 1, shows the utilities for the knee condition. Results by quartile are given because the estimates were not normally distributed (so the mean would not have been representative).

Table 10.6: Utilities for health states with knee condition

Survey version	25th percentile	50th percentile	75th percentile
RS–self	0.400	0.500	0.750
RS–other	0.250	0.600	0.750
RS–other/cure	0.250	0.500	0.250
PTO–comparison	0.900	0.995	0.900

Source: Based on Ubel et al. (1998)

Table 10.6 indicates that the variation among the RS results was small relative to PTO–RS differences. Therefore the fact that PTOs include preferences other than one's own (recorded in RS–other scores), and relate to treatment improvements and not just conditions (recorded in RS–other/ cure scores), does not account for differences between RS and PTO estimates. By default, differences thus had to be mainly due to PTOs eliciting values in the context of comparing equivalent numbers, which is something absent from a RS valuation. Note that Ubel et al. explicitly did not include a numbers version of RS in their study because it does not make sense to ask the question: 'How many of *yourself* would you need to cure of knee pain to equal the benefits of saving 10 people's lives?'.

10.5 APPLICATIONS

We include two studies that apply the PTO method and two studies that relate to the use of DALYs. The PTO method has been used to test both dimensions of the equal weights approach to equation (10.3). That is, to test whether a QALY weight varies according to how many QALYs one will get (whether $\tau = 0$), and to test whether a QALY weight to one group differs from a QALY weight to some other group (whether $\alpha_i = \alpha_2$). The first two applications deal with these equal weights tests. Then we present a CUA that uses DALYs as the outcome measure for evaluating treatments for sleeping sickness; and we close with a study that examines the implications of using DALYs to measure the global burden of a particular disease, HIV.

10.5.1 Weights that Vary According to the Size of the QALYs

Olsen (1994) set up a PTO estimation of weights in the following way. The question was how many people p with a long time interval of T years gained (i.e., having a larger number of QALYs) would be judged equivalent to P people with a short time interval t years (i.e., having a smaller number of QALYs). The equivalence being sought was:

$$p.T = P.t \qquad (10.4)$$

Note that this is an exact equation only if all units for the variables are valued equally; for example, five two-year periods equals ten one-year periods.

In a sample of 44 economics students and 40 doctors, P was set equal to 100, T equal to 20 and t equal to 5. Hence (10.4) would reduce to: $p.20 = 500$. In this relation, a respondent setting a p value of 25 would be one benchmark. For this would mean that 500 total years made up of long time periods was equal to the same total years made up of short time years. In other words, it did not matter the duration as long as the total was the same. In this case, the distribution of the years (QALYs) over time was not important and thus this implies equal weighting to a year (QALY). The other benchmark would be if a respondent set a p value of 100. This would entail fixing $p = P$. In this case, the person would *not* take into account the length of the time period people gain. Each QALY gained could not then have an equal weight.

To summarize: people who set $p = 25$ are using equal weights; people who set $p = 100$ are using zero weights; and p values between 25 and 100 imply weights between 0 and 1, i.e., both duration (the number of QALYs) and their distribution are important. Olson found that 11.5% of his sample chose p values that implied unit weights, 11.5% chose p values that implied zero weights, and 77% chose p values implying that they would use less than unit weights. Most people were willing to make a trade-off between total QALYs and their distribution. Using equation (10.3), the implication is that $\tau \neq 0$.

This result was consistent with the Johannesson and Gerdtham (1996) study which found that individuals were willing to give up one discounted QALY in the group with more QALYs to gain 0.58 discounted QALYs in the group with fewer QALYs (using a 5% discount rate). But note that neither study gives empirical support for a particular τ value. Johannesson and Gerdtham found that the trade-off was not affected by the size of the differences in QALYs between the two groups. So, for example, it does not follow that if one group had twice the QALYs of another then they would get any lower weight than if they had three times the number of QALYs. All one knows is that the group with the higher number of QALYs gets a lower weight. Similarly, the Olsen et al. study found that a trade-off existed, not that the trade-off was of any particular functional form, such as the iso-elastic one in equation (10.3).

10.5.2 Weights that Vary According to Who Receives the QALY

Johannesson and Johansson (1997) tested whether the judgment that a QALY gained should have the same value independent of age was consistent with the views of society at large. They asked a sample of a thousand people whether they would choose program A which saves 100 lives among 50-year-olds or program B which saves 50 lives among 30-year-olds.

If, for example, the person was indifferent, then saving two 50-year-olds was equivalent to saving one 30-year-old. If the person thought that they would rather save the 50 30-year-olds, the number of 50-year-olds specified was increased from 100 until the person was indifferent. In this way, the number of 50-year-olds equivalent to one 30-year-old could be determined.

The exercise was then repeated by comparing numbers of 70-year-olds equivalent to 50 30-year-olds. The results (for the median person in the sample) are given in Table 10.7 (their Table 3) using two alternative estimation techniques: EQ (logistic regression) and NP (non-parametric method). The discount rate used was 5%.

Table 10.7: *The number of lives, life years and QALYs saved among 50-year-olds and 70-year-olds equivalent to saving one life, life year and QALY among 30-year-olds*

Age	Lives saved		Life year gained		QALYs gained	
	EQ	NP	EQ	NP	EQ	NP
50-year-olds	7.7	4.9	7.7	4.9	7.7	4.9
70-year-olds	40.8	34.5	40.8	34.5	40.8	34.5

Source: Johannesson and Johansson (1997)

Concentrate on the QALYs gained result using the EQ method. This says that one QALY gained by one 30-year-old was valued equal to 7.7 50-year-olds gaining one QALY each, which in turn was equal to 40.8 70-year-olds gaining one QALY each. We can express these results alternatively by saying that a QALY to a 50-year-old was worth 0.14 a QALY to a 30-year-old, and a QALY to a 70-year-old was worth 0.02 a QALY to a 30-year-old. On the basis of these individual preferences, Johannesson and Johansson concluded that equal weighting as required by the QALY maximization rule does involve age discrimination – against the young!

What this means in terms of equation (10.3) is that, with α_1 being the weight to the young and α_2 being the weight to the old, not only do 30-year-olds have more QALYs than 70-year-olds ($QALY_1 > QALY_2$), because their life expectancies are greater, but also each QALY that they gain should be given a greater weight ($\alpha_1 > \alpha_2$).

10.5.3   DALYs and Treatments for Sleeping Sickness in Uganda

Politi et al. (1995) used DALYs in their evaluation of African trypanosomiasis, which is one of two main types of sleeping sickness caused by tsetse flies in Uganda, a disease that is fatal if untreated. Trypanosomiasis is endemic in 36 Sub-Saharan countries where some 50 million people are at risk. The emphasis of the study was only on choosing the appropriate drug for late stage disease (which comprised about 60% of the new cases in 1991 and 1992). The main (and cheapest) drug was melarsoprol. This drug has severe side-effects (the treatment itself has a fatality rate of between 1 and 5% of the treated cases). A new drug (eflormithine) has been developed that is more effective, but more expensive. So a CUA of the alternative treatments was carried out. The implications for affordability were also included in the analysis.

Melarsoprol was the baseline treatment. When it is used on its own and instead of doing nothing, it is called alternative A. When melarsoprol is initially used and is found to be ineffective, patients are then switched to the more expensive drug eflormithine. This joint melarsoprol and eflormithine treatment is alternative B. When eflormithine is used on its own it is called treatment C.

On the basis of the DALYs lost (which depended in part on the DALY losses by age at death in Uganda previously given in Table 10.2) and indirect and direct costs, the best-case incremental cost-effective ratios for the three alternatives were as shown in Table 10.8 (their Table 3).

The calculations are based on 1000 hypothetical patients, which is approximately the actual annual number treated in Uganda between 1990 and 1992. Table 10.8 shows that melarsoprol (alternative A) was extremely cost-effective with a cost per DALY saved of only $8. As with any CUA, one then has to ask whether this result means that the treatment is worthwhile. Politi et al. returned to the standard CUA solution to this question by referring to accepted benchmarks. This time the benchmarks had to be expressed in terms of DALYs and not QALYs as before. Politi et al. referred

Table 10.8:   *Incremental cost-effectiveness analysis for sleeping sickness in Uganda*

Alternative treatments	Incremental costs ($)	Additional lives	Additional DALYs	Incremental cost per life saved ($)	Incremental cost per DALY saved ($)
A	189376	906	23668	209	8.0
B	22727	22	556	1033	40.9
C	262172	59	1572	4444	166.8

Source: Politi et al. (1995)

to the dollar per DALY bands established by Jamison et al. (1993) for the World Bank. The most cost-effective programs that the World Bank evaluated had costs per DALY less than $25. The $8 cost of alternative A meant that melarsoprol had a cost-effectiveness ratio that was comparable to most forms of childhood immunization and blood screening for HIV, for example. Alternative B, which cost an extra $41 per DALY, would put it in the second tier of World Bank interventions of 'very good buys' which comprise the $25–$70 range.

Alternative C posed what they called an 'ethical dilemma'. If melarsoprol did not exist (or was made illegal because the treatment itself causes deaths) then eflormithine would have a cost per DALY gained of $18 and not the $167 cost given in Table 10.8. At $18, eflormithine would be included in the top group of cost-effectiveness interventions. But melarsoprol *does* exist and *is* very cost-effective. So at $167 per additional DALY, there are many treatments that would be more cost-effective, such as the prevention of helminthic diseases (parasitic infections).

As we can see from Table 10.8, the ethical issue translates into the fundamental health care evaluation decision regarding the value of a life. With eflormithine instead of melarsoprol, one can save 59 additional lives if one is prepared to pay an additional $262 172. If a life is worth more than $4444 on average, then alternative C is worthwhile. As Politi et al. recognize, this evaluation depends on the 'combined willingness to pay of government, donors and patients'. As WTP is an evaluation component that is in the domain of CBA and not CUA, CUA cannot adequately address this issue.

The $189 376 cost of alternative A was financed by the government paying $96 840 (a 51% share) and donors paying $64 560 (a 34% share), with the remaining $27 975 coming from patients (a 15% share). Their judgment was that the Ugandan government may be reluctant to expand drug treatment for trypanosomiasis for fear of foreign exchange shortage, and private patients are unable to pay more because their incomes are so low. They concluded that: 'It thus seems that the adoption of new treatments depends finally on donors' willingness to pay', the main donor in the Ugandan case being the Danish government.

Since most governments are notoriously reluctant to expand foreign aid, we can interpret Politi et al.'s judgment to mean that the budget constraint is binding. From this it follows that alternatives B and C would be unfeasible no matter the social net benefits. CUAs are not even permitted to contemplate whether adjustments to the budget constraint are worthwhile. Only a CBA can evaluate whether exceeding the budget constraint could be justified by the benefits this generates.

10.5.4   DALYs and the Global Burden of AIDS

On the basis of DALYs, one can identify the three main causes of disease for 1990 in developed countries to be heart disease, unipolar major depression and cerebrovascular disease (which caused 21.9% of the DALY total); while the three main causes of disease in developing countries were lower respiratory infections, diarrheal diseases and conditions arising during the perinatal period (which caused 24.5% of the DALY total).

The question is to what extent rankings would be different if an alternative outcome measure had been used. To address this issue, Hyder et al. (1998) and Hyder and Morrow (1999) made comparisons between DALYs and an outcome measure called a healthy life year (HeaLY), which was first constructed by the Ghana Health Assessment Project Team (1981). Calculations were made using the same basic data as employed by the World Bank burden of disease study, except that age weights were not used in HeaLYs.

In this case study we focus on comparisons related to HIV, a disease that caused 0.8% of the world's DALY loss in 1990, and which was projected to cause 1.8% of the DALY loss in 2020. This disease was chosen by Hyder and Morrow because it highlights differences that arise whenever diseases are not at their standard ('steady state') level of virulence. A DALY can be split into its two constituent parts, the loss from premature mortality (or years of life lost, YLL) and the loss from morbidity (or years of life lived with the disability, YLD). Abstracting from age weighting, DALYs and HeaLYs give similar outcomes over the YLD component. So it is to the mortality component YLL that we now turn our attention.

Estimates of YLL rely on three variables: the number of deaths, the age at death, and the expectation of life. If people get HIV around the age of 31, and they would have been expected to live till 80, except that they die at 38 due to the disease, then there are 42 years lost per infected person (i.e., the loss of 42 years is the 49 years that they would have lived if they did not get infected at age 31minus the 7 years they actually did live with the infection). This is the way that HeaLYs calculate losses and this relies on the *age of onset* perspective for premature mortality, which is 31 in this example.

HeaLYs use the age of onset perspective for both mortality and morbidity, but DALYs use this perspective only for morbidity. For premature mortality DALYs use the *current year* perspective (the life expectancy forgone as at the time of death), which is going to be a year later than 31 when a disease is in a growth phase. In a steady state, the numbers recorded of new cases and deaths due to HIV would be the same each year. But, when a disease is in a growth phase, the later the year one is considering, the more one underestimates the true number of cases and deaths that exist at the age of onset. In sum, when diseases are in growth phases DALYs under-record the YLL relative to HeaLYs. To see the extent that this underestimation matters with HIV, refer to Table 10.9 (Hyder and Morrow's Table 1).

Table 10.9: Apparent impact of HIV on mortality: DALYs as compared with HeaLYs, 1990

Indicator of impact	Middle Eastern Crescent	India	Sub-Saharan Africa
DALYs in thousands	16	17	7020
HeaLYs in thousands	642	4554	28493
Annual incidence (per 1000 per year)	0.05	0.21	2.1
Case fatality ratio	1	1	1
Average age of onset (y)	31.6	31	27.5
Average duration of disease (y)	7	7	6.5
Average age of fatality (y)	38.6	38	34
Deaths from HIV (thousands)	1	1	239

Source: Hyder and Morrow (1999)

HIV is growing throughout the world with its strongest impact in Sub-Saharan Africa. If one compares the regional burden of HIV disease on the basis of DALYs, India is comparable to the Middle Eastern Crescent (which includes the Middle East, North Africa, Central Asia, and Pakistan) and has 0.24% (17/7020) of the burden of Sub-Saharan Africa. Given the worldwide rising trend, all countries would be expected to have a higher number of HeaLYs lost due to HIV. But for the non Sub-Saharan countries that are only now starting to experience full exposure to the HIV epidemic, the relative increase would be much greater using the HeaLY measure. Thus India has 15.98% (4554/28493) of the Sub-Saharan Africa burden judged by HeaLYs, which is 66.58 times larger than the DALY HIV burden ratio. Clearly, as Hyder and Morrow emphasize, when diseases are not in their steady state, and on a strong secular trend, DALYs are not a good measure of their relative burden.

10.6 FINAL SECTION

As usual, we wrap up the discussion with some problems, provide a summary and give a preview for what is to follow.

10.6.1 Problems

Refer again to the Olsen study given as the first case study where his focus was on trying to value a QALY in the context of how many QALYs a person has. In addition to the PTO method covered in the application, he also used a TTO method. Recall that in his formulations when he mentions time T and t as a number of years he is really talking about numbers of QALYs as he is assuming that the quality of a life year is unity. The PTO comparison was expressed as: $p \; T = P \; t$, as explained in equation (10.4), where $T > t$ and $P > p$, and one wants to establish how many persons p would bring about the equality for fixed P, T and t. The TTO question was the standard one asking how many more years in an inferior health state is equivalent to a fewer number of years in a better health state.

The questions are about the rate at which the value of QALYs declines over time in alternative contexts and using different techniques. To help you answer the questions, be aware that Olsen gave three reasons why the value of QALYs may decline over time. The reasons were: (1) there exists a rate of time preference i; (2) there is diminishing marginal utility for an individual as the number of QALYs rises, with β as the rate of fall in an individual value of a QALY; and (3) there is diminishing marginal utility for society (others) as the number of QALYs rises (due to distributional preferences against those with a larger number of QALYs), with α as the rate of fall in social value of a QALY. Refer to these parameters in your explanations.

1. Which technique PTO or TTO would you use to measure α and why?
2. If one uses the PTO and finds that the value of QALYs falls at a rate of 15%, while if one uses the TTO one finds that the value of QALYs falls at a rate of 13%:
    (a) What is the social diminishing rate of marginal utility and why?

(b) Can one tell what is the individual's diminishing rate of marginal utility? Explain.

10.6.2 Summary

QALYs, as measured by the methods explained in the last chapter, use individual utilities. When we use the individual utilities we can think of the total QALYs as being an unweighted sum. Strictly, this simply means that equal, unit weights are applied. However, the QALYs are to be used to help determine social decisions. Social decisions also depend on equity as viewed as a distributional issue. To reflect distribution concerns, non-unity weights can be applied to the individual QALYs. Weighted total QALYs incorporate both efficiency and distribution as social objectives. The weights indicate the trade-off of distribution for efficiency. A unity weight signifies that distribution is unimportant and that only efficiency matters as recorded by the total number of QALYs.

There are two types of weights that can be attached to a QALY. One set is due to the characteristics of the persons receiving the QALYs. Age and gender may be cases in point. The second set is due to how many QALYs a person has. Just as individuals have diminishing marginal utilities for goods, the additional value of an additional QALY may decline as the number of QALYs increases. Though, as the problems made clear, it is the social value of these additional QALYs that matters, which need not be the same as individual evaluations.

It is in terms of DALYs that the CUA literature has mainly delved into QALY weighting. Weights for DALYs gained (QALYs lost) were devised to depend on age and gender. However, as we saw when we analyzed DALYs as formulated by their creators, DALY weights are really efficiency based. Women live longer than males, so their lives saved generate a larger quantity of life years. Similarly, middle-aged persons get a higher weight not because quality of life is highest at middle age, but because, in addition to the years of life that they have, they generate via their care-giving more years of life to others. Again, the total quantity of life years is enhanced by promoting this social group. It is not the case that any social group is considered to be inherently more important than any other.

This logic also helps us understand why it is that maximizing unweighted QALYs is not ageist from the point of view of discriminating against the elderly. The young have more QALYs to look forward to than the elderly and this is the only reason why they contribute more to the total number of QALYs. From a life cycle point of view, everyone can expect to be young and given priority and subsequently be old and no longer given priority. So counting the greater number of QALYs for the young is really being fair to all. The fair innings argument fits in with the life cycle view of QALYs to the extent that someone, the young, have not yet had a fair innings. When there is a threshold for a fair innings, say 70 years, and someone lives longer than 70, then their subsequent QALYs would not count at all. In this case efficiency would not matter at all. More generally, one would want to have weights that are neither unity nor zero if both social objectives are to count.

To determine the social weights, a social utility measurement instrument is required. The method suggested for this purpose has been the PTO. This method has been advocated because it explicitly asks people to value distribution, i.e., it asks how many of one type of treatment is worth the same as a given number of people being treated by some other type of treatment. It is because DALYs use PTOs to measure utilities that the technique can be said to reflect equity, despite the fact that its age and gender weighting system reflects only efficiency.

When the PTO methods were used to estimate QALY weights, there was support for both dimensions of distribution weighting. The more QALYs one has, the less is the additional social value to obtaining more QALYs; and the older the person, the less their QALYs were worth.

When we presented the DALY evaluation of sleeping sickness, we uncovered the complete impasse that CUA faces. One needed to know WTP to discover whether certain treatments would be worthwhile. One could not ignore having to value a life. Evaluating with a fixed budget constraint was not very helpful if one desperately needed additional funds to save lives. Some way of assessing the benefits of acquiring additional funding had to be a part of the evaluation. In short, what was needed was CBA.

10.6.3   Looking Ahead

We have come as far as we can without using monetary measures of the consequences of treatment. Economists have found that using monetary valuations can bring a wider range of effects into consideration. CBA is based on the monetary valuation of both inputs and outputs and it is this that we will now analyze. Chapter 11 covers measures of benefits using the human capital approach, and Chapter 12 deals with measures of benefits based on WTP. Equity as a social objective was introduced in this chapter by using non-unity utility weights. As we shall see in Chapter 13, we can ensure that CBA also does not ignore equity by using distribution weights applied to WTPs.

PART V

CBA

11. Cost–benefit analysis and the human capital approach

11.1 INTRODUCTION

CBA requires that outputs and inputs be measured in comparable units. With inputs measured in monetary units forming costs, the main way that CBA is made operational is for the outputs also to be measured in monetary terms and become benefits. In this chapter we look at the traditional, human capital approach to benefit estimation that places monetary valuations by way of individual earnings affected by health care interventions. This approach can be used for estimating indirect benefits, but it can also be used to measure lives lost or saved. The main alternative approach to valuing a life is to find out what people are willing to pay for reductions in the probability of losing one's life. This modern approach, called valuing a 'statistical life', typically relies on revealed preferences in the labor market and is the main way that intangible benefits are estimated.

We start by reviewing the three main components of benefits and then define intangible benefits and list the main methods by which they can be estimated. In section 11.2 we explain the logic of the human capital approach. Section 11.3 examines the alternative approach that is based on WTP and an expression is presented that relates the two methodologies. Section 11.4 covers ways of converting CUAs into CBAs that put a price on a QALY. In the conversions both human capital and revealed preference WTP estimates are used. The applications focus on these two valuation approaches.

11.1.1 Three Components of Benefits

In Chapter 1 we explained that the typical health care evaluation splits costs into three categories: direct (the health expenditures), indirect (forgone earnings) and intangible (the pain and suffering associated with treatment). If a cost is considered to be a negative benefit, then a benefit can be regarded as a negative cost. So the benefits of treatment are the avoided costs and there are three corresponding categories: direct (savings in health expenditures), indirect (restored earnings) and intangible (any reduction in pain and suffering from the illness no longer existing).

The human capital approach (HK) focuses on earnings (forgone or restored) and so is primarily used to measure indirect effects. As such, restored earnings from treatment constitute just a part of total benefits. This is important to understand because WTP is inherently the more comprehensive measure. If a patient is willing to pay, say, $100 to eliminate an illness (by having it successfully treated) then this conceptually would cover all three categories of benefits. This applies to any person's WTP, whether s/he is a primary beneficiary or an external gainer, as we now illustrate.

Zarkin et al. (2000), using a mall survey, found that on average people would be willing to pay $37 per respondent for an expansion in drug treatment that would lead to the successful treatment of 100 drug users. This $37 WTP valuation for drug treatment for others is all-inclusive and measures both the tangible external benefits (reduced crime and health care costs) and the intangible external benefits (a reduction in the fear of criminalization and an increase in psychic well-being attributable to knowing that drug addicts are being treated). The alternative HK approach would have to identify each and every possible crime committed by drug users (and the consequential impact of each crime on the victims' earnings), and add this to the saved medical costs (from not being mugged, etc.) and then lastly incorporate the intangible effects (presumably using some other evaluation method).

11.1.2   Measuring Intangibles

Some people confuse 'intangible' with the idea of 'immeasurable' (or non-quantifiable). 'Intangible' means difficult to measure in monetary terms. Often measurement is just a matter of time. They used to consider that heat was unmeasurable until Fahrenheit invented his scale. Once the output has been measured in physical terms, by some means a monetary valuation can be attached.

The main methods for measuring intangibles are:

1. *Using similar markets.* For example, the value of housewives' services that are lost if they have syphilis was measured by Klarman (1965) by the wages of domestic servants. The problem is: how similar is 'similar'? The syphilis case study presented in the applications provides an example of the good use of this method.
2. *Adjusting market prices.* The aim is to use market prices as a point of departure, but allow for considerations that are not reflected in market prices, especially 'external effects'. Much of modern industry takes place imposing pollution costs on the rest of society (e.g., acid rain).

The value of the industrial output can be valued at market prices, and then one adjusts this for the costs imposed by the pollution. A major problem with this approach is obtaining relevant information.

3. *Using implicit markets.* If somebody's behavior is such that they choose to accept an option that has a monetary gain, but puts the person at a particular risk, then the person implicitly values the risk at no more than that monetary amount. This method can be applied to both government decisions and individual decisions:

   (a) For government decisions, this method has been criticized for providing too wide a range of estimates. For example, a standard set by the Occupational Safety and Health Administration on the use of acrylonitrile is estimated to save a life at the cost of $11 million, while mandating the use of seat belts in automobiles saves a life at the cost of $88 (according to Graham and Vaupol (1980)).

   (b) For private decisions, it is the labor market (via compensating wage differences) that has most been used to obtain the implicit values. Section 11.3.1 explains the theory behind this approach and the third case study shows how this approach has been applied. Section 11.3.2 relates the theory of implicit markets to the HK approach. The relative magnitudes of estimates of the value of a life using implicit markets compared to those using the HK approach are presented in section 11.4.1.

11.2   HUMAN CAPITAL APPROACH

We first explain the standard rationale for using the HK approach in health care evaluations. Then we supply an alternative justification for the approach that gives it wider applicability.

11.2.1   Human Capital Measures of Benefits

When a person is very sick they cannot work. A treatment can allow that person to return to work and earn income. But in what sense is this restored income a benefit to society? That is, what is the social significance of this income?

In competitive markets, workers are paid the value of their marginal product. Marginal product (MP) is the extra output that a worker produces. The value that this generates for the firm is given by the market price of the output P. The value of the marginal product is thus $MP.P$ and we have:

$$\text{Wage} = P\,(\text{MP}) \tag{11.1}$$

So if a newly signed US baseball player will attract an extra 10000 fans into the stadium for each game, and there are 81 home games in a season, then the MP would be 10000 times 81 = 810000 attendees. If the average ticket price that a person pays to enter the stadium is $10, then the value of the marginal product would be $8.1 million for that season. This $8.1 million is the size of the value of the player to the firm (baseball owner). But it is also a measure of satisfaction because fans would only be willing to pay this sum if they feel better off to this extent. Of course, any increase in individual satisfaction will be treated as an increase in social satisfaction only if the individuals are regarded as the best judges of their own welfare.

Mishan (1976) argued that this evaluation method based on variations in earnings, called the human capital approach, is inconsistent with the basics of CBA, which tries to incorporate measures of individual preferences. It is true that some persons' preferences are recorded (those of the fans in the baseball example); but it is not the preferences of the persons most affected that are included, in our case, the preferences of the sick people. So it is more accurate to say that the HK approach measures just a part of the benefits of treatment, i.e., the benefits of individuals other than the persons most affected by treatment. One should therefore expect that the HK measures *underestimate* the benefits of treatment as reflected by WTP. In this chapter we will see this underestimation in both theory and practice.

The essence of the HK calculation of the value of a person's life is the following. The age of the person involved is noted and the difference between his/her current age and the retirement age (when earnings cease) is calculated. This produces the number of remaining years of working life. Information on the amount of the average yearly earnings is then obtained. If we multiply the number of working years by the average annual earnings, then we obtain the figure for remaining lifetime earnings. When these earnings are discounted, the result is the present value of the stream of lifetime earnings, which is the estimated value of the person's life.

It is not the case that the WTP approach asks a person: 'what is your life worth to you?', for this would typically extract a response in terms of an infinite monetary amount. Rather the question would be that in order to avoid a particular reduction in the probability of losing your life (by seeking medical treatment), 'what would you be willing to pay for that probability reduction?'. Individuals are used to buying life insurance, so would have some experience in answering such questions. The WTP approach uses the preferences of individuals personally affected and not just indirectly affected as with the HK approach.

11.2.2 Human Capital and Mental Health

In CBA, benefits and costs should reflect individual preferences. When individuals are the best judges of their own welfare, we can ask what they are willing to pay, or willing to receive as compensation, for the health care intervention. But what should be done if individuals are clearly not the best judges of their welfare, as is the case with patients in mental hospitals? Certainly the law in most countries does not treat them as responsible for their actions. So it would seem to be inappropriate for CBA to base treatment choices related to mental health options on patient preferences.

The particular choice we are considering is whether to house a mental patient in a hospital, or allow the person out into the community under supervision. One advantage of permitting patients outside the hospital setting is that they can work and earn income. As we just saw, this consideration is central to the traditional (human capital) approach to health care evaluations, which measures economic benefits in terms of production effects (lifetime earnings of those affected). This approach does not attempt to measure the WTP of those concerned. For most evaluations, this is a major drawback (even though under some conditions the WTP for improved health of other people may be a function of the productivity improvement of the latter). But, in the context where one has ruled out the validity of the WTP of those personally involved on competency grounds (as with mental patients), or ruled out the WTP approach on equity grounds because poor consumers are constrained by their ability to pay (as in the health care field where evaluators are reluctant to use explicit distribution weights), the traditional approach still may be useful.

This is especially true if one concentrates precisely on the justification given by Weisbrod et al. (1980, p. 404) for using earned income as a measure of the benefits of non-institutional care for mental patients. They argue that earnings can be thought of as an indicator of program success, 'with higher earnings reflecting a greater ability to get along with people and to behave as a responsible person'. Thus if one of the objectives of mental health treatment is to help get a patient back into playing an active role in society, then earnings are a sign that progress has been made. (For details of the Weisbrod et al. evaluation see the second case study.)

11.3 THE RELATION BETWEEN WTP AND HUMAN CAPITAL

Human capital is reflected in a person's lifetime income. WTP can be measured by the implicit labor market trade-off between wages and the risk of losing one's life. Linnerooth (1979) explains how the two approaches can be directly related.

11.3.1 Linnerooth Model

Assume that the individual regards his/her lifetime as fixed if s/he survives the initial period. Let Π be the probability of surviving into the future, in which case $(1 - \Pi)$ is the probability of dying. If there is no saving, then lifetime income Y equals lifetime consumption. The individual is an expected lifetime utility maximizer. With E[U] as expected lifetime utility, and $U(Y)$ the utility of lifetime income, we have:

$$E[U] = \Pi . U(Y) \tag{11.2}$$

Changes in both Π and U (i.e., $\Delta\Pi$ and ΔU) will bring about changes in expected lifetime utility $\Delta E[U]$. As a (linear) approximation, the change in lifetime utility corresponding to changes in both variables will be:

$$\Delta E[U] = \Pi . \Delta U(Y) + \Delta \Pi . U(Y) \tag{11.3}$$

The first term on the right-hand side of (11.3) can be written alternatively, by dividing and multiplying by ΔY. In which case, we can express this term in units of the marginal utility of income MU(Y):

$$\Pi . \Delta U(Y) = \Pi . [\Delta U(Y)/\Delta Y] \Delta Y = \Pi . MU(Y). \Delta Y \tag{11.4}$$

Substituting (11.4) into equation (11.3) produces:

$$\Delta E[U] = \Pi . MU(Y). \Delta Y + \Delta \Pi . U(Y) \tag{11.5}$$

By setting equation (11.5) equal to zero, we can obtain how much a change in one variable (the probability) will lead to a change in the other variable (income) holding lifetime utility constant. The result (called a 'marginal rate of substitution' by economists) is shown in equation (11.6):

$$\frac{\Delta Y}{\Delta \Pi} = (-) \frac{U(Y)}{\Pi MU(Y)} \tag{11.6}$$

Equation (11.6) measures the marginal rate of substitution between changes in Y and changes in Π. This is what is called 'the value of a human life'. That is, it is what one is willing to pay (lifetime income one will sacrifice) for a marginal risk reduction. Note that this equation is in the same form as the Garber and Phelps' utility maximization equation (6.4), where the change in the effect ΔE is defined in the present context by the percentage change in the risk of dying $\Delta\Pi/\Pi$.

The value of a life can be shown diagrammatically as the slope of the graph relating Π to Y: see Figure 11.1. Economists call such a graph an 'indifference curve' because it records when the individual is indifferent between changes in Y and Π. A person is indifferent when (expected) utility is held constant (i.e., equation (11.5) does not change (set equal to zero)). The figure shows, for example, that the individual is willing to pay \$200 for a reduction in mortality risk from 10^{-6} to 10^{-9} (a reduction of $1/1000$). This trade-off produces a value of life of \$200000 only in the sense that the CBA we are dealing with is a health care intervention that produces a *per capita* reduction in risk from 10^{-6} to 10^{-9} for a population of 1000. The expectation here is that one would be saving one life (i.e., a $1/1000$ reduction in dying for a group of 1000 equals 1 life saved on average).

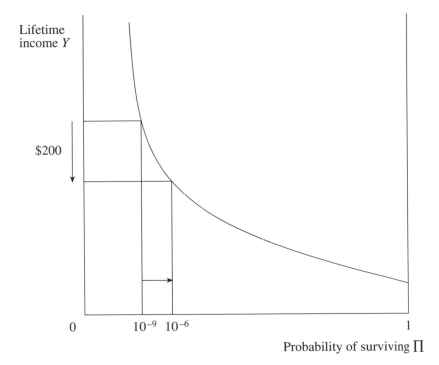

Note: The curve shows the trade-off of lifetime income Y for survival probability Π. For a risk reduction from 10^{-6} to 10^{-9}, one would be willing to pay (give up) \$200 for utility to be unchanged and remain on the curve.

Figure 11.1:   The trade-off of lifetime income for survival probabilities

Note that the slope is a *non-linear* relation between WTP and changes in the survival probabilities. As survival chances decrease, WTP increases at an increasing rate. This means that the indifference curve will approach asymptotically, but will never intersect, the Y axis. This has two important implications:

1. One can resolve the paradox that a person places an infinite value on his/her life, but willingly accept small probabilities of death for finite compensation. The individual will not accept \$200000 for $\Pi=0$. The slope is much steeper at low values of Π and infinite at $\Pi=0$.
2. Strictly, it means \$200000 is the value for the expectation of saving one life, only when the risk reduction is from 10^{-6} to 10^{-9}. For a reduction in risk from 10^{-7} to 10^{-10} the value will be much greater (because the slope is steeper over that range) even though the risk reduction is again $1/1000$. Knowing the starting risk level is very important, not just knowing the size of the risk change. If one starts off with a low probability of survival, one would be willing to pay a lot for additional security.

11.3.2 Conley Model

Linnerooth extends her model of the value of a statistical life to the analysis by Conley (1976). Conley derives the value of a human life V as discounted lifetime income, Y, divided by the elasticity of lifetime utility with respect to lifetime income, α:

$$V = \frac{U(Y)}{\Pi MU(Y)} = \frac{Y}{\alpha} \qquad (11.7)$$

where α is the percentage change in utility divided by the percentage change in income: $(\Delta U/U)/(\Delta Y/Y)$. By assuming a value for the elasticity of utility with respect to income, one can obtain from equation (11.7) a simple relation between the value of a life in a WTP sense with the value of a life as recorded by lifetime earnings. This works as follows.

Assume diminishing marginal utility of lifetime income, as in Figure 11.2 based on Linnerooth's Figure 2. Then there are three regions. In the first U is negative, and so $\alpha<0$. In the second region, $U>0$ and $\alpha>1$. In this case $V<Y$. In the third region, $1>\alpha>0$ and we have $V>Y$. The conclusion therefore is that, as long as expected lifetime income Y is above a certain critical level Y^* where $\alpha=1$, then the WTP measure of value of a life will exceed the human capital measure of life (given by lifetime income).

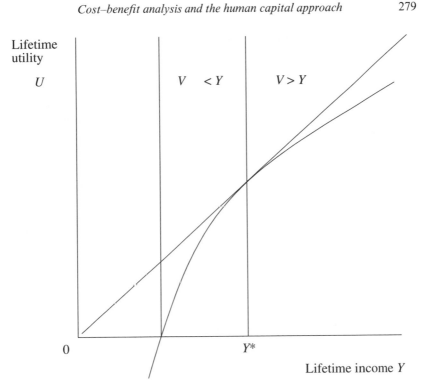

Note: The curve shows that with diminishing marginal utility of lifetime income, the relation between WTP and lifetime earnings depends on the size of the elasticity of lifetime utility with respect to income α.

Figure 11.2:   The relation between WTP and lifetime earnings

11.4 METHODS FOR CONVERTING A CUA INTO A CBA

In section 6.4, we presented various methods to convert a CEA into a CBA. These methods can be applied to any type of CEA, so they are equally applicable to CUA where outcomes happen to be measured in terms of QALYs. We now consider some additional conversion techniques that have QALYs explicitly in mind (though it should be recognized that even the Garber and Phelps' theoretical model covered in Chapter 6 did actually specify QALYs as its unit of effect).

11.4.1   Using QALYs for Both Benefits and Costs

Strictly, the only requirement to be able to tell if a health care expenditure is worthwhile, that is, to know whether the Bs are greater than the Cs, is for inputs and outputs to be valued in the *same* units. In standard CBA, the units are monetary ones, but other common measurement units (called numeraires) are possible. QALYs basically use time as the numeraire (having adjusted for the different values of time in alternative health states). A first step in converting a CUA into a CBA would be to stick with QALYs on the consequences side, but translate the inputs into QALYs on the costs side. This is implicitly the approach proposed by Brent (1991).

To see how this works, let us restate the definition of a benefit that applies to a CEA context, that was given in Chapter 1: $B \equiv P.E.$ In a CUA context, QALYs are the measures of the effects, and so the identity becomes:

$$B = P . QALY(B) \tag{11.8}$$

where $QALY(B)$ are the number of QALYs on the consequences (benefits) side and P is now the price of a QALY. The corresponding CUA definition of a cost would be:

$$C = P . QALY(C) \tag{11.9}$$

where $QALY(C)$ are the number of QALYs on the inputs (costs) side. The efficiency criterion that $B > C$ using equations (11.8) and (11.9) translates into the condition for a worthwhile project if:

$$QALY(B) > QALY(C) \tag{11.10}$$

Note that in the relation (11.10), the monetary price of a QALY does not appear, as the Ps on both the input and output sides are divided out. Time units are on both sides and thus the two sides are commensurate. It is just a matter of how much time is gained relative to how much time is given up.

The obvious questions to ask are under what circumstances, and how often, the costs could be expressed in terms of time. In the applications we show an example of a safety precaution (a driving speed limit) that causes time to be used up complying with the regulation. Many types of regulation impose such a time cost, whether it is involved with buckling one's seatbelt or bicycle helmet, or taking extra time to unscrew a child-protected bottle of aspirins. But the general case is that money is a more useful numeraire than time, so approaches that use Ps must be considered.

11.4.2 Deriving the Price of a QALY from a Measure of Benefits

Let us return to the situation where costs are measured in dollar terms and where equation (11.8) specifies the benefits as: $B = P . QALY$. The health care evaluation literature seems to have operationalized this representation by dividing both sides by the number of QALYs to obtain:

$$P = \frac{B}{QALY} = \frac{B}{\bar{U}.T} \tag{11.11}$$

Hirth et al. (2000) implicitly employ (11.11) as their way of valuing a QALY. They recognize that since T (they call it x) corresponds to the number of years of life remaining, it makes most sense to apply equation (11.11) to a situation where the benefits one is considering relate to a person's lifetime. In which case, the value of life literature supplies the most relevant estimates of B. To measure $\bar{U}$ (they denote it by q) they used age specific quality of life weights derived from Fryback et al. (1993) (the Beaver Dam Health Outcomes Study). To see how the Hirth et al. method works, consider an illustrative calculation that abstracts from discounting (in their study they used the 3% rate recommended by the US CUA panel).

Say a particular value of life study comes up with a $3 million per person estimate. Hirth et al. then investigate that study to identify the age group of the persons being evaluated. If the study was represented as applying to the US population as a whole, then they assumed that the typical person had an average age of 40. For a person aged 40, life tables indicate that s/he would have 38.1 years of life remaining (the life expectancy was set at 78.1 years for both males and females). For a person aged 40, the Fryback et al. study gives the age specific utility score. Hirth et al. do not report the 40-year-old score. But let us say it is the same as the 45-year-old score of 0.9 that they do report. So this means that the typical person being valued has a QALY total of 34.29 (38.1 times 0.9). If 34.9 QALYs are worth $3 million, then one QALY must be worth $87 489 ($3 million divided by 34.9).

The method just explained can be used to determine the price of a QALY conditional on a given value for B. It thus can be used irrespective of the particular methodology used to measure B, whether it is HK or WTP. On the basis of this method, and incorporating a 3% discount rate, Table 11.1 (based on Hirth et al.'s Table 1) shows the values of a QALY (P) that correspond to four different methodologies used to estimate the value of life (B) (41 different estimates of B were obtained by Hirth et al. based on 38 value of life studies). The four different methodologies were HK and

Table 11.1:   *The value of a quality adjusted life year (1997 dollars)by study type*

Study selected	Value for B	Derived value for P
Human capital (N=6)		
Lowest	458029	21294
Highest	2079796	76326
Median		24777
WTP (RP2) (N=8)		
Lowest	679224	32359
Highest	6026998	287137
Median		93402
WTP (CV) (N=8)		
Lowest	458029	58639
Highest	2079796	1176171
Median		161305
WTP (RP1) (N=19)		
Lowest	923425	46965
Highest	19352894	904679
Median		428286

Source: Based on Hirth et al. (2000)

three WTP versions: WTP (CV), WTP (RP1) and WTP (RP2), where CV is contingent valuation and RP stands for revealed preference (with RP1 relating to job risk decisions, and RP2 relating to safety decisions).

Table 11.1 reveals that the implied value of a QALY depends critically on the methodology adopted to make the benefits estimate. The median for HK was $25000, which is about one-tenth of the valuation of $265 345 derived from the median value for the 35 estimates based on the WTP approach. These valuations seriously challenge the validity of the CUA benchmarks, by which a cost per QALY of less than $20000 is considered good, $20000–$100000 is judged acceptable and anything over $100000 is questionable. Apart from the HK estimates, most valuations of a QALY far exceed the typical benchmarks suggested in CUA. For example, an intervention obtaining a QALY for as high as, say, $200000 would be socially worthwhile using a median WTP valuation.

Note that the QALY valuations using this method are very sensitive to the discount rate used. If instead of the 3% rate no discount rate were used, the estimates would fall by 40%. A 5% discount rate would raise estimates by 30%, and a 7% rate would raise the estimates by 60%.

11.4.3   Deriving Benefits from the Price of a QALY

A second way to work with the definition $B = P$. QALY is to use it in a direct way to estimate benefits by multiplying the price P by the number of QALYs involved. Although equation (11.11) is just a rearrangement of equation (11.8), both expressions can be used if one uses different measures of the variables in each equation. This is the approach taken by French et al. (1996) in their valuation of benefits of avoiding a two-month bout of hepatitis B mentioned in Chapter 9. First equation (11.11) was used to obtain the price of a QALY in a general setting independent of hepatitis B. Then this value for P is fed back into equation (11.8) to be used on the number of QALYs lost by hepatitis B.

One way of understanding the details of the French et al. calculations is to recognize that the price that they are working with is the value of a year of life *in full health*. So they treat $\bar{U}$ as equal to unity. This means that their version of equation (11.11), their equation (3), was: $P = B / T$. They took B to be $5 million, which was the value of a statistical life for an average individual, as estimated by Moore and Viscusi (1988) – see the fourth application below. A white male at age 38 has a maximum life span of 90 years, and so has 52 more years remaining, which equates to 624 months. If one discounts these months at a rate of 5%, and allows for the probability of dying at each year until 90, then the discounted expected life months were 192.59. Dividing $5m by 192.59, along the line of equation (11.11), produces a price per quality adjusted life month (QALM) of $25 961. As we saw in section 9.2.2, the Rosser and Kind index applied to hepatitis B gives a 0.956 utility value. Two months with this disease leads to 0.08457 QALMs (again when discounted at 5% and adjusted for the probability of survival from one month to the next). Using (11.8), one multiplies the price of $25 961 times the quantity of 0.08457 to obtain a $2196 estimate of the benefits of avoiding a moderate case of hepatitis B.

11.5   APPLICATIONS

The first case study is a traditional, human capital CBA that provides estimates for all three categories of benefits. Then we cover an evaluation that uses the HK approach in a non-traditional way. From there we present an application based on the rival revealed preference WTP approach and close with a CBA study that has benefits and costs, but they are measured in non-monetary units.

Table 11.2: Costs of syphilis prevention (*in millions of dollars, except for cost per case*)

Type of cost	Total	P and S stages		Early latent stage	Late latent stage	Late stage
		Reported	Not reported			
Medical care expenditures	19.5	3.0	5.0	1.8	2.5	7.2
Output loss due to treatment	40.7	1.5	1.9	0.8	1.2	35.3
Reduction in earnings due to stigma	51.0	11.9	11.1	7.8	19.3	0.9
Consumer benefit loss	6.3	1.0	1.7	0.4	1.2	2.0
Total cost	117.5	17.4	19.7	10.8	24.2	45.4
No. of cases (in thousands)	119.6	20.0	33.4	17.0	48.2	1.0
Cost per case (dollars)	985	870	590	635	500	45400

Source: Klarman (1965)

11.5.1   A CBA of Syphilis Prevention

One of the biggest problems in evaluating the benefits of health care programs is to disentangle investment from consumption effects. By obtaining treatment, a person can go back (or continue) to work. This is an investment dimension to the health expenditure, and is reflected in the person's earnings. But how does one estimate the benefit that is obtained from removing the pain and anxiety from not having the health problem? It is this that can be called the 'consumption benefit', and is not included in the earnings figure. Usually, the consumption benefits are ignored in CBAs in the health care field. Klarman's (1965) syphilis study is important because it tried to put a dollar amount on it. The study is also worth considering because it tried to measure other intangibles, such as the 'stigma' of having had syphilis.

In 1962, the prevalence of the disease was 1.2 million, and the incidence (the new cases occurring) was 60 000. 124 000 are newly reported each year, most of them years after the onset of the disease. This shows that the (then) existing syphilis control programs were not completely effective. There are a number of stages with the disease. The primary stage (P) is the first symptomatic stage after the disease is acquired and lasts 2–13 weeks. The secondary stage (S) follows, and lasts 6–25 weeks. In both stages, patients are infectious to sex partners. The later, tertiary, non-infectious stages, are called early latent, late latent, and late. The tertiary stages come 10–30 years after the others. Each stage was costed separately by Klarman.

The aim was to measure the benefits of syphilis prevention by looking at the existing costs that this would eliminate. This then has to be compared with the costs of an actual program that would prevent the disease (which was not identified in Klarman's study). The benefits (costs avoided) are listed in Table 11.2 (his Table 7). There are three categories of costs: loss of production (indirect costs), expenditures for medical care (direct costs), and the pain and discomfort from the disease (intangible costs).

The total benefits were $117.5 million into perpetuity. Dividing this by a discount rate of 4% produces a present value of $2.95 billion. (To understand why one divides by r, refer back to the present value formula in Chapter 2, given as equation (2.7). Assume annual effects are the same in each year and so S_t is fixed, equal to, say, S. Now let n approach infinity. The infinite sum becomes equal to $S(1/r)$. Here $1/r$ is called the 'annuity factor' for a constant sum into perpetuity.)

An explanation of how the intangible benefits in Table 11.2 were calculated will now be given.

1. 'Consumer benefits': The approach adopted was to use the method of an 'analogous disease'. This focused on the symptoms of syphilis and

not any treatment given. Klarman describes the approach as follows. Consider a disease with symptoms that are similar to those of syphilis, which involves expenditures that do not have any prospect of curing the disease (or are undertaken when the person is retired). The expenditures have no output (earnings) benefits, and they do not reduce the medical expenditures. The expenditures must therefore be incurred for consumption purposes only. *By analogy*, these expenditures measure the value of the consumption benefits of syphilis. The analogous disease selected was psoriasis, a skin disease. Psoriasis usually entails no disability, but a permanent cure is not likely. With four visits per episode, and a cost per episode of $50, including drugs, for 20 000 cases, the calculated cost was $1 million (when discounted).

2. 'Reductions on earnings due to stigma': Here we explain how the $11.9 million loss during the P and S stages was obtained. It was estimated (guessed) that 1% of the present value of a person's earnings would be lost due to the stigma of having had syphilis. The total earnings for all cases amounted to $1376.1 million. This was adjusted downward by 4%, to allow for the possibility of unemployment, and 10%, which reflected the chances of being reinfected. The combined adjustment was to take 0.864 of the earnings (.96 times .90). The total earnings were therefore taken to be $1190 million. 1% of this is $11.9 million. The costs due to stigma were particularly high, equal to 44% of the total economic costs.

It is interesting to note that Klarman (1982) wrote: 'I put a great deal of effort into an attempt to value intangible benefits in the paper on syphilis for the first Brookings conference (Klarman, 1965). The subsequent literature frequently cites this effort but does not repeat it.'!

11.5.2   A CBA of Alternative Treatments for Mental Health

The size of earnings was the largest category of benefits valued in monetary terms in the study of alternative mental health treatments by Weisbrod et al. As we can see from Table 11.3, mental health patients had annual earnings of $2364 if treated in a community based program (identified as the experimental program *E*), and only $1168 if treated in a hospital (the control program *C*). There were therefore extra benefits of $1196 per patient if treatment takes place outside the hospital setting.

Earnings were not the only category of benefits that were valued. Patients in the *E* program were (surprisingly) less likely to get involved with breaking the law. The lower law enforcement costs were registered as a cost saving of the *E* program. In aggregate though, the costs (direct and indirect

Table 11.3:   Costs and benefits of alternative mental health programs

Unit of analysis	Community program E	Hospital program C	Difference $E - C$
Benefits (earnings)	$2364	$1168	$1196
Costs	$8093	$7296	$797
Net benefits	−$5729	−$6128	$399

Source: Weisbrod et al. (1980)

as defined in Chapter 1, law enforcement, maintenance and family burden) were higher in the E program (by $797) as supervision costs were obviously greater.

The figures in Table 11.3 relate to a period 12 months after admission. They are therefore on a recurring annual basis (which means that they are the same in each year). The net benefits per year for either program were negative. This need not imply that no mental treatment should be provided, seeing that not all benefits (or cost savings) were valued in monetary terms (e.g., burdens on neighbors, co-workers, and family members). However, if these non-valued effects were the same for both programs, then the preferred option would be program E. Its negative net benefits were $399 lower than for program C.

11.5.3   An Estimate of the Value of a Statistical Life from Worker Occupation Choices

We have already seen in Chapter 7 how the revealed preference approach can be used to extract the trade-off between behavioral variables and thereby uncover implicit preferences. In that chapter the labor market choice was between having a higher wage and a higher, discounted number of life years. The estimation framework was captured by equation (7.8):

$$\text{Wage rate} = \alpha_1 \, (\text{Expected Life Years Lost}) + \alpha_2 \, (\text{Other Variables})$$

and the discount rate, which was our prime concern, was one of the other variables in the equation.

In the current application, based on Moore and Viscusi (1988b), we are again considering labor market choices, but this time from an annual point of view, in which case discounting is not an issue. Also instead of focusing on how many expected years one is willing to give up to obtain the extra wages, one can key in on the expectation part itself, in terms of the risk of not surviving to the future. In this way one is exactly in the value of a statistical life framework summarized by Figure 11.1, where lifetime income (or Y) was being traded off against a survival probability Π.

In line with the annual point of view that we are now taking, it is the (net of tax) wage rate and not lifetime income that is the dependent variable and the risk of *not* surviving that is the independent variable (and so job risk is equal to $1 - \Pi$). Equation (7.8) can then be replaced by:

$$\text{Wage rate} = \alpha_1 \text{ (Job Risk)} + \alpha_2 \text{ (Other Variables)} \qquad (11.12)$$

In equation (11.12) the other variables reflect personal characteristics (e.g., age and gender) that may account for why risk-taking behavior may differ across individuals and labor market determinants (e.g., years of experience or union membership) that could cause wage rates to be different independently of occupational risk.

It is the size of α_1 that interests us now, for the expectation is that workers need to obtain higher wages to accept greater job risk. Hence this coefficient should be positive if the theory of compensating wage differences is to hold. The main estimate of α_1 by Moore and Viscusi was +0.021667, thus they did come up with an estimate with the expected sign. Moreover, from α_1, and the measured size of the risk involved, one can obtain an estimate of the statistical value of a life. The regression coefficient tells us that a person needs $0.021667 in extra wages per hour to put up with the additional *annual* risk of being in a particular occupation. Since the typical employee works 2000 hours a year, this translates into a required extra annual compensation of $43.4 ($0.021667 times 2000). The risk units were the annual number of deaths per 100 000 workers in an industry. So, if in order to accept a 1/100000 chance of dying a person typically needs $43.4, this implies that society would accept $4.34 million ($43.4 times 100000) to accept the loss of one worker (assuming linearity). This $4.34 million estimate related to 1981. Moore and Viscusi wished to work with current 1986 prices, so they updated the value to $5.235 million (using the GNP deflator). This thus explains how the $5 million value that French et al. used to price a QALY in section 11.3.2 was originally obtained.

A controversial issue in the value of a statistical life literature involves what data to use to measure occupational risk. It is not simply a matter of trying to obtain the most accurate measure of occupational risk, though this is clearly important. What is also crucial is how aware are workers of these job risks. If workers think the risks are of a given size, even though objectively the information is different, then their behavior will be driven by the subjective measures and not the objective ones. One is again confronted with the fundamental value judgment of CBA as to whether to accept the assumption of consumer sovereignty. If one does not accept that individuals are the best judge of their own welfare, either because they are unable to discern small risk probabilities, or because they are not well informed about job risk probabilities, then one would question the usefulness of value of life estimates based on occupational choices.

This discussion has particular relevance for the Moore and Viscusi study because one of their contributions was to utilize a new, and much more refined, data series, on occupational death risks issued by the National Traumatic Occupational Fatality (NTOF) project. The standard data source for most value of life calculations was the occupational risk of death figures supplied by the US Bureau of Labor Statistics (BLS). The main difference between the BLS data and the NTOF data was that the latter source was not a partial survey as it covered the whole population. This means that the NTOF data were more reliable they did not have any sampling error. In the BLS data source the average fatality rate reported was 5.2 per 100 000 workers. However, the mean NTOF death risk rate was 7.9 deaths per 100 000 workers, which is 52% higher than the BLS rate.

It is not the case that because the NTOF death risk was higher by 52% that therefore the NTOF value of life estimate would be 52% higher than the BLS value. This is because the NTOF risks were not proportionally higher for every occupation. For example, in services the NTOF rate was almost four times as high as the BLS rate (3.428 versus 0.866), but it was only 14% higher for the construction industry (32.738 versus 28.698). When the regressions were repeated using the BLS data, the implied value of life for 1986 was around $2 million. The overall difference therefore was that the NTOF data produced value of life estimates that were more statistically significant and were over twice as large as those given by the BLS data.

Moore and Viscusi acknowledged that they did not have any data to be able to test whether NTOF data were closer than BLS data to individual subjective risk evaluations (which is the basis for the behavior recorded in the equations). Nonetheless, they interpreted their finding from two alternative perspectives. In either case the $5 million is considered to be more reliable than the $2 million estimate.

If one accepts consumer sovereignty and judges that individuals can make sound assessments of occupational risk rates, then the more accurate NTOF risk variable should enhance the reliability of the empirical estimates of the value of life. On the other hand, if one does not accept consumer sovereignty and judges that individuals have biased assessments of risks, the $5 million valuation is unlikely to be an overestimate. In the literature, any systematic bias in risk perceptions is such that individuals tend to overestimate small probabilities and underestimate large probabilities. The fact that the NTOF risk rates were *higher* than the BLS rates would therefore suggest that the NTOF measures would be more likely to be underestimates of perceived risks. The NTOF figure for the value of life should be considered to be more of a minimum estimate – the value of life was at least $5 million.

An illustrative calculation might help here. When the average measured NOTF risk was 7.9 deaths per 100000 workers, and worker behavior implies that they needed $43.4 to compensate for it, the value of life would be $4.34 times 100000. If the workers perceived the risk to be lower at say 7.9 deaths per 120000, then the $43.4 would have to be multiplied by 120000 to produce a larger estimate.

11.5.4   A CBA of the 55 mph Speed Limit

The main advantage of the US government imposing the 55 mph speed limit was that it saved lives. The speed limit would not save a person's life forever, as life expectancy is finite. So avoiding a road fatality saves a period of time, i.e., a person's life expectancy. On the other hand, the main drawback of the speed limit was that people would take much more time traveling to their destinations. Overall then, travelers had to forgo time in order to expect to gain time. Since the units of measurement for both the gains and the losses were expressed in terms of time, Brent (1991) decided to quantify the size of the time gain and the time lost to see which was greater. In this way he carried out a CBA that had time as the numeraire along the lines of the criterion specified by relation (11.10). Brent used a simplified version of (11.10) as he assumed that $\bar{U} = 1$ for both the benefits and costs and therefore did not make any utility adjustment to the numbers of life years.

The CBA of the 55 mph speed limit as evaluated with 1981 as the starting date and expressed in time units was carried out as follows. The speed limit saved approximately 7466 lives per year. The average driver was 33.5 years old. With an average life expectancy of 76 years, avoiding a road fatality preserves 42.5 years per person. The 7466 people, each saving 42.5 years, amounted to 316558 life years gained. These were the (undiscounted) benefits of the speed limit.

The costs were due to the fact that drivers typically had to go 4.8 mph slower than they did before the imposition of the speed limit. Given the distance (total mileage) traveled in 1981, the slower speed caused car users and their passengers to spend an extra 456 279 life years on the road. These benefits and costs are recorded in Table 11.4. As the number of life years gained was less than the number of life years lost (by 139 721 life years) the speed limit decision was not worthwhile, viewed from the time perspective.

Table 11.4:   *Costs and benefits of the 55 mph speed limit decision using different numeraires*

Category	Money as the numeraire ($ millions)	Time as the numeraire (years)
Benefits	4188	316558
Costs	16543	456279
Net-benefits	−12355	−139721
Benefit–cost ratio	0.25	0.69

Source: Constructed by the author from Forester et al. (1984) and Brent (1991)

We can compare this time evaluation with a monetary evaluation of the 55 mph speed limit decision that was carried out by Forester et al. (1984). They did not report benefits and costs separately, but their individual amounts can be approximated from the data they presented (and checked against the 0.24 *B/C* ratio which they did report). A part of their evaluation included a traditional CBA. From the human capital point of view, a person's life is valued by the net present value of the stream of lifetime earnings. Average earnings in 1981 were $15 496. Assuming a person retires at 65 years, a person aged 33.5 would have earned $527 200 over their lifetime at a 'net discount rate' of 0.5% (i.e., average earnings are expected to grow at 0.5% more than the opportunity cost of capital, which is another way of estimating the discount rate). So $527 200 is the HK value of a life. With 7466 lives at stake, the total monetary benefits were $4188 million. Drivers spent an extra 2220.556 million hours on the road because they were forced to travel at reduced speeds. The market value of this lost time, valuing each hour at the average wage rate of $7.45, was $16 543 million. This, then, is the size of the monetary costs. The monetary B and C figures are also included in Table 11.4. As $4188 million is less than $16 543 million (by $12 355 million) the monetary net benefits of the speed limit decision were negative and this legislation would not be considered worthwhile.

The CBA outcomes using the time and monetary numeraires were the same. Neither would have approved of the 55 mph speed limit. This correspondence is reassuring when, as is the case with the HK approach, a methodology is used that is under widespread criticism. For one cannot in this case argue that it was only because an inegalitarian CBA approach was used that the speed limit decision was not considered worthwhile.

When the direction of the results of alternative numeraires is being compared, the signs of the net benefits are important. But, if one wants to compare the magnitudes by which CBAs using different numeraires support a particular outcome, then the benefit–cost ratios can be used. For the B/C ratio is simply a pure number and can be compared on a numerical scale. As we explained in Chapter 1, when we presented the relation (1.3), the requirement that $B > C$ is equivalent to the need to have $B/C > 1$. Table 11.4 shows that the benefit–cost ratio was less than 1 for the speed limit using either numeraire. But the monetary numeraire ratio (0.24) was much lower than the time numeraire ratio (0.69) and as a consequence would give much less support for the speed limit decision.

As we acknowledged in section 11.3.1, the time numeraire is not as readily applicable as a monetary numeraire. But, when it can be utilized, as with the 55 mph speed limit decision, it does have egalitarian properties not shared by monetary numeraires, especially those based on the human capital approach. With time as the numeraire, a person's remaining life years count the same whether the person is rich or poor, working or not working. In the HK approach, one's life years count only for the working years and when one is in paid employment. Life years of housewives (or househusbands) or of those retired are given a zero weight. In the context of the 55 mph speed decision, although people were expected to live 76 years, the 11 years after 65 were ignored completely in the HK calculations. Moreover, in the HK approach persons who earn 10 times the average have their lives valued at 10 times the average.

11.6   FINAL SECTION

We now present the problems, summary and looking ahead sections.

11.6.1   Problems

The aim of the problems is to check the reader's understanding of some of the findings in this chapter and to collect a number of results from studies included in this and previous chapters so that they can be easily compared.

1. Explain precisely why it is that, in section 11.3.2, the value of a QALY goes up as the size of the discount rate increases. (Use equation (11.4) to help you with your explanation and think about how T in this equation would be affected by the discount rate. For help, look at the details of the French et al. calculation.)
2. Could the lifespan and adjustments made for annual survival rates used by French et al. for an average male in section 11.4.3 be consistent with the life expectancy figure used by Hirth et al. in section 11.4.2? What then are the differences in which they measure T in their methods?

3. Refer back to the Garber and Phelps' method for converting a CEA into a CBA explained in Chapter 6 (the method is explained in section 6.3.1 and the application is covered in section 6.4.2).
    (a) Assuming one uses the human capital approach to value a life year, what value for a QALY could be extracted from the Garber and Phelps study?
    (b) In summarizing their analysis, what relation did Garber and Phelps say existed between annual income and their utility-based measure of the cut-off ratio?
    (c) On the basis of your answers to (a) and (b), what relation between human capital measures and utility measures of QALYs could be deduced from the Garber and Phelps study?
    (d) What needs to be assumed in the Linnerooth extension of her model, as expressed in equation (11.7), to make her relation between human capital and WTP consistent with the Garber and Phelps relation?

11.6.2 Summary

In this chapter we began our discussion of the last of the main evaluation methods, i.e., CBA. Central to this method is benefit estimation, which involves the need to obtain a price for the health care output. The main output we analyzed in this chapter was a saved life or a QALY. In the traditional, human capital approach, a life saved or a QALY is valued in terms of an individual's earnings. This approach has the merit of being easy to use as earnings data are readily available. But it has the drawback of ignoring the preferences of those directly involved with the health care treatment. And the HK approach also fosters inequity, as those who are economically vulnerable often do not have earnings, and the richest workers' lives would be valued the most. However, when the HK approach is applied to mental health evaluations, it takes on a very different interpretation, for earnings then become a proxy for the success by which patients are being re-assimilated into 'normal' everyday (working) life.

A variation of the HK approach, that is consistent with the use of QALYs in CUA, is to use time as the numeraire. When inputs and outputs are mainly in this form, which is not generally the case but is true of life-safety interventions (such as the 55 mph speed limit regulation in the US), a policy can be determined to be worthwhile in terms of time alone. This numeraire is more egalitarian as everyone's life expectancies are treated the same, whether they are rich or poor, employed, unemployed or retired.

Modern CBA uses WTP to measure benefits. In this chapter we concentrated only on the WTP version based on implicit market behavior, as this method facilitates comparison with the HK approach. Both approaches use wage rate data, but the interpretation of the use of earnings is very different in the two approaches. In the HK framework, earnings are obtained because the workers satisfy the preferences of others (the consumers). In the revealed preference approach, the workers' preferences themselves are being utilized. The workers are choosing to give up earnings in order to obtain less risk of losing their lives.

The relative sizes of HK and WTP estimates were examined in theory and in practice. In the Linnerooth model, the two methods were compared from a lifetime perspective. Lifetime utility, or WTP, was found to be equal to lifetime income, divided by the elasticity of lifetime utility with respect to income. Under the assumption that this elasticity is greater than one, one obtains the result that WTP will exceed the amount of lifetime income. This expectation derived from expected utility theory was confirmed by the estimates of Hirth et al. that were based on annual estimates. Median WTP estimates were 10 times that of median HK estimates. The central conclusion of this chapter therefore is that, if HK estimates are to be used to value benefits, then one is likely to be *underestimating* the true size of benefits. Any evaluation that comes up with positive net benefits using the HK approach would be even more likely to be judged worthwhile if a WTP estimation of benefits had been used. This finding is consistent with the conclusion of the Garber and Phelps model given in Chapter 6, where they suggested that a WTP benchmark for a CEA would be twice the size of annual income.

The second major conclusion of this chapter follows from the section explaining how to price a QALY. The method involved working backwards from values of a person's lifetime utility or income to obtain annual valuations (by dividing by the present value of the number of years of remaining life expectancy). Conventional CUA guidelines suggest that if a QALY obtained by an intervention costs more than $100000, then that treatment is unlikely to be worthwhile. But the QALY prices obtained were, on the basis of the median WTP estimates, over twice this amount. This means that the value of a QALY was much higher than the recommended cut-off cost of a QALY. We obtained this realization only because we left the CUA domain and turned to the more comprehensive evaluation method CBA. CUA benchmarks are only valid if they have first been established by benefit estimation that is a central part of CBA. CUA cannot ignore benefit estimation as is commonly thought.

11.6.3   Looking Ahead

The HK approach has many weaknesses as a method of measuring benefits for use in a CBA. The WTP approach is more consistent with the consumer sovereignty basis of CBA. The consumer sovereignty dimension to WTP will be analyzed further in Chapter 12. The implicit markets (revealed preference approach) covered in this chapter is just one way of obtaining WTP magnitudes. Other methods for deriving WTP estimates need to be explained and this will also take place in the next chapter.

12. Cost–benefit analysis and willingness to pay

12.1 INTRODUCTION

WTP is at the core of CBA and in this chapter we explain why this is so. WTP should be used when consumer sovereignty holds. Consumer sovereignty requires rationality and full information. When we explain the principles of WTP, and discuss applications, we will do so with the requirements of consumer sovereignty explicitly in mind. We start by affirming how WTP relies on consumer sovereignty and go on to review the main methods for valuing WTP. Because WTP is constructed differently for some health care goods that are public goods, this difference needs explaining. Section 12.2 presents the welfare economic base to WTP in CBA. Section 12.3 deals with the special case where WTP is being used in the context of rationing by time rather than by price. The applications highlight the many considerations that need to be understood when using WTP for health care CBAs.

12.1.1 WTP and Consumer Sovereignty

To maximize utility the individual equates $P = MU$. The price that someone is willing to pay therefore measures the satisfaction from consuming a good. The total satisfaction, i.e., the benefits, from consumption is the aggregate WTP for all units of the good.

In most circumstances, both within and outside the health care field, WTP is the correct approach to measure benefits. Only this method is consistent with one of the fundamental principles of modern economics based on consumer utility maximization. With resources (income) limited, purchasing health care precludes the purchase of other goods and services that also give satisfaction. As we pointed out in Chapter 1, because it is the individuals themselves who are to decide how to spend their income, and in the process make themselves better off, the main value judgment behind WTP is the assumption of consumer sovereignty.

As a general rule, CBA in health care should be based on consumer sovereignty. However, in this book there have been three occasions when consumer sovereignty was in dispute:

1. We saw with immunization programs that individuals, in some cases, were *actually* vaccinating at rates not only less than the social optimum, but also below rates that were privately optimal. The suggestion was that people might not have been well enough informed to bring about their own utility maximization.
2. In the context of explaining the determination of the social discount rate, we recognized that individual preferences for long-term decisions might not be reliable (i.e., were myopic) as they ignore the cost and benefits of future generations. For this reason a *social* time preference rate was formulated that was different from an individual's time preference rate.
3. When we covered an evaluation related to those who were severely mentally ill, consumer sovereignty was not the starting point for measuring benefits. Earnings (as proposed by the human capital approach) were utilized as a proxy measure for a person being integrated back into the community.

Whatever the reason, it is a fact that many health care evaluations are not consistent with accepting the consumer sovereignty value judgment. For example, CUA guidelines required that 'community', not individual, preferences be used to measure utilities. Interestingly, in the Propper study that we shall be referring to below, she was able to specify precisely whose preferences are to count. As she said (Propper (1900), p. 196): 'The under-25s were excluded to limit the possibility of inclusion of individuals who have no experience of waiting lists. Over-70s were excluded, as it was thought that this group might include some individuals who could give unreliable responses.' The many further adjustments that need to be made to health care CBAs because of reservations about accepting consumer sovereignty are highlighted in the applications.

12.1.2   Methods for Valuing WTP

1. *Direct demand*: These are revealed preference measures that reflect prices actually charged or implicitly charged. The first application in this chapter includes an example of this direct measure that relates to topical cortisone paid for over the counter in a pharmacy. But often in health care a non-monetary price is used. It is still the relation between price and quantity demanded that is being estimated, only now it is a *time* price that is determining usage. For example, Martin and Smith (1999) found that the number of elective surgery episodes in the UK fell by 2.063% for every 10% increase in the average number of waiting days (the average wait across England in 1991–92 was 114.8 days).

2. *Contingent valuation (CV)*: These measures record preferences expressed in response to hypothetical circumstances as specified in a questionnaire. Economists do not normally use surveys, preferring instead to rely on recorded behavior (what people actually do, rather than what they say they will do). However, for health care evaluations such surveys are often the only source of information about preferences because market prices do not always exist. Market prices may be absent for goods and services that are 'pure public goods' (explained below).

3. *Conjoint analysis (CA)*: These measures are really a special kind of CV. Instead of asking people to value hypothetical circumstances explicitly, one asks them to express their choice of options given those circumstances and then one infers valuations from those choices. The simplest way to understand the essentials of CA is to refer to section 6.3.3 where the revealed preference approach to evaluating alcohol treatment programs was first explained.

Recall equation (6.10), which stated that decisions related to treatment effectiveness (where $D=1$ is an effective outcome and $D=0$ is an ineffective outcome) were based on two main determinants, a change in a non-monetary effect E_1 (changes in drinking consumption) and a monetary effect or benefit Y (changes in income):

$$D = a_0 + a_1 E_1 + a_2 Y \qquad (12.1)$$

The regression coefficients in this equation were $a_1 = \Delta D / \Delta E_1$ and $a_2 = \Delta D / \Delta Y$. So the ratio of the coefficients, which was expressed in equation (6.11), gave the value of the effect in money income terms:

$$a_1 / a_2 = \Delta Y / \Delta E_1 \qquad (12.2)$$

What is crucial in this approach is the specification of the dependent variable D as a *discrete* variable taking on the values 0 or 1. In the revealed preference approach, D relates to actual behavior, i.e., a choice was made to do (or decide) something. For the alcohol treatment program, the decision was related to the change in effects before and after treatment. So $D=1$ meant that there was sufficient change in the effects to warrant a verdict that the treatment was effective, while $D=0$ meant the changes in effects were not enough to be called effective.

In the CA approach, D is a hypothetical choice, i.e., what the individual purportedly would choose under specified conditions (given certain information about prices and outcomes such as pain and time to recovery, etc.).

When there is a choice between two alternative treatments, the changes involve the *difference* between the two sets of outcomes. So if one of the effects is the difference in time till recovery between the two treatments, T, and another effect is the difference in price charged, P, then the CA equation appears as:

$$D = b_0 + b_1\, T + b_2\, P \tag{12.3}$$

Given the specifications of the independent variables in equation (12.3) as treatment differences, the dependent variable D has a particular interpretation. $D = 0$ means that, say, treatment A would be chosen and $D = 1$ means that treatment B would be chosen. So D represents a chosen *change* in the form of treatment from A to B. With D, T and P already expressed as changes, the ratio of the regression coefficients directly give the WTP for (avoiding) recovery time as:

$$b_1/b_2 = P/T \tag{12.4}$$

An important consequence of specifying the dependent variable as a chosen difference in treatments is that the constant term b_0 in the regression equation (12.3) has special meaning. Assume that the two treatments have identical effects in all respects. This would mean that T and P in equation (12.3), being the difference in effects, would both be zero. Equation (12.3) then reduces to: $D = b_0$. So the size of b_0 tells us what is the inherent value of having one treatment over another, independent of the outcomes that flow from treatment. In this way CA can measure the value of processes (the way things are done) and not just the value of outcomes (what things are done). Individuals care about means as well as ends. Preferences for means are estimated jointly with preferences for ends in a conjoint analysis.

12.1.3   WTP and Public Goods

Economists (following Samuelson (1954)) distinguish two categories of goods. The first category are called 'private goods' whereby what one person consumes comes at the expense of what someone else consumes. Thus, if there is an artificial hip and one person obtains this in a transplant operation, then that prosthesis cannot go to someone else. However, there is a second category called 'public goods' that are equally consumed by all. Once a disease-carrying pest has been destroyed (vector control), each and every member of society simultaneously receives the benefit of a reduced chance of getting infected. People receive benefits whether they pay for them or not. So private markers fail to provide for such goods, and government provision is required.

For private goods, many of which were evaluated in this text, the demand curve is the horizontal sum of all individuals' demands. So if a doctor's visit has a price of $100, and person A wants to make three visits per month, and person B wants to make five visits per month, then the total quantity demanded at a price of $100 is eight visits. In other words, the WTP for the eighth visit is $100. But, for a public good, everyone by definition consumes each unit simultaneously. So if person A is willing to pay $10 for one acre to be sprayed for mosquitoes, and person B is willing to pay $20 for one acre to be sprayed, then total quantity demanded is only for one acre (as an acre sprayed for one is an acre sprayed for all). The WTP for this one-acre spraying is the sum of the individual WTPs and amounts to $30. Public good demand curves are then obtained by vertically summing individual demand curves.

Let us return to Zarkin et al.'s (2000) CV study of the value of treatment for illegal drugs reported in the last chapter to illustrate how WTP must be calculated for public goods. They estimated that there was a $37.48 per resident WTP for 100 others to be successfully treated. Now if 100 persons are successfully treated then each resident gains the psychic satisfaction from this treatment. The more residents there are, the more is the total satisfaction. Zarkin et al. calculated that there were 828 199 households in Brooklyn and 74 905 in Greensboro, the communities where the proposed treatments were being evaluated. So the total number of residents affected was 903 104. Multiplying the total number of residents by $37.48 produced a total benefit of drug treatment of $33.8 million. This sum far exceeded the total cost of treatment in the two communities of $12.04 million.

Although we will not be emphasizing this point in this text, one needs to be aware that when researchers ask questions in CVs about the WTP for public goods, such as drug treatment programs for others, they are careful to ask questions about WTP that minimize the chances that responders will intentionally understate their preferences for such goods (because they will benefit, get a 'free ride', even if they do not pay for the goods themselves).

12.2   WILLINGNESS TO PAY APPROACH

Benefits and costs are measured in terms of WTP. When benefits are greater than costs, compensation can take place and there need be no losers. The potential absence of losers is a requirement for economic efficiency. However, what one person will be willing to pay for something will not always be the same as what that same person will be willing to accept as compensation for not having something, and this difference needs to be recognized.

12.2.1 WTP and Compensation Tests

Benefits (in welfare economics) are defined as the maximum that a person is willing to pay for a change. The costs are correspondingly to be measured by the minimum amount that people must receive to accept the change. From this it follows that when there are positive net benefits, i.e., $B - C > 0$, there are sufficient gains that everyone incurring losses can be compensated for putting up with the change. The traditional CBA criterion has therefore been interpreted as a 'compensation test'. Positive net benefits indicate that sufficient funds for compensation are produced by the intervention and there is a positive sum left over that makes people better off. This is what makes the intervention 'worthwhile'.

12.2.2 WTP and Economic Efficiency

It turns out that when one concludes that a change is worthwhile in the traditional CBA sense, one is also saying that the change is 'efficient'. In economics, the efficiency concept is defined in Paretian terms. According to Pareto, a change is efficient (the existing situation is inefficient) if at least one person can be made better off and no one is made worse off. Obviously, in the real world there are hardly any situations of change where no one loses. But this is where compensation tests have a role to play. For if there are positive net benefits, *potentially* there need be no losers as there are sufficient gains to compensate everyone and a Pareto improvement could result. This explains the strategic significance of WTP in CBA.

    Of course, a potential Pareto improvement need not be an actual Pareto improvement. This would be the case if redistribution does not take place (which is almost always). So one should expect losers to exist. When the losers are low income people, the efficiency principle is questioned on equity grounds. How CBA can incorporate a concern for losers in general, and low income losers in particular, will be subjects covered in the next chapter dealing with equity in CBA.

12.2.3 WTP and Willingness to Accept (WTA) Compensation

An important question arises in the context of compensation tests: is there a difference between what I am willing to pay *to have* something and what I would be willing to accept as compensation *not to have* something? Say I am in a hospital and want to move into a nursing home. Is the amount that I am willing to pay for a nursing home equal to the amount of money I am willing to accept as compensation assuming that I am already in the nursing home and being asked to move back into a hospital?

The answer is that it depends on the shape of the marginal utility of income curve and where a person is on this curve. As we saw in earlier chapters, the marginal utility of income declines as a person's income increases. So it matters whether one's income is decreasing or increasing. Figure 12.1 (similar to Figure 6.2) explains the difference it makes as to whether one is moving left or moving right along the marginal utility of income curve.

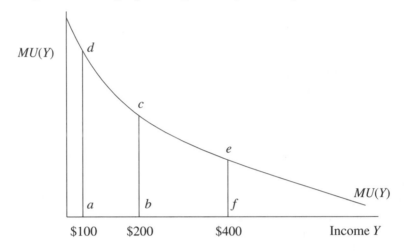

Note: The starting point is where one has an income of $200 on a curve where the marginal utility of income declines with income. Assume that one values a health care treatment in terms of utility by the area *abcd*. If one has to give up income for this change, this would mean moving from an income of $200 to an income of $100. So $100 would be the monetary value of this utility change. However, this same area would translate to *bfec* if one were receiving income. The monetary equivalent of the same size utility change would now be $200 (i.e., $400 − $200). So what one is willing to pay and what one is willing to accept as compensation would be different.

Figure 12.1:   The relation between WTP and willingness to accept

Say one is at point *b* where income is $200. Consider a change that has a utility value of a given size ΔU. This is represented as an area under the curve in Figure 12.1. If one moves left from Y = $100, we can designate the area *abcd* as the utility change ΔU. The income equivalent to this utility change is $100 (i.e., $200 − $100). Alternatively, if one moves to the right of Y = $100, the same size utility change, corresponding to area *bfec* (equal to area *abcd*), has an income equivalent of $200 (the difference between $400 and $200). The point is that, if a dollar is valued highly, then one only needs a few dollars to represent a utility change. But, if a dollar is valued lowly, then one needs a lot more dollars to represent the same utility change.

The significance of this for valuation purposes is that, when there is an increase in output, it is as if consumers have increased incomes, and those who have to supply the resources have decreased incomes. What the gainers are willing to pay for additional output will be greater (they move to the right in Figure 12.1) than what the losers are willing to accept as compensation for the change (they move to the left in the diagram), even though the utility change to the gainers and losers may be exactly the same.

This explanation of why WTP>WTA is predicated on the assumption that one is dealing with a change that affects people positively, which corresponds to an *increase* in output. For a negative change, where output is being contracted, the income effect is reversed. Consumers now have less (effective) income after the change and those who do not have to supply the resources have more income than before the change. In this case, paying for the change (not to happen) means going to the left in Figure 12.1 and receiving compensation means going to the right. Consequently the difference between WTP and WTA is altered and WTP is less than WTA. The third application, which is an evaluation of personal care for the elderly, illustrates the reduction in output case and so this has WTP<WTA.

Of course, if the marginal utility of income were constant (a horizontal straight line), then there would be no difference between WTP and WTA. As drawn in Figure 12.1, the downward slope is greater the lower the income. So the lower one's income, the greater would be the difference between WTP and WTA. (This needs to be understood to answer one of the problems below.)

12.3   WTP AND RATIONING BY TIME

The British NHS was set up in 1944 to ensure that individuals should receive medical care, advice and treatment irrespective of whether they can pay for these services or not. In such a system, the government determines the supply and the consumer does not pay a user price. Health care is rationed by a non-price mechanism, basically by using either waiting times or waiting lists. In this section we look at both rationing methods. The waiting time analysis focuses on the opportunity cost of time forgone by waiting. The waiting list analysis concentrates on the fact that benefits may decay over the time one is waiting.

12.3.1   WTP and Waiting Times

When we covered CM, we pointed out that the time involved with a health care intervention is a cost (an indirect cost) just like the health care expenditures that constitute the direct cost of treatment. If this time is valued by the opportunity cost of time (in terms of the wage rate) it can be expressed in money terms and can be added to the direct cost to form total monetary costs. In the analysis that is to follow, there is no user charge (explicit price) and the time cost is the only monetary consideration influencing purchases. Waiting time can be viewed as a proxy for price in the sense that when demand rises, or supply falls, waiting times rise and this chokes off the excess demand. Figure 12.1 explains this rationing process. We use some ideas and numbers from Martin and Smith (1999) to provide the context.

Figure 12.2 shows the demand for elective surgical episodes as inversely related to price as expressed by the length of waiting time. A wait for elective surgery can be calculated as the number of days between a decision by a hospital surgeon to admit a patient and the patient's admission to hospital. The average wait for elective surgery was about four months. In the absence of restrictions, patients would choose a number of surgical epi-

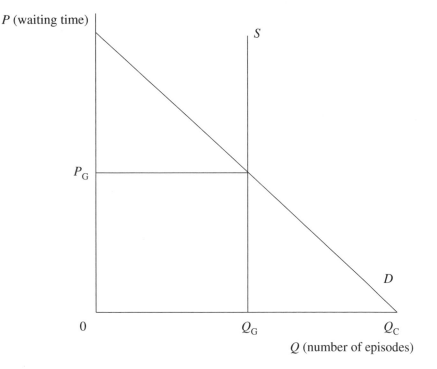

Note: The government only supplies Q_G even though at a zero price individuals would demand a larger quantity Q_C. People have to wait to be treated and the opportunity cost (forgone wage rate) of this waiting time is the time price P_G that rations the quantity Q_G.

Figure 12.2:   Demand and supply with waiting time as the price

sodes equal to Q_C. However, the government decides how many surgeries that they are willing to finance. This quantity Q_G is independent of the price and so the supply curve S is drawn as a vertical straight line.

Because not everyone who wants surgery now can get surgery now, waiting times rise. The rise in waiting times causes the quantity demanded to be reduced. The reduction continues until enough people are discouraged by the waiting time to satisfy the government's available quantity of surgeries. P_G is the resulting waiting time that corresponds to the available quantity Q_G.

The issue is how to value that waiting time P_G that amounts to around four months. The human capital approach would use the wage rate. This would be most relevant for those who are employed, but what about the rest? A more comprehensive approach to valuing time would try to find out what each person on the list would be willing to pay for a reduction in waiting time. The CA study by Propper (1990) estimated these time evaluations and they are reported in Table 12.1 (part of her Table 3). The hypothetical choice was basically between paying more and having less of a wait, or paying less and waiting more.

Table 12.1:   Estimated value of waiting list time (£ per month)

Segment	Weekly household income below £350 per month	Weekly household income above £350 per month
Full-time employed	41.90	49.43
Part-time employed	35.70	42.11
Housewife	20.40	24.06
Retired	43.43	49.90

Source: Based on Propper (1990)

Propper's study found that people were, on average, willing to pay £38 to avoid a month on the NHS waiting list. Table 12.1 reveals that different groups systematically valued time higher or lower than average. Those employed and with a higher income have a greater WTP for time and thus incur a greater cost of having to wait. This might be what was desired by those who devised replacing a price rationing system with one related to time rationing. On the other hand, the finding that the elderly also incur a higher cost would not seem to be socially desirable. (The reason for the higher WTP by the elderly group is explained in the next section.)

The key assumption in the above analysis is that the demand for treatment stays constant over the time that the patient is waiting. This assumption is relaxed in the next section.

12.3.2   Rationing by Waiting Lists

Rationing by waiting lists is a very different system than the one that rations by waiting times. According to Lindsay and Feigenbaum (1984), the key difference is that if one is on a waiting list, one need not personally be forgoing one's use of time. So there is not an opportunity cost involved as there is when sacrificing time. Rather the issue is that being on a waiting list means that one is postponing till later when treatment is taking place. The effect of being on the list is a loss of benefits and not a rise in costs.

The nature of the loss of benefits is more tied up in *decay* rather than delay. Postponing treatment delays treatment and because of time preference constitutes a loss. But Lindsay and Feigenbaum argue that most of the loss occurs because current benefits decay when one has to postpone treatment. Just as today's newspaper is worth more delivered today than it is delivered next week, treatment today has higher value than treatment in the future even without discounting, that is, future treatment is a diminished product. If we define B_0 as the benefit of treatment today and B_1 as the benefit in the future, then $B_0 - B_1$ measures the diminished benefit. It is this component of the loss of benefits that we will now analyze in the context of waiting lists under the NHS.

Figure 12.3 shows two different benefit curves, with WTP for treatment on the vertical axis and time that treatment takes place on the horizontal axis. B_0 is the total benefit of treatment if it takes place today (time t_0). The government decides that there is a waiting list and treatment will take place at time t_1. The total benefit of treatment at this later date is B_1. Certain types of diseases (which we call category a), such as hernias or cataracts, do not get much worse with delays in treatment. Total benefits for these diseases at time t_1 are virtually the same as at time t_0 and we denote these benefits as $B_1{}^a$. The benefit curve for type a diseases is thus shown as the horizontal straight line $B_0 B_1{}^a$. Other types of diseases (which we call category b), such as infective and parasitic diseases, have a faster rate of decay and the total benefits for these diseases at time t_1, denoted $B_1{}^b$, are well below B_0. The benefit curve for type b diseases is depicted as the downward sloping line $B_0 B_1{}^b$. Lindsay and Feigenbaum estimate that the rate of decay of type b diseases is twice that of type a diseases.

Cullis and Jones (1986) use the above Lindsay and Feigenbaum framework to estimate the cost of being on a NHS waiting list in 1981. In order to be on a waiting list certain conditions must hold. These conditions specify limiting cases, from which minimum and maximum benefit values are derived. The average of these limiting values is to be used to estimate the average cost of waiting. The total cost is the product of the average cost

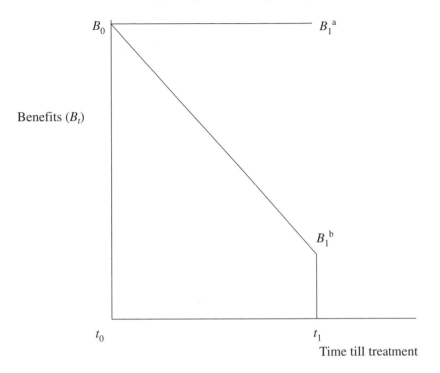

Benefits (B_t)

B_0 $B_1{}^a$

$B_1{}^b$

t_0 t_1

Time till treatment

Note: The size of the total benefits of treatment depends on when treatment takes place. At time t_0, if treatment were to take place now, total benefits are B_0. If patients are required to join a waiting list, they do not receive treatment until some time in the future, say t_0. For some diseases (type *a*) waiting does not affect the size of benefits. So the benefits in the future $B_1{}^a$ are basically the same as the benefits if treatment were to take place now. For other diseases (type *b*) benefits decay at a faster rate over time and future benefits would be much lower at $B_1{}^b$.

Figure 12.3: Benefits as a function of time till treatment

times the number of persons on the waiting list. The maximum and minimum values are obtained as follows:

1. *The maximum value of having to wait*: The alternative to being put on a NHS waiting list and getting treatment at time t_1 is for a patient to transfer to the private sector, pay a market price P and get treatment now, at time t_0. The advantage of the transfer is that one avoids the decay of benefits of $B_0 - B_1$. The disadvantage is that one has to pay the price P. Any person who is on the waiting list, but has the most benefits to lose from waiting, will be (almost) indifferent between paying the price and incurring the loss of benefits from waiting. For patients

having type *b* diseases with a falling benefits curve, and where the advantage of the transfer to the private sector equals the disadvantage, we have: $B_0 - B_1 = P$. This means that the maximum value of the loss of benefits by being forced to wait is the price P. If the loss of benefits is any more than this, the patient will not wait and will incur the cost P. In other words, any persons who are actually on the waiting list must not have been willing to pay the price P and so this must be the upper bound.

2.   *The minimum value of having to wait*: Anyone who has the least benefits to lose from waiting will value benefits today the same as benefits in the future. With $B_0 = B_1$, it follows that: $B_0 - B_1 = 0$. So, when there is a horizontal benefits curve, which corresponds to type *a* diseases, patients incur a zero cost from being forced to receive treatment later. Stated simply, people who are unaffected by waiting would have a zero WTP to avoid waiting.

Cullis and Jones assume that people on the waiting list are equally likely to have valuations within the limits of the minimum and maximum values. The mean μ of a continuous uniform distribution is shown in any elementary statistics text (such as Weiers (1998, p. 192)) to be:

$$\mu = \frac{Lowest\ value + Highest\ value}{2} \tag{12.5}$$

Since we have just seen that 0 is the lowest value and P is the highest value, then the average value of the loss of benefits from equation (12.5) is $P/2$.

The typical private health plan price for 18 various types of treatment in 1984 ranged between £1048 and £1874. So half these sums were the average cost per person waiting, i.e., between £524 and £937. With 2.3 million being the estimate of the annual number of people on the NHS waiting list, the range of estimates for the total cost of waiting was between £1205.2 million (2.3 million times £524) and £2155.1 million (i.e., 2.3 million times £937).

So far, we have concentrated on the cost of decay part of the loss of benefits due to postponing treatment. This ignores the second component of the loss of benefits mentioned above that involves a cost of delay due to time preference (seeing that a unit of benefits today is worth more than a unit of benefits in the future). Propper's CA estimates of the value of time cited earlier abstracts from the cost of decay (by specifying a medical condition with a near zero decay rate in her CV of time spent on NHS waiting lists). But her estimates nonetheless include the time preference dimension. Recall that she found that the elderly had an above-average WTP (i.e., over £43 per month for those with a weekly income below £350 and over £49 for those with a weekly income above £350). In opportunity cost terms, this higher than average evaluation does not make sense, since retired people do not work. But from a time preference perspective this evaluation is easily explained. Retired people are older people. They can be expected to put a higher value on time as they have fewer years remaining.

12.4 APPLICATIONS

The first reason for violating consumer sovereignty (that individuals may not have the necessary information) will be examined in the first application. The second reason (that individuals may not be capable of making rational decisions) is covered in the second study. Both these applications use direct estimates of the demand curve. The third case study uses a CV to measure WTP within a compensation tests framework, and the fourth one relies on CA to value processes as well as outcomes.

12.4.1 A CBA of Switching Drugs from Prescription to Over the Counter

The analysis is based on Temin (1983) who, as a part of his evaluation of switching from prescription to over-the-counter drugs, highlighted two methods to measure benefits. The first is based on consumer preferences as revealed by observed market demand curves. This is the direct, consumer sovereignty, WTP approach. The alternative method is to rely on the 'net medical benefit'. This bases benefits on what a fully informed consumer would know from epidemiological evidence. This second method, as we shall see, effectively relies on an indirect measure of WTP based on the implicit value of a life. We explain these two WTP approaches (direct and indirect) in turn and identify the circumstances under which each approach is more appropriate.

1. *When a direct estimate of WTP is more appropriate*
    Market demand curves assume that people have a thorough under-standing of the drugs that they are taking. When individuals know all the side-effects of a drug they incorporate these effects in their WTP. The side-effects are therefore not a cost that has to be measured separately. The simpler the drug, and the more immediate the condition it is designed to alleviate, the more appropriate is the WTP approach. Temin selected topical hydrocortisone as an example of a drug for which WTP would apply. He gave four reasons:
    (a) Topical cortisone is a simple drug such that one can assume that people know what they are doing when they use it.

(b) As the drug is topical, its effects (both good and bad) are also local. One does not therefore have to understand how the human body works as a system.

(c) The drug does not involve much of a risk of hiding a more serious disease because there are very few serious diseases that could be alleviated by topical hydrocortisone.

(d) The medical benefit is hard to measure. There are very few data on the more rapid healing of local injuries.

The way to conceptualize the CBA of a regulation change that switches drugs from a prescription (Rx) status to being purchased over the counter (OTC) is to think of it as a cost reduction leading to a price decrease that benefits consumers. There are two reasons why the drug price falls: first, the cost of selling OTC drugs is lower than filling prescriptions, and second, consumers can obtain the drug without having to incur the time and expense of visiting a doctor to write the prescription for the drug. There are no important investment costs because it merely involves an administrative action that changes the terms under which the drug is sold. The analysis of the price change brought about by the switch in status for topical cortisone is summarized in Figure 12.4. The figures all correspond to the year 1981.

The price in the diagram corresponds to the 'full price'. This consists of the price paid at the drug store plus the time and other costs associated with buying a good. The initial price (labeled P_1) consisted of an average purchase price of $3.57 at drug stores, plus a $10 value of the consumer's time, plus $30 for a doctor's visit to obtain the prescription. The initial price therefore was $43.57 and the sum of the elements other than the purchase price was $40. It is this $40 amount that constituted the price reduction brought about by the switch in status as the purchase price was assumed to be the same before and after the change. Thus the new price P_2 was equal to the initial price P_1 minus $40.

Prescription sales in 1980 were around 12 million and they did not fall due to the switch. This meant that the increased volume of sales of 11.8 million was all due to OTC sales. In the WTP approach, the benefits of the increased output are equal to the area under the demand curve. Similarly, costs are equal to the area under the MC curve. Net benefits are given by the triangle *abc* in Figure 12.4. Assuming that the demand curve is linear (i.e., we can join the initial price and quantity with the new price and quantity by a straight line), the net benefits are equal to $236 million, i.e., (1/2) (11.8 million) times ($40).

2. *When an implicit estimate of WTP is more appropriate*
Temin chose thiazide diuretics as the alternative case for switching drug status where the medical net benefit method would be more applicable.

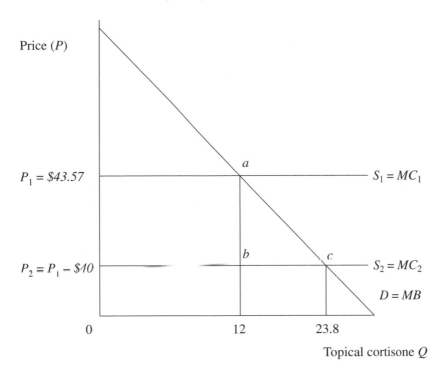

Note: The full price for topical cortisone consists of the medication itself ($3.57) and the time and cost necessary to go to a physician in order to get a prescription ($40). When this medication can be obtained over the counter, there would be a cost saving of $40 as a doctor's visit would no longer be necessary. With sales of 12 million when a prescription was required, and sales of 23.8 million after the change, two points on the demand curve are known. Assuming linearity, we can join the two points and form the demand curve.

Figure 12.4: Demand and supply as functions of the full price

This drug was chosen because there was the potential for much consumer confusion involved with the use of this drug. At the time, half of the use was for mild hypertension. The switched drug would have to be labeled as suitable for hypertension only. Hypertension is asymptomatic; so treatment would not be designed to reduce symptoms that are easily discerned. Eventually, if the consumer takes the medication regularly, there would be a decrease in the risk of coronary heart disease and stroke. This means that the effects of treatment were not apparent in the short run. People persevering with treatment would have some idea of the benefits and costs, but not in great detail. The crucial unknown was whether consumers would persist with the drug without a doctor's repeated urging.

To apply the medical net benefit approach, Temin took as his unit of analysis a 40-year-old male with diastolic blood pressure of 90 mm Hg who will have a 10 mm Hg reduction in blood pressure if he persists with thiazide diuretics. Lowering blood pressure by this amount yields an expected gain of 1% in discounted QALYs (at a discount rate of 5%). The quality adjustment was due to a reduction in non-fatal strokes and myocardial infarctions. If the 40-year-old has a discounted life span of 15 years, the expected gain translates into 0.15 years.

The present value of lifetime costs of treatment was estimated to be $1500. If a person values his/her life at $150000, then the person should be willing to spend $1500 to increase its length by 1%. So, $150000 would be the switching value for a life in order for thiazide diuretics to be worthwhile. Temin refers to the $300000 implicit value that people place on their life as estimated by Thaler and Rosen (1975). He therefore concludes: 'This is twice the value needed to make a diuretic worthwhile. If people act consistently in choosing jobs and medicines, then we would expect a mildly hypertensive person making this calculation to use a diuretic.'

12.4.2   WTP and Need for Drug Abuse Treatment Programs

Individuals with drug abuse problems have inadequate information as well as impaired decision-making capabilities due to brain disorder. Such individuals are classic examples of those for whom the assumption of consumer sovereignty is not valid. Thus drug treatment programs in the US have heavy government subsidies and price is set below market clearing levels. As a result the standard demand and supply apparatus cannot be used to evaluate these treatment programs.

Because there are many who require help that do not seek treatment, there is also a distinction between demand and 'need', which can be defined as medical demand (what public health experts say is required). Figure 12.5 summarizes the position for demand, supply and need for the US according to Cartwright and Solano (2001). This figure neatly brings together the various considerations that are discussed in national policy.

The supply curve is not the usual one as the government largely sets it. It is called the 'constrained' supply curve and is assumed to be perfectly price inelastic. According to the Uniform Facility Data Set, 1997, there were 299593 patients with drug problems, and 376 482 patients with joint drug and alcohol problems. So there were in total about 676 075 patients receiving treatment in public specialty facilities. If a typical patient on average gets treated twice during a year, this means that there were around 1.352 million annual treatment episodes. In addition, there were a further 143 661

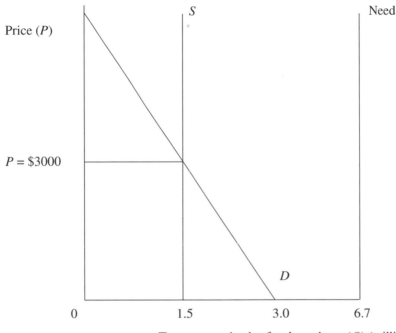

Note: Supply is constrained and set by the government at 1.5 million episodes. Patient demand for drug abuse treatments has a non-zero price elasticity. So the quantity demanded at $3000, which is the price that corresponds to the constrained quantity of 1.5 million episodes, is less than the 3 million demanded at a zero price. Need is determined independently of price. Public health experts fix it at 6.7 million episodes based on epidemiological studies and clinical data.

Figure 12.5:   Demand, government supply and need

private patients, which makes the total number of treatment episodes around 1.5 million. This is the supply figure appearing in Figure 12.5. Note that 87.5% of these treatments took place in outpatient facilities.

By construction, need depends on an expert's judgment. The judgment is based on epidemiological and clinical data. Typically, a clinical standard is set as to how many dependency problems of various types constitute a person in need of drug treatment and then one applies this standard to the population as a whole to see how many people meet the standard. Epstein and Grfeoror (1995) estimated the need for treatment in 1995 to be 6.7 million individuals over the age of 12. Being based on judgment, need is independent of price and is therefore also represented by a vertical line in the diagram.

The demand curve as drawn by Cartwright and Solano is a linear approximation. The price was approximately $3000 (equal to total drug abuse expenditures of $4.7 billion divided by the quantity of 1.5 million). As demand is constrained by supply, quantity demanded at the price of $3000 would be equal to the 1.5 million supply estimate. The quantity demanded at zero price would be greater than 1.5 million. If the elasticity of public and private demand is assumed to be −1 (between the figures of −0.43 for outpatient care and −1.14 for inpatient care based on private demand estimates), moving from the $3000 price to a zero price (a 100% price reduction) would lead to an additional quantity of 1.5 million (a 100% quantity increase from 1.5 million). So the total quantity at a zero price would be 3 million.

In Figure 12.5 there is an aggregate treatment gap of 5.2 million episodes between the (supply-constrained) demand of 1.5 million and the need of 6.7 million. This gap is made up of two components:

1. The difference between the quantity of 3 million and the quantity of 1.5 million, equal to 1.5 million, is attributable to price rationing. That is, if a zero price had been used, 1.5 million more would have demanded treatment.
2. The difference between the quantity of 6.7 million and the quantity of 3 million, equal to 3.7 million, is latent (hidden) demand. It is due to the denial that drug addicts have regarding their condition. This difference measures the extent to which those who fixed need independent of consumer preferences are questioning the assumption of consumer sovereignty.

The 5.2 million aggregate treatment gap for drug abuse treatment poses an enormous incentives problem for those who would make health care evaluation decisions on the basis of need and not WTP. Assume that the cost per treatment was constant at $3000. A CBA using WTP would decide that 1.5 million should be provided as this maximizes net benefits. An evaluation using need instead of demand, might decide that consumers underestimate the benefits of treatment by as much as 5.2 million. If the demand curve D in Figure 12.5 were to shift to the right by 5.2 million, the new demand curve would intersect the need quantity of 6.7 million exactly at $3000. So the quantity that would maximize needs-based net benefits would be 6.7 million. If the government bases its health care expenditure decisions on need, it would agree to provide treatment for all 6.7 million. Since WTP relates to actual demand, only 1.5 million spaces would be taken up voluntarily. The problem then would be how to eliminate the 5.2 million excess capacity.

Lowering the treatment price to zero could solve some of the excess capacity. Figure 12.5 tells us that 1.5 million would respond to this price incentive. However, this still leaves 3.7 million slots to fill. Only if the government can actually change preferences by some intervention (such as providing information, support, or medication) will the rest of the excess capacity be reduced. Interventions of this type may be costly and are unlikely to be successful.

The main message from this study is that even if one would rather base health care evaluations on need than demand, one still needs to estimate WTP in order to plan a strategy for ensuring that people choose the quantity that they need rather than the quantity that they demand.

12.4.3   A CBA of Nursing Home versus Hospital Care

In the British National Health Service (NHS), the government provides (finances) most of the health care. People do not have any experience of paying for care. In these circumstances, where behavior-based, revealed preferences cannot be used, how is one to construct a WTP measure? Donaldson's (1990) answer is to carry out a questionnaire and ask clients not what they are willing to pay, but ask what they think the government *ought to* pay for health care. The choice for an elderly person needing assistance was between living in a nursing home and staying in a hospital. Not only did the elderly people in NHS hospitals not have any experience of health care markets, they were also thought to find a question about their type of care to be too stressful. So Donaldson devised his questionnaire for relatives of the patients (family members or friends). His approach then was to devise a WTP measure that did not rely on consumer sovereignty and see whether this was feasible. Before explaining the details of his methods, let us first focus on Donaldson's CBA criterion.

When options are mutually exclusive (when the adoption of one precludes the adoption of the other) it is not sufficient that an option have positive net benefits. It is necessary that one alternative have greater net benefits than the other. Define the subscript N for nursing home care and H for hospital care. For nursing home care to be worthwhile, the net benefits must exceed those for hospital care, or, equivalently:

$$(B_N - C_N) - (B_H - C_H) > 0 \tag{12.6}$$

This is an aggregate criterion. That is, equation (12.6) tries to establish whether there is a positive difference between the *total* net benefits for nursing home care and the *total* net benefits for hospital care. A part of the total B_N, for instance, are the WTP for some individuals who have greater net benefits for nursing home care, but the other part consists of the WTP of the other individuals who have greater net benefits for hospital care. Let everyone who has greater net-benefits (NB) for nursing homes be grouped under NB_N, and all those who have greater net benefits for hospital care be grouped under NB_H. Then equation (12.6) can be decomposed into:

$$NB_N - NB_H > 0 \qquad (12.7)$$

In this context, all those who have a net WTP greater for nursing home care can be classed as gainers, and those who have a net WTP larger for hospital care can be classed as losers. Donaldson found that in his sample there were 59 gainers with $NB_N = £11\,837.50$ and there were 10 losers with $NB_H = £2145$. The gainers of moving to nursing home care could compensate the losers (but not vice versa). Thus, Donaldson concluded that nursing home care was the more Pareto efficient option.

Now we address the issue of how he obtained his estimates of the benefits in order to find the net benefits. To help fix orders of magnitude, Donaldson informed those surveyed about the relative costs of the two kinds of care to the government. It cost the government £215 per week (at 1985 prices) for a continuing care hospital bed and £225 per week for a NHS nursing home place. The first question asked of the relatives was which type of care they preferred. If they preferred nursing-home care, they were then asked whether this was worth more than the £215 per week cost of hospital care and, if so, how much more (in £5 per week intervals); while if they thought that nursing home care was worth less than £215 per week, they were then asked how much less. Similar kinds of questions were then asked of those who preferred hospital care. The monetary valuations given by the 83 respondents for those who preferred nursing home care (12 preferred hospital care) are listed in Table 12.2.

Note that in Table 12.2, 51 of the 83 said they would not choose a hospital bed even if the costs were zero. If C_H is set equal to zero in equation (12.6), then this implies that:

$$(B_N - C_N) > B_H \qquad (12.8)$$

The upper bound for the hospital benefits is therefore the amount of the net benefits for nursing home care, something established from the first set of questions in the survey. The lower bound for B_H is zero. Donaldson effectively treated the two bounds as equally likely, which meant that he took the average of the two to determine B_H:

$$B_H = (B_N - C_N)/2 \qquad (12.9)$$

Table 12.2:   *Monetary valuations of NHS nursing home care and hospital care for respondents with a preference for NHS nursing home care (n = 83)*

Valuation (£ per week)	Type of care			
	NHS nursing home care		Hospital care	
	Number	%	Number	%
Less than 215	1	1	8	10
215–234	26	32	0	0
235–254	42	51	0	0
More than 255	9	11	0	0
Cannot value it in monetary terms	2	2	9	11
Don't know	1	1	2	2
No response	2	2	8	10
Would not choose at any cost	0	0	51	61
Not applicable	0	0	5	6
Total	83	100	83	100

Source: Donaldson (1990)

On the basis of equation (12.9), the 51 answers were converted to exact estimates of benefits. These 51, together with the 8 in Table 12.2 who provided valuations less than £215, contributed to there being 59 out of the 83 who provided usable estimates of WTP. In addition, there were 10 out of 12 in the group who preferred hospital care who provided usable estimates and 8 were indifferent between the two types of care.

Because, in total, there were 77 respondents out of 109 that supplied meaningful results, Donaldson concluded that his methods were worth exploring further. WTP may be able to be used even when consumer sovereignty is ruled out. But the biggest weakness of the Donaldson measure is that he asks what people ought to be willing to pay. So he confuses 'positive' economic measures (what people *are* willing to pay) with 'normative' economic measures (what people *should be* willing to pay).

12.4.4   WTP for Medication versus Surgery for the Management of Miscarriage

WTP measures people's strength of preference for something. However, WTP also depends on people's ability to pay, since the more income one has, the more dollars one can afford to set aside to buy something. This greater ability to pay applies to all things that people purchase, including time, which is used to ration resources in the NHS. It follows therefore that if time is considered to be a price, and WTP varies positively with income, then the time price charged to a high-income person is greater than for a low-income person. In the CA study by Ryan and Hughes (1997) they included income as an interactive term with price and time and so were able to quantify the magnitude by which ability to pay impacts WTP for time and health effects.

The Ryan and Hughes study used CA to assess women's preferences for miscarriage management. The standard treatment was surgery. The alternative treatment was medical which involved taking drugs. The dependent variable was therefore specified as the change in utility from moving from surgical management of miscarriage to medical, where $D = 1$ signifies that a person has chosen medicine as his/her preferred management method. All other things held constant, a positive coefficient to the intercept means that medicine would be the preferred process, while a negative intercept signifies that surgical management was inherently preferable.

The selection of the list of independent variables was determined from a controlled clinical trial that identified all the statistically significant differences between the two management methods. These determinants ('attributes') were: the amount of pain experienced; time taken to return to normal household activities; time in hospital receiving treatment; and whether (yes or no) complications from treatment followed. In addition, the change in price (called 'cost') to the woman being treated was included. The regression they used corresponded to equation (12.3) with two time variables and a complications variable added. Table 12.3, based on their Table 4, gives the results.

As we explained earlier, the constant term has special importance in a CA. The fact that it was significantly negative meant that, when all attributes were held constant, people were willing to pay a premium for surgical over medical treatment. This process preference depends on the income level of the woman. Whether it was for the process itself, or the outcomes of treatment, the higher the income, the greater the WTP. For example, to reduce pain, low-income people are willing to pay £231, middle-income people are willing to pay £353, and high-income people are willing to pay £375. WTP is also positively related to income for both time variables. These sets of results support the critics of WTP, i.e., WTP is affected by ability to pay, and using a time price rather than a monetary price is more egalitarian, as the poor pay less when time does the rationing.

In an extension of the CA methodology applied to *in vitro* fertilization by Ryan (1999), she tried to control explicitly for the characteristics that makes one process different from another by suppressing the constant term and including instead two dummy (0 or 1) independent variables. The two process attributes were 'attitudes of staff towards you' (caring or not) and

Table 12.3: *Conjoint analysis results for the choice of medication versus surgery for the management of miscarriage*

Variable	Coefficient	Marginal WTP (£)
Constant	−0.239	
Income group 1		−92
Income group 2		−142
Income group 3		−149
Level of pain experienced	−0.600	
Income group 1		−231
Income group 2		−353
Income group 3		−375
Complications following treatment	−1.153	
Income group 1		−443
Income group 2		−678
Income group 3		−721
Cost to you of treatment		
Income group 1	−0.0026	Not applicable
Income group 2	−0.0017	Not applicable
Income group 3	−0.0016	Not applicable
Time in hospital		
Income group 1	−0.255	−98
Income group 2	−0.219	−129
Income group 3	−0.392	−245
Time taken to return to normal activities		
Income group 1	−0.126	−48
Income group 2	−0.135	−79
Income group 3	−0.125	−78

Source: Based on Ryan and Hughes (1997)

'continuity of contact with the same staff' (yes or no). Continuity of care is of paramount importance for mental health improvements and is a key component of 'quality' in many types of health care. So CA has an important role in allowing WTP to estimate quality as well as quantity of care.

Ryan's *in vitro* fertilization results support all the main findings of CA reported in this chapter. The WTP for both the process attributes and the health outcomes were greater the higher the income of the respondent. Because she decomposed the waiting time variable by age as well as income, she was able to confirm that WTP for time saved waiting was related to age. For example, for all persons on a low income, younger people were willing to pay £52 for a month reduction in waiting time (other things being equal), middle-aged people were willing to pay £78, and the older group were willing to pay £73.

12.5   FINAL SECTION

We now present the problems, summary and looking ahead sections.

12.5.1   Problems

In this problems set we focus on the CV study by Garbacz and Thayer (1983) on the difference between WTP and WTA for measuring the benefits of senior companion program (SCP) services. The evaluation involved a proposed reduction in services. To simplify, we report just one set of point estimates (related to a 75% reduction in service). The program aim was not just to provide basic services for the elderly, such as light household chores and transportation, but also to supply social contact (friendship) and advocacy. The basic services component of the program could be purchased on the labor market for around $160993 per year. The companionship component cannot directly be bought on a market and this is why a CV evaluation was undertaken. The WTP per hour was valued at $2.00 and the WTA was valued at $4.70. To be conservative, Garbacz and Thayer used the mid-point of these hourly estimates to obtain an annual total benefits measure of $248 306 (which amounts to $397 for each of the 625 clients in the program). The annual costs that would be saved by reducing the program would be $136 500.

1.   For a reduction in service that makes the elderly worse off, where it is likely that they have less income, and they have to pay for the adverse change *not* to happen, would you expect the elderly's WTP to be higher or lower than their WTA compensation? (Hint: re-read section 12.2.3.) Do Garbacz and Thayer's WTP and WTA estimates confirm your expectation? Does the fact that 76% of the elderly people in the SCP have yearly incomes of $5000 or less affect the size by which WTP and WTA differ in this case?
2.   The CV evaluation of $248 306 measures the total benefits of the SCP, which includes both the basic services and the companionship components. Is there any way of estimating from this amount what are the benefits of just the companionship (the non-market) component?
3.   On the basis of your answer to question 2, would the proposed reduction in the level of the SCP be socially worthwhile? Would the SCP reduction be worthwhile if one excluded the non-market benefits?

12.5.2 Summary

In this chapter we showed that WTP can be used to measure many different kinds of health outcome, whether it be the pain involved with surgery for a miscarriage, or the time taken up by waiting for the operation to take place, or even companionship. However, contrary to what is often thought, CBA is not restricted to measuring only the benefits of health care outcomes. Processes, or means to ends, can also be valued. Even if surgery and medication were to generate an identical set of outcomes, individuals were willing to pay for one over the other and this can be estimated using conjoint analysis. Also, Ryan found in her study of *in vitro* fertilization that people were willing to pay for non-health outcomes in addition to health care outcomes and processes. Specifically, people were willing to pay for follow-up support.

Logically, there is nothing that excludes researchers from seeking utility valuations for all these consequences in a CUA questionnaire. But people have experience of spending their incomes on pain relievers and personal services, and virtually no practice of putting utility values on these aspects. So WTP-based CBA has a big practical advantage over CUA. Moreover, WTP has the advantage of providing an organizational framework for estimation. WTP is reflected in the demand curve. Because demand interacts with supply to determine price and quantity, we can predict what benefits would correspond to alternative output levels, whether they be competitive market equilibria or output levels chosen by governments. Thus, we could predict what benefits would be at the treatment levels chosen by clients even if drug treatments were supplied free of user charge or set at levels that correspond with medically defined levels of need.

The WTP concept is at the core of CBA because it is the way by which the objective of efficiency is made operational. When $B > C$, buyers are willing to pay more than what owners of resources are willing to accept as compensation. A worthwhile project is therefore one that is a potential Pareto improvement, where at least one person gains and no one need lose. It is true that the sizes of the gains and losses are conditional on the income levels of the two parties involved. But once distributional aspects have been explicitly brought into the analysis (as we intend) there is no reason to try to ignore efficiency considerations altogether. That is, provided that consumer sovereignty is accepted, WTP should be accepted.

However, as we know, in the health care field the use of WTP is often resisted. Acceptance of consumer sovereignty is not universal and rationing by price is questioned even when prices do exist. Because of this fact, we thought the reader would have a better grasp of the strengths of WTP by examining it in situations where it is being most challenged, viz., in the context of the NHS in the UK. So we have focused in both the theory and applications on areas where there have been misgivings over WTP.

Time can be used instead of price as the rationing mechanism. When prices are used to ration resources, differences in abilities to pay dominate WTP. For example, the richest group would be willing to pay 50% more for the relief of pain from miscarriage treatment than the poorest group. However, rationing by time does not 'price' services equally to all. Those persons who have the highest value (opportunity cost) of time would pay the highest prices. It is true that the higher-income groups value time more (in the case of miscarriages, time in hospital treatment was valued three times more than for the poorest group) and so would pay a higher price, which is considered to be fair by many. But we also saw that the elderly value time more and would have to pay more, which would not be considered fair.

In the last chapter we explained how we could obtain indirect measures of WTP (related to labor market choices). The question arises as to when one should use these measures and when to use the direct measures of WTP covered in this chapter. The answer was supplied in the Temin case study in the context of when OTC medications can be used to replace physician pre-scribed medications. He proposed that: (1) when patients had good infor-mation of the effects of drugs (as with topical cortisone) direct WTP can be used; and (2) when patients do not have detailed knowledge of drug effects and do not understand the benefits of persistence (as with thiazide diuretics), then indirect measures of WTP can be used. But the message is that even when questioning consumer sovereignty in a particular context is justified (buying OTC medications), one can still use other valuations by the same individuals where consumer sovereignty is not questioned (making labor market choices).

Possibly the most important point made in this chapter about the virtues of thinking in WTP terms was what happens if one tries to ignore it com-pletely and rely on notions of medically defined need instead. It may be understandable that, for drug addicts, one may wish to superimpose expert judgments on client preferences when deciding how many treatments to fund publicly. But, if the number provided significantly exceeds what people think they want, then services could be grossly underutilized and valuable resources would be wasted.

12.5.3 Looking Ahead

We have seen in the applications that what one is willing to pay depends on the income one has and thus on one's ability to pay. Our account of CBA will be complete when we cover equity and its role in CBA. Thus in the final chapter we explain how to combine ability to pay with WTP in CBA.

13. Cost–benefit analysis and equity

13.1 INTRODUCTION

In this chapter we add equity considerations to the efficiency objective. Instead of going into first principles of what equity means in health economics, along the lines of Williams and Cookson (2000), we will simply build on the discussion of equity in CUA in Chapter 10. The two building blocks are the QALY weights and the person trade-offs. In a CBA context these blocks transform into the use of income distribution weights and the inclusion of a 'numbers effect'. We devote a section to each of these blocks after providing the necessary introductory background.

13.1.1 A Re-Examination of QALY Weights in CUA

In equation (10.2), we defined the weighted total number of QALYs as:

$$\text{Weighted total QALYs} = a_1\,\text{QALY}_1 + a_2\,\text{QALY}_2 \qquad (13.1)$$

where 1 was the 'poor' group (with the lower number of QALYs), 2 was the 'rich' group (with the larger number of QALYs) and the weights a_1 and a_2 recorded the relative QALY weights for the two groups with $a_1 > a_2$. If we multiply both sides of equation (13.1) by P (the price of a QALY), and acknowledge the way we converted QALYs into monetary terms, via $B = P.\text{QALY}$, equation (13.1) becomes:

$$\text{Weighted total benefits} = a_1\,B_1 + a_2\,B_2 \qquad (13.2)$$

Equations (13.1) and (13.2) tell us that, if one wishes to use weights for outcomes that are in QALYs, one should also be willing to use weights when outcomes are measured in monetary units. So when benefits are in terms of WTP, we can rewrite equation (13.2) as:

$$\text{Weighted total benefits} = a_1\,\text{WTP}_1 + a_2\,\text{WTP}_2 \qquad (13.3)$$

We will mainly use QALYs in this chapter to explain the process of weighting because this is the unit used by most of the literature we will be referring to. Since CUA assumes that the price of a QALY is the same irrespective of who is involved, no *relative* difference among groups results from working with QALYs or benefits defined as the product of P times the number of QALYs.

Note that the weights in equation (13.3) are due to distributional considerations; group 1 gain a lower number of QALYs than group 2 and therefore their QALYs attract a higher weight. However, Nord's person trade-off (PTO) method, covered in Chapter 10, interprets group 1 as being patients with more serious ailments. A patient is judged 'more serious' if he/she starts off with a lower number of QALYs before treatment takes place. Given that group 1's condition is more serious, Nord's PTO then asks how many *more* people in group 2 with the lesser condition need to be treated to have the same social value as treating a fewer number with the more serious condition. This consideration can be integrated into a utility framework as follows.

Define the average amount of QALYs that a group i receives as $\overline{QALY}_i$, where $\overline{QALY}_i = QALY_i / N_i$ and N_i is the number of persons in the group. Obviously total QALYs are just the product of the average amount of QALYs and the number involved: $QALY_i = N_i \cdot \overline{QALY}_i$. As was pointed out below equation (10.4), 5 people receiving two QALYs each was equivalent to 10 people each receiving one QALY only if equity were not important. If equity now is to be considered important, we can apply a weight to the numbers involved a_{Ni}. Weighted QALYs then become equal to $(a_{Ni} N_i)$ $(\overline{QALY}_i)$, or simply $a_{Ni} QALY_i$. Let us again consider two groups with group QALY totals equal to $QALY_1$ and $QALY_2$. Then total weighted QALYs would be:

$$\text{Weighted total QALYs} = a_{N1} N_1 \overline{QALY}_1 + a_{N2} N_2 \overline{QALY}_2 \quad (13.4)$$

Or:

$$\text{Weighted total QALYs} = a_{N1} QALY_1 + a_{N2} QALY_2 \quad (13.5)$$

Clearly (13.5) is in the same form as equation (13.1), with numbers weights replacing distribution weights. Once again we can reconstruct versions of (13.2) and (13.3) to apply to group WTPs and benefits.

The PTO exercise can be expressed in terms of equation (13.4). The aim is to see for what value of N_2 (the numbers in group 2) are the two components of total weighted QALYs equal:

$$a_{N2} N_2 \overline{QALY}_2 = a_{N1} N_1 \overline{QALY}_1 \quad (13.6)$$

From this the relative value of the weights can be determined as:

$$\frac{a_{N1}}{a_{N2}} = \frac{N_2 \overline{QALY_2}}{N_1 \overline{QALY_1}}$$ (13.7)

In the special case where the average number of QALYs gained by the two groups is the same, equation (13.7) reduces to:

$$\frac{a_{N1}}{a_{N2}} = \frac{N_2}{N_1}$$ (13.8)

The greater one wants to weight the seriousness of group 1 relative to group 2, the more people in group 2 will have to be treated relative to the number in group 1 in order for society to be indifferent between treating the two sets of groups. In the applications we explain how both (13.7) and (13.8) can be used to derive estimates of weights.

To summarize: we have shown that those in the literature who want equity to be included in health care evaluations, and are against QALY maximization in CUA, logically should be against equal weights for group benefits in a CBA. The equity weights that they would think relevant would be of two kinds: one set for distributional reasons and another set for the numbers involved due to the different seriousness of patients prior to treatment.

13.1.2   Equity Weights as an Externality

Individuals have preferences about what happens to them. But they also have preferences about what happens to others. This is true whether we are discussing QALYs or whether we are dealing with benefits. What happens to others is an effect in addition to what happens personally to the people themselves. This effect on others is thus an external effect. As we saw in Chapter 4, markets often fail to include external effects and these must be measured separately in a CBA and then incorporated into a total, i.e., social, effect.

As evidence that these external effects are real, consider two estimates in studies that we have covered previously, one by Dolan (1998) related to QALYs and the other by Zarkin et al. (2000) involving WTP. Dolan's students gave *twice* the weight to a utility change that doubled the utilities of a group in a low health state (with a starting utility value of 0.2) as they did to doubling the utilities of a group in a higher health state (with a starting utility value of 0.4). Zarkin et al.'s survey found that people were willing to pay $37 per respondent for the drug treatment of others. It is true, as pointed out by Johannesson (1999), that estimates such as the one in the Dolan study consist only of the external effects. But this does not make the estimates theoretically invalid as suggested. It only means that the external effects are one part of the benefits and require the direct benefits to be added to them to obtain the total benefits.

There are three points that we wish to emphasize regarding these external preference effects:

1. Given that people have these external preferences, and one accepts consumer sovereignty, CBA has to include these external effects. It is a secondary issue as to why people have these preferences. It could be due to altruism; but it could also be 'enlightened self interest' as when people help drug addicts in order to avoid crime and so on. We should not assume that these external effects are just special cases that arise only in rare circumstances.

2. As Brent (1996, section 6.2) makes clear, recognizing external effects and using distribution weights is one and the same process. Assume that: individuals value a dollar to themselves as $1, value a dollar to poor people as $0.20, and a project generates $1 of benefits for the poor. These preferences can be included in a CBA of the project in either of two equivalent forms: one can say the direct benefits are $1 and the external benefit are $0.20, making a total benefit of $1.20; or else one can say that the benefits are $1 and, because they go to a deserving group who have a weight of 1.2, the weighted benefits are 1.2 ($1), i.e., $1.20. In either case there is an amount of $1.20 to be compared with any costs. If every time one does a CBA one wants to explicitly measure the income distributional gains generated by a project, then one can use the direct + external benefit version. But if, as we assume in this chapter, those distributional preferences are set in advance and hence independent of individual projects, then distributional weights is the version to use to incorporate external effects.

3. In Chapter 10, when we dealt with QALY weights, there were two external effects that researchers tried to include. First, due to age or other considerations, one group had more QALYs than another and the disparity in the relative number of QALYs needed to be allowed for. Second, in the PTO technique, the *number* of people being treated was of concern to individuals. It was shown that either of these external effects could be used to justify not weighting QALYs equally. In this chapter we will explain how each of the equity considerations requires a weight in its own right. Before proceeding, we need to clarify exactly what a weighted cost–benefit criterion represents.

13.1.3   A Weighted Cost–Benefit Criterion

The traditional criterion that aims to maximize net benefits $B - C$ is not really an 'unweighted' decision rule. As we saw in the context of QALY weights there are no unweighted criteria. Traditional CUA and CBA adopt unit weights. So if one sets $a_1 = a_2 = 1$ in equation (13.2) one obtains B as total benefits. Unit values are just one set of weights and they depend on a value judgment being made just like any other choice of weights. We will not be proposing any restrictions on the choice of weights, other than to suggest that: (a) equal weights are not correct and that (b) if group 1 has a lower income (or fewer QALYs) than group 2, then a concern for equity requires only that $a_1 > a_2$. The reader is not required to accept any particular formulation that says that a_1 should exceed a_2 by a specified amount, as analyzed in the next section.

What is the problem with setting $a_1 = a_2 = 1$ as in the traditional approach? The answer is that of all the possible values for the weights, it can be proven that only equal weights *must be* wrong! Before we demonstrate this proposition, we need to explain first why the traditional school opted for equal weights.

It was never the case that traditional economists considered distributional matters to be unimportant. The argument was only that distribution concerns should not be introduced in any type of expenditure decisions. The tax-transfer system (for example, having the rich pay an income tax and the proceeds be transferred to the poor through some sort of welfare system) would be the appropriate instrument for bringing about a fair distribution of income.

The problem with this justification for the traditional CBA criterion is that the tax-transfer system cannot be relied upon to achieve a situation where the social value of a dollar would be the same no matter who receives it. There are administrative costs in executing tax-transfer programs and these will drive a wedge in between equal weights. Let us explain how this comes about.

Assume that society wishes to transfer T dollars from the rich (group 2) to the poor (group 1). The poor will gain by the amount T, but the rich will have to give up T plus the administrative costs, denoted by A. Society's redistribution will be optimal when the weighted gain of any change in transfers is equal to the weighted loss:

$$a_1 T = a_2 (T + A) \tag{13.9}$$

As $(T + A)$ is greater than T, it follows that a_1 must be greater than a_2. Equal weights violate the optimality condition (13.9) and so unequal weights must be used.

How does one interpret a weighted net cost–benefit outcome? A positive number simply means that the health care expenditure is socially worth-while, where a treatment's 'worth' corresponds to a joint objective that combines equity with efficiency. This is different than trying to pursue either of these objectives separately. What is the point in having complete equity when everyone is equitably being allocated no QALYs or no benefits? Similarly why should society care about having the largest possible equally weighted net benefits if these net-benefits all go to one person who was already rich and healthy? The weights enable the two objectives to be combined in a trade-off situation. The greater one sets a_1 relative to a_2, the more one is willing to sacrifice efficiency for distribution. In the real world, choices have to be made. So let us make these choices explicitly by setting the weights in advance rather than letting them be determined implicitly (equal to unity).

A weighted CBA criterion is therefore necessary to acknowledge the fact that there are two social objectives, efficiency and equity, and not just one. The weights then record the trade-off between the two objectives. The traditional equally weighted benefit measure (or QALY maximization rule) is simply the case where equity is given no weight at all. No matter whether one labels the weighted benefits 'equity-adjusted efficiency' or 'equificiency', as suggested by Dowie (1998), or 'health-related social value CUA', as proposed by Nord et al. (1999), the consequence records *social* benefits'. Equally weighted benefits are only '*economic*' benefits'.

13.2   DISTRIBUTION WEIGHTS

Weighted total benefits are given as the sum of $a_1 B_1$ and $a_2 B_2$. Thus to apply distribution weights there are two tasks: measuring the group benefits, B_1 and B_2, and deciding on a set of distribution weights, a_1 and a_2.

13.2.1   Disaggregating Total Benefits by Income Group

To form B_1 and B_2 from total benefits one cannot just divide B by the share of the total population in each group, for WTP varies for the various income groups. The overall shapes of demand curves can be summarized by the size of the (own) price elasticities. Gertler et al. (1987) have argued (and demonstrated for Peru) that lower income groups have larger price elasticities of demand than higher income groups.

This result just assumes that health care is what economists call a 'normal' good, i.e., the quantity bought goes up as income goes up. From there the argument is very subtle, though also very simple. Quantity of health care can be thought to be a discrete random variable – either one has had an accident or an illness or one has not. Let $Q = 1$ if one has been sick. Quantity does not vary. So expenditures on health (PQ) can only go up if the sick person goes to a higher priced provider. Price here acts as an index of quality; the expected health status from treatment is higher for higher quality providers. From this it follows that health care will only be a normal good if people go to higher priced providers and in the process spend more as their income rises. When prices rise and people spend more this is equivalent in economics to saying that the good is price inelastic. Hence as income rises, demand becomes more inelastic.

Gertler et al. estimated the relationship between income and price elasticity in Peru by focusing on groups defined by income quintile. The lowest income quintile is 'poor' and the highest income quintile is 'rich'. There were three categories of provider (other than self-treatment): public clinics, public hospitals and private doctors. The hospitals and the private doctors were perceived to have higher quality than the clinics. Table 13.1 (based on their Table 3) shows how estimated price elasticities varied by income quintile, quality and the size of the price increases (measured in thousands of soles). Prices for public services are called 'user fees' because they collect revenues from those who use the services rather than from the general taxpayer.

Table 13.1:   *Price elasticities for health in Peru by income quintile*

Price (user fee) change		(Lowest) Quintile 1	Quintile 2	Quintile 3	Quintile 4	(Highest) Quintile 5
Clinic	0–10	−0.17	−0.12	−0.09	−0.06	−0.03
	10–20	−0.62	−0.42	−0.23	−0.15	−0.09
	20–30	−1.43	−0.58	−1.38	−0.26	−0.14
Hospital	0–10	−0.15	−0.12	−0.08	−0.05	−0.03
	10–20	−0.57	−0.34	−0.23	−0.15	−0.09
	20–30	−1.52	−0.56	−0.39	−0.26	−0.13
Private doctor	0–10	−0.17	−0.12	−0.07	−0.06	−0.03
	10–20	−0.53	−0.35	−0.21	−0.14	−0.08
	20–30	−1.36	−0.60	−0.35	−0.25	−0.12

Source: Gertler et al. (1987)

We see from Table 13.1 that the price elasticities for the poor are uniformly much higher than for the rich. The highest quintile have price elasticities close to zero, while the lowest quintile actually have elastic demand curves (values greater than 1) over some price ranges.

13.2.2   Determining the Distribution Weights

In this section we discuss determining the distribution weights in the context of the restriction that $a_1 > a_2$. In a continuous form, this restriction is called the assumption of 'diminishing social marginal utility of income', that is, the higher is a group's income, the lower is the social value of an increase in that group's income. There are two main ways of deriving estimates of the weights. One is empirical whereby one looks at survey results to see what preferences are actually expressed. The other method is to appeal to (normative) economic theory to see what weights one should apply if one accepts various assumptions. We cover each method in turn.

1.   *Empirical estimates of the distribution weights*: In the health care field, unlike other areas of application of CBA, there have not been any revealed preference estimates of distribution weights derived from behavior, whether they be from individual or government decisions (for an example in the transport field see Brent (1979, 1980)). We will therefore refer to explicit preferences that are recorded in questionnaires. We start with QALY weights and then proceed to income weights.

     In Chapter 10 we discussed the 'fair innings' argument for unequal QALY weights. That is, the elderly have had more QALYs than the young and so a QALY to a young person should be given more weight than to an elderly person. It is true that some versions would only have elderly people's QALYs devalued after a prescribed number of years (say, reaching 70) and that after this period their weight would drop to zero. But the essential idea is still connected to the assumption that the more QALYs one has had the lower the weight. In this way the QALY weighting approach exactly mirrors the diminishing social marginal utility of income assumption, where the more income one has the lower is the weight.

     The case studies in Chapter 10 on determining QALY weights were in the context of age differentials. There are other case studies that deal more generally with the existence of QALY differences. For example, in the study by Johannesson et al. (1996) they tried to estimate QALY weights due to QALY differences derived from life expectancies caused by hereditary factors. This study is especially relevant because it provides explicit empirical support for the diminishing social marginal utility per QALY assumption.

     Johannesson et al. asked respondents to choose between two societies containing two groups: one society with a higher average life expectancy and the other society with a larger difference in life expectancy between the two groups. The respondents were asked to consider both efficiency and distribution. Their choices revealed that individuals were willing to give up 1 discounted QALY in the group with more QALYs to gain 0.58 discounted QALYs in the group with fewer QALYs. We can deduce from this trade-off that if a QALY to the group with more QALYs is given a weight of 1, then the weight to the lower QALY group would be 1.724 (that is, $1/0.58$).

The Zarkin et al. estimate of the external benefit of drug treatment programs can be converted into an estimate of the distribution weight attached to benefits as follows. The only tricky part is to pin down the unit of analysis to a single person. Recall that they found that people were willing to pay $37 per respondent for the successful drug treatment of 100 others. This averages to 37 cents per person successfully treated. Zarkin et al. use 62% as their success rate. So the average treatment cost of $12 440 has to be multiplied by 1.38 (as 38% extra has to be spent on unsuccessful cases) to obtain $17 167 as the cost of treating successfully a drug addict. Presumably respondents would value treatment benefits going to themselves (if they were addicted) as $17 167. In other words, they would value a dollar of direct benefits to themselves as a dollar. But they would have to pay $17 167 to have an external benefit of 37 cents. An external dollar of expenditure going to others would therefore be worth 0.0022 cents ($0.37/ $17 167). Given that there were 903 104 people in the local area who each receive the external benefit, the total external benefit per dollar spent on treatment amounts to $19.46. The total benefit of a dollar spent on treatment would be $1 of direct benefits and $19.46 of external benefits for a total benefit of $20.46. As explained in section 13.1.2, this implies that a dollar to a drug addict's treatment has a social weight of 20.46.

2. *Estimates of the weights derived from economic theory*: Here we explain how one can obtain estimates using *a priori* reasoning. This involves specifying in advance a set of reasonable assumptions and then deriving weights from these assumptions. A good example of this approach can be seen in the World Bank's approach to weighting, as explained by Squire and van der Tak (1975). They make two key assumptions:
   (a) Everyone has the same utility function. This is equivalent to assuming that everyone makes the same contribution to society's satisfaction, in which case one can use individual evaluations of the marginal utility of income. With all individual preferences the same, one can choose just one individual's marginal utility of income curve to represent society's preferences.
   (b) Let the one (representative) individual's utility function exhibit

diminishing marginal utility of income. Economic theorists often assume that the value of income diminishes at a constant rate. The rate of decline is represented by the size of the income inequality aversion parameter η, which we first introduced in section 7.2.1 when determining the social rate of time preference. (It was represented by τ in equation (10.3) as applied to QALYs.) In the Squire and van der Tak version, they specify a group's income Y_i relative to average income $\overline{Y}$. The distribution weight a_i for a group with an income Y_i is given by:

$$a_i = (\overline{Y} / Y_i)^{\eta} \qquad\qquad (13.10)$$

This function has the same shape as in Figure 6.2, except that relative income and not just Y is on the horizontal axis.

For the special case where $\eta = 1$, we have $a_i = \overline{Y} / Y_i$. This implies that the distribution weight of a group with one quarter of the income of the average would be 4, and a group with four times the average would have a weight of 0.25. More generally, the greater the aversion of society to inequality, the higher will be the value of η, and the steeper will be the slope of the curve.

The traditional approach to distribution weighting in CBA is to apply equal weights. In terms of equation (13.10) this translates into a zero value for η. Since we have ruled out equal weights, any positive value for η could be valid. Squire and van der Tak recommended a value of $\eta = 1$. The author has advocated elsewhere (see Brent (1996, 1998a)) a value of $\eta = \frac{1}{2}$ because this seems to be more in line with the upper bound of policy practice regarding income redistribution. However, in terms of theory, one can insist only on diminishing marginal utility of income, not the rate it declines.

13.3   NUMBERS EFFECT

Equity weights exist not only for distributional considerations. The numbers affected also determine people's views of fairness. In this section we analyze three different ways that one can think about the importance of numbers when making economic evaluations.

13.3.1   Numbers and PTOs

We saw in Chapter 10 that Nord criticized the SG, TTO and RS methods for deriving utility values based solely on personal preferences. He advocated the use of PTOs because he thought that this method was more in line with social preferences. Although Dolan criticized the PTO method because it combined four main considerations (the severity of the illness that a group has before and after treatment, the size of the health gain, and the numbers being treated), we learned from Ubel et al.'s (1998) study that each of these four ingredients could be isolated in the questions and therefore estimated separately. What Ubel et al. found is vitally important for this chapter because, of the four ingredients, only the numbers being treated was significant.

There is evidence therefore that it is the numbers affected that may drive the PTO estimates, not necessarily the other ingredients. When the other ingredients are not significant, then the numbers affected would be important in their own right and not only as an indicator of a concern for distribution. Of course, more generally, people may also be concerned with the relative sizes of group QALYs when expressing PTO preferences and so distribution would then play a role in the estimates. We are suggesting only that the numbers being treated could be a consideration additional to distribution.

When Nord explained his justification for the PTO he was careful to specify that conventional CUA was deficient by ignoring the *seriousness* of those affected and focusing only on the size of QALY improvements. As we saw earlier, a concern for distribution would be captured by weights attached to the group QALYs to reflect the diminishing marginal utility requirement for social decisions. But what would follow in the Nord framework if, *because* one group was more seriously ill, they had more QALYs to gain from treatment than other groups? Allowing for diminishing marginal utility of income would not reflect 'seriousness' and would go against giving priority to the more deserving group (which is the essence of the argument mentioned earlier). Relative numbers in a PTO context incorporate the missing seriousness dimension.

13.3.2   Numbers as a Third Social Objective

In a series of papers, Brent (1984b, 1986, 1991b, 1992, 1994b) argued that trying to reduce the numbers *adversely affected* was a third social objective, in addition to efficiency and equity. A theorem was presented that showed that, under specified conditions, a concern for numbers was inconsistent with giving greater weight to low-income groups. Also, empirical support was supplied for the existence of a numbers effect that was both separate from efficiency considerations (the larger the numbers affected the greater the benefits) and was not a proxy for a political objective such as vote maximization (the greater the number affected, the more votes at stake). The basic rationale addresses the central weakness of the economic foundation of CBA, as we now explain.

In the WTP approach, B is what the gainers are willing to pay for the program, and C is what the losers must receive in compensation to put up with the program. As we saw in the previous chapter, when $B > C$ there are sufficient funds for the gainers to compensate the losers and someone can be made better off and no one worse off (i.e., there is a potential Pareto improvement). This, of course, does not imply that an actual Pareto improvement will take place. Compensation is hypothetical. That is, *if* compensation takes place, there would be *no* losers.

There are fundamental difficulties with efficiency-based compensation tests. It is important to note that the B and C used in this test are measured on the basis of the existing distribution of income. If this is not optimal, then one may question the validity of the test – even if compensation takes place and there is an actual Pareto improvement. Of course, if compensation does not take place, a potential Pareto improvement can be criticized on equity grounds because some of those who are made worse off may have low incomes. Thus, to the extent that income distribution is considered important, Pareto improvements have weaknesses *whether or not* compensation takes place. Thus, to acknowledge that efficiency needs to be adjusted to accommodate distributional issues, weighted WTP must be the criterion: $a_1 B_1 + a_2 B_2$.

On the other hand, one should expect that compensation would *not* take place. It is not feasible to ensure that there are no losers whenever resources are reallocated. Since compensation tests are constructed around a concern for the existence of losers, the fact that losers will take place means that we should allow for the number of losers in our criteria about what is socially worthwhile. Note that efficiency-based compensation tests are violated by the existence of any type of loser (whether they be rich or poor). It is the existence of losers that is important not distribution *per se.*

13.3.3   Numbers and Access

There is no doubt that numbers count in a general sense in health care. For example, there is a great concern at this time in the US that there are around 40 million without any kind of health insurance. Increasing access to health care is a prime goal of many social groups and organizations and access is measured in terms of numbers.

In fact, the Oregon plan that we discussed in earlier chapters was all about numbers and access. The aim was to increase the number of low-income people under Medicaid who would now have public health insurance. For a given sized budget, increased access must come at the expense of reducing the average amount of services that people could receive – hence the need for the priority setting exercise known as the Oregon plan.

Everything was reduced to this thought experiment by Eddy (1991c): was treating 105 dental cap worth the same as treating one ectopic pregnancies when these two alternatives cost the same in total? The philosophy of the Oregon plan was that treating the 105 people was socially more worthwhile than treating the one. This judgment is simply saying that the weight to the numbers affected should be greater than unity if access is to be considered important as a separate social objective.

13.4 APPLICATIONS

We first outline two studies that use distributional weights in CBAs of health care. Both rely on the van der Tak formula, one explicitly and one implicitly. Then we turn to numbers weights and see how PTO responses reveal estimates of these equity weights. The final case study starts with an efficiency benefit calculation and subsequently decomposes this to form an implicit weighted benefit estimate.

13.4.1 Distributional Weights and Case Management Programs in Mental Health

We have already covered in section 5.4.4 the complete CBA by Brent (2002b) of four case management programs that integrated medical and supportive services to psychiatric patients in the community. Every dollar transferred to the patients from the public sector had a MCF loss of 1.3 and a distributional gain of 2.28, which meant that every dollar transferred from the public sector generated a social net benefit of around a dollar (that is, 2.28 − 1.3). Here we examine the distribution weighting part of the evaluation. In our reporting of the Brent study we focused on a single estimate of the weights to the beneficiaries and concentrated only on the weight attached to money income. Now we consider alternative estimates for the weights and include an analysis of weights in-kind as well as in money income (cash) form.

The recipients of the public transfer are the psychiatric patients (the severely mentally ill, SMI) and they are designated as group 1. The people paying the transfers are the taxpayers, group 2. $1 of the income received by the patients was judged to have a social value greater than $1 because their income was below the average and they were regarded as a more socially deserving group than the taxpayers. The income-weighting scheme used was Squire and van der Tak's equation (13.10). We rewrite this as equation (13.11), which inserts the subscript m to all variables, to indicate that this expression is to be used for weights attached to *money* income:

$$a_{mi} = (\bar{Y}_m / Y_{mi})^{\eta} \tag{13.11}$$

An obvious problem with trying to use equation (13.11) for weighting the income of the SMI is to know how to measure their income Y_{m1}. Typically, the SMI do not earn income. The solution adopted by Brent is to count as income all the payments (transfers) made on their behalf that do not involve medical treatment. Even prior to choosing to be placed into case management programs, the clients had sums transferred to them (or their care givers) to be spent looking after them. These sums determine the living standards of the SMI, just as persons without mental problems have their purchasing power linked to their incomes.

Thus Y_{m1} will be defined as the total transfers (private plus public) per client to the SMI in the baseline period, which amounted to \$8038 for fiscal year 1990–91. Assuming that the average income earner is the representative taxpayer (group 2), and with the mean *per capita* income of California in 1991 being \$18 343, this sets the weight for the SMI as $a_{m1} = (\$18\ 343/\$8038) = 2.28$ with $\eta = 1$, and $a_{m1} = (\$18\ 343/\$8038)^{0.5} = 1.51$ with $\eta = 0.5$. All subsequent analysis will rely on these two estimates for a_{m1}. The weight to the income of the taxpayers, a_{m2}, is always fixed at unity in this weighting scheme (as their income equals the average and unity raised to any power is always equal to 1).

In the Hochman and Rodgers (1971) analysis of in-kind transfers, the preferences of the rich must be considered if transfers are to be voluntarily voted for by the rich. The rich may care about how income is redistributed. They may prefer that any assistance be given in kind, since none of this will be spent on goods for which the rich do not have a positive externality. For instance, in-kind transfers, such as providing food, education and housing for the SMI, generate positive externalities; while cash given can be spent on alcohol and cigarettes, items that do not promote psychic benefits for the taxpayers.

Brent (1980) adapted the Hochman and Rodgers theory of transfers to distribution weighting in CBA. There should be now two sets of distribution weights: one set in cash a_{mi} and another set in kind a_{ki}. The weight to cash income given to the needy would be expected to have a value lower than for income in kind from the donor's point of view, i.e., $a_{m1} < a_{k1}$. In the CM context in which the weighted CBA criterion was applied in Chapter 5, benefits are costs avoided. So all benefits are in cash form. No in-kind elements are involved. Similarly with the public transfers, R_G, cash payments from the taxpayers become cash receipts to the beneficiaries, so there are no in-kind effects to weight. On the other hand private transfers are monies spent by family members for goods and services received by the SMI. In this case, cash is given up for in-kind benefits and so the two sets of weights could be relevant for this category of transfers.

Each \$1 of private transfers R_P generates a gain of a_{k1} and a loss of a_{m2}. The net benefit per dollar is the difference $a_{k1} - a_{m2}$. The loss of cash of the family member is treated like any taxpayer's contribution and thus has a weight of unity. The resulting weight on private transfers becomes $a_{k1} - 1$. The problem now is how to fix a_{k1}. The solution depends on how one classifies the family members of the SMI. Are they group 1 or group 2? What it is necessary to recognize is that, in this context, family members play a dual role. As custodians for the SMI, they spend the transfers; but they also act as taxpayers in that they provide the funds for the spending.

To allow for this dual role, we will incorporate two special cases for the in-kind weights. In the first, we assume that family members identify themselves fully with the SMI and thus their preferences as taxpayers (preferring in-kind transfers) are not important. The in-kind weight to the SMI would then be the same as the SMI's money income weight, $a_{k1} = a_{m1}$. As $a_{m1} > 1$ for either value of η, we have the net gain attached to private transfers $a_{k1} - 1$ as always positive. In the second case, we assume that family members see themselves as primarily taxpayers. Private transfers would then be viewed as cash transfers from themselves to themselves. This implies that $a_{k1} = a_{m2} = 1$, which means that private transfers would make no net contribution to the CBA outcome ($a_{k1} - 1 = 1 - 1 = 0$).

There are four sets of weights that follow from the considerations just presented. All four sets include $a_{m2} = 1$ as this is the numeraire weight. The first two sets are determined when family members are treated like beneficiaries and $a_{k1} = a_{m1}$. So when $a_{m1} = 2.28$, we have $a_{k1} = 2.28$, and when $a_{m1} = 1.51$, we have $a_{k1} = 1.51$. The remaining sets appear when family members are treated like taxpayers and $a_{k1} = a_{m2}$. As $a_{m2} = 1$, we have $a_{k1} = 1$. This value for a_{k1} is then paired with the two values for a_{m1} of 2.28 and 1.52 to form sets three and four. To summarize, the four sets of weights are:

$$\text{Set 1: } (a_{m1} = 2.28, \ a_{k1} = 2.28, \ a_{m2} = 1.00);$$
$$\text{Set 2: } (a_{m1} = 1.51, \ a_{k1} = 1.51, \ a_{m2} = 1.00);$$
$$\text{Set 3: } (a_{m1} = 2.28, \ a_{k1} = 1.00, \ a_{m2} = 1.00); \text{ and}$$
$$\text{Set 4: } (a_{m1} = 1.51, \ a_{k1} = 1.00, \ a_{m2} = 1.00).$$

The weighted net benefits of the case management programs in Table 5.7 were based on weight set 3. The other sets can be used to provide a sensitivity analysis to the main results. Table 13.2 (based on Brent's Table 3) shows the alternative results for the weighted net benefits where there is both a MCF (equal to 1.3) and four different sets of distributional weights (in cash and in kind). The robustness of the earlier result pointing to the relative social desirability of the PACT program carries over to the case where alternative sets of distribution weights are tried.

Table 13.2: Weighted net benefits of case management programs with alternative sets of distribution weights ($)

CBA category	Intensive broker	Clinical team	PACT adaption
Weight set 1	30404	31173	34301
Weight set 2	19001	19405	21277
Weight set 3	30462	31331	34481
Weight set 4	19024	19468	21349

Source: Based on Brent (2002c)

13.4.2 Distributional Weights and the Benefits of Eliminating Arthritis

One CV study that did try to adjust WTP for equity reasons was by Thompson et al. (1984) which related to the elimination of arthritis. As we shall see, their method of adjustment involved the implicit assignment of (money) income distribution weights. Their justification for making their adjustment is the key to our interpretation of their methods.

184 patients with osteoarthritis and rheumatoid arthritis were asked their WTP per week for hypothetical *complete* cure. Although only 27% were able to give plausible answers, this response rate was not judged unacceptably low because responses were given without prompting about what their incomes are and what alternative uses of funds they might have. The main three factors determining whether patients would respond were their education level, whether they worked for money or not, and the number of treatments undergone.

On average, patients with arthritis were willing to pay $35 per week for a complete cure. However, as one would expect, WTP was positively related to income. Therefore Thompson et al. presented patient WTP responses as a percent of their family incomes and these ratios are recorded in Table 13.3 (based on their Table 6). We see that WTP as a percent of income did rise as one moves up the income scale, but not in a continuous way. However, for a band of income (between $5000 and $29999) there was no clear pattern between the WTP % and income.

Table 13.3: Number responding and stated willingness to pay as percent of family income

Annual income	Number	Mean stated WTP (% of income)
Less than $3000	8	10
$3000–$4999	26	17
$5000–$9999	42	35
$10000–$14999	34	38
$15000–$19999	20	27
$20000–$29999	22	33
$30000 or more	15	54
No response	17	42
Total	184	35

Source: Based on Thompson et al. (1984)

Thompson et al. were concerned that, given that WTP depends on income, the aggregate WTP for arthritis elimination would be dominated by the WTP of the rich. They recommended that the problem 'might be avoided if willingness to pay is expressed as a proportion of personal income, if the mean proportional willingness to pay is calculated, and if this proportion is multiplied by total, adjusted, societal willingness to pay'. For two income groups, their recommended procedure can be stated as:

$$\text{Social WTP} = (\text{WTP}_1 / Y_1)\ \bar{Y} + (\text{WTP}_2 / Y_2)\ \bar{Y}$$

or:

$$\text{Social WTP} = \text{WTP}_1 (\bar{Y} / Y_1) + \text{WTP}_2 (\bar{Y} / Y_2) \qquad (13.12)$$

Equation (13.12) is exactly equal to the weighted total benefit criterion expressed by equation (13.3) when the group distribution weights are determined on the basis of equation (13.10) with $\eta = 1$. This means that, although Thompson et al. do not state this, their equity adjustment is equivalent to advocating a particular set of distributional weights. The weights they recommend are exactly those based on economic theory. Thompson et al.'s procedure therefore has all the strengths and weaknesses of this weighting approach – see Brent (1984a).

13.4.3   Deriving Numbers Weights from a PTO of the Ability to Walk Freely

Nord (1995) used a survey related to the ability to function, that is, walk freely, to estimate his PTO measures. In a subsequent paper, Nord et al. (1999) outlined various calculations that convert the PTO estimates into weights. The methods described are basically captured by the two equations (13.8) and (13.9) given earlier. The only real difference is that Nord was trying to obtain utility weights so he suggested ways of confining the estimates to the 0–1 interval, while we are dealing with equity weights applied to QALYs or benefits. As a result we take unity as the benchmark and make all the calculations from this base. Treatment costs were assumed to be equal, so it was only weighted QALYs that was the issue for estimation.

The ability to walk freely was expressed in terms of two end-states, 1: having 'No problems walking' and 7: being 'Completely bedridden'. In between these end-states there were five intermediate levels, 2: 'Can move about without difficulty anywhere, but has difficulties walking more than 1 K'; 3: 'Can move about without difficulty at home, but has difficulties in stairs and outdoors'; 4: 'Moves about with difficulty at home. Needs assistance in stairs and outdoors'; 5: 'Can sit. Needs assistance to move about – both at home and outdoors'; and 6: 'To some degree bedridden. Can sit in a chair if helped up by others.'

It was claimed that differences between these seven levels were 'equally significant'. So moving from level 1 to level 4 (denoted 4–1) meant the same as moving from level 4 to level 7 (denoted 7–4). To fit in with our formulae (and also to be consistent with Nord et al.) we will interpret these two equally significant changes as ones producing equal numbers of QALYs to the two groups, whereby $QALY_1 = QALY_2$. What was different about moving from 1 to 4 and moving from 4 to 7 was that the former change starts from a lower level. As we pointed out earlier, Nord defined patients starting at lower levels (group 1) as 'more severely ill' (than group 2).

Nord presented two main scenarios to respondents (called 'pairs'). In the first, there were 10 people in group 1 who were seriously ill, an unknown number N_2 in group 2, and both groups had equally significant changes; and in the second scenario, again $N_1 = 10$ and N_2 was unknown, but this time group 1 gained more QALYs from treatment than group 2. Each scenario was presented to the respondents in two different questionnaires. In the first questionnaire just the information necessary to form a PTO was presented. In the second questionnaire (sent two to three months later) the exact same data were provided but, in addition, there was a commentary suggesting arguments *why* the respondent should react differently to the specified changes to the two groups. The resulting equivalent numbers in group 2, i.e., N_2, are presented in Table 13.4 (Nord's Table 1), for both questionnaires, for each of the scenarios. We examine the results of each of these scenarios in turn.

Table 13.4: *Equivalence numbers in questionnaires without and with explicit arguments*

	Subjects													
	1	2	3	4	5	6	7	8	9	10	11	12	13	14
Pair (7–4) versus (4–1)														
W/O explicit arguments	30	350	200	35	35	100	100	50	20	40	50	300	200	350
With explicit arguments	15	200	30	10	10	20	75	30	30	15	15	50	100	10
Pair (7–2) versus (7–5)														
W/O explicit arguments	20	35	25	30	20	40	15	100	35	50	15	15	15	20
With explicit arguments	10	10	200	30	15	20	20	50	50	35	20	10	10	10

Source: Nord (1995)

In the first scenario, $\overline{QALY_1} = \overline{QALY_2}$. The PTO question in questionnaire A was: how many in group 2 need to be treated to be equivalent to 10 severely ill persons being treated? Line 1 of Table 13.4 lists the responses given by 14 individuals placed in the role of social planners by Nord. As one would expect, N_2 is always greater than 10, which means that respondents were willing to trade off more than one person in group 2 in order to treat one more person who is seriously ill. The range is from 20 to 350 with the median person in the survey responding $N_2 = 75$.

If one substitutes $N_1 = 10$ into equation (13.8), one obtains: $a_{N1}/a_{N2} = N_2/10$. Thus if the weight on group 2 is fixed equal to unity, then the weight on group 1 is just one-tenth of the N_2 number that is expressed in the PTO. Dividing every number on the first line of Table 13.4 by 10 produces the first line of weights presented in Table 13.5. The range is from 2 to 35 with the median person's response implying $a_{N1} = 7.5$.

When the initial questionnaire was repeated, but with words added giving an argument why the respondent should answer more than 10 for N_2, the numbers and weights were greatly reduced.

The added words (in questionnaire B) advocated giving priority to the 10 persons moving from 7 to 4 ('who are worse off to start with') unless 'considerably more people would be helped' when moving from 4 to 1. In response to this prompting, the N_2 responses are recorded in line 2 of Table 13.4. The range is now from 10 to 200 with a median of 25. Dividing

Table 13.5:   *Numbers weights for severity of illness corresponding to PTO*
             estimates

								Subjects						
	1	2	3	4	5	6	7	8	9	10	11	12	13	14
Pair (7–4) versus (4–1)														
W/O explicit arguments	3	35	20	3.5	3.5	10	10	5	2	4	5	30	20	35
With explicit arguments	1.5	20	3	1	1	2	7.5	3	3	1.5	1.5	5	10	1
Pair (7–2) versus (7–5)														
W/O explicit arguments	5	8.8	6.3	7.5	5	10	3.8	25	8.8	12.5	3.8	3.8	3.8	5
With explicit arguments	2.5	2.5	50	7.5	3.8	5	5	12.5	12.5	8.8	5	2.5	2.5	2.5

Source: Derived by the author from Nord (1995)

all the N_2 values by 10 as before produces the second line of weights in Table 13.5. The range of weights is from 1 to 20 with a median weight of 2.5. Interestingly, three persons now would give equal weights to both groups.

In the second scenario, the 10 persons in group 1 move up five levels when the unknown number in group 2 moves up only two levels. Assuming again that each level change has equal significance, then group 1's QALYs would change relative to group 2's QALYs in the ratio of 5 to 2, i.e., $QALY_1/QALY_2 = 2.5$. The PTO responses to the second scenario are recorded in line 3 of Table 13.4. As one would expect when group 1 is getting a larger treatment effect, it would take fewer people in group 2 to get treatment than in the first scenario in order to equalize the social value of the two sets of group treatments. The range of N_2 values is from 15 to 100, with a median of 22.5.

The weights that correspond with line 3 of Table 13.4 can be obtained by substituting $N_1 = 10$, $a_{N2} = 1$, and $\overline{QALY_1/QALY_2} = 2.5$ into equation (13.7). The result is: $a_{N1} = 2.5 \ N_2/10 = N_2/4$. One obtains weights by dividing the N_2 numbers by 4. These weights are displayed in line 3 of Table 13.5. The weights are in the band from 3.8 to 12.5, with a median weight of $a_{N1} = 5.7$.

The second questionnaire for the second scenario (questionnaire C) adds words of explanation to the first questionnaire to highlight to the respondents that in the alternative sets of treatments, group 1's 'health benefit is clearly greater' and so they 'should have priority unless considerably more people would be helped' in group 2. Respondents are therefore to be aware of making an explicit trade-off between group 1 being severely ill and group 1 having larger benefits, and that this trade-off should be expressed relative to the numbers to be treated in group 2. Line 4 of Table 13.4 presents the equivalent numbers and line 4 of Table 13.5 displays the weights. The range for the N_2 numbers is between 15 and 100, with a median of 20; while the range for the severity weights is from 2.5 to 50, with a median of $a_{N1} = 5$.

Nord concludes that the PTO estimates are very much dependent on how questions are framed and what information is given to the respondents. Nord is correct to point out that the larger the sample of respondents, the smaller will be the sampling error. We just wish to emphasize that, even with such a small sample, the median weights lay in the narrow range of 2.5 to 7.5 and did not admit equal weights.

13.4.4 An Evaluation of Raising User Fees in Peru

In developing countries, tax sources for financing public expenditures are limited. At the same time, social services are heavily subsidized and near zero user fees are in effect. In response to this severe public funds constraint, many have advocated raising user fees in order to generate revenues to recover the cost of the social services and, perhaps, to fund other much needed public expenditures.

Gertler et al. (1987) wanted to know how raising user fees for public hospitals would impact the poor in Peru. Increasing revenues R will be advantageous, but this will be accompanied by a loss of benefit B, called 'welfare losses', which include the excess burdens, as analyzed in Chapter 5. The magnitudes for B and R depended on the estimated reductions in quantity demanded by each quintile. Gertler et al. estimated B and R for two levels of user fees in Peru, viz., 10 and 20 thousand soles. To test how much of a difference it makes when the private sector matches any public sector fee raises, Gertler et al. considered two scenarios: one with 'no private doctor price response' and a second with an 'equal private doctor price response'. The aggregate results for the user fee changes for each of the scenarios are given in Table 13.6 (their Table 4). The benefit losses rose with the size of the fee increases and were greater when private doctors matched the public sector's fee increases.

The results were then disaggregated by quintile. Given that the poorer the quintile the larger the price elasticity (recall section 13.1.1), it follows that, for a specified price increase, the quantity reductions and the benefit losses would be greater for the poorer quintiles. The reduction in quantity demanded was expressed as a share of the total reduction in demand. Thus D_i/D is the share of the quantity reduction experienced by quintile i. These quantity reductions are recorded as percentages in Table 13.7 (a part of their Table 5). The table shows that around 40% of the reduction

Table 13.6: *Aggregate results: percentage change in total demand accounted for by each income quintile and consumers' welfare loss as a percentage of income by income quintile*

Scenario	User fee change (thousands soles)	Cumulative % reduction in total demand	Public revenue increase, R (millions soles)	Loss of benefits, B (millions soles)
No private doctor	1–10	−7.3	6390	6390
Price response	1–20	−14.2	11518	13692
Equal private doctor	1–10	−11.9	6510	11918
Price response	1–20	−23.5	11890	23590

Source: Based on Gertler et al. (1987)

Table 13.7: *Disaggregated results for quantity reductions (D_i/D) by quintile*

Scenario	User fee change (thousands soles)	Quintile 1 (Lowest)	Quintile 2	Quintile 3	Quintile 4	Quintile 5 (Highest)
No private doctor price response	1–10	37.4%	27.8%	17.4%	11.6%	5.8%
	1–20	36.8%	27.1%	17.8%	12.0%	6.2%
Equal private doctor price response	1–10	38.6%	25.7%	17.2%	12.0%	6.5%
	1–20	37.9%	25.1%	17.6%	12.5%	6.9%

Source: Based on Gertler et al. (1987)

in quantity demanded was borne by the poorest quintile, while the richest quintile reduced their quantity by only 5%. Gertler et al. interpreted the greater relative reduction in quantity by the poor as a decrease in their 'access' to health care.

Gertler et al. also disaggregated the total reduction in benefits. Interestingly they did not detail what were the absolute sizes of the group benefit losses. Instead they expressed these losses as a percentage of a quintile's income. A group's losses were therefore expressed as B_i/Y_i. These losses are presented in Table 13.8 (again a part of their Table 5). Mirroring the quantity losses, the benefit losses were much larger for the poorer quintiles.

Table 13.8: Disaggregated results for benefit losses as a percentage of income (B_i/Y_i) by quintile

Scenario	User fee change (thousands soles)	Quintile 1 (Lowest)	Quintile 2	Quintile 3	Quintile 4	Quintile 5 (Highest)
No private doctor price response	1–10	2.7%	1.3%	0.6%	0.3%	0.1%
	1–20	5.5%	2.3%	1.2%	0.7%	0.2%
Equal private doctor price response	1–10	5.6%	1.9%	1.2%	0.6%	0.2%
	1–20	12.0%	3.5%	2.0%	1.2%	0.5%

Source: Based on Gertler et al. (1987)

Gertler et al.'s conclusion was that although there was a potential to raise significant revenues from user fees in Peru, this would be inequitable ('regressive') in terms of both access and loss of benefits. They recommended that the rich be charged higher prices than the poor. Because demand curves are more inelastic for the rich, the higher prices for the rich would lead to greater revenues *and* lower benefit losses.

Although Gertler et al. are undoubtedly right to suggest that one can do *better* than introducing equal user fees for all, one still does not know from their analysis whether raising any type of user fee system would be *any good* (i.e., socially worthwhile). Only a full CBA with distribution weights can tell whether the gain in revenues can offset the benefit losses. We leave such an economic evaluation as an exercise in the problems section. Here we just emphasize that, although Gertler et al. did not say exactly why they expressed quintile benefits relative to incomes, the *effect* of doing so is to apply distributional weights (as in the previous case study).

Specifically, the weight to a quintile is inversely related to their income, or $a_i = (1/Y_i)$. This is equivalent to the Squire and van der Tak weighting system when the risk aversion parameter in equation (13.10) is set equal to 1 *and* $\bar{Y}$ is replaced by 1. This implies that what Gertler et al. designate in Table 13.7 as B_i/Y_i is really the loss of weighted benefits of each quintile, i.e., $a_i B_i$.

There is nothing inherently wrong with using non-standardized values for benefit weights (arbitrarily replacing $\bar{Y}$ by 1) if one just wants to focus on the benefits in isolation of costs and try to find which group lost the most when user fees are raised. But if one wishes to use the weighted benefits in a CBA, one needs to standardize the weights and make the weighted benefit units comparable to the costs. So a CBA would use *relative* income weights by multiplying each B_i / Y_i by average income $\bar{Y}$. In this case, each group effect is $(B_i / Y_i) \bar{Y}$, or after arranging, $(\bar{Y} / Y_i) B_i$. Clearly now each group effect becomes the weighted benefit $a_i B_i$, where $a_i = \bar{Y} / Y_i$ as in the Squire and van der Tak framework with $\eta = 1$.

13.5   FINAL SECTION

We present for the final time the problems and summary sections. As this is the last chapter, instead of looking forward, we close by reviewing the main conclusions of the book.

13.5.1   Problems

The problems use data presented by Gertler et al. to illustrate how to carry out a complete CBA of whether to raise user fees for public services in Peru. Gertler et al. in their article did not detail all of their findings by quintile, so we have interpolated some numbers that are consistent with their aggregative data. In addition, because no indication was given of any cost savings from reduced quantities, we have made up some estimates that are necessary to complete the evaluation.

Table 13.9 presents the main ingredients for the CBA. All figures are in thousands of soles. They correspond only to the case where the user fees change was 1–10 and there was no private doctor price response. In addition one needs to know (in order to derive the distribution weights) that $\bar{Y}$ was 223 031. Use a figure of 1.5 for the MCF.

The complete CBA criterion takes the form stated in equation (5.4), which is based on B, C and R (and the MCF), and applies income distribution weights to it. The resulting criterion is:

$$\Sigma \, a_i \, B_i - a_2 \, (\text{MCF}) \, C + (\text{MCF} - 1) \, \Sigma \, a_i \, R_i > 0 \qquad (13.13)$$

The third element warrants some explanation. In this application the repayments R represent the amount of the user fees collected by the government. They add to social desirability because the funds go to the government and so they reduce the need for taxes, thereby avoiding the excess burden, $\text{MCF} - 1$. On the other hand, the value of monies given up by any quintile depends on the social values of the income group involved and this depends on their distributional weight. The questions simply take you through the criterion (13.13) element by element.

Table 13.9: Disaggregated costs and benefits of raising user fees in Peru by quintile

Category	Quintile 1 (Lowest)	Quintile 2	Quintile 3	Quintile 4	Quintile 5 (Highest)	Totals
1. Loss of benefits B_i	2592	1926	1206	804	402	6930
2. Rise in revenues R_i	2360	1760	1120	760	390	6390
3. Savings in costs C_i	2700	2000	1200	800	400	7100
4. Income of quintile Y_i	96000	148154	201000	268000	402000	1115154
5. Distribution weights a_i						
6. Weighted benefits $a_i B_i$						

Source: Constructed by the author related to Gertler et al. (1987)

1. Use the Squire and van der Tak formula, i.e., equation (13.10), to obtain estimates of the distribution weights for the five quintile groups and thereby fill in rows 5 and 6 of Table 13.9.
2. Assuming costs are paid by taxpayers who have incomes equal to the quintile average, what is the amount of weighted costs? (Note that there is a cost saving so reductions in costs are a positive effect in this case study.)
3. What is the social value of the revenues R given to the government?
4. Would raising user fees in Peru be socially desirable if one considers the weighted benefits, costs and revenues? Would the outcome be different if a simple $B - C$ criterion were used?

13.5.2 Summary

This chapter dealt with equity in CBA by interpreting it to be a simple extension of the theory of equity in CUA. Equity in CUA was incorporated by employing unequal weights to utilities accruing to different individuals or groups. The equity weights were based on a concern with, first, distribution (who had more QALYs than whom) and, second, the level of group utilities before health interventions changed them. This second dimension of equity was a central part of PTOs and was expressed in terms of the relative numbers affected by treatment. One can appeal to the same set of considerations that have already been accepted in CUA, and just transpose them to CBA to advocate that unequal equity weights for distribution and numbers be employed.

Distribution and numbers weights share a lot of characteristics in common. They reflect equity considerations and have significance only to the extent that they deviate from unity. Traditional approaches to economic evaluation, relying on QALY maximization or efficiency-based CBA, both weight group effects the same irrespective of the group involved. Setting any equity weights inherently involves making value judgments. Implicitly using equal weights is no less of a value judgment than adopting any other set. However, equal weights are much more likely to be wrong if one recognizes that there are administrative costs in redistributing resources from rich to poor. So, whether or not to use equal weights is not the issue (the answer is unambiguously affirmative). What is very much the issue is how to determine the 'right' set of weights. Many different methods exist in the CBA literature. No matter the method, the essential requirement is only that any effects on the poor be given a higher weight than for the rich.

Distribution and numbers weights deviate from each other when the groups that start off with the least QALYs (benefits) have a larger improvement than the groups with the most QALYs (benefits). In this case one would not necessarily ague that the more QALYs (benefits) one group has, the less is the social value of any additions. Diminishing social marginal utility would not now seem to apply. The way forward seems to be to acknowledge that numbers are a third consideration (in addition to efficiency and distribution). Using distribution *and* numbers weights can allow for both the severity of illness that groups start off with and the extent of improvement from treatment.

Using equity weights is not an *ad hoc* exercise. It is clear from the questionnaires used in CUA studies that people do, in fact, have preferences about effects related to others (external effects). Central to CBA is the value judgment that individuals are the best judges of their own welfare. If one adopts that value judgment, it is entirely consistent to include these preferences for others in the social evaluation. *Not* to do so would be *ad hoc*. Attaching the equity weights to group QALYs (benefits) ensures that the CBA criterion is a social one. This is not the same as trying to achieve efficiency on its own, or promoting equity on its own. The social criterion records a concern for efficiency and distribution jointly, with the weights indicating the trade-off that society is willing to make for improvements in one objective at the expense of reductions in the other.

Weighting benefits involves fixing the relative values for different groups of beneficiaries. In order to be able to determine the overall desirability of an intervention, one also needs to ensure that the weighted benefits are in comparable units to the costs. For this purpose it is important to anchor the evaluation by setting the equity weight attached to costs equal to unity. This does not mean that the overall weight on costs will be unity for, as we know from earlier chapters, costs incurred by the public sector that require taxes to finance them attract a MCF that will exceed unity.

The CBA criterion is simply that weighted benefits should exceed weighted costs.

13.5.3 Looking Back

CBA is the umbrella under which all other types of economic evaluation in health care exist. CM requires estimates of costs. Without an economic framework there are just too many unanswered questions. Does one include patient costs, non-health care costs, external costs, and discounted costs? How does one measure each of these if one does include them? With opportunity costs as the measure and the principle that the costs of everyone who is affected should be included (that is, social costs) one has a consistent framework, which makes many different types of intervention comparable.

CEA includes effects with costs. But again one faces a whole stream of questions: How does one compare an intervention that has an intermediate effect (e.g., a diagnostic test) with one where there is a final effect (e.g., the patient regains mobility)? What happens when there are a large number of effects per intervention and the interventions do not have one main effect in common? A comprehensive effects measure like WTP would provide the necessary comparability.

CUA also includes a comprehensive effects measure, the QALY. Why not regard this as the centerpiece for economic evaluations? What else is there as an effect other than quantity and quality of life? Although CUA clearly dominates over CM and CEA, it still does not take us far enough. Fundamental measurement issues are left unresolved. Whose utility measure should one use: the patient's, family member's, the doctor's, or the government's? One cannot just hope that the estimates will be roughly the same independent of the source. CBA assumes consumer sovereignty. It is the individuals who are affected that one should use to make the utility estimates. Effects that affect patients should be valued by patients. Effects that affect family members (for example, their time) should be included and valued by these people. Resources that government uses to make health expenditures that are taken from the private sector should be valued by the people affected by the taxes given up. There is a straightforward assignment to individuals for every effect, even if measurement will not always be straightforward. Furthermore, estimating a social discount rate is difficult enough when there is just one rate to be applied to benefits and costs. One does not need the complication of having one rate for effects and another one for costs.

The fundamental problem with relying on CUA is that it does not, just like CM and CUA, tell us whether an intervention should be undertaken or not. We get the best 'bang for the buck', but should more 'bucks' be acquired to generate even more 'bangs'? Is a health care 'bang' equal to an education 'bang'? Resources are limited; we need to spend them in areas where they are most worthwhile. One cannot ensure this if one puts blinkers on and simply assumes that a fixed budget has been set to do one type of activity and one chooses just from a narrow set that relates to the activity. Fortunately, health care evaluators have recently realized this and there is now a literature that tries to put a price on QALYs. With such a price one can compare health, education, transport, environmental and defense expenditures (to list just a few).

To use a single QALY price one has to assume that all those affected value a QALY the same and that the value of a QALY does not vary with the scale of the effects. Why not just relax these two assumptions and allow value to vary by individual and by size? In which case one might just as well go all the way into the economist's domain and incorporate WTP. WTP is based on consumer sovereignty and so should be used when it can, rather than the human capital approach to benefit measurement. This latter approach is useful when one is sure that consumer sovereignty is untenable (as with the severely mentally ill). Whenever human capital estimates are used it must be realized that they, in general, underestimate the size of the benefits. Human capital CBAs that come up with positive net benefits are all likely to be socially worthwhile judged by WTP, though the reverse will not necessarily be true.

The real advantage of employing WTP-based CBA is that it provides a framework for estimating benefits and costs. Data are organized around demand and supply. This does not mean that one is restricted to assuming that only competitive markets exist. Rather one has a starting point for estimation. Some kind of market outcome exists and can therefore be observed. At that market outcome one has readily available measures of benefits and costs. Then when one wishes to contemplate changes in output levels one has a benchmark for telling us what would happen in the absence of interventions one wishes to evaluate. It is true that private markets may exclude external benefits and costs. But this simply means that we add to, or subtract from, the market-based estimates. We do not have to start from scratch and devise a set of interviews to obtain the relevant estimates.

Now that the book is complete and we have established just exactly what is CBA, and have seen it in action via the applications, we are in a position to evaluate a common criticism of CBA that purports to go to the heart of the welfare base of the subject. The criticism involves identifying CBA with utilitarianism and attributing all the defects of this philosophy to CBA. This is not the place to give a full account of utilitarianism. The aim is only to defend the theory and practice of CBA.

If there are two groups, 1 the gainers and 2 the losers, then it is correct to say that a CBA that defines $B = U_1$ and $C = (-)U_2$ is following utilitarianism in the sense of trying to obtain the greatest sum of total utility equal to $U_1 + U_2$ in the guise of maximizing net benefits $B - C$. What is not true is that CBA constructed in this way is indifferent to the distribution of income and is consequentialist (judges outcomes only by their results). There are absolutely no restrictions in CBA as to what is contained in the utility functions that one is summing. If individuals care about the utilities or incomes of others, and we have seen that this is indeed the case in health care, then income distribution will affect CBA outcomes. It is true that the criterion $B - C$ transforms into $a_1B - a_2C$, but the underlying principle is still $U_1 + U_2$. Though, with numbers weights, the CBA criterion is the purest form of utilitarianism, as it follows Bentham's maxim of seeking 'the greatest social good for the greatest number'.

Similarly, if people care about processes, then processes will affect CBA outcomes. In the last chapter we covered conjoint analysis, which was especially designed to allow for the *method* that treatment is carried out to be valued in monetary terms. Also in this chapter we saw that distribution weights can be constructed in kind as well as in cash to record individual preferences as to how income is redistributed.

CBA is inherently a very flexible evaluation approach. It not only makes the best use of what data are available, it also is a framework that informs us as to what new types of data need to be collected before evaluation can proceed. The aim of this text was to help people identify the necessary ingredients and show how they can be put together.

References

Ashton, T. (1991), 'Cost-Effectiveness of Alternative Medications in the Treatment of Duodenal Ulcer', *Scandinavian Journal of Gastroenterology*, **26**, 82–8.

Axnick, N.W., Shavell, S.M. and Witte, J.J. (1969), 'Benefits due to Immunization against Measles', *Public Health Reports*, **84**, 673–80.

Ballard, C.L., Shoven, J.B. and Whalley, J. (1985), 'General Equilibrium Computations of the Marginal Welfare Costs of Taxes in the United States', *American Economic Review*, **75**, 128–38.

Bayoumi, A.M. and Redelmeier, D.A. (1999), 'Economic Methods for Measuring the Quality of Life Associated with HIV Infection', *Quality of Life Research*, **8**, 471–80.

Bleichrodt, H. and Johannesson, M. (1997), 'Standard Gamble, Time Trade-off and Rating Scale: Experimental Results on the Ranking Properties of QALYs', *Journal of Health Economics*, **16**, 155–75.

Bombardier et al. (1982), 'Comparisons of Three Preference Measurement Methodologies in the Evaluation of a Functional Status Index', in *Choices in Health Care*, edited by Deber, D.B. and Thompson, G.G., Department of Health Administration, University of Toronto.

Boyle, M.H., Torrance, G.W., Sinclair, J.C. and Horwood, J.C. (1983), 'Economic Evaluation of Neonatal Intensive Care of Very Low Birth-Weight Infants', *New England Journal of Medicine*, **308**, 1300–7.

Brent, R.J. (1979), 'Imputing Weights Behind Past Railway Closure Decisions Within a Cost–Benefit Framework', *Applied Economics*, **9**, 157–70.

Brent, R.J. (1980), 'Distinguishing Between Money Income and Utility Income in Cost–Benefit Analysis', *Public Finance Quarterly*, **8**, 131–52.

Brent, R.J. (1984a), 'On the Use of Distributional Weights in Cost–Benefit Analysis: A Survey of Schools', *Public Finance Quarterly*, **12**, 213–30.

Brent, R.J. (1984b), 'A Three Objective Social Welfare Function for Cost–Benefit Analysis', *Applied Economics*, **16**, 369–78.

Brent, R.J. (1986), 'An Axiomatic Basis for the Three Objective Social Welfare Functions Within a Poverty Context', *Economics Letters*, **20**, 89–94.

Brent, R.J. (1991a), 'A New Approach to Valuing a Life', *Journal of Public Economics*, **44**, 165–71.

Brent, R.J. (1991b), 'The Numbers Effect and the Shadow Wage in Project Appraisal', *Public Finance*, **46**, 118–27.

Brent, R.J. (1992), 'The Consumption Rate of Interest and the Numbers Effect', *Public Finance*, **47**, 367–77.

Brent, R.J. (1993), 'Country Estimates of Social Discount Rates based on Changes in Life Expectancies', *Kyklos*, **46**, 399–409.

Brent, R.J. (1994a), 'Shadow Prices for a Physician's Services', *Applied Economics*, **26**, 669–76.

Brent, R.J. (1994b),'Counting and Double-Counting in Project Appraisal', *Project Appraisal*, **9**, 275–81.

Brent, R.J. (1996), *Applied Cost–Benefit Analysis*, Cheltenham: Edward Elgar.

Brent, R.J. (1998a), *Cost–Benefit Analysis for Developing Countries*, Cheltenham: Edward Elgar.

Brent, R.J. (1998b), 'Estimating the Effectiveness and Benefits of Alcohol Treatment Programmes for Use in Economic Evaluations', *Applied Economics*, **30**, 217–26.

Brent, R.J. (2000a), 'An Economic Evaluation of the Privatization of Inpatient Psychiatric Services for Non-Federal General Hospitals', Department of Economics, Fordham University.

Brent, R.J. (2000b), 'The Role of Public and Private Transfers in the Cost–Benefit Analysis of Mental Health Programs', Department of Economics, Fordham University.

Brent, R.J. (2002), 'A Simple Method for Converting a Cost-Effectiveness Analysis into a Cost–Benefit Analysis with an Application to State Mental Health Expenditures', *Public Finance Review*, **30**, 144–60.

Brent, R.J. (2003), 'The Tax Implications of Cost Shifting in Cost–Benefit Analysis in Mental Health', *Applied Economics* (forthcoming).

Brent, R.J. and Patel, M. (1997), 'Physician Rewards for Different Kinds of Service', *Journal of Plastic and Reconstructive Surgery*, **100**, 51–7.

Brown, G.C. (1999), 'Vision and Quality-of-Life', *Transactions of the American Ophthalmological Society*, **97**, 473–511.

Brown, K. and Burrows, C. (1990), 'The Sixth Stool Guaiac Test, $47 Million that Never Was', *Journal of Health Economics*, **9**, 429–45.

Browning, E.K. and Browning, J.M. (1994), *Public Finance and the Price System*, (4th edn), New Jersey: Prentice Hall.

Buchanan, J.M. and Stubblebine, C. (1962), 'Externality', *Economica*, **29**, 371–84.

Buchanan, J.M. and Tullock, G. (1962), *The Calculus of Consent*, Ann Arbor: University of Michigan Press.

Cairns, J.A. and Van Der Pol, M.M. (1997), 'Saving Future Lives: A Comparison of Three Discounting Models', *Health Economics*, **6**, 341–50.

Cartwright, W.S. and Solano, P. (2001), 'The Economics of Public Health: Financing Drug Abuse Treatment Services', National Institute on Drug Abuse and University of Delaware.

Chang, R.W., Pellissier, J.M. and Hazen, G.H. (1996), 'A Cost-Effective Analysis of Total Hip Arthroplasty for Osteoarthritis of the Hip', *Journal of the American Medical Association*, **275**, 858–65.

Churchill, D.N., Torrance, G.W., Taylor, D.W., Barnes, C.C., Ludwin, D., Shimizu, A. and Smith, E.K.M. (1987), 'Measurement of Quality of Life in End-Stage Renal Disease: The Time Trade-Off Approach', *Clinical and Investigative Medicine*, **10**, 14–20.

Clarke, R.E., Teague, G.B., Ricketts, S.K., Bush, P.W., Keller, A.M., Zubkoff, M. and Drake, R.E. (1994), 'Measuring Resource Use in Economic Evaluations: Determining the Social Costs of Mental Illness', *The Journal of Mental Health Administration*, **21**, 32–41.

Conley, B.C. (1976), 'The Value of Human Life in the Demand for Safety', *American Economic Review*, **66**, 45–55.

Cook, J., Richardson, J. and Street, A. (1994), 'A Cost Utility Analysis of Treatment Options for Gallstone Disease, Methodological Issues and Results', *Health Economics*, **3**, 157–68.

Cullis, J.G. and Jones, P.G. (1986), 'Rationing by Waiting Lists: An Implication', *American Economic Review*, **74**, 250–6.

Culyer, A.J. (1982), 'Health Care and the Market, A British Lament', *Journal of Health Economics*, **1**, 299–303.

Dickey, B. (1995), unpublished paper, Belmont, Massachusetts: Mental Health Services Research.

Dolan, P. (1998), 'The Measurement of Individual Utility and Social Welfare', *Journal of Health Economics*, **17**, 39–52.

Dolan, P. and Green, C. (1998), 'Using the Person Trade-Off approach to Examine Differences between Individual and Social Values', *Health Economics*, **7**, 307–12.

Donaldson, C. (1990), 'Willingness to Pay for Publicly-Provided Goods: A Possible Measure of Benefit?', *Journal of Health Economics'*, **9**, 103–18.

Doubilet, P., Weinstein, M.C. and McNeil, B.J. (1986), 'Use and Misuse of the Term "Cost-Effective" in Medicine', *New England Journal of Medicine*, **314**, 253–6.

Dranove, D. (1995), 'Measuring Costs', in Sloan, F.A. (ed.), *Valuing Health Care*, New York: Cambridge University Press.

Drummond, M.F. (1981), 'Welfare Economics and Cost–Benefit Analysis in Health Care', *Scottish Journal of Political Economy*, **28**, 125–45.

Drummond, M.F. (1990), 'Priority Setting for AIDS and Other Health Care Programmes', in Drummond, M.F. and Davies, L.M. (eds), *AIDS:*

The Challenge for Economic Analysis, Birmingham: Health Services Management Centre in collaboration with the WHO.

Drummond, M.F., O'Brien, B., Stoddart, G.L. and Torrance, G.W. (1987), *Methods for Economic Evaluation of Health Care Programmes* (2nd edn), New York: Oxford University Press.

Drummond, M.F., Stoddart, G.L. and Torrance, G.W. (1987), *Methods for Economic Evaluation of Health Care Programmes*, New York: Oxford University Press.

Drummond, M., Torrance, G. and Mason, J. (1993), 'Cost-Effectiveness League Tables: More Harm than Good', *Social Science and Medicine*, **37**, 33–40.

Eddy, D.M. (1991a), 'Oregon's Methods. Did Cost-Effectiveness Analysis Fail?', *Journal of the American Medical Association*, **266**, 2135–41.

Eddy, D.M. (1991b), 'Oregon's Methods. Should it be Approved?', *Journal of the American Medical Association*, **266**, 2439–45.

Elixhauser, A., Luce, B.R., Taylor, W.R. and Reblando, J. (1993), 'Health Care CBA/CEA, An Update on the Growth and Composition of the Literature', *Medical Care*, **31**, JS1–JS11.

Epstein, J.F. and Grfeorer, J.C. (1995), 'Estimating Substance Abuse Treatment Need from a National Household Survey', paper presented at the 37th *International Congress on Alcohol and Drug Dependence*.

Fingarette, H. (1988), *Heavy Drinking*, Berkeley: University of California Press.

Finkler, S.A. (1982), 'The Distinction Between Cost and Charges', *Annals of Internal Medicine*, **96**, 102–9.

Forester, T.H., McNown, R.F. and Singell, L.D. (1984), 'A Cost–Benefit Analysis of the 55 MPH Speed Limit', *Southern Economic Journal*, **50**, 631–41.

Frank, R.G. (1991), 'Clozapines Cost–Benefits' [letter], *Hospital and Community Psychiatry*, **42**, 92.

French, M.T., Mauskopf, J.A., Teague, J.L. and Roland, E.J. (1996), 'Estimating the Dollar Value of Health Outcomes from Drug Abuse Interventions', *Medical Care*, **34**, 890–910.

Fryback, D.G., Dasbach, E.J. and Klein, R. (1993), 'The Beaver Dam Health Outcomes Study: Initial Catalog of Health-State Quality Factors', *Medical Decision Making*, **13**, 89–102.

Garbacz, C. and Thayer, M.A. (1983), 'An Experiment in Valuing Senior Companion Program Services', *Journal of Human Resources*, **18**, 147–53.

Garber, A.M. and Phelps, C.E. (1997), 'Economic Foundations of Cost-Effectiveness Analysis', *Journal of Health Economics*, **16**, 1–31.

Gardiner, J., Hogan, A., Holmes-Rovner, M., Rovner, D., Griffith, L. and

Kupersmith, J. (1995), 'Confidence Intervals for Cost-Effectiveness Ratios', *Medical Decision Making*, **15**, 254–63.

Gatsonis, C. (1990), 'The Long Debate on the Sixth Stool Guaiac Test, Time to Move on to New Grounds', *Journal of Health Economics*, **9**, 495–7.

Gerard, K. and Mooney, G. (1993), 'QALY League Tables: Handle with Care', *Health Economics*, **2**, 59–64.

Gertler, P.J., Locay, L. and Sanderson, W. (1987), 'Are User Fees Regressive? The Welfare Implications of Health Care Financing Proposals in Peru', *Journal of Econometrics*, **36**, 67–88.

Getzen, T.E. (1997), *Health Economics, Fundamentals and Flow of Funds*, New York: John Wiley & Sons.

Ghana Health Assessment Project Team (1981), 'A Quantitative Method of Assessing the Health Impact of Different Diseases in Less Developed Countries', *International Journal of Epidemiology*, **10**, 73–80.

Gold, M.R., Siegel, J.E., Russel, L.B. and Weinstein, M.C. (1996), *Cost-Effectiveness in Health and Medicine*, New York: Oxford University Press.

Grannemann, T.W., Brown, R.S. and Pauly, M.V. (1986), 'Estimating Hospital Costs, A Multiple-Output Approach', *Journal of Health Economics*, **5**, 107–27.

Grob, G.N. (1994), 'Government and Mental Health Policy: A Structural Analysis', *Millbank Quarterly*, **72**, 471–500.

Gwatkin, D.R., Guillot, M. and Heuveline, P. (1999), 'The Burden of Disease Among the Global Poor', *The Lancet*, **354**, 586–9.

Hadley, J. (1991), 'Theoretical and Empirical Foundations of the Resource-Based Relative Value Scale', Ch. 5 in Frech III, H.E. (ed.), *Regulating Doctors' Fees: Competition, Benefits, and Controls under Medicare*, Washington D.C.: AEI Press.

Hadorn, D.C. (1991), 'Setting Health Care Priorities in Oregon. Cost-Effectiveness Analysis Meets the Rule of Reason', *Journal of the American Medical Association*, **265**, 2218–25.

Hannum, R.J. (1997), 'Using an Expected Utility Model to Analyze the Social Costs and Benefits of Childhood Immunizations', PhD Thesis, Department of Economics, Fordham University, New York.

Harper, D.R. (1979), 'Disease Costing in a Surgical Ward', *British Medical Journal*, **1**, 647–9.

Harris, J. (1985), *The Value of Life: An Introduction to Medical Ethics*, London: Routledge.

Hellinger, F.J. (1993), 'The Lifetime Cost of Treating a Person with HIV', *Journal of the American Medical Association*, **270**, 474–8.

Hinman, A.R. and Koplan, J.P. (1984), 'Pertussis and Pertussis Vaccine,

Reanalysis of Benefits, Risks and Costs', *Journal of the American Medical Association*, **251**, 3109–13.

Hirth, R.A., Chernew, M.E., Miller, E., Fendrick, M. and Weissert, W.G. (2000), 'Willingness to Pay for a Quality-Adjusted Life Year: In Search for a Standard', *Medical Decision Making*, **20**, 332–42.

Hochman, H.M. and Rodgers, J.D. (1971), 'Is Efficiency a Criterion for Judging Redistribution?', *Public Finance*, **26**, 76–98.

Horngren, C.T. (1982), *Cost Accounting* (5th edn), New Jersey: Prentice-Hall.

Hsiao, W.C., Braun, P., Kelly, N.L. and Becker, E.R. (1988), 'Results, Potential Effects, and Implementation Issues of the Resource-Based Relative Value Scale', *Journal of the American Medical Association*, **260**, 2429–38.

Hsiao, W.C. and Dunn, D.L. (1991), 'The Resource-Based Relative Value Scale for Pricing Physicians' Services', Ch. 9 in Frech III, H.E. (ed.), *Regulating Doctors' Fees, Competition, Benefits, and Controls under Medicare*, Washington D.C.: AEI Press.

Hull, R., Hirsh, J., Sackett, D.L. and Stoddart, G. (1981), 'Cost Effectiveness of Clinical Diagnosis, Venography, and Noninvasive Testing in Patients with Symptomatic Deep-Vein Thrombosis', *New England Journal of Medicine*, **304**, 1561–7.

Hurley, S., Kaldor, J.M., Gardiner, S., Carlin, J.B., Assuncao, R.M. and Evans, D.B. (1996), 'Lifetime Cost of Human Immunodeficiency Virus-Related Health Care', *Journal of Acquired Immune Deficiency Syndromes and Human Retrovirology*, **12**, 371–8.

Hyder, A.A. and Morrow, R.H. (1999), 'Steady State Assumptions in DALYs: Effect on Estimates of HIV Impact', *Journal of Epidemiology and Community Health*, **53**, 43–5.

Hyder, A.A., Rotllant, G. and Morrow, R.H. (1998), 'Measuring the Burden of Disease: Healthy Life-Years', *American Journal of Public Health*, **88**, 196–202.

Jerrell, J.M. and Hu, T-W. (1989), 'Cost-Effectiveness of Intensive Clinical and Case Management Compared with an Existing System of Care', *Inquiry*, **26**, 224–34.

Johannesson, M. (1999), 'On Aggregating QALYs: a Comment on Dolan', *Journal of Health Economics*, **18**, 381–6.

Johannesson, M. and Gerdtham, U.-G. (1996), 'A Note on the Estimation of the Equity–Efficiency Trade-off for QALYs', *Journal of Health Economics*, **15**, 359–68.

Johannesson and Johansson (1997), 'Is the Valuation of a QALY Gained Independent of Age? Some Empirical Evidence', *Journal of Health Economics*, **16**, 589–99.

Kaplan, R.M. (1995), 'Utility Assessment for Estimating Quality-Adjusted Life Years', in Sloan, F.A. (ed.), *Valuing Health Care*, New York: Cambridge University Press.

Kaplan, R.M. and Bush, J.W. (1982), 'Health Related Quality of Life Measurement for Evaluation Research and Policy Analysis', *Health Psychology*, **1**, 61–80.

Kaplan, R.M., Bush, J.W. and Berry, C.C. (1979), 'Health Status Index', *Medical Care*, **17**, 501–25.

Keeler, E.B. and Cretin, S.B. (1983), 'Discounting of Life-Saving and other Non-Monetary Effects', *Management Science*, **29**, 300–6.

Kind, P., Rosser, R.M. and Williams, A.H. (1982), 'Valuations of Quality of Life: Some Psychometric Evidence', in Jones-Lee, M.W. (ed.), *The Value of Life and Safety*, Amsterdam: North Holland.

Klarman, H.E. (1965), 'Syphilis Control Programs', in Dorfman, R. (ed.), *Measuring Benefits of Government Investments*, Washington D.C.: Brookings Institution.

Klarman, H.E. (1982), 'The Road to Cost-Effectiveness Analysis', *Milbank Memorial Fund Quarterly*, **60**, 1–16.

Klarman, H.E., Francis, J. and Rosenthal, G. (1968), 'Cost-Effectiveness Applied to the Treatment of Chronic Renal Disease', *Medical Care*, **6**, 48–54.

Klevit, H.D., Bates, A.C., Castanares, T., Kirk, E.P., Sipes-Metzler, P.R. and Wopat, R. (1991), 'Prioritization of Health Care Services. A Progress Report by the Oregon Health Services Commission', *Archives of Internal Medicine*, **151**, 912–16.

Koplan, J.P. and Preblud, S.R. (1982), 'A Benefit–Cost Analysis of Mumps Vaccine', *American Journal of Diseases in Children*, **136**, 362–4.

Koplan, J.P., Schoenbaum, S.C., Weinstein, M.C. and Fraser, D.W. (1979), 'Pertussis Vaccine, An Analysis of Benefits, Risks and Costs', *New England Journal of Medicine*, **301**, 906–11.

Lasker, E.M., Meisner, M. and Siegel, C. (1997), 'Statistical Inference for Cost-Effectiveness Ratios', *Health Economics*, **6**, 229–42.

Lightwood, J.M. and Glantz, S.A. (1997), 'Short-Term Economic and Health Benefits of Smoking Cessation, Myocardial Infarction and Stroke', *Circulation*, **96**, 1089–96.

Lindsay, C.M. and Feigenbaum, B. (1984), 'Rationing by Waiting Lists', *American Economic Review*, **74**, 405–17.

Linnerooth, J. (1979), 'The Value of Life: A Review of the Models', *Economic Inquiry*, **17**, 52–74.

Llewellyn-Thomas, H. et al. (1984), 'Describing Health States. Methodological Issues in Obtaining Values for Health States', *Medical Care*, **22**, 543–52.

Logan, A.G., Milne, B.J., Achber, R.N., Campbell, W.P. and Haynes, R.B. (1981), 'Cost-Effectiveness of a Worksite Hypertension Treatment Program', *Hypertension*, **3**, 211–18.

Martin, S. and Smith, P. (1999), 'Rationing by Waiting Lists: An Empirical Investigation', *Journal of Public Economics*, **71**, 141–64.

Maynard, A. (1991), 'Developing the Health Care Market', *The Economic Journal*, **101**, 1277–86.

Mehrez, A. and Gafni, A. (1989), 'Quality-adjusted Life Years, Utility Theory, and Healthy-years Equivalents', *Medical Decision Making*, **9**, 142–9.

Meltzer, H.Y., Cola, P., Way, L., Thompson, P.A., Bastani, B., Davies, M.A. and Switz, B. (1993), 'Cost-Effectiveness of Clozapine in Neuroleptic-Resistant Schizophrenia', *American Journal of Psychiatry*, **150**, 1630–8.

Mishan, E.J. (1976), *Cost–Benefit Analysis* (3rd edn), New York: Praeger.

Moore, M.J. and Viscusi, W.K. (1988a), 'The Quantity-Adjusted Value of Life', *Economic Inquiry*, **26**, 369–88.

Moore, M.J. and Viscusi, W.K. (1988b), 'Doubling the Estimated Value of Life: Results using New Occupational Fatality Data', *Journal of Policy Analysis and Management*, **7**, 476–90.

Morrison, G.C. (1997), 'HYE and TTO: What is the Difference?', *Journal of Health Economics*, **16**, 563–78.

Murray, C.J.L. and Acharya, A.K. (1997), 'Understanding DALYs', *Journal of Health Economics*, **16**, 703–30.

Murray, C.J.L. and Lopez, A.D. (1996), *The Global Burden of Disease. A Comprehensive Assessment of Mortality and Disability from Diseases, Injuries and Risk Factors in 1990 and Projected to 2020*, Cambridge: Harvard University Press.

Musgrove, P. (1992), 'Cost–Benefit Analysis of a Regional System for Vaccination Against Pneumonia, Meningitis Type B, and Typhoid Fever', *Bulletin of the Pan American Health Organization*, **26**, 173–91.

Neuhauser, D. (1990), 'The Sixth Stool Guaiac Test, A Reply', *Journal of Health Economics*, **9**, 493–4.

Neuhauser, D. and Lewicki, M. (1975), 'What Do We Gain from the Sixth Stool Guaiac?', *New England Journal of Medicine*, **293**, 226–8.

Nord, E. (1992), 'Methods for Quality Adjustment of Life Years', *Social Science and Medicine*, **34**, 559–69.

Nord, E. (1993), 'The Trade-off between Severity of Illness and Treatment Effect in Cost–Value Analysis of Health Care', *Health Policy*, **24**, 227–38.

Nord, E. (1995), 'The Person-Trade-Off Approach to Valuing Health Care Programs', *Medical Decision Making*, **15**, 201–8.

Nord, E., Pinto, J.P., Richardson, J., Menzel, P. and Ubel, P. (1999),

'Incorporating Societal Concerns for Fairness in Numerical Valuations of Health Programmes', *Health Economics*, **8**, 25–39.

O'Brien, B.J., Drummond, M.F., Labelle, R.J. and Willan, A. (1994), 'In Search of Power and Significance: Issues in the Design and Analysis of Stochastic Cost-Effectiveness Studies in Health Care', *Medical Care*, **32**, 150–63.

Olsen, J.A. (1994), 'Person vs Years: Two Ways of Eliciting Implicit Weights', *Health Economics*, **3**, 39–46.

Patrick, D.L., Bush, J.W. and Chen, M.M. (1973), 'Methods for Measuring Well-being for a Health Status Index', *Health Services Research*, **8**, 228–45.

Pauly, M.V. (1995), 'Valuing Health Care Benefits in Money Terms', in Sloan, F.A. (ed.), *Valuing Health Care*, New York: Cambridge University Press.

Phelps, C.E. (1988), 'Death and Taxes', *Journal of Health Economics*, **7**, 1–24.

Pigou, A.C. (1920), *The Economics of Welfare*, London: Macmillan.

Politi, C., Carrin, G., Evans, D., Kuzoe, F.A.S. and Cattand, P.D. (1995), 'Cost-Effectiveness Analysis of Alternative Treatments of African Gambiense Trypanosomiasis in Uganda', *Health Economics*, **4**, 273–87.

Propper, C. (1990), 'Contingent Valuation of Time Spent on NHS Waiting Lists', *Economic Journal*, **100**, 193–9.

Read, J.L. et al. (1984), 'Preferences for Health Outcomes. Comparison of Assessment Methods', *Medical Decision Making*, **4**, 315–29.

Revicki, D.A., Luce, B.R., Wechsler, J.M., Brown, R.E. and Adler, M.A. (1990), 'Cost-Effectiveness of Clozapine for Treatment-Resistant Schizophrenic Patients', *Hospital and Community Psychiatry*, **41**, 870–4.

Rice, D.P., Kelman, S. and Miller, L.S. (1992), 'The Economic Burden of Mental Illness', *Hospital and Community Psychiatry*, **43**, 1227–32.

Richardson, J., Hall, J., and Salkeld, G. (1989), 'Cost Utility Analysis: The Compatibility of Measurement Techniques and the Measurement of Utility through Time', in Smith, S.C. (ed.), *Economics and Health, Proceedings of the Eleventh Australian Conference of Health Economists*.

Ried, W. (1998), 'QALYs versus HYEs – What's Right and What's Wrong. A Review of the Controversy', *Journal of Health Economics*, **17**, 607–25.

Rosser, R. and Kind, P. (1978), 'A Scale of Valuations of States of Illness: Is there a Social Consensus?', *International Journal of Epidemiology*, **7**, 347–58.

Russell, L.B., Gold, M.R., Siegel, J.E., Daniels, N. and Weinstein, M.C. (1996), 'The Role of Cost-Effectiveness Analysis in Health and Medicine', *Journal of the American Medical Association*, **276**, 1172–7.

Ryan, M. (1999), 'Using Conjoint Analysis to Take Account of Patient

Preferences and Go Beyond Outcomes: An Application to In Vitro Fertilization', *Social Science and Medicine*, **48**, 535–46.

Ryan, M. and Hughes, J. (1997), 'Using Conjoint Analysis to Assess Women's Preferences for Miscarriage Management', *Health Economics*, **6**, 261–73.

Sackette, D.L. and Torrance, G.W. (1978), 'The Utility of Different Health States as Perceived by the General Public', *Journal of Chronic Diseases*, **31**, 697–704.

Samuelson, P.A. (1954), 'The Pure Theory of Public Expenditure', *Review of Economics and Statistics*, **36**, 350–6.

Schimmel, V.E., Alley, C. and Heath, A.M. (1987), 'Measuring Costs, Product Line Accounting Versus Ratio of Cost to Charges', *Journal of Health Care Finance*, **13**, 76–86.

Shwartz, M., Young, D.W. and Siegrist, R. (1995), 'The Ratio of Costs to Charges, How Good a Basis for Estimating Costs?', *Inquiry*, **32**, 476–81.

Siegel, C., Laska, E.M. and Meisner, M. (1996), 'Statistical Methods for Cost-Effectiveness Analysis', *Controlled Clinical Trials*, **17**, 387–406.

Siegel, J.E., Weinstein, M.C., Russell, L.B. and Gold, M.R. (1996), 'Recommendations for Reporting Cost-Effectiveness Analyses', *Journal of the American Medical Association*, **276**, 1339–41.

Siraprapasiri, T., Sawaddiwudhipong, W. and Rojanasuphot, S. (1997), 'Cost Benefit Analysis of Japanese Encephalitis Vaccination Program in Thailand', *The Southeast Journal of Tropical Medicine and Public Health*, **28**, 143–8.

Squire, L. and van der Tak, H. (1975), *Economic Analysis of Projects*, Baltimore: Johns Hopkins.

Starmer, C. (2000), 'Developments in Non-Expected Utility Theory: The Hunt for a Descriptive Theory of Choice under Risk', *Journal of Economic Literature*, **38**, 332–82.

Stason, W.B. and Weinstein, M.C. (1977), 'Allocation of Resources to Manage Hypertension', *New England Journal of Medicine*, **296**, 732–9.

Stern, S.H., Singer, L.B. and Weissman, M.M. (1995), 'Analysis of Hospital Cost in Total Knee Arthroplasty', *Clinical Orthopaedics and Related Research*, **321**, 36–44.

Temin, P. (1983), 'Costs and Benefits in Switching Drugs from Rx to OTC', *Journal of Health Economics*, **2**, 187–205.

Thaler, R. and Rosen, S. (1975), 'The Value of Saving a Life: Evidence from the Labor Market', in Terleckyj, N. (ed.), *Household Production and Consumption*, New York: NBER.

Thompson, M.S., Read, J.S. and Liang, M. (1984), 'Feasibility of Willingness to Pay Measurement in Chronic Arthritis', *Medical Decision Making*, **4**, 195–215.

Torrance, G.W. (1976), 'Social Preferences for Health States: An Empirical Evaluation of Three Measurement Techniques', *Socio-Economic Planning Sciences*, **10**, 129–36.

Torrance, G.W. (1986), 'Measurement of Health State Utilities for Economic Appraisal', *Journal of Health Economics*, **5**, 1–30.

Torrance, G.W., Boyle, M.H. and Horwood, S.P. (1982), 'Application of Multi-Attribute Utility Theory to Measure Social Preferences for Health States', *Operations Research*, **30**, 1043–69.

Torrance, G.W. and Feeny, D. (1989), 'Utilities and Quality-Adjusted Life Years', *International Journal of Technology Assessment in Health Care*, **5**, 559–75.

Torrance, G.W., Thomas, W.H. and Sackette, D.L. (1972), 'A Utility Maximization Model for Evaluation of Health Care Programs', *Health Services Research*, **7**, 118–33.

Tsuchiya, A. (2000), 'QALYs and Ageism: Philosophical Theories and Age Weighting', *Health Economics*, **9**, 57–68.

Ubel, P.A., Loewenstein, G., Scanlon, D. and Kamlet, M. (1998), 'Value Measurement in Cost-Utility Analysis: Explaining the Discrepancy between Rating Scale and Person Trade-off Elicitations', *Health Policy*, **43**, 33–44.

Vaillant, G.E. (1983), *The Natural History of Alcoholism*, Cambridge, Mass.: Harvard University Press.

Van Hout, B.A. (1998), 'Discounting Costs and Effects: A Reconsideration', *Health Economics*, **7**, 581–94.

Viscusi, W.K. (1995), 'Discounting Health Effects for Medical Decisions', in Sloan, F.A. (ed.), *Valuing Health Care*, New York: Cambridge University Press.

Von Neuman, J. and Morgenstern, O. (1944), *The Theory of Games and Economic Behavior*, Princeton: Princeton University Press.

Wagstaff, A. (1991), 'QALYs and the Equity–Efficiency Trade-off', *Journal of Health Economics*, **10**, 21–41.

Weiers, R.M. (1998), *Introduction to Business Statistics* (3rd edn), New York: Duxbury.

Weimer, C. (1987), 'Optimal Disease Control Through Combined Use of Preventative and Curative Measures', *Journal of Development Economics*, **25**, 301–19.

Weinstein, M.C. (1980), 'Estrogen Use in Postmenopausal Women: Costs, Risks and Benefits', *New England Journal of Medicine*, **303**, 308–16.

Weinstein, M.C. (1995), 'From Cost-Effectiveness Ratios to Resource Allocation', in Sloan, F.A. (ed.), *Valuing Health Care*, New York: Cambridge University Press.

Weinstein, M.C., Siegel, J.E., Gold, M.R., Kamlet, M. and Russell, L.B.

(1996),'Recommendations of the Panel on Cost-Effectiveness in Health and Medicine', *Journal of the American Medical Association*, **276**, 1253–8.

Weinstein, M.C. and Stason, W.B. (1977), 'Foundations of Cost-Effectiveness Analysis for Health and Medical Practices', *New England Journal of Medicine*, **296**, 716–21.

Weintraub, W.S., Mauldin, P.D., Becker, E., Kosinski, A.S. and King III, S.B. (1995), 'A Comparison of the Costs of and Quality of Life after Coronary Artery Disease', *Circulation*, **92**, 2831–40.

Weisbrod, B.A. (1961), *Economics of Public Health*, University of Pennsylvania Press.

Weisbrod, B.A. (1971), 'Costs and Benefits of Medical Research', *Journal of Political Economy*, **79**, 527–44.

Weisbrod, B.A., Test, M.A. and Stein, L.I. (1980), 'Alternative to Mental Hospital Treatment', *Archives of General Psychiatry*, **37**, 400–5.

White, C.C., Koplan, J.P. and Orenstein, W.A. (1985), 'Benefits, Risks and Costs of Immunization for Measles, Mumps and Rubella', *American Journal of Public Health*, **75**, 739–44.

Wildasin, D.E. (1992), 'The Marginal Cost of Public Funds with an Aging Population', in Dressen, E. and van Winden, F. (eds), *Fiscal Implications of an Aging Population*, Berlin: Springer-Verlag.

Willan, A.R. and O'Brien, B.J. (1996), 'Confidence Intervals for Cost-Effectiveness Ratios: An Application of Fieller's Theorem', *Health Economics*, **5**, 297–305.

Williams, A. (1997), 'Intergenerational Equity: an Exploration of the "Fair Innings" Argument', *Health Economics*, **6**, 117–32.

Williams, A. and Cookson, R. (2000), 'Equity in Health', in Culyer, A.J. and Newhouse, J.P. (eds), *Handbook of Health Economics*, Vol. 1B, Amsterdam: Elsevier.

World Bank (1993), *World Development Report, 1993*, New York: Oxford University Press.

Wyatt, R.J., Henter, I., Leary, M.C. and Taylor, E. (1995), 'An Economic Evaluation of Schizophrenia—1991', *Social Psychiatry and Psychiatric Epidemiology*, **30**, 196–205.

Zarkin, G.A., Cates, S.C. and Bala, M.V. (2000), 'Estimating the Willingness to Pay for Drug Abuse Treatment', *Journal of Substance Abuse Treatment*, **18**, 149–59.

Index